# A HISTORY OF THE IRISH ARMY

# A HISTORY OF THE IRISH ARMY

JOHN P. DUGGAN

GILL AND MACMILLAN

Published in Ireland by
Gill and Macmillan Ltd
Goldenbridge
Dublin 8
with associated companies in
Auckland, Delhi, Gaborone, Hamburg, Harare,
Hong Kong, Johannesburg, Kuala Lumpur, Lagos,
London, Manzini, Melbourne, Mexico City,
Nairobi, New York, Singapore, Tokyo

Index compiled by Helen Litton
Print origination by
Seton Music Graphics Ltd, Bantry, Co. Cork
Printed by
Billing & Sons Ltd, Worcester



**British Library Cataloguing in Publication Data**
Duggan, John P. *1918–*
A history of the Irish Army.
1. Ireland (Republic). Army, history
I. Title
355.009417

ISBN 0–7171–1582–8

# Contents

*What feat of arms will we perform today?*

from *The Táin*

A Ardcheannasaithe, a Oifigeacha, a Oifigeacha Neamhchoimisiúnta agus a fheara de chuid Óglaigh na hÉireann, bíodh sibh ar shlí na Fírinne, bíodh sibh inár measc nó le teacht inár measc.

To Commanders-in-Chief, Officers, NCOs and Men of *Óglaigh na hÉireann,* past, present and future.

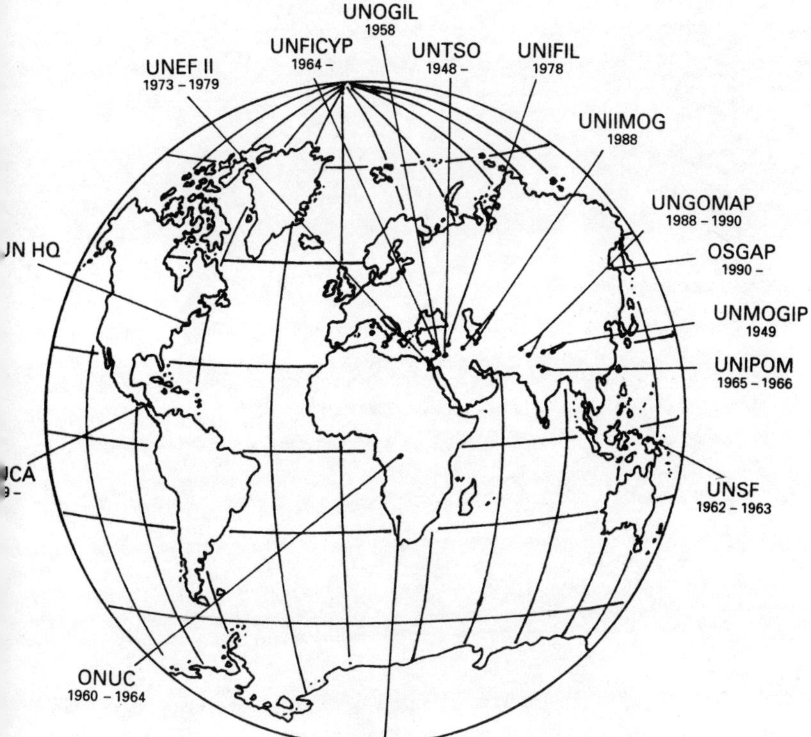

# Foreword

## F.X. Martin

Lt Col. Duggan's *A History of the Irish Army* is a landmark volume.

It is the first published comprehensive history of the Irish Army. It required considerable courage to undertake the task, since he had to plot an accurate, fearful course across a minefield of Irish history, particularly dangerous with trip wires for the period 1913–39. During those traumatic twenty-six years dedicated men and women on both sides suffered and died for what they believed was the best way to solve the burning problem of Ireland's national identity.

Indeed, it was not a question of two but of at least three sides, since there were fearless Irish men and women — notable on the nationalist side were the Home Rulers led by John Redmond — who believed that Ireland's prospects would be best served by a distinct Irish State but as a member of the British Commonwealth (like India later under Nehru).

On the other hand the Unionists in Ireland, ably and eloquently led by Carson and Craigavon, and strongly supported by the Conservative Party in England, literally to a militant degree, believed in a United Kingdom of Great Britain and Ireland.

Nehru, the Indian leader, acknowledged that it was de Valera's inspiration — his concept of the inner circle of Ireland and Great Britain within the greater international circle of the British Commonwealth — which decided Nehru to remain in the Commonwealth but as a sovereign republic. In fact, this arrangement has proved feasible for India — today the largest democratic state in the world.

Lt Col. Duggan is exceptionally qualified, one might say uniquely so in present circumstances, for the task on two scores.

First, he was a serving member of the Irish Army, 1939–76, with active experience abroad in three places, Germany, Great Britain and Cyprus. He saw and served the military machine from the inside, and observed its bureaucratic face, warts and all. Secondly, he then subjected himself to the rigours of a demanding basic history degree at University College, Dublin. This he completed with distinction in 1973. At my suggestion he then transferred to Trinity College, Dublin, in order to appreciate different views and standards in pursuit of his further historical research. There he studied fruitfully for an M.Litt. degree which he secured in 1980 under the supervision of Dr Patrick Keatinge in the Department of Political Science. Lt Col. Duggan rose to the challenge successfully. His Trinity College, Dublin, findings were published as *Neutral Ireland and the Third Reich*, Dublin and New Jersey, USA, 1985. It is a standard work, still unsurpassed.

As a true soldier he is not dismayed by difficult circumstances. For the present task he had to convince (even to cajole) Irish army authorities to allow him have a limited access to official records. His difficulty can be appreciated from the fact that the official highly enlightening and detailed records about the courts-martial of the rebel leaders of the Easter 1916 Rising in Ireland are — with the remarkable exception of those for Eoin MacNeil — not yet available to historians in Dublin or London. For the later period, 1918–32, Lt Col. Duggan has had to utilise not merely official records, but (discreetly) has had recourse to valuable information which he garnered along the grapevine of Irish army (and Civil Service) friends.

One notable feature emerges from this history. The modern Irish army began and has sustained without compromise the principle that, as called into existence by Professor Eoin MacNeill in 1913, it is a Defence (not an aggressive) Force.

Significantly the term still used officially by the government of the Irish Republic is that its army is a Defence Force. By direct implication it is not aggressive. This helps to explain the role which the Irish army has readily adopted overseas since the 1960s, for example, in the Congo, the Middle East and the Lebanon, as UN mediators for peace.

Let it be admitted frankly that the despatch of Irish troops overseas is also a fruitful release for adventuresome Irish soldiers who otherwise would have no outlet in their own peaceful country for experience of war conditions. Men like the stimulus of war, Irish men more than most!

It is not irrelevant to note that Eoin MacNeill, who was founder of the Irish Volunteers in 1913 — the embryo national Irish army and the first in almost 300 years — was also a member of the Provisional Government of Southern Ireland in 1922, which decided that the new police force, the Gardaí (unlike the RUC and the 'B Specials' in Northern Ireland) should be unarmed.

Many Gardaí during the next troubled years, 1922–32, died as a result of the decision, as a monument at the Garda Headquarters in the Phoenix Park testifies. Other unarmed colleagues of theirs have died similarly in recent years while maintaining law and order within the Republic of Ireland against subversive paramilitary and criminal elements.

It is a bitter harvest but let it be stated with the deepest regret that it is well worth the sacrifice, however painful the short-term result has been for the wives and families of the murdered Gardaí, who were well aware of the possible consequences of being Gardaí.

The firm stand taken unhesitatingly by the Irish Republic is in the best tradition of parliamentary democracy.

In 1990 the Republic of Ireland still stands by the principle, first expressed in 1913 for the Irish Volunteers, that its army is a Defence, not an aggressive, Force. It is for peace and reconciliation, at home and abroad, not for war and sectarian divisions.

# Preface

Piaras Béaslaí suggested the title *Óglaigh na hÉireann* for the Volunteers, and Pearse and MacNeill agreed. A carry-over from a counter-proposal to name the organisation *Fianna Fáil* is traceable in the FF lettering in the cap badge, and in the National Anthem ('*Sinne Fianna Fáil*'). *Óglaigh na hÉireann* was adopted and became the official name of the Volunteers of 1913 and the army of 1919 to 1922. The name stuck, and the Defence Act of 1954 reaffirmed it.

An independent Irish parliament on Irish soil was set up following success in the 1918 General Election. The autonomous Volunteers with its own executive gave allegiance to the Dáil and so became the army of the lawfully constituted government elected by the people. From this time on it may be referred to as the Irish Republican Army, though that term did not gain currency until much later on. The name 'IRA' was unknown to Béaslaí and his comrades at that period and was never officially adopted. The official title of the Force today remains what it was in the beginning: *Óglaigh na hÉireann.*

The following is an editorial comment in *An tÓglach* of 20 February 1926:

> A History of the Irish Army
>
> Many a long day must pass before a history, properly so-called, of *Óglaigh na hÉireann* can be written. When that time comes, the historian will have as his theme one of the most soul-stirring epochs in the chequered history of Ireland — an epoch of tragedy, comedy, and glorious achievement.
>
> While none of us — the actual participants — can hope to live to see that day of publication, we have, at least, the consolation of knowing that we have now available to our

hand in the bound volumes of *An t-Oglach* what is to all practical purposes a history of the Irish Army.

From its inception the Army Journal has consistently 'marched with the Army'. The development, the trials, the tragedies and the achievements of the Army have been faithfully mirrored in its pages. It has shared all the dangers, and outlived them, too. Many a good man and true has in the old days faced prison for the mere possession of a copy.

By a piece of good fortune we have come into possession of a number of back issues of *An t-Oglach.* This series of very scarce numbers runs from 1921 to 1923. In the earlier issues some numbers are missing, and every effort is being made to fill the gaps.

Early efforts had been made to fill the gaps. Archives operated — albeit fitfully — since 1923. In 1924 Col. M. J. Costello, Director of Intelligence, proposed its formal establishment to the Chief of Staff, Lt Gen. Peadar MacMahon. No one knew what to do with the valuable historical documents on hands. Capt. A. Blake was given the job.

In 1929 the Irish Manuscripts Commission was consulted. In 1936 it recommended the transference from Military Archives to the National Library of the Kilmainham papers, *Correspondence and papers of the Commander-in-Chief of the Forces in Ireland 1784-1894.* They are still there. Interestingly, the Minister for Defence accepted the Commission's recommendation.

Initially Col. J.J. ('Ginger') O'Connell, Director No. 2 Bureau, Intelligence Branch, was a driving force in setting up archives. Without his interest valuable source material would never have been collected. His overriding ambition, however, was to write a history of the War of Independence. That did not materialise.

The situation remained static until 1935 when the Historical Bureau was set up to collect Irish military historical material, particularly for the period 1913-21. Between then and 1939 — when on the outbreak of war it ceased to function — that bureau collected many valuable documents.

After the 'Emergency' the Historical Bureau was reconstituted as an Archives Sub-section but its quota of appointments was never filled. In 1946 it was superseded by the Bureau of Military History whose task was to collect material from the survivors of the 1913-21 period which would not be released during their lifetime. The material collected lies in the Taoiseach's office awaiting processing in due course.

The 1986 National Archives Act has finally formalised archival practice here to conform with that in other modern democracies. The professional Irish Military Archives are zealously in the vanguard of this movement. Churchill's quip can at long last be laid to rest: in 1922 when he heard of the loss of priceless records in the Four Courts he made the crack, 'Better a State without archives than archives without a State'.

There is no pretence at being the last word. It is hoped that this book will stimulate a progressive and scientific study of Irish military history and leadership in order, in the words of Clausewitz, to 'produce searching rather than inventive minds and cool rather than hot heads' to whom the security and the defence of our country can be safely entrusted in time of emergency or war. Historical events are evaluated and analysed to determine what lessons can be drawn from the past. Blow-by-blow accounts of each and every incident are obviously outside the scope and span of this survey which covers the years 1913 to 1990.

J.P. Duggan
October 1990

# Acknowledgments

I can only begin to thank the many many people, too numerous to mention here, for their generous assistance when they heard the words '*Óglaigh na hÉireann*' mentioned. Rev. Professor F.X. Martin OSA first suggested the undertaking. The then Minister for Defence, Mr Paddy Cooney, kindly acceded to a request for co-operation and wished the project every success.

Founding fathers of the Forces contributed gold dust: Lt Gen. Seán Collins-Powell; Major Gen. Jim Lillis; Col. James Flynn; Col. Jim Cogan; Capt. Martin Bell; Lt Col. Seán Clancy. Eamonn de Barra gave other viewpoints, which also threw light on the first *Óglaigh na hÉireann* female soldiers, *Cumann na mBan*, a heroic band who made their mark in history.

Capt. R.N. Cooke SC looked over the legalisation chapter on which subject contact with the late Judge Cahir Davitt were indispensible. Col. John Kane encouraged and imparted crucial information. Lt Col. Ned Barry took great trouble to assemble first-hand information on the Ack-Ack. Comdt Jim Dukes provided FCA insights, while Comdt Owen Quinn expertly outlined the Coast Watching operation. Capt. John Meehan clarified the material on the Construction Corps. Lt Gen. Bill Callaghan DSM and Lt Gen. Louis Hogan DSM patiently read the pieces on the United Nations and internal security.

The wholehearted co-operation of Comdt Peter Young's Military Archives staff and associates was deeply appreciated. Without it, this work could not have been completed. The international reputation earned by dedicated Military Archives brings credit to the Defence Forces. Nothing is too much trouble for Comdt Young and his most helpful comrades: Captain Victor Laing, Sergeant Joe White, Corporals Bertie Egerton, Brendan Mahony and Private Paul Reilly. Words cannot express my gratitude to them all. The friendly response from individual serving officers was also heartening. I will not embarrass them or rub off my own interpretative fallibility by mentioning their names: they know. A trawl too through the pleasant Public Records Office in Kew was a rewarding pleasure — if only to throw a little light on the controversial 'W' plan.

Sergeant John Duffy of the Garda Museum could not have been more helpful in trying to track down Goertz's call to the army.

Professor Martin's *History of the Irish Volunteers 1913-1915* is a basic text; *The Irish Defence Forces Handbook*, together with James J. Hogan's *Badges: Medals: Insignia*, are recommended accompaniments. *An Cosantóir* is a worthy successor to *An tÓglach* as a rich source.

Eibhlín Nic Dhonncha heroically accomplished the typing. Go raibh míle míle maith aici. Tá mé thar a bheith buíoch dí.

Responsibility is mine alone. *Telum iactum est.*

# List of Illustrations

## Maps



## Photographs

*between pp. 120 and 121*

All photographs are copyright Military Archives, except for that of the Niemba funerals which is copyright *Irish Times* and those of the Air Corps helicopters and Fougas, which were kindly supplied by Capt. Kevin Byrne, Baldonnel. The author and publishers gratefully acknowledge permission to reproduce all illustrations.

General Map of Ireland

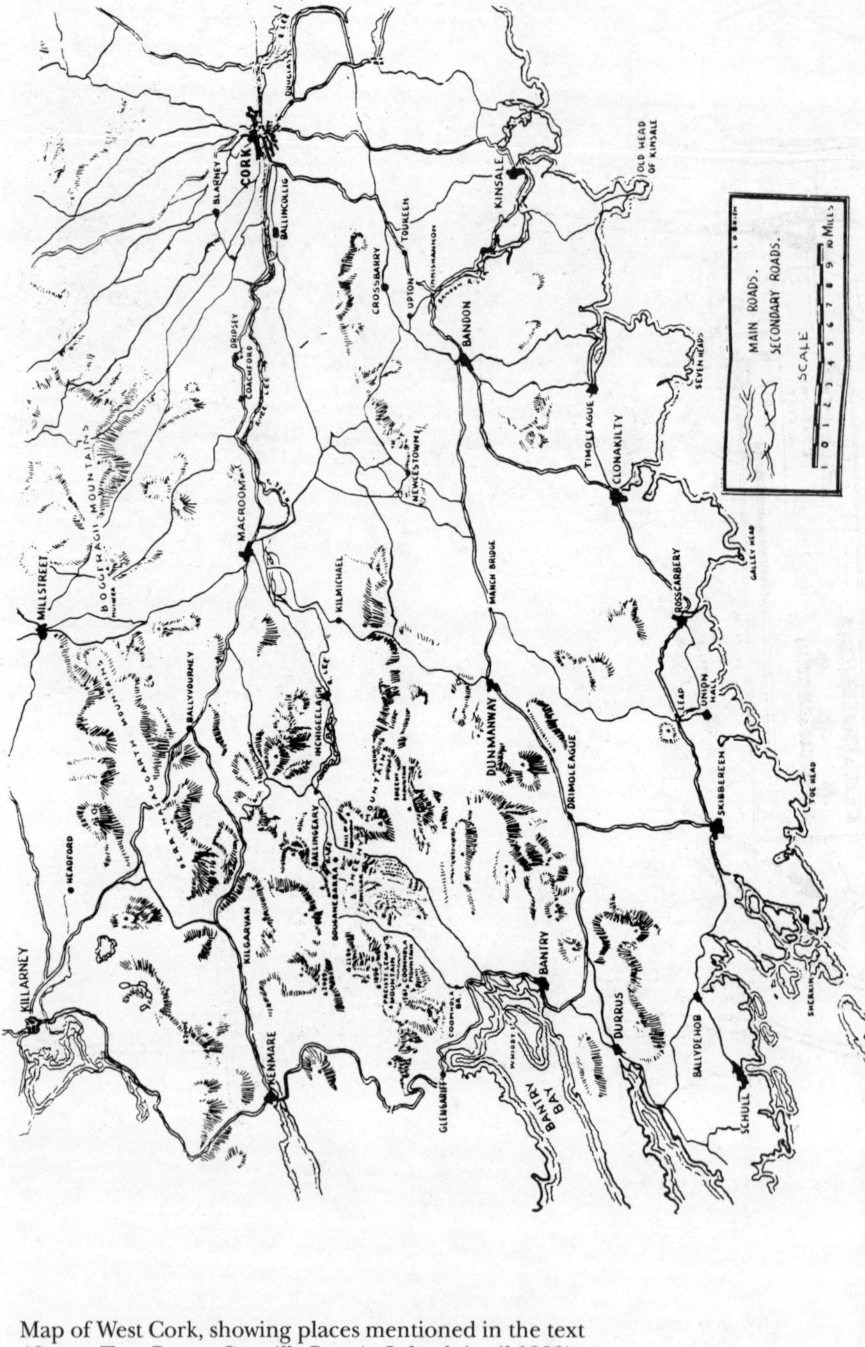


Map of West Cork, showing places mentioned in the text
(*Source*: Tom Barry, *Guerrilla Days in Ireland*, Anvil 1989)

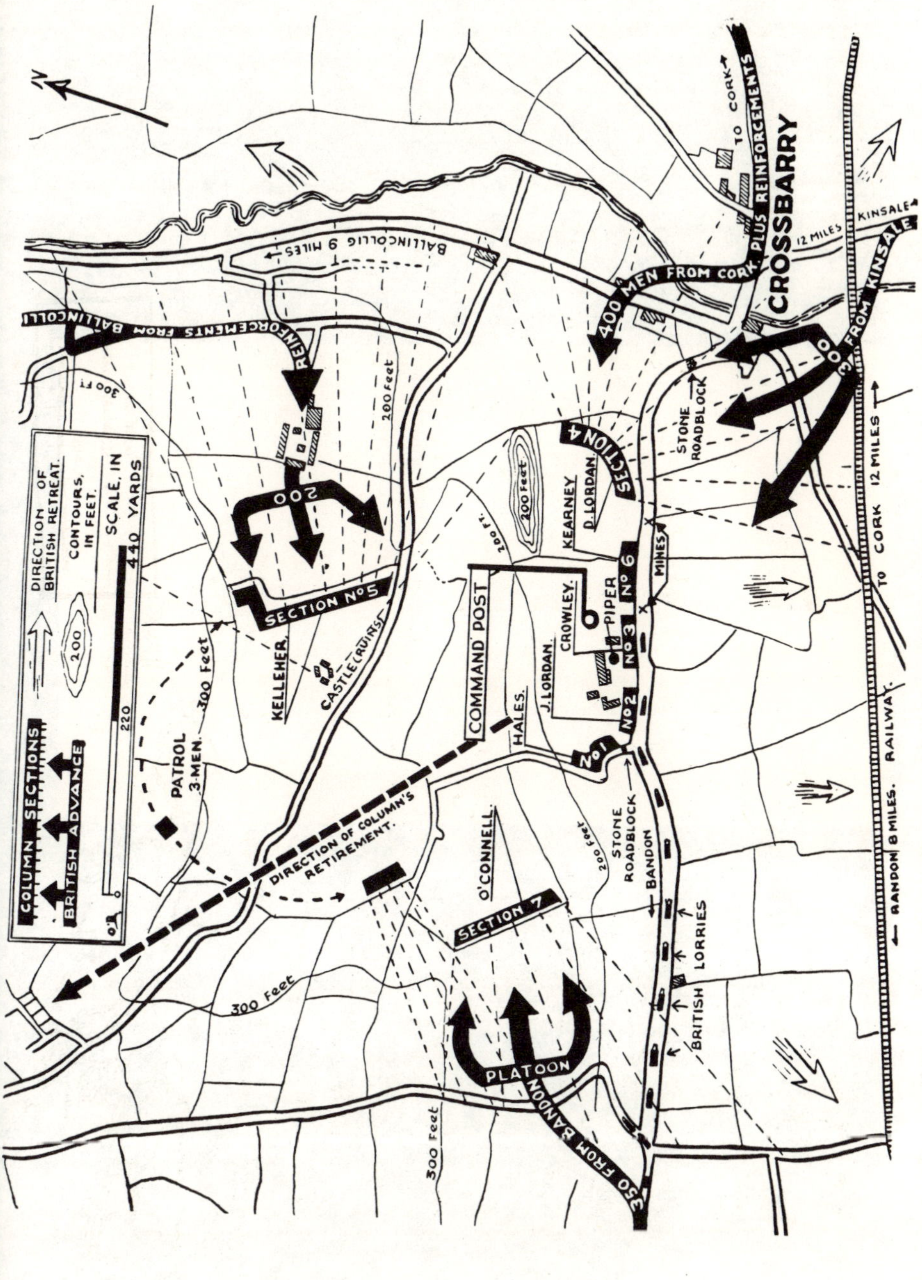


Detailed map of Crossbarry action (*Source*: Tom Barry, *Guerrilla Days in Ireland*, Anvil 1989)

**ERRATA**

| | | |
|---|---|---|
| p. 89 | Line 15 | "Kilmacon" should be "Kilmacow" |
| p. 92 | Line 17 | "Kilmagonny" should be "Kilmaganny" |
| p.192 | Line 17 | "eighty-nine" should be "eighty-three" |
| p.224 | Line 23 | "1969" should be "1963" |
| p.249 | Line 18 | "1956" should be "1955" |
| p.252 | Line 8 | "1966" should be "1960" |
| p.269 | Line 18 | "Haule" should be "Houle" |
| p.271 | Line 9 | "Kevin" should be "Aengus" |
| p.271 | Line 33 | "been" should be "being" |
| p.290 | Line 2 | "Connemara" should be "Co. Cork" |

# 1

## Roots and Rebellion
## (1913–16)

*Óglaigh na hÉireann,*[1] forerunner of the modern Irish army, was called into being in the Rotunda Rink, Dublin, on 25 November 1913. It was a volunteer force, a people's army, formed to secure and maintain the rights and liberties common to all the people of Ireland without distinction of creed, class or politics. It subsequently embodied a women's auxiliary organisation, *Cumann na mBan.*[2] It was prepared to fraternise and co-operate with the Ulster Volunteer Force, the inspiration of its inception. The inceptor, Eoin MacNeill, an Ulsterman, declared:

> We do not contemplate any hostility to the Volunteer movement that has already been initiated in parts of Ulster. The strength of that movement consists in men whose kinsfolk were amongst the foremost and the most resolute in winning freedom for the United States of America, in descendants of the Irish Volunteers of 1782, of the United Irishmen, of the Antrim and Down insurgents of 1798, of the Ulster Protestants who protested in thousands against the destruction of the Irish Parliament in 1800. *The more genuine and successful the local Volunteer movement in Ulster becomes, the more completely does it establish the principle that Irishmen have the right to decide and govern their own national affairs. We have nothing to fear from the existing Volunteers in Ulster nor they from us. We gladly acknowledge the evident truth that they have opened the way for a National Volunteer movement, and we trust that the day is near when their own services to the cause of an Irish Nation will become as memorable as the services of their forefathers.*[3]

He viewed Ulster Volunteers as fundamentally home rulers,

albeit Orange ones. He was well aware of the lineage and pretensions of the Ulster Protestants but he was also conscious of their strong sense of separate identity. It was, nevertheless, a fond hope that the Ulster Volunteers would stand shoulder to shoulder with the Irish Volunteers in defence of a motherland they disdained to recognise as a separate political entity.

The Ulster Volunteers had been called into being by a Dublin unionist, Edward Carson, and the Ulster Unionist Council to prevent the Protestants of Ulster being ruled by an all-Ireland home rule government located in Dublin. Aided and abetted by a powerful and unscrupulous section of the Conservative Party, they threatened rebellion and civil war to thwart the rule of law. The 'Orange Card' — a phrase used originally by Lord Randolph Churchill, father of Sir Winston — was cynically played to the full. A blind eye was turned to a mutiny of the officers of the 3rd Cavalry Brigade in the Curragh (on 20 March 1914) who collectively declined to undertake active operations against Ulster. The majority of the Irish people were to be denied the fruits of decades of patient constitutional endeavours. Many in the newly founded *Óglaigh na hÉireann* took the point: if force would prevent home rule, then a greater force could secure it. If granting home rule was going to cause a civil war, not granting it was also going to cause a civil war. Nevertheless they forebore to openly criticise the Ulster Volunteers. In his Ulster speech in the Rotunda Rink on 25 November 1913 Pearse stressed the point that the movement they were inaugurating was not one in antagonism to the Volunteer companies which had been raised by the unionists in the north east of Ulster. He recognised that they might differ as to the degree of autonomy which was desirable for Ireland but emphasised that it was for Ireland herself and not for any external power to determine that degree. On 12 February 1915 Eoin MacNeill addressed a general muster of the four battalions of the Dublin regiment as follows:

> I wish to say a word to you about those whom we may call our separated brethren. It is altogether out of the question, it would be giving the lie to the first principles of our

organisation, if we were to regard these men with any feelings of enmity or ill-will. For my part, I hope and trust that they will keep before them the same purpose as we keep before ourselves, and that they will never rest content until they, as well as we, are fully armed, trained, instructed, organised and equipped for national defence. If you can do no more at present, my advice to you is to give them also every encouragement and every incitement to that end.[4]

After years of agitation the Irish Parliamentary Party under John Redmond had finally in 1912 pushed forward a home rule bill in the British Parliament, which was passed into law in 1914 but suspended for the duration of the Great War.

Both Redmond and Carson believed in the benefits of belonging to the British empire. But Carson believed that Irish home rule would be disastrous for the imperial connection whereas Redmond, in common with Gladstone before him, believed that home rule would copperfasten the union and enhance the empire. Redmond simply wanted Irishmen to get the credit which was rightfully theirs for their significant contribution to building up that empire. He recognised the imperial commonwealth of states as a reality and felt that within one commonwealth there could not be two standards of justice.

It was only natural that MacNeill should endeavour to enlist the support of the most powerful Irish political leader of the day, but Redmond was less than forthcoming. He regarded the mere existence of the Volunteers as a threat to his authority. Grassroots rumblings that the faith of a number of the younger generation in constitutional politics was beginning to waver contributed to his reservations. It was true that Pearse had welcomed the home rule bill as a measure of independence but he had also sternly warned that if they were tricked and cheated once more there would be 'red war in Ireland'. Redmond feared that such rhetoric might rob him of the home rule prize, now within his grasp. He was losing his touch, failing to understand the sea changes taking place in nationalist public opinion.

The outbreak of the Great War in August 1914 relegated the implementation of his home rule bill until the war was over. The Irish people felt betrayed by what they regarded as political chicanery. Redmond's credibility diminished as a result and he lost some of his following and much of his flair. The real rupture came on 20 September 1914, when he made a speech at Woodenbridge, Co. Wicklow, publicly announcing that the Volunteers should be prepared to fight as members of the British army to prove that they were worthy of home rule. By the end of October 1914 the Volunteers following him had fallen to 165,000 and continued to shrink. Those following MacNeill went up to 13,500 including over 2,000 in Dublin of whom a few belonged to the Citizen Army.[5] The close association between the Citizen Army and the Irish Volunteers only dated from the end of 1915 when the Citizen Army's policy urging violent action received wider acceptance. From the middle of October to the middle of December 1914 the Volunteers were estimated to be about 14,000 strong and they were increased by about 2,000 men from the provinces. By 1916 the estimate went up to 15,000, including 2,850 in the provinces who actually enrolled as Irish Volunteers although calling themselves National Volunteers. Some of the more militant who seceded actively canvassed to procure equipment for a defence force and on 31 October 1914 Sir Roger Casement reached Berlin from America on an arms purchasing mission. On top of that, ingenious smuggling of revolvers and pistols was set in train, rifles were purchased from soldiers on leave and there were thefts of rifles from the National Volunteers (a hundred were also stolen from warehouses of the London and North Western Company). There were considerable thefts of explosives throughout the country (Enniscorthy 1913, Sligo, Cork, Castlebellingham and Lanarkshire in 1915) and the manufacture of bombs continued. English manufacturers continued to trade. Five hundred bayonets were detected on their way from a Sheffield cutler to a Sinn Féin manager. On 5 August 1914 the restriction on the importation of arms into Ireland had been removed. The British later knew of an Irish Volunteer, Monteith, recruiting in Germany and of a contemplated landing from a disguised German ship of arms and ammunition on the south-west coast. But they had no fear of any rising by Volunteers standing alone. In British eyes, 55,000 Irish Catholics were fighting for the Empire. No notice was taken of a sham attack on Dublin Castle on 6 October 1915.

The majority (149,000 out of 180,000), renamed the National Volunteers, had followed Redmond's advice. Largely from them came the Tenth and Sixteenth Divisions of the British army which, with the Tyneside Irish battalions, took their places alongside the Thirty-Sixth Ulster Division to fight gallantly in the now legendary Somme battles, at Messines and at Ypres.

Stories of the valour of the Munster Fusiliers and the Irish Guards abounded. They marched into battle singing 'God Save Ireland', convinced that they were fighting for home rule. At the same time the Ulster Division at the Somme went over the top wearing Orange sashes and ribbons shouting 'No surrender' and 'Remember 1690' in memory of the battle of the Boyne, when the army of Dutch William of Orange defeated the inept English Catholic King, James II.[6] Notwithstanding all that, Capt. Willie Redmond, MP, John's brother (later to be killed in action in France), assured a receptive House of Commons that the Northern and Southern divisions got on very well together when they rubbed shoulders in the trenches. Southern unionist opinion allowed itself to be impressed; Northern unionist opinion did not want to know. A small but significant number of the Volunteers (effectively around 3,000) were openly unimpressed and aggressively opted to remain with MacNeill in *Óglaigh na hÉireann*.

Their numbers grew and in the early months of 1916 they were enrolling six new companies per week throughout the country, including Dublin. Their policy remained the arming, training, instruction, organisation and equipping of the men and women of Ireland for the defence of Ireland. For them Redmond's day was done. They saw him as having been duped by 'perfidious Albion'. His heady utterances in Woodenbridge, echoing enthusiasm for the war, had done less than justice to his earlier insistence that he would co-operate with the War Office only on condition that there would be no oath of allegiance and no overseas service. In Belfast he declaimed in a turnabout that the proper place to guard Ireland was on the fields of France.

*Óglaigh na hÉireann* saw no merit whatsoever to their cause in serving the imperial government in defence of the British empire. They remained pledged to the cause of Ireland, of all Ireland, and Ireland only. They adhered to the declaration of policy adopted at their First Irish Volunteer Convention in the Abbey Theatre Dublin on Sunday 25 October 1914:

1. To maintain the right and duty of the Irish Nation henceforward to provide for its own defence by means of a permanent armed and trained Volunteer Force.
2. To unite the people of Ireland on the basis of Irish Nationality and a common national interest; to maintain the integrity of the Nation and to resist with all our strength any measures tending to bring about or perpetuate disunion or the partition of our country.
3. To resist any attempt to force the men of Ireland into military service under any Government until a free national Government of Ireland is empowered by the Irish people themselves to deal with it.
4. To secure the abolition of the system of governing Ireland through Dublin Castle and the British military power and the establishment of a National Government in its place.

From the beginning the necessity for professional soldier training was stressed; ex-military instructors from the British army were used wherever possible by the Irish Volunteers. Discipline was strict. Men were imbued with the spirit of securing and maintaining the rights common to the whole people of Ireland. There was to be no suggestion that any one section of Irishmen should gain a political advantage over any other section, such as the people of Ulster.

Each member was required to purchase his own uniform and rifle. P.H. Pearse, as director of organisation, drew up a scheme of military organisation for the Volunteers in December 1914.[7] Colours and flags for regiments were authorised. The national flag showed on a green ground the golden harp of Ireland with its nine silver strings. It represented the mystic harp of *Dagda* — a symbol of life joyously renewing itself. In deference to the devices of the Volunteers of 1782 and on the advice of the noted Celtic studies scholar, Dr Sigerson, the carved harp or *cláirseach* was chosen in preference to the plain harp or *cruit.* All colours were to be made of Irish material, preferably poplin. Pearse laid down that no other flag except the authorised regimental colours was to be carried and that companies should be trained to salute the flag.[8]

Great care was given to the design and cloth for a uniform, which it was decided should consist of tunic, two-buttoned knickers and puttees. A grey-green cloth suitable for field work in Ireland was selected. The headdress for the Dublin regiment was after the Cossack style. It was left undecided for other regiments. Buttons and badges were agreed and orders were placed. Eoin MacNeill designed the cap badge.[9] F.F. stood for *Fianna Fáil*, the legendary standing army of Ireland. The stage was being set for the 1916 rebellion, which gave *Óglaigh na hÉireann* its baptism of fire and charted the future course of Irish history.

It had been plain that the political process in Westminster would continue to deny the majority of the Irish people their political rights. The time had come to take a stand for Ireland's freedom by asserting in arms their right to national freedom and sovereignty, but it was not the intention of MacNeill and the majority of the Irish Volunteers leaders that an armed revolt was inevitable.

The secret society, the Irish Republican Brotherhood (IRB), the Fenian physical force movement, had got a firm grip on much of the active military leadership of the Irish Volunteers in order to have a trained force at its disposal for a planned rising. The IRB plan was based on an arrangement to land on the Kerry coast a cargo of German arms. Lack of adequate communications prevented proper synchronisation of the operation, which was part of an unrealistic plan for a national uprising. Sir Roger Casement, who landed at Bannow Strand on Good Friday morning 1916 from an accompanying submarine, *U-19*, was immediately arrested. The German arms ship, the *Aud*, was captured by the British and scuttled by its captain, Spindler, off Cobh (Queenstown) on 21 April 1916. Casement was hanged for high treason in Pentonville prison, London on the following 4 August.

MacNeill, the official head of the Irish Volunteers, was instinctively and on principle opposed to the aggressive, militant role now being thrust upon him. Only by chance had he learned on Thursday 20 April that a full-scale insurrection was planned for the following Easter Sunday (23 April). Angered at being kept in the dark and at the far-reaching implications of such a momentous decision he tried — and failed — to dissuade Pearse. In turn, MacDonagh and MacDermott persuaded him that the landing of the German arms would inevitably produce a confrontation between the Irish Volunteers and the British forces. MacNeill did not believe a pre-emptive strike would, even in those circumstances, be justified. It would be up to the British to try and disarm the Volunteers. That prospect released him from the stigma of the immorality attaching to an unjustified rebellion. The disastrous news from Kerry, however, was decisive for him. After much agonising he countermanded orders for the general manoeuvres, under cover of which the Rising had been planned. The military maxim of order, counter-order, disorder was duly borne out.

It now fell to a military committee consisting of Pearse, Ceannt, Plunkett, Clarke, MacDermott, Connolly and MacDonagh to meet hurriedly in Liberty Hall that Easter Sunday to endeavour to restore order and direction to the movement. Command by committee violated the unity of command principle of war but there was no help for it in the circumtances.

Early next morning MacDonagh, the Brigade Commandant, issued orders to the five battalions of his Dublin Brigade units to parade for inspection and a route march at 10 a.m. In the order Pearse, as a code, underlined the words '*full arms and equipment*'. One day's rations were to be carried. He also specifically stipulated that E Company of the 3rd Battalion (his own past pupils from St Enda's College) should parade outside Liberty Hall, to form part of a headquarters protective battalion. He also called half of the 2nd Battalion into the GPO.

The outline plan of the Rising[10] was that the Volunteers in the provinces, armed with German rifles and their own scanty equipment, were to keep the British troops and the Royal Irish Constabulary from advancing into Dublin, whilst strategic positions in the capital were being seized and fortified by the four battalions of the Dublin Brigade.

The British garrison at Enniskillen was to be cut off by Volunteers from Belfast. Other sections of Volunteers were to deal with the British troops at the Curragh and in Athlone. As soon as Volunteers could be spared from the provinces, reinforcements were to be sent to Dublin.

The main road leading from Dun Laoghaire to Dublin, along which troops landing from England would pass, was to be covered from Boland's Bakery by the 3rd Battalion, Dublin Brigade. This battalion was to cover, also, the railway line from Lansdowne Road to Westland Row.

The task of the 2nd Battalion was to secure Jacob's Factory, and to protect the approaches from Portobello (Cathal Brugha) and Wellington (Griffith) Barracks. Kingsbridge (Heuston) Station, the terminus of the railways from the south, was to be controlled from the South Dublin Union by the 4th Battalion. This unit was to occupy Marrowbone Lane Distillery and advanced sniping positions covering the railway. It also had the task of covering Richmond Barracks. Dublin Castle was to be seized by a contingent from the Citizen Army.

The Military Council was to occupy the General Post Office and establish the headquarters of the Provisional Government there. The seizing of the GPO was to be carried out by a force composed of Volunteers and Citizen Army.

The 1st Battalion had the task of occupying the Four Courts, Broadstone Station, the terminus of the railways from the west, and of covering the approaches from the Royal (Collins), Islandbridge (Clancy) and Marlborough (McKee) Barracks. The Linenhall Barracks was also in its area. The Citizen Army was to occupy St Stephen's Green and cover the approaches to the city from that quarter.

It is generally known[11] that the Kerrymen were to transport the arms from the *Aud* to various parts of the country. Limerick men were to arrange to receive them and get them to Clare and Galway. Liam Mellowes was to return to Galway from England and march on Athlone to seize the artillery there. The Northerners were to rendezvous in Tyrone; Wexford was to rise. But the British had previous information that a Rising was planned for Easter Sunday.[12] The Admiralty had intercepted transatlantic cables to that effect between Arthur Zimmermann, the German Foreign Minister, and

Bernstoff, the German Minister in Mexico, having already broken the German code.

The ad hoc headquarters battalion set out from Liberty Hall to march on the General Post Office shortly before noon. It numbered around 150. About a quarter of the marchers wore the dark green uniform of the Citizen Army or the grey-green of the Irish Volunteers. Others attempted a military appearance by wearing puttees, riding breeches, bandoliers or yellow brassards. They were armed with short service Lee Enfields, Mausers, German sniping rifles, Sniders, Martinis,[13] shotguns, pickaxes and pikes. The bombs, borne in boxes, were made out of condensed milk tins, jam jars, lengths of piping and receptacles of all kinds. A spirit of intense determination pervaded the group.

Leading the parade in full uniform, his leggings splendidly polished as befitted an alleged ex-NCO of the British army, was Comdt Gen. James Connolly. On his left, casually dressed, was the Rising's amateur strategist,[14] the ailing Joseph Plunkett. His acting aide-de-camp, Michael Collins, uncharacteristically silent and morose, stuck close to him. Dublin, in contrast, was gay and lively that Easter Monday morning. Nearby, Fairyhouse Races contributed to the gaiety. Morning strollers viewed with amusement and contempt the motley dress and variety of armament of the passing parade. Pearse kept step on Connolly's right. Then came Plunkett; a pace to the rear on the left marched Collins. At the GPO Connolly stridently commanded: 'Halt; Left turn; the GPO, Charge.' Surprise was complete. One unintended effect of MacNeill's cancellation order was that Dublin Castle was caught napping. The armed guards surrendered without a struggle (they had no ammunition!). From the steps of the GPO Pearse read — to a largely indifferent audience — the proclamation of the Republic, one of the great documents of Irish history. He assumed the office of President of the Provisional Government and became the first Commander-in-Chief of the Irish army, named in the Fenian tradition as the Army of the Irish Republic.[15] Above the royal arms of the pediment floated proudly and historically the flag of a new egalitarian Ireland — the green, white and orange tricolour.[16]

Unfortunately, the combat effectiveness of the units to be deployed had been critically reduced by the mobilisation confusion. Only about one-third of the Dublin Brigade reported, around 1,000 at most. Two hundred and twenty men of the Citizen Army turned out. The combined force were roughly distributed as follows:[17]

| | | |
|---|---|---|
| 1st Battalion | —Four Courts, Church St, King St | 120 |
| 2nd Battalion | —Jacob's, Kevin St, Camden St | 150 |
| 3rd Battalion | —Boland's Bakery, Grand Canal St, Westland Row, Northumberland Rd | 130 |
| 4th Battalion | —South Dublin Union, Marrowbone Lane, Roe's Malt House, Watkins Brewery | 150 |
| 5th Battalion | —Ashbourne (20 men to GPO) | 39 |
| Citizen Army | —Stephen's Green — City Hall Area | 180 |
| Hibernian Rifles | — GPO | 20 |
| Special Force | — Mendicity Institute | 30 |
| Headquarters Battalion | — GPO/O'Connell St, Henry St Area (mixed Citizen Army and Volunteers from 5th Bn plus 20 men from E Coy 4th Bn) | 170 |
| Total | | 989 |

The opposing forces were better situated. On Day 1 the British Dublin garrison consisted of 2,827: the 6th Reserve Calvary Regiment (886 strong) comprising squadrons of the 5th and 12th Lancers was in Marlborough (McKee) Barracks; the 3rd Battalion (Special Reserve) of the Royal Irish Regiment (403 strong) was in Richmond (Keogh) Barracks — it supplied drafts to the active service battalions on the Western front and in Macedonia; the 10th Battalion of the Royal Dublin Fusiliers (467 strong) *en route* to the Somme battles was in Royal (Collins) Barracks, the 3rd Battalion of the Royal Irish Rifles, an Ulster militia battalion (671 strong) was in Portobello (Cathal Brugha) Barracks. In addition there were four stand-to parties (400 strong). Most of those troops — all of the Infantry — were Irish.

This force was reinforced at once by a mobile column of 1,600 from the Curragh (the 3rd Reserve Cavalry Brigade, earmarked to repel a German invasion). This was augmented by an additional 1,000 men on Day 2 (Tuesday 25 April). A battery of four 18-pounder quick-firing guns from the Reserve Artillery Brigade in Athlone, the 4th Dublin Fusiliers from Templemore and a composite battalion from Belfast made up of Royal Inniskilling Fusiliers and Royal Irish Fusiliers, also arrived on that day, making the following opposing forces available for action in Dublin:

| | |
|---|---|
| Dublin garrison | 2,827 |
| Curragh garrison | 2,600 |
| Athlone garrison | 100 |
| Templemore garrison | 500 |
| Belfast battalion, composite | 1,000 |
| Total | 7,027 |

The 25th Irish Infantry Brigade, made up of the 5th Battalion Royal Dublin Fusiliers and the 5th Battalion Leinster Regiment (an extra 1000 men), arrived with Brig. Gen. W.H.M. Lowe on the Tuesday and Wednesday. This strength was increased by the arrival from Hertfordshire, England, of further reinforcements (approx. 10,000) of the 176th and 178th Brigades of the 50th (North Midland) Division. They concentrated in Kingstown (Dun Laoghaire) by nightfall on Day 4, Thursday 27 April, bringing to over 16,000 the numbers available to the British to put down the Rising. Lt Gen. Sir John Maxwell, late Commander-in-Chief, Egypt, and now Commander-in-Chief, Ireland, arrived the following day to take command. His was a military estimate of what was in many ways fundamentally a political problem.

The Dublin Metropolitan Police estimated numbers of the Volunteers in Dublin at 2,225 with 825 rifles, the Citizen Army at 100 with 125 rifles, the AOH (American Alliance) at 140 with 25 rifles. Gen. Maxwell's eventual total superiority was in the region of twenty to one — an uneven order of battle.

Gen. Connolly ordered civilians out of the GPO. Collins arrested a British officer found in the building. General headquarters of Ireland's army in the field was set up in the heart of the capital[18] although at that point chances of conventional military success were incalculable. A blood sacrifice had been perhaps one course of action, but that was theoretical now. There was a battle to be won. Connolly, the man of action, gave military orders to barricade the doors, break the windows and fortify them. Plunkett studied his maps. On the representation of Gen. Connolly, Patrick Pearse, the Commander-in-Chief, detailed Comdt Brennan-Whitmore and Collins to assist in the fortification. Flags were flown, bombs redistributed and reserve ammunition and demolition tools were rearranged in convenient dumps. Orders were given that any man found taking intoxicating drink without permission would be shot, a measure which proved effective. The dependants of British soldiers, unable to draw their Separation Allowance, told the rebels in no uncertain terms what they thought of them. Fights broke out between them and lady Sinn Féin supporters in the crowd of onlookers. Reports that unsuccessful attempts were made to blow up Nelson Pillar were untrue. Such a thought never crossed their minds.

The first attack on General Headquarters was repulsed. The garrison held their fire until the Lancers galloped abreast of the GPO. On the Tuesday 44 Parnell St (Kevin Barry Hall) was raided to seize the arms belonging to the National (Redmondite) Volunteers. (Pat McCrea, later Colonel, was a member of that party.)

On The O'Rahilly's suggestion Pearse ordered the occupation of the upper stories. Day 2, the Tuesday, was a quiet day. A couple of seafaring men, a Finn and a Swede, joined the garrison because they did not like England. Reinforcements trickled in. *Cumann na mBan* ferried in arms from surrounding caches. Permission was refused to deal drastically with looters: unless the Volunteers were actually attacked by civilians, they were not to fire on them. Day 3, Wednesday, saw sniping intensified and Connolly was seriously wounded. Thereafter he commanded with great confidence and authority from a stretcher. By Thursday the enemy had come into effective strength in College St, Trinity College, Tara St, the Custom House, Liberty Hall, Amiens St and by Parnell St to Findlater Place. Childers's Howth Rifles with their comforting 'boom' proved to be excellent weapons but were outgunned. An incendiary shell sent the offices of the *Freeman's Journal* up in flames. The Volunteers took pleasure in seeing this happen to their old enemy. The gunboat, *Helga*, moored in the Liffey, had laboriously reduced the vacant Liberty Hall the day before. A direct bombardment from a 9-pounder was next brought by the British from a position at Trinity College, facing D'Olier St. The heat from the burning buildings across the road was almost unbearable. All that side of O'Connell St was ablaze. The artillery got the range and poured incendiary shells into the GPO building. Evacuation through fires and under fire began.

The gallant defence of the GPO was at an end. The remainder of the actions were, with the exception of the occupation of the North Earl St area, unco-ordinated, and until the final surrender had separate lives of their own.

Connolly had ordered Comdt Brennan-Whitmore to occupy and fortify Tylers shop (across the road), together with the block of buildings between the Pillar Café and the Imperial Hotel, and to build and man a barricade across North Earl St.[19] The enemy had occupied Amiens St station as a forming-up point for an attack on the GPO. Luckily for the rebels the British held back from attacking North Earl St so fortification continued unchecked on the Tuesday. Pearse came across, but his inspection consisted of chatting. Connolly was more trenchant and did not rest until he had satisfied himself as to the strength of the barricade; he then commended the party. Three members of *Cumann na mBan* arrived with medical supplies and worked like slaves to help.

Everything had to be improvised. A ball of twine with a condensed milk tin attached to it provided communication across the street. But all the ingenuity could not compensate for the lack of machine-guns. British reluctance to take offensive action in spite of their superior fire power did not reflect much martial credit on them. It reinforced Connolly's fallacious conviction that the British would never shell private property. (He had planned an independent rising a month before Easter on that premise.)

Connolly had also ordered Oscar Traynor with a party recalled from Fairview (on Tuesday) to occupy and fortify the Metropole Hotel.[20] They had to depend entirely on revolvers, automatics, rifles and a rather weird assortment of bombs against machine-gun and artillery fire. Oscar Traynor worked indefatigably all the week. On Friday they assembled on the first floor to meet a massed attack on their position with only their rifles and a number of bombs with a lighted candle to touch them off. When the GPO was engulfed their position became untenable and they were ordered to withdraw. Hopkins and Hopkins,[21] a jewellers' shop in O'Connell St, was also heroically defended and only evacuated because a verbal message got garbled in the time-honoured manner.

Connolly continued to give incisive orders. As his Order of the Day on 28 April 1916, 'the fifth day of the establishment of the Irish Republic', indicates, he remained optimistic to the end, endeavouring to impose order and purpose on the unco-ordinated situation. The headquarters protective battalion was a piecemeal organisation cobbled together in a hurry. No commander had been appointed, so Connolly in addition to his other duties as *de facto* Commander-in-Chief — as Commandant General of the Citizen Army he was given command of the forces in Dublin for the Rising — assumed control. He displayed great courage and character in the conduct of the battle. Pearse called him the guiding brain of the resistance. The imaginative Plunkett, with Michael Collins as his staff officer, provided operational support. Michael Collins was one of the contingent from Great Britain who had rendezvoused in Kimmage[22] prior to the Rising.

The 1st Battalion under Comdt O'Daly occupied the Four Courts and the Church St area on the north west of the city and blocked the approaches from Royal (Collins) Barracks and Marlborough (McKee) Barracks. They had raided first the Magazine Fort in the Phoenix Park at noon on the Monday and disarmed the garrison of fifteen (the sentry was killed). They held the Fort for a half hour and destroyed 150 tons of .303 ammunition by burning it.

They then returned to Four Courts where they held out for the rest of the week. Maxwell later reported that with the one exception of the place in Ballsbridge where the Sherwood Foresters were ambushed this was by far the worst fighting that occurred in the whole of Dublin.

Barricades were skilfully constructed and manned with determination. Pearse sent ten of the best armed of the recalled Kimmage garrison to the Four Courts where they reinforced the men holding the barricade at Church St Bridge.

The British plan was to establish a cordon from Kingsbridge (Heuston) Station — Infirmary Rd — North Circular Rd — Amiens St — Butt Bridge to Trinity College. On the west a cordon was thrown up in Bridgefoot St — Queen St — King St — Capel St. They concentrated their attack on the North King St area but the final surrender, after two days of incessant fighting, did not come until 10 a.m. on Sunday. The Volunteers there continued to hold out under arms and only reluctantly surrendered when ordered to do so.[23]

The 2nd Battalion[24] under Comdt MacDonagh had been split by Pearse. One half seized Jacob's Factory to defend the southern approach to the city centre while the other half reported as ordered to the GPO. They occupied Ardee St Brewery and also took up a position to seal off Wellington (Griffith) Barracks. There were lively encounters in Marrowbone Lane. By the Thursday they were hemmed in, but easily repulsed dilatory British attacks. They too found it hard to accept the order to surrender on the Saturday.

The 3rd Battalion, de Valera's, was allocated 'the Ringsend area'.[25] It was the first area to be occupied and the last to be evacuated. There were not enough men to close the circle in the south east of the city. Only 112 men turned out on the Easter Monday — eighty of them from B Company, and de Valera rejected women soldiers.[26] Personal initiatives rather than organised action made it possible for such a small force to cover such a large area.

De Valera made his headquarters in an apartment attached to the Union Dispensary — not in Boland's Mill which was only held by a token force of Lt Joseph O'Byrne and a few men. Possession was taken of Westland Row Station, the railway lines at various points and Boland's Bakery. From the archways stretching across South Lotts Rd and Bath Avenue, Beggars Bush Barracks was dominated. Nothing much happened on the Monday. Most outposts were withdrawn into HQ in the Bakery for the night. It was 'flourbagged' to make it shell-proof. The next day (Tuesday) occupation proceeded; walls were loopholed, houses telescoped, outposts positioned.

Wednesday 30 April brought the most memorable conflict of Easter Week. The mobilisation of Dun Laoghaire and Blackrock Volunteers had failed so the 'Third' had to extend the men at its disposal along Northumberland, Shelbourne and Lansdowne Roads. De Valera gave that job to Lt Michael Malone who had originally taken over No. 25 Northumberland Rd (not Clanwilliam House)[27] with three men on the Monday morning. For the first couple of days he had maintained communications with the main body via the Parochial Hall and Clanwilliam House.

The 178th Brigade was made up of four battalions of the Sherwood Foresters (Nottinghamshire and Derbyshire Regiment). One set out to march on Dublin from Kingstown (Dun Laoghaire); the 2nd Battalion, sent to Kilmainham on the Stillorgan-Donnybrook axis, got through, but the two battalions (7th and 8th) ordered to Trinity College by Merrion Rd, Ballsbridge and Merrion Square, ran up against the Mount St Bridge outpost. (The 2/6th South Staffords also suffered heavy casualties — over forty in the South King St area — from O'Daly's 1st Battalion.)

Malone and one man (Grace) inflicted heavy casualties until Malone fell and Grace by some miracle got out. The second line of defence was Clanwilliam House held by seven Volunteers (the Sherwood Foresters were 800 strong). The Volunteers never wasted a round. When the British neared the bridge they dropped their rifles and emptied their revolvers into them. Maxwell reported that four officers were killed, fourteen were wounded and 216 other ranks killed and wounded (more than half the total British casualties).

De Valera has been criticised for not keeping a reserve with which to influence the Mount St battle. If full mobilisation had worked he would have had over 400 men. As it was he had only barely over 100. He had also been criticised for being too histrionic. He led the way to take over the dispensary with a drawn sword. He roared and cheered when British shells missed. The men remained phlegmatic. He worked himself, with little sleep, to the point of exhaustion. His zeal and personal bravery were remarkable. He knew every inch of the area under his command with mathematical accuracy. He was a lone figure in a position of intense responsibility. His Vice-Commandant had failed to turn out. The next senior officer, an ex-British and Boer War veteran, deserted within a week. There were other officer defections, and so he had to attend to everything himself.

He summoned all boys and youths under eighteen years of age on the Tuesday morning, explaining to them that this was a real war, not manoeuvres, and urged them to go home. On a lighter note, a member of a patrol detailed for the dangerous task of creating a diversion to relieve the pressure on the Citizen Army in Stephen's Green rushed back to try to find his hat. If he was going to die for Ireland he wanted to be properly dressed! Time was of the essence. 'Here's a hat for you', cried de Valera, pitching the man his own headgear. He went hatless for the rest of the engagement.

By the end of the week the position had become untenable. O/C explosives had failed to deliver the material. They did not even have hand grenades. On Sunday two girls of *Cumann na mBan* brought Pearse's order to surrender. De Valera complained that if the people had only come to help them, even with knives and forks, they would not be in the predicament of having to surrender.

The 4th Battalion extended from the Rathfarnham area in the south to the Inchicore area in the west (a portion of the south west was also included until the formation of a sixth battalion, later the 2nd Dublin Brigade). E company of the battalion (Rathfarnham) was commanded by Capt. Willie Pearse and was stationed in the GPO.

The depleted unit under the command of the Battalion Commandant, Eamonn Ceannt, then endeavoured to make a strong point of its principal post in the South Dublin Union area.[28] It did not have enough men to seize the key Kingsbridge (Heuston) Station, and Connolly made a commander's decision to compensate: he ordered some of his reserve under Capt. Heuston to seize and hold the Mendicity Institute, where they performed heroically.

The little garrison in the Union repulsed attack after attack. The Battalion Vice-Commandant, Cathal Brugha, although lying on the kitchen floor, a mass of wounds, fearessly and singlehandedly prevented the enemy from crossing the barricades and inspired the defenders to further efforts. It took a long hard consultation between Comdt MacDonagh (2nd Battalion) and Comdt Ceannt before they could persuade themselves to accept the general surrender order at the end of the week. They were both signatories of the Proclamation of the Republic and were executed in Kilmainham Jail. Con Colbert, who was in command of the Marrowbone Lane Distillery, was also executed there.

Before the Rising the four companies of the 5th Dublin Brigade[29] were organised into a battalion under Comdt Thomas Ashe in succession to Dr R. Hayes, who became Battalion Adjutant. Mr Lawless senior was the Quartermaster.

On the Sunday the battalion mobilised as ordered almost to a man. The official cancellation of the general mobilisation order caused confusion. On remustering, depleted units went into camp in Knockshedan and Killeck. It rained persistently and the men were soaked through.

On the Tuesday, as detailed, twenty men were sent to the GPO with the aim of creating a diversion in the city. On Wednesday the remaining battle force captured Swords Police Barracks. No resistance was offered. The police in Donabate surrendered after firing a few shots. Twelve carbines, 1000 rounds of carbine ammunition, three Webley revolvers and 300 rounds of ammunition were thus added to the armament of the party. Ashe, who was nominally in charge, placed himself in Mulcahy's hands. He (Mulcahy) quickly put a stop to the grumbling that the Rising was not an official act of the Volunteer organisation, the President of the Executive having publicly signified his dissent.

The next objective was Ashbourne Police Barracks. In that action eleven police were killed and up to forty wounded. Volunteer casualties were: one killed in action (Jack Crinnigan), one died of wounds (Tom Rafferty) and five wounded (Joe Taylor, Matt Kelly, Ned Rooney, Pat Walshe, Jack Rafferty). The battalion thought very badly of having to lay down its arms in the general surrender. It had defeated a well-equipped body of more than double its number.

The Maynooth Volunteers[30] under Domhnall O Buachalla immediately mobilised on getting word of the Rising at 3 p.m.

on the Monday (communication with the North Kildare Volunteers having broken down). Their mission was to relieve members of the Citizen Army surrounded in the *Evening Mail* office in Parliament St. They got as far as the nearby Exchange Hotel where they were surrounded. The attacks were beaten off, enemy losses amounting to about thirty killed and wounded. They evacuated and eventually fought their way back to the GPO.

Shortly after the foundation of the Irish Volunteers in 1913 the women's auxiliary organisation was created under the title of *Cumann na mBan* to aid the Volunteer movement in a number of ways, the chief of which were by:

(*a*) compiling regular intelligence reports on activities of enemy forces such as projected raids, movement of troops;

(*b*) the carrying of dispatches;

(*c*) training in first aid and elementary nursing care in secret in the event of casualties;

(*d*) helping in fund-raising activities, especially on behalf of comrades 'on the run'.

In the carrying out of their duties the members of *Cumann na mBan* endured many hardships (travelling long journeys in inclement weather), frequent terms of imprisonment, hunger-striking, etc. The value of their dedicated service during the Black and Tan fight received the highest commendation, especially from Michael Collins who as Director of Intelligence had first-hand knowledge of their valuable contribution. However, de Valera later (1976) referred to them as 'unmanageable revolutionaries'.

The work of *Cumann na mBan*[31] during the 1916 fighting was heroic. They ran crucial courier missions, attended to casualties and established a field hospital at the back of the main building in the GPO. (They gave generous praise for the assistance rendered by a British medical officer who was a prisoner in the building. Two British soldiers, who were prisoners also, assisted with the cooking during the week for the entire garrison.) It was the 3rd Battalion's loss when de Valera spurned the girls' advances. His motives for doing so have been variously ascribed: 'girl-shyness' in one of his advisors; anti-feminism; old-fashioned chivalry. He did not want to add to his anxieties by being lumbered with women untrained for soldiering. He saw their uses for cooking and first aid but they wanted to fight and he would not give them arms as he had barely enough for his own men. None of them came to him.

About ninety women took part in the Rising — sixty *Cumann na mBan*, with the balance made up of Citizen Army and the seldom-mentioned *Clan na Gael* Girl Scouts. The Countess Markievicz (Citizen Army) was the only one to carry a rifle, but forty *Cumann na mBan* were in the GPO during the fighting. About thirty left on Pearse's order on the Friday, but fourteen remained and were among the last batch to leave at 7 p.m.

Their principal study was first aid but some of them (in Fairview for instance) did some elementary rifle marksmanship and drill — anything to help the men of the 2nd Battalion to which they were 'attached'. They were run by an executive and committees. They had their own ideas of how a chain of command should work. When, on verification of the countermanding order, they refused to go home without orders from 'our own Commandant', the battalion commander, Comdt Tom Hunter, said plaintively, 'But I am your Commandant: I am in charge of the second battalion'. The complainant, Mrs Nora O'Daly, hadn't the heart to tell him that she was very well aware of that fact but that it was Comdt Molly Reynolds she was referring to.

Insurgent positions[32] in the GPO, Four Courts, Jacob's Factory, St Stephen's Green and Boland's Bakery encircled the weakly held central city, including Dublin Castle. Outside the ring troops were located in the following barracks: Marlborough (McKee), Royal (Collins), Richmond (Keogh) and Portobello (Cathal Brugha). Token forces were based in Wellington (Griffith), Beggars Bush, Linenhall, Islandbridge (Clancy) and in the small training camp at Bull Island.

The rebels were too thin on the ground to set up effective road blocks to prevent enemy movement. In the absence of a spontaneous national uprising there were no realistic prospects for protracted defence. The amateur army lacked the unity of command, staff structure, armament and equipment necessary to conduct prolonged perimeter defence. Opposing forces were trained, combat-experienced, well-equipped professional soldiers. Their counter-attack planned to secure the Castle, clear the south bank of the river and, from the area of Trinity College, to attack and capture the GPO while cordoning off the north city from Parkgate St to the North Wall. Artillery fire support would be augmented by fire from the *SS Helga.* Intense street fighting resulted.

Earlier bungling with a traditional cavalry charge down Sackville (O'Connell) St from Marlborough (McKee) Barracks, and the later driving up Northumberland Rd by the Sherwood Foresters now gave way to solid if plodding fire and movement drills. On the other hand, the only professionalism left to the rebels[33] to display was in the realms of personal bravery and localised leadership. They had virtually no reserves and no artillery. After the first die was cast they had no capability to influence the battle. Nominal command control was however maintained throughout.

The Citizen Army[34] under Comdt Michael Mallin, with Countess Markievicz as second-in-command, did not initially display the same military expertise in their actions and orders as did *Óglaigh na hÉireann.* This may have reflected Connolly's conviction that they had no chance whatsoever of success. The decision to restrain Connolly from premature insurrection in January 1916 had been based on Plunkett's feelings that the time would rarely be riper than at the coming Easter to roll the dice of war with a prospect of success. At that time there were about 6,000 troops and 10,000 armed policemen to be opposed by a possible 18,000 Volunteers, who would be armed with German rifles if the *Aud* landing plans worked out. Connolly's concept did not appear to go beyond confrontation. Others (notably Comdt Brennan-Whitmore, who controlled the buildings in North Earl St opposite the GPO) felt that nothing more elaborate than the seizing, fortifying and holding of key buildings was 'on'. After that manoeuvre they would slip out again and engage in hit and run tactics. Plunkett on the other hand, somewhat fancifully, deduced a possible national military success and conceived a theoretical course of action to accomplish it.[35]

Connolly was a revolutionary, and there were class tensions between the Irish Citizen Army and the Irish Volunteers. But he was a Nationalist first and an Internationalist second. He was a born soldier also and the man of action in the GPO. But he could not be everywhere.

Digging in on St Stephen's Green by his Citizen Army without seizing the Shelbourne Hotel or Trinity College made no military sense. But Comdt Mallin quickly recomposed himself and seized the City Hall, the bridges at Portobello, Harcourt St Station and the guardroom at Dublin Castle. Erroneously he failed to secure the Castle foothold.[36]

After the first wave of aggression the insurgents concentrated on defence. The only further offensive action taken was at the Magazine Fort in the Phoenix Park and at Dublin Castle. The Fort was captured by ruse and that limited mission was accomplished. The Castle operation was bungled in a manner painfully reminiscent of Robert Emmet's rebellion of 1803. Faulty intelligence, bad planning and inexperience were the reasons for the failure.

Some of Capt. Sean Connolly's small Irish Citizen Army detachment attacked the Castle, shot the gate policeman, overpowered the guard and entered the Upper Castle Yard. The deserted Castle was theirs for the taking if they but knew it. Sean Connolly reckoned (erroneously) that it would be hard to hold and he withdrew to occupy the City Hall instead: a fatal decision. At 12.15 p.m. the DMP had telephoned that Dublin Castle was being attacked by armed Sinn Féin. Col. Kennard, the Garrison Commander, who had left his office shortly before, was prevented from returning. All available troops from Portobello, Richmond and Royal Barracks were ordered to proceed to the Castle and the 6th Reserve Cavalry Regiment were moved towards Sackville St.

The 3rd Royal Irish Regiment on their way to the Castle were held up at Dublin South Union. At 9.35 p.m. Col. Kennard with another party of the 3rd Royal Irish secured the critical telephone exchange in Crown Alley and reached the Castle vicinity. It had been a grievous mistake not to have captured the exchange in time and cut off crucial telephone communications. The British spent the first day's military activity securing it and Trinity College. By midnight, however, the Volunteers still held the approaches to the Castle itself.

In order to relieve the garrison and get ground communication with the Castle, Col. Portal, commanding the Curragh Mobile Column, was ordered to establish a line of posts from Kingsbridge (Heuston) Station to Trinity College via the Castle. This was completed by 12 noon on 25 April, with very little loss. It divided the Volunteers into two and permitted enemy communication by dispatch rider. Heavy fire on the Castle from Volunteers in the Corporation Buildings and City Hall was still kept up so those buildings were attacked and captured.

Also on the second day two or three hundred Royal Irish Rifles and Dublin Fusiliers had slipped in by the Ship St gate to reinforce the small number in the Castle. From then on the strength of the garrison increased and so did the casualties on both sides. A historic opportunity had been lost.

The Castle had a deep symbolism in Irish history. To recapture it would have required as much destruction as the Sackville (O'Connell) St situation demanded. It would have made a better bastion than the GPO. The presence of a Red Cross hospital there might have inhibited enemy artillery fire. The Volunteer leadership did not have the necessary military intelligence to make a proper estimate of the situation.

The pre-rising intelligence put together by Connolly and MacDonagh — especially about Beggars Bush and the Castle — was not accurate.[37] The party detailed to seize the Crown Alley Exchange did not mobilise in time but Comdt Mallin then seized the College of Surgeons and other buildings on the west side of St Stephen's Green, where his men fought extremely well and were one of the last posts to surrender. They pinned down troops and restricted the passage of reinforcements from England into the city.

Men who were later to take opposite sides in the Civil War outdid each other in valour. W.T. Cosgrave, later President of the Executive Council of the Free State (1922–32), distinguished himself in the South Union area. He was on Eamonn Ceannt's staff and was in touch with everything that happened. He was sentenced to death and later reprieved. Desmond Fitzgerald and his wife looked after the commissariat in the Post Office. Cathal Brugha was bravery personified. But courage alone could not overcome enemy firepower. In addition to their integral machine-guns and mortars the British had four 18-pounder guns, a 9-pounder and a 1-pounder naval gun fired from a truck, together with shells from the *Helga*, a gunboat armed with a 12-pounder. Not mass artillery by any means, but too much, especially with the use of incendiary shells, for the ramshackle weaponry of the hastily mobilised hotch-potch rebel force.

The British progressively and professionally, albeit pedestrianly, co-ordinated their fire plans. In support were machine-guns from Trinity College and snipers from advantageous surrounding rooftop positions; 18-pounders were used effectively as single guns to neutralise posts. However, all the *Óglaigh na hEireann* battalions with their Citizen Army and Hibernian comrades-in-arms fought extremely well and none of them surrendered until categorically ordered to do so. They performed well under fire. But they did not have a significant counter-attack capability. Individual efforts at offensive action came to nothing.

Oscar Traynor's gallant band withdrawing from the Metropole found the GPO an inferno. Early on the Saturday morning the British barricades were within 250 yards so they decided to fling a bayonet charge against them. It was in that bayonet charge that The O'Rahilly and several others lost their lives. There was nothing left but to do or die in the open streets. Pearse decided not to take that course of action as it would involve not only the lives of his own men but of all the people in the densely populated area. That was the thought that persuaded him to surrender.

Shortly before four o'clock on the Sunday (Day 6) Patrick Pearse, President of the Provisional Government of the Republic, agreed to an unconditional surrender and ordered the commandants of the various districts in the city and county to lay down their arms. His hemmed-in headquarters was ablaze from incendiary shells; the wounded and the women were evacuated;[38] arrangements for further evacuation and possible re-grouping were set in train. At 3 p.m. Pearse surrendered unconditionally to Lowe on the north side of the Moore St barricade. The simultaneous rising in other parts of Ireland[39] had not materialised. The failure to secure arms from Germany dissipated whatever understandings may have existed. The fundamental need for secrecy and the incidental requirement of dissimulation with MacNeill obscured clear-cut intentions. Plans to distribute the German arms, involving a need to work in and link up between neighbouring Volunteers, almost certainly were considered. A plan to hold the line of the Shannon was discussed (in the context perhaps of an original idea of an arms landing in Limerick).

In the event, action was confined to Counties Galway and Wexford and north Co. Dublin. No fighting apart from blocking was contemplated in Ulster. The Ulster Volunteers were supposed to come under the command of Liam Mellowes in Galway. He mobilised up to 600 men who were armed with twenty-five rifles, sixty revolvers, about 300 shotguns and sixty pikes. They unsuccessfully attacked police barracks in Gort, Clarenbridge and Oranmore but made no attempt to move towards the Shannon. There was no firm prearranged plan. Mellowes had no specific orders. In Wexford, however, they had. Connolly ordered the Wexford Brigade Commandant, Paul Galligan, to prevent British reinforcements from moving on Dublin from Rosslare. The Volunteers took over Enniscorthy but no attempt to move reinforcements was made. The British reacted by sending a small force by sea to guard the explosives factory at Arklow. In Galway the sloop *HMS Laburnian* fired nine rounds at an imaginary rebel force advancing in Galway. The cruiser *HMS Gloucester* landed 100 troops in Galway.

Up to the Redmondite split Dundalk had one of the strongest Volunteer contingents in that command (Louth, Meath, South Down, South Armagh and South Monaghan). Sean MacEntee (later Tanaiste) was a member of one of them. When the split occurred all rifles in the different companies were placed for safe keeping in RIC barracks except when training (the factions being a bigger menace then to each other than the British were to either of them). On Easter Sunday morning the Volunteers captured thirty Redmondite rifles stored in Ardee. Through no fault of theirs they did not take any vital part of the Rising; Sean MacEntee was sent to Dublin to keep contact and got involved. He was sentenced to death, commuted to penal servitude for life.

The fire fight had been lost but the battle for the hearts and minds had only begun. The Rising was over. The War of Independence was yet to come. That guerilla campaign would have been unthinkable without the support of the people, won over to the cause of the Volunteers by the dramatic sequel to the Rising of executions and imprisonments. Casualties on both combat sides totalled about 500 killed and 2,500 wounded. 300 civilians were killed; 2,000 wounded. The troops and police had 132 killed and 397 wounded. The insurgents had around sixty killed and 200 wounded: sixteen were executed.

Executions[40] served to highlight the outstanding personal qualities of the insurgent leaders. Between 3 and 15 May fifteen of them, including the seven signatories of the proclamation of the Republic, were tried by court-martial and executed. Joseph Plunkett was shot, although he was on the verge of death. Poignantly, he was given permission to wed the night before and was granted ten minutes alone with his bride. James Connolly was too ill from his wounds to stand up and was shot sitting down. All were idealists who were not afraid to die for their cause. Two commandants, Ashe and de Valera, were reprieved from the death sentence (Brennan-Whitmore had not been sentenced to death). De Valera later did not accept that he was reprieved because of his American citizenship. He felt that the British, too late, were beginning to perceive the adverse effect of the executions on public opinion. The real reason why de Valera, alone among the Commandants of the Rising, was not executed may have been due to prosecuting counsel Wylie's advice to Maxwell that Dev was not important enough to execute. This and pressure from Westminster probably saved him. The British did not seem to consider his American citizenship.

The leaders of the Rising displayed high qualities of humanitarianism, chivalry and valour, the hallmark of *Óglaigh na hÉireann*; qualities, indeed, also displayed by the British, Irish and German troops during the bloody battles in France in 1916.

The Rising provided invaluable under-fire experience for the newly emerging Irish army. There were many lessons to be learned: that an ambush could be as effective in a city street as in a mountain pass; that a counter-attack capability was an essential; that small highly trained flying columns were the answer to difficulties encountered in training large-scale units; that there was no substitute for up-to-the-minute intelligence. The military action was a curtain-raiser, a reconnaissance-in-force.

The Irish army had come through its baptism of fire. Under fire it showed military competence, supreme self-confidence, determination, leadership and a remarkable facility to extemporise and improvise. It was not at all intimidated by the overwhelming might of the enemy — the contrary was the case, even to the point of foolhardiness. The people came to be proud of the Rising. It achieved its main objective: to win public opinion. The outcome was the eclipse of the Irish Party and a coolness towards those Volunteers who had joined the British army to fight for Redmond's home rule. They still sang 'God Save Ireland' going into battle but no longer with the same certitudes as in Redmond's heyday. Their sacrifices were devalued.

The goal posts had shifted. In Easter Week 1916 the Sixteenth Irish Division was subjected to two harrowing attacks of poison gas in France. The 47th Irish Brigade relieved them in the line. But it no longer made heroes of them at home in Ireland. The ground had been cut from under them by British politicians, who had dragged their feet in implementing the home rule bill already on the statute book, condoned Maxwell's mishandling of the Rising and ill-advisedly called for conscription.

One of the Volunteers in Flanders, an ex-pupil of Pearse's St Enda's School, Stephen Gwynn, visited fellow officer, Willie Redmond,[41] in his neighbouring company commander's dug-out opposite '*Puits 14 bis*'. Willie remarked: 'Don't imagine that what you and I have done is going to make us popular with our people. On the contrary, we shall both be sent to the right about at the next General Election.'

A year earlier the Royal Dublin Fusiliers and the Munster Fusiliers suffered appalling casualties while landing at Sedd

El Bahr on the Gallipoli peninsula in Turkey. Grief was national. Black crepe hung from every single door in the Coombe in Dublin and from many more throughout Ireland. The pain of loss remained, but fighting in France for the freedom of small nations was losing its meaning. A new nationalism was awakening, based on Sinn Féin, 'Ourselves Alone':

'All changed, changed utterly'
'A terrible beauty is born'.[42]

In two dispatches, dated 20 and 26 May 1916, Gen. Maxwell reported the British version of the fighting. On 2 May 1916 he ordered the surrender of all arms, ammunition and explosives. Brig. Gen. Blackadder ordered the 177th Infantry Brigade to withdraw the cordon of troops surrounding Dublin at 7 p.m. on Friday 12 May.[43] The houses of families of the prisoners continued to be ransacked. The duties of guards and picquets were to prevent any recurrence of the disturbance and to assist the civil police if called upon.

Even their most hidebound enemies paid sincere tribute to the determined professionalism and temperate, chivalrous behaviour of *Óglaigh n hÉireann*.[44]

A direct result of the Rising was the resignation of Lord Wimborne, the Lord Lieutenant, Mr Birrell, the Chief Secretary and Sir Matthew Nathan, the Under Secretary. Birrell admitted that he had underestimated the Sinn Féin movement. Redmond said that he felt that he had incurred some of the blame as Birrell might have been influenced by what he said. Asquith, the British Prime Minister, belatedly visited Dublin (and Belfast) from 12 to 18 May. He spoke to some of the prisoners in Richmond Barracks.

Redmond proposed, on 10 June 1916, that the home rule bill be brought into immediate operation. Lord Lansdowne in the House of Lords responded on 11 July in bellicose terms. He invoked Gen. Maxwell, 40,000 soldiers and the Defence of the Realm Act to preserve order in Ireland. Redmond was shocked. On 12 July he described Lansdowne's statement as a 'gross insult to Ireland . . . a declaration of war on the Irish people . . . the announcement of a policy of coercion.[45]

# 2

## The War of Independence
## (1917-21)

Although the 1916 Rising was not supported throughout the country its aftermath increased Sinn Féin's power. By August 1916 the majority of internees arrested after the rebellion was released. The following Christmas most of the unconvicted prisoners interned in Frongoch were freed. This aided the spread of separatist ideas, and Frongoch got the name of being the nursery of the IRA.

Fighting for the freedom of small nations in Flanders patently failed to deliver on home rule. The Rising, the executions,[1] the imprisonments, the conscription threat, all contributed to the sweeping victory of the separatist republicans over the Parliamentary Party in the General Election of 1918. Subsequently Sinn Féin established an alliance with the militant Irish Republican Brotherhood.

The Irish Parliamentary Party and its recruiting policy for the British army became largely[2] discredited in the popular mind. Even returning ex-soldiers were disenchanted and rejoined the parent *Óglaigh na hÉireann* organisation.

After the Rising, the prospect of American intervention in the war tempered British belief in more colonial-type executions; instead they resorted to internment. De Valera emerged as the leader of his imprisoned compatriots in Britain. The prisoners there knew little of how Lloyd George, who had replaced Asquith, tried to placate Irish-American sentiment which had been outraged by the executions. They began to identify more closely with the cause, ideals and aspirations of their comrades who had died in 1916. De Valera's preoccupation in prison was for the future of *Óglaigh na hÉireann*. He wrote:

> The armed force started in 1913 must not be allowed to disappear. The Irish Volunteers, or whatever you like to call them, must be kept as a permanent force at the country's back. That it seems to us is our mission as a body and we must allow nothing to make us forget it.[3]

However, when the Volunteers were re-formed in November 1917 it was Michael Collins and not de Valera who was appointed Director of Organisation. He straight away began preparations for guerilla warfare against government forces. Ruthless and efficient, he quickly established discipline.

De Valera stuck to politics. He expected that the Americans, who had entered the war on the Allied side in April 1917, would support Irish national aspirations. Reflecting converted public opinion, he was emphatic that their demand at the post-war peace conference should be nothing less than independence.

After a strike the rest of the prisoners were released from British jails in June 1917. To underline the extent of their victory in winning over the people, the same men who had been reviled in the Dublin streets on their way to internment now received a tumultuous welcome. It was a historic u-turn and an index of the success of *Óglaigh na hÉireann.*

After his release, de Valera set about running politics on military lines. He attempted to harmonise the political and military movements of Sinn Féin. He did not resume relations with the secret Irish Republican Brotherhood, of which his rival, Collins, was President. He made known his conviction that the secret organisation had served its purpose and was no longer necessary since *Óglaigh na hÉireann*, with the backing of the people, could now work openly for Irish independence. The contradictory orders of Easter 1916 exemplified for him the problem arising between a democratic and a secret organisation, and he also disliked having to obey a faceless executive. Cathal Brugha, who objected to Collins in any case, agreed.

The aims of the Irish Volunteer 1914 constitution remained unchanged: the republican ideal was now taken for granted. The military and political wings of the national movement were nominally combined under one man, Eamon de Valera.

The underground IRB, however, quite distinct from Sinn Féin, maintained its claims to absolute national independence and the establishment by force of arms of a permanent republican government.[4] Until that came about it regarded itself as the proper government. The presence of British troops in Ireland, it held, rendered void the Dáil's pretensions to full status of government. It did not need to infiltrate Sinn Féin. A duality of appointments provided an overlap: four of the eleven known members (including Collins) of the IRB'S Supreme Council were leading members of the Sinn Féin executive: at least another three were well-known sympathisers. The path was paved for a takeover, and de Valera was out of the way in America from June 1919 to December 1920.[5]

The attempt by England in 1917 to extend conscription to Ireland had hastened the triumph of Sinn Féin, the political wing of *Óglaigh na hÉireann*, bringing the Irish Catholic hierarchy in support of them on this issue. During the conscription crisis young men of every class and creed flocked to join *Óglaigh na hÉireann*. They denied the right of the British government to impose conscription in Ireland. Drilling took place openly; arms were improvised, blacksmiths turning metal 'slide' rakes into pikes. The Sinn Féin/IRB policy of physical force now seemed justified. Support for the Irish Party finally withered away, and in March 1918 John Redmond died a broken man, let down by Westminster, his policies out of date.

The November armistice was followed by the general election in December 1918, in which the old Irish Parliamentary Party was reduced to six; twenty-six unionists were returned; seventy-three Sinn Féin candidates were successful, representing legitimately the majority opinion in Ireland. They had got their mandate and on 21 January 1919 proclaimed themselves the parliament of the Irish people, Dáil Eireann.

The first Dáil, in a private session, elected Cathal Brugha as President and he appointed Michael Collins Minister of Home Affairs, Professor Eoin MacNeill Finance Minister and Count Plunkett Minister of Foreign Affairs. Most significant of all, he appointed the Chief of Staff of the Volunteers, Gen. Richard Mulcahy, as Minister of Defence, by which appointment the army of the Republic came formally into being. The outline structures of a nation were formalised. At its second meeting in April an executive government was established with de Valera as President, claiming — in spite of ominous rumblings from Belfast — jurisdiction over a 32-county Republic. This was seen as the political fulfilment of the proclamation of independence of 1916 which was re-affirmed. A constitution was adopted and delegates to the peace conference at Versailles appointed. They failed to secure a hearing and the home rule solution lost its residual relevance.

*Óglaigh na hÉireann* was reconstituted as the army of the Republic. Two of its principal commanders were Cabinet members in the Dáil: Michael Collins was Minister of Finance and Cathal Brugha was now Minister of Defence. These dual appointments raised awkward questions of military jurisdiction that became aggravated as time went on. Brugha sought to maintain Dáil control over the army, but for many leading GHQ officers their prior allegiance was to the IRB in which Collins was dominant. Ironically, those roles, broadly speaking, reversed when the Civil War split came in 1922. Again, Collins, as Director of Intelligence, was subordinate to Brugha, but as Minister for Finance he was a Cabinet colleague who held the purse strings and an upper hand. The relative positions of the President, the Commander-in-Chief and the Minister for Defence were never clearly defined. However, the pressure of active service compelled a *modus vivendi.* By mid-1920 the War of Independence was in full spate, demanding total dedication from all nationalists. In 1919 the armed rebel movement was in a minority: by the end of 1920 it dominated the country. Ad hoc organisations sprang up accordingly.

The Dublin Brigade, launched to counter the renewed campaign of terror, drew its strengths from survivors of the 1916 Rising. It was 'made up in the main of Dublin artisans', according to Oscar Traynor, with a sprinkling of students from the National University and Trinity College representing practically every county and profession. The paper strength was around 3,500, of which 15 per cent could be counted on for action — if they could get off work!

The brigade consisted of five battalions: 1st, 2nd 3rd, 4th and 5th. The 5th was an engineering battalion and contained four companies of all kinds of tradesmen corresponding to each of the other four battalions. It was administered by a brigade staff and was disposed as follows:[6]

1st Battalion: North Liffey and West O'Connell St area;
2nd Battalion: North Liffey and East O'Connell St area;
3rd Battalion: South Liffey area;
4th Battalion: South townships, Rathmines, etc.
5th Battalion: Engineers only.

In April-May 1921 the 6th and 7th Battalions were added, covering the area of South Co. Dublin and Dun Laoghaire. Each battalion was made up of six or seven companies designated 'A', 'B', 'C', etc. The company was divided into four sections of about twenty-five men each, grouped according to locality. They came from all walks of life 'but were mainly unskilled workers', according to Charles Dalton. They had practically no arms and relied on a .22 miniature rifle for musketry training. Charles Dalton, a volunteer, acquired a Mauser belonging to his brother, Emmet, who had been an officer with the British army. The Brigade was commanded by Dick McKee. The Vice-Brigadier was Peadar Clancy. After the death of these two men in the Castle on the 21 November 1920 Oscar Traynor became Brigadier, and Sean Mooney Vice-Brigadier.

The Active Service Unit which co-operated with the original 'Squad' of less than a dozen Volunteers was organised towards the end of 1920. It acted as a separate unit until the truce in July 1921, and in 1922 formed the nucleus of the emergent Regular Army. There were about fifty Volunteers in the Active Service Unit. They were whole-time men, having left their employment to serve. Their pay in each case was at the same rate as they had been earning in civil employment.

Civil and military affairs were inextricably intertwined. The Sinn Féin government used the Irish Volunteers as an armed instrument for the establishment of a republic. The two main objectives were the destruction of the RIC (the principal instrument of British authority) and the influencing of public opinion (a principle of war).

During the winter of 1917–18 the country was in turmoil, with arms searches, arrests of suspected republicans and suppression of papers. The slide into war was irreversible. The British held their fire. Lloyd George wanted the rebels to be the first to fire. He was obsessed with an American Civil War analogy, wherein the North managed to treat the Southern rebels according to the laws and customs of war, without definitely recognising them as belligerents. Although there was a large body of British troops in the country, they were only called upon for duties in aid of the civil power.

The first shots in the War of Independence were fired on 21 January 1919 in Soloheadbeg, Co. Tipperary. Members of the 3rd Tipperary Brigade IRA, led by Dan Breen, Seamus Robinson, Sean Hogan and Sean Treacy, ambushed a party of RIC men, killing two and capturing army gelignite, to be used for manufacturing grenades. Coincidentally the new Dáil met for the first time in the Mansion House on the same day. There was no connection: the Tipperary men had acted on their own. A short time previously in an impromptu engagement, Barry O'Brian and a couple of the 'Boys' hijacked and burned out a British army vehicle a few miles from Soloheadbeg. Guerilla warfare had begun. Martial law was proclaimed in South Tipperary.

The new Dáil went about its business in a less arbitrary fashion. It inaugurated a system covering all facets of civil administration. Arbitration courts dealt with agrarian disputes, and with persons acting in ways detrimental to the Cause. Pigs were seized, slaughtered (and compensated for) to stop their export when factories at home were lying idle.

On 13 May following came the famous rescue of Sean Hogan at Knocklong, Co. Limerick. Two RIC were killed and one wounded, and four of the rescue party were wounded — Dan Breen badly.

The Volunteer Force under IRB control was elaborated on army lines. The Dáil sat and issued decrees. Effective propaganda was disseminated at home and abroad in America and France. The Volunteers came round to swearing allegiance to the Dáil.

The Dáil in turn took full responsibility for all the acts of its army[7] and determined to secure international belligerent rights for its soldiers, since Irish Volunteers, captured in action, were still being illegally 'executed' by the British.[8] Notwithstanding these executions, the dedication and discipline of all ranks of *Óglaigh na hÉireann* remained rocklike. They drew sustenance from the support of the people. Desmond Fitzgerald, the gifted director of propaganda, successfully managed the appeal to national pride and patriotic spirit. When he was arrested President de Valera arranged for Erskine Childers to succeed him. Childers had had a distinguished career as an officer in the British army, and in July 1914 had brought in arms for the Volunteers in his yacht, *The Asgard.* With his American wife, dynamic despite the fact that she was semi-crippled, he was a notable addition to the Irish publicity machine (see Chapters 3 and 4). Psychological operations were an essential form of combat support to redress the relative combat power imbalances, coupled with an improving enemy intelligence capability.[9]

Up until the end of 1918 the British had made no attempt to compile an IRA order of battle and the 'black list' made in 1916 was not kept up to date. During the Great War military intelligence in Ireland was controlled by the RIC officer at GHQ who had no military training and was ignorant of military organisation and up-to-date methods of processing information into intelligence. His duties were concerned mainly with the war in Europe and centred on counter-espionage against potential spies. Military intelligence about Ireland had been a secondary consideration.

At the beginning of 1919 the RIC officer was replaced by a regular and trained General Staff Officer. The Irish Volunteers began to be studied as a hostile force and efforts were made to discover details about their organisation, armament and strength. Towards the end of 1919, when the troops in Ireland were reorganised into divisions and brigades, intelligence officers were gradually appointed to the various headquarters. It was later laid down that battalion intelligence officers were to be nominated (without extra pay). In addition agents were projected into Ireland who were directly controlled from London by the Scotland House Organisation, e.g. the 'Cairo gang', so called from the name of a Dublin cafe they frequented. The G Branch of the Dublin Metropolitan Police were not linked up with this scheme as Collins had practically neutralised them. Several of the best detectives of G Division had been killed by the Volunteers and (after a report by Sir Basil Thompson, Director of Intelligence, Home Office), the Superintendent of the Division was put on retired pay and replaced by a Belfast RIC officer named Redmond who became Assistant Commissioner DMP, with the principal task of reorganising G Division. He at once increased the number of 'outdoor' men and started to bring the registry up to date. He was anxious to work at the military side of Sinn Féin and to collaborate with military intelligence. He was shot in January 1920 and that effectively snuffed out G division intelligence gathering. Thereafter, during 1920–21, it did little more than point duty! That did not deter the military. They decided that guerilla action and not a general rebellion was the only military action to be expected. Therefore the immediate requirement was for a professional military organisation working on independent lines whose principal objective was to find out the opponents' order of battle. A fairly accurate picture of formations and units in and about Dublin and in Cork was built up. They found it practically impossible to obtain definite evidence of the subsections of the staff of GHQ. The RIC were more of a hindrance than a help in the development of and organisation of intelligence in country districts, being set in their ways and sceptical of military intelligence. The military reckoned that IRA staff work was primitive and that its GHQ did not know which units comprised their own Second Southern Division.

Up to the end of 1919 the British relied on the police forces for suppression. Now, however, Crown agents were being systematically eliminated, and information on rebel activities was harder to come by. The Dublin Metropolitan Police was unable to prevent an attempt at Ashtown to assassinate the Lord Lieutenant on 19 December 1919. (The General Headquarters staff of the army of the Irish Republic had decided to shoot Lord French as the head and symbol of English forces and institutions in Ireland. Their claim to hold and control the country was repudiated by the *elected* Parliament — Dáil Éireann — and government.) Tom Kehoe, Paddy Daly, Joe Leonard, Tom Kilcoyne, Mick MacDonnell,

Dan Breen, Seamus Robinson, Sean Treacy and Sean Hogan participated. Dan Breen was wounded, and Lt Martin Savage killed. In the New Year RIC barracks were attacked at Newmarket-on-Fergus (by Brennan), Drumlish (by MacEoin) and Ballytrain (by O'Duffy and Dan Hogan). The British government decided that the police could no longer cope on their own and that troops must be called in.

British troops in Ireland at the beginning of 1920 were distributed as follows:

The Fifth Division, with headquarters at the Curragh, consisted of three infantry brigades:

13th Infantry Brigade (three battalions) — Counties Westmeath, Longford, Roscommon, Galway, Mayo and South Leitrim.

14th Infantry Brigade (three battalions) — Counties Carlow, Kildare, King's County (Laois), Queen's County (Offaly) and part of Wicklow.

15th Infantry Brigade (four battalions) — the six 'Ulster' counties and Counties Donegal, Cavan, Monaghan, Louth, Sligo and North Leitrim.

The Sixth Division, with headquarters at Cork, consisted of three infantry brigades:

16th Infantry Brigade ( four battalions) — Counties Waterford, Wexford, Kilkenny and South Tipperary.

17th Infantry Brigade (four battalions) — Counties Cork and Kerry.

18th Infantry Brigade (four battalions) — Counties Limerick, Clare and North Tipperary.

Dublin District had recently been converted from a brigade of the Fifth Division into a district, under the command of a Major General.

By the end of January this consisted of two infantry brigades:

24th (Provisional) Infantry Brigade (four battalions) — Dublin City north of the River Liffey, and, later, Co. Meath.

25th (Provisional) Infantry Brigade (three battalions) — Dublin City south of the River Liffey, and part of Co. Wicklow.

There were also in the country:

Six young soldier battalions.
A cavalry brigade at the Curragh.
The 5th and 6th Divisional Artillery.
One brigade, Royal Horse Artillery.
Two medium brigades, Royal Garrison Artillery.
Four field companies, Royal Engineers.
One fortress company, Royal Engineers.
One machine-gun battalion.
One armoured-car company, to which were attached a few tanks.
The Irish wing of the RAF consisting of two squadrons, each with three flights — thirty-six aeroplanes in all.

Division were briefed on procedures for 'snatching' prominent Volunteers. On 30–31 January sixty-four were rounded up: sixty-one were deported for internment in England. The targeting of the RIC, however, was beginning to have effect and information leading to the arrests was drying up.

The RIC had been the eyes and ears of British governments for generations. Many now resigned: some through fear, some for patriotic reasons; others were dismissed suspected of being too sympathetic to the rebel cause. The government had to look elsewhere for recruits. In March 1920, to stiffen the declining RIC, they started to recruit a force which became known as the 'Black and Tans' (they were originally clothed partly in khaki and partly in black RIC uniforms, hence their nickname). They were a mixed bag of ex-soldiers and some ex-convicts attracted by the high rate of pay for stamping out rebellion in Ireland. Their Commanding Officers told them that the more they killed the more they would love them. Lord French, the Lord Lieutenant, added: 'the Irish should be crushed as one would crush a poisonous insect.'

To buttress the 'Black and Tans' recruitment started around July 1920 for another force, the Auxiliaries. These were recruited from ex-officers and organised into fifteen companies of 100 men each. In September 1920 the Auxiliary Division RIC formed, and companies filtered out to areas. The mission of both groups was to terrorise.

Curfew was imposed in Dublin on 20 February 1920. During this period twenty police barracks were attacked, and around Easter 1920 240 vacated ones were burned. By May 317 leaders had been arrested and over 250 deported to England for internment. Tomás Mac Curtain,[10] Lord Mayor of Cork and Officer Commanding 1st Mid-Cork Brigade was murdered; by the police, a coroner's jury said; possibly by his own hand, the British countered, giving out that he was very unpopular in Sinn Féin circles for denouncing assassinations. In another voice it claimed that all efforts to suppress lawlessness would have been stultified had it not been for the firm stand made by the government in the case of the Lord Mayor of Cork.

The Commander-in-Chief called for 25,000 bayonets. By mid-March 1920 he was 5,000 short of that figure. This affected his operation, particularly in Galway, Mayo and Kerry. An application was made to the War Office at the beginning of April for an additional four battalions, each 800 strong. The War Office were unable at the time to make four battalions available but agreed to send four cavalry regiments instead. Three of these (the 10th Hussars, 17th Lancers and 1st Dragoons) arrived during April, and the fourth (the 9th Lancers) arrived in May. Two infantry battalions (the 1st Battalion Lancashire Fusiliers and 1st Battalion Manchester Regiment) were also sent to Ireland during April and allocated for duty in Dublin and in the 6th Divisional Area (Munster) respectively.

In April prisoners in Mountjoy Jail awaiting trial and those awaiting deportation began a hunger strike. Crowds assembled outside the prison saying rosaries, singing hymns and waving handkerchiefs. It took troops (a company of the 1st Battalion Lancashire Fusiliers with two tanks and a company of the 1st Battalion Wiltshire Regiment) to disperse them. A general strike began in Dublin on 13 April, and the hunger strikers were released the following day. Coincidentally, on 14 April Gen. Sir Nevil Macready took over the appointment of Commander-in-Chief of the Forces in Ireland from Lt Gen. Sir Frederick Shaw. A few weeks later a new Chief Secretary, Sir Hamar Greenwood, replaced Mr Ian Macpherson. Sir John Anderson shared Mr James McMahon's duties and Alfred ('Andy') Cope replaced Sir John Taylor as Assistant Under Secretary. Greenwood's new team attempted conciliation. The troops were restricted to the old position of carrying out duties in aid of the civil power.

There was no let-up in the guerilla campaign. Ambushes using concealment, camouflage and deception were stepped up. Roads were blocked by felled trees or stone walls in order to hold up lorries conveying small bodies of troops. Telegraph and telephone wires were cut, trains held up and mail disrupted. Attacks on police barracks and raids for arms continued.

The attack on the RIC Barracks in Ballylanders, Co. Limerick on 29 April 1920 brought booty of seven carbines, five Webley revolvers, hundreds of rounds of .303 and a few rounds of .45 revolver ammunition. It was not generally realised how poorly armed the IRA in the provinces were. Service rifles were few and far between. Some twenty rifles were scattered through the East Limerick and South Tipperary districts. They were the ones (typically old German 7 mm Mauser) that had been retained and concealed following the countermanding order of 1916.

Encouraged by the success of the Ballylanders operation sights were set on the strongly fortified Kilmallock RIC barracks.[11] A night attack was launched on 27 May. From the roof of an adjacent building three 56 lb weights were sent crashing through the slates of the barrack roof. Petrol and paraffin were poured in through the gaping hole and quickly the building was aflame. Meanwhile a fire fight ranged all round the barracks. The large garrison manned every loophole and hotly returned the attackers' fire. They fought with remarkable courage and pertinacity and repeatedly refused to surrender even though the building was ablaze all around them. They were all Irishmen.

The IRA lost one man, Liam Scully. The RIC officially reported one sergeant and one constable killed, and six constables wounded. Unofficially it was accepted that three others were killed and burned beyond recognition. The barracks was gutted. No arms or ammunition were captured. The IRA withdrew when its meagre stock of ammunition was expended. The other side of that story is the sadness it brought to the Morton family and the Kilmallock community. Sergeant Morton was killed in action defending the barracks. His son, John, also an RIC man, lived as a recluse for the rest of his life.

Savage reprisals followed and most of the prominent buildings in Kilmallock were reduced to ashes. The people subjected to such brutalities had nothing whatsoever to do with the attack, nor would they have condoned any actions which put their property at risk. The IRA readily acknowledged the magnificent stand made by the RIC garrison in a hopeless situation.

Generally, however, the police were boycotted and women who associated with any of the Crown forces had their hair cut off. Several engine drivers refused to drive trains conveying British troops and RIC.

All fronts were active now. Two military officers were kidnapped on 26 June, Brig. Gen. C.H.T. Lucas and Lt Cols Danford and Tyrrell were in Liam Lynch's custody, but Lucas escaped. The notorious one-armed Col. Smyth, newly appointed Divisional Commissioner of the RIC, who advocated a shoot on sight to kill policy, was himself shot dead in the Cork County Club at the end of June. 'Andy' Cope, the Assistant Under Secretary, commented that he had asked for it.

Much valuable information was obtained by holding up trains and military vehicles. This forced the British to employ escorts to protect dispatches. One of these escorts was ambushed at Oola. The Volunteers, armed with assorted weapons for which there was only a limited supply of ammunition, were forced to retire on the arrival of enemy reinforcements. Unknown to them, Lucas was one of the party attacked. He escaped again. The previously seized Martini rifles proved useless — a bigger danger to themselves than to the enemy.

In the 3rd Tipperary Brigade area alone there were big detachments of British military (in Tipperary town, Cahir, Clonmel, Carrick-on-Suir, Clogheen, and Fethard) with hundreds of RIC units dotted around, five to eight miles apart.

It was difficult to operate. In August 1920 a Brigade Council meeting at Blackcastle (on the Cashel-Clonmel road) was surrounded by Lancers.

That brigade suffered a serious loss when one of its best officers, Sean Allis Treacy, was killed in action in Dublin on 14 October 1920 — just eleven days before his planned wedding day and two days after the epic fight at 'Fernside' Drumcondra, in which he and Dan Breen shot their way out of a death-trap when surrounded by the military. Battalion active service units were formed in the brigade area for blocking roads, raiding mails and harassing the enemy generally. The First Brigade flying column consisted of fifty men, drawn from all the eight battalions but mainly the 4th (Tipperary town and district), commanded by the magnificent leader, Dinny Lacey. An engagement in Thomastown followed soon after, in which five or six soldiers were killed and several wounded. The next successful ambush was staged in Lisnagaul in the Glen of Aherlow about mid-November 1920. The British burned farmhouses as reprisals. On 20 September 1920 Balbriggan was sacked by the Black and Tans and Ballyhaise (Co. Cavan) RIC barracks was burned down.

Meanwhile no form of resistance was neglected. Labour unrest was fomented. At the end of July the state of Cork and some other towns in Munster was such that curfew restrictions were extended. Sinn Féin courts were functioning openly, and increasingly Sinn Féin projected itself as the *de facto* government. The thirty enemy battalions in the country were stretched and feeling the strain.

In May the War Office were asked to send four additional battalions to Ireland from the eight battalions which were held as a reserve in England for duty in Ireland when necessity arose. The Sixth Division area required two of these, while the other two were to deal with the area outside Dublin.

During May and June four battalions arrived and were distributed as follows:

| | |
|---|---|
| 2nd Bn Cameron Highlanders<br>1st Bn Devonshire Regiment | to Sixth Division (Cork) |
| 1st Bn Cheshire Regiment<br>1st Bn South Wales Borderers | to Dublin District |

In addition, the following reliefs were carried out during June and July:

- 2nd Battalion Duke of Wellington's Regiment relieved 1st Battalion East Surrey Regiment in Dublin District;
- 2nd Battalion Welsh Regiment relieved 2nd Battalion South Lancashire Regiment in Dublin District;
- 2nd Battalion Royal Scots relieved 2nd Battalion Highland Light Infantry in 6th Division.

The necessity for employing lorries for the rapid movement of patrols led to a demand for additional mechanical transport. This was gradually provided by the War Office and became the normal method of patrol work in the country areas, and, to a certain extent, in towns.

The next addition to the troops in the country arose from the serious riots which broke out in Derry. The following battalions arrived at the end of June and early in July:

- 1st Battalion The Queen's Royal Regiment for Derry;
- 2nd Battalion Rifle Brigade for Belfast;
- 1st Battalion Bedfordshire and Hertfordshire Regiment for Belfast.

It was not enough. The question of imposing martial law throughout the land had to be faced.

In order to carry out this policy a further addition was required to the number of troops in Ireland. Two battalions and an additional infantry brigade headquarters were requested for the Sixth Division, and one battalion and an additional infantry brigade headquarters for Co. Galway in the Fifth Division. The additional brigade headquarters became necessary owing to the increase of troops and the abnormal extent of the brigade areas. The following arrived at the end of July:

- 1st Battalion King's Liverpool Regiment for Sixth Division;
- 1st Battalion Royal Fusiliers for Sixth Division;
- 2nd Battalion Argyll and Sutherland Highlanders for Fifth Division.

New formations emerged. The Kerry Infantry Brigade was formed on 13 July 1920, and included Co. Kerry and a portion of Co. Cork transferred from the 17th Infantry Brigade. The Galway Infantry Brigade was formed in September 1920, and included Co. Galway and Co. Mayo, transferred from 13th Infantry Brigade.

Before the end of July it was found necessary to ask for an additional divisional headquarters for Northern Ireland, up to now controlled by the 15th Infantry Brigade of the Fifth Division. This area comprised the six Ulster counties together with Counties Sligo, North Leitrim, Donegal, Monaghan, Cavan and Louth. It was decided to divide this into two infantry brigade areas, making an additional infantry brigade headquarters at Derry. On 7 August 1920 the headquarters of the First Division was established at Belfast. On 14 August the Londonderry Brigade was established, comprising Counties Donegal, Derry, Tyrone, Cavan, Fermanagh, North Leitrim and Sligo, the 15th Infantry Brigade retaining its headquarters at Belfast, and consisting of Counties Antrim, Armagh, Louth, Down and Monaghan.

Thus by the middle of August 1920 the distribution of troops in Ireland was as follows:

| | |
|---|---|
| *First Division:* | |
| 15th Infantry Brigade (Belfast) | 2 battalions |
| Londonderry Brigade | 4 battalions |
| *Fifth (Fourth) Division:* | |
| Galway Brigade | 1 battalion<br>2 cavalry regiments |
| 13th Infantry Brigade (Athlone) | 3 battalions<br>1 cavalry regiment |
| 14th Infantry Brigade (Curragh) | 3 battalions<br>1 cavalry regiment |
| *Sixth Division:* | |
| 18th Infantry Brigade (Limerick) | 4 battalions<br>1 cavalry regiment |
| Kerry Brigade | 2 battalions |
| 17th Infantry Brigade (Cork) | 5 battalions<br>1 cavalry regiment |
| 16th Infantry Brigade (Fermoy) | 5 battalions |

*Dublin District*:

| | |
|---|---|
| | 1 cavalry regiment |
| 24th (Provisional) Infantry Brigade | 5 battalions |

This gave a total of thirty-four battalions and seven cavalry regiments. The scale of commitment reflects the scope and intensity of the campaign. All these units (with the exception of the Black and Tans and the Auxiliaries and the Essex Regiment) had proud battle traditions. They had a job to do, but it was militarily indefinable. Every unit listed in the order of battle had its own story to tell of the frustrations of unconventional war. A piebald horse is still a horse. Unconventional war was, withal, war.

There was no comparison in relative combat power terms between the two armies. The hard-pressed Irish army had to draw on spiritual rather than material resources for reinforcements. It was inspired and motivated by the demeanour of patriots like Terence MacSwiney,[12] Lord Mayor of Cork and Commandant 1st Cork Brigade, who died on hunger strike on 25 October 1920, having been in captivity since 7 August of the previous year.

The pressure was eased slightly when ten battalions were taken out of battle and redeployed for service in Britain during a coal strike (August to November 1920). On the other hand, the Restoration of Order in Ireland Act came into operation on 13 August 1920. In pursuance of that Act a memorandum from the Commander-in-Chief on 27 September 1920 called for a declaration of martial law throughout the country and for an acknowledgement that a state of insurrection existed with organised forces in active opposition, and that peace could not be restored without military measures taken under martial law. He got no answer and on 17 October he wrote again recommending a draconian reprisals policy. The formation of the Auxiliary Division, RIC, coincided with the request.

The rebel response was to organise flying columns and active service units. Flying columns were grouped from men on the run — like Rapparees of yore.[13] They moved about, billeted here and there and requisitioning necessary supplies for which the elected Sinn Féin government paid. They carried out large-scale attacks and ambushes throughout the country. The Dublin Active Service Unit (ASU) confined itself mainly to urban guerilla warfare. This entire guerilla force constituted the armed combat element of the resistance movement. It depended on civilian support. Morale was of prime importance. The Volunteers possessed the most important of morale factors: belief in their Cause. The enemy's cause by comparison was essentially repressive: 'Croppy lie down!' The British were seen as invaders. This entitled the Volunteers to belligerent status, whereas inhabitants of occupied areas who rise against an occupier as distinct from an invader are not so entitled. However, there was no way in which the Imperial government would recognise an Irish Republic — which is what according belligerent status would entail. Consequently a dirty war was inevitable.

The shady 'Cairo gang' were sent from London to Dublin by The Scotland House Organisation to assassinate Sinn Féin leaders. At 9 a.m. on Sunday 21 November 1920 the Active Service Unit anticipated them in a surprise raid. Twelve were killed. That afternoon ('Bloody Sunday') angry troops descended on the spectators at a gaelic football match between Tipperary and Dublin in Croke Park. They killed ten civilians and wounded sixty-five. Among those shot down was the Captain of the Tipperary team, Michael Hogan (the Hogan stand is named after him). The Commandant and Vice-Commandant of the Dublin Brigade, Dick McKee and Peadar Clancy, who had played a principal part in organising the foiling of the 'Cairo gang' and other coups, were cruelly treated in captivity and finally murdered. The loss of these two fine soldiers was a grievous loss to the army (McKee Barracks and Clancy Barracks are named after them).

A new British government policy was introduced, sanctioning the widespread arrest of all known IRA leaders and their internment in Ballykinlar Camp in Co. Down. Eight hundred officers were apprehended at once. A second camp was opened there. Due to sea transport difficulties a third camp was set up in Bere Island in the Sixth Divisional area. Arthur Griffith was arrested on 26 November 1920.[14]

The British were committed to a military solution. To that end the Auxiliaries were given a free hand to strike terror into the hearts of the people. Tom Barry resolved to put a stop to that. In a brilliant operation his West Cork flying column wiped out two lorry loads of Auxiliaries on 28 November at Kilmichael on the Macroom-Dunmanway road. The first lorry slowed down, distracted by a decoy; then a grenade and rifle attack, followed by hand-to-hand fighting, wiped them out. Using the old 'we surrender' ruse the second lorry inflicted casualties: it was then that the enraged Barry shouted his famous command 'Keep firing until I whistle'. No more phoney surrender offers were believed. Of the eighteen Auxiliaries sixteen were killed, one missing and one wounded. Three Irish army men were dead. Eighteen rifles and 1800 rounds of ammunition, thirty revolvers and ammunition, and a quantity of Mills bombs were captured.

The proclamation of martial law accorded some recognition of the Irish army as an army in the field. The Kilmichael column had gone thirty hours without food; had marched twenty-six miles and had lain soaked and frozen on exposed rocks waiting for battle. To remind them that they were soldiers who could not wallow in the luxury of shock Barry drilled them severely amidst the dead immediately after the action. The Auxiliaries' 'superman' image was well dented.

Martial law was proclaimed on 10 December covering Counties Cork, Kerry, Tipperary and Limerick. Generals or other Officers Commanding the Sixth Division, 16th, 17th, 18th and Kerry Infantry Brigades were appointed as military governors. The forces of the Crown in Ireland were declared to be on active service. A series of proclamations under martial law followed.

Towards the end of 1920 twelve members of the active Tipperary Brigade were killed. During the first three months of 1921 they made about twenty attacks on enemy forces, including Glenbower in the valley near Slievenamon; Coach Road, Tipperary town (breaking through an encircling movement of the Yorkshire Light Infantry, without loss, after half an hour's fighting); Ballinahow; Bansha; Limerick Junction and Thomastown again. A second column, under Seán Hogan of Knocklong fame, was formed. It operated mainly in the Galtee — Knockmealdown — Comeragh mountains area. Lacey's and Hogan's columns, which had become too big and unwieldy, were also split into battalion active service units. In May 1921 various brigades throughout the country were grouped into divisions and an elaborate system of dug-outs was planned and constructed. The 3rd Tipperary Brigade then came under the 2nd Southern Command (O/C Ernie O'Malley, succeeded by Seamus Robinson) and a number of its officers were appointed to the Divisional Staff. Immediately prior to the truce (11 July 1921) that brigade numbered 3,500 men, of whom 350 were on whole-time active service and 250 imprisoned. The armament available included 100 Lee Enfield rifles, 200 Martinis (single shot), 12 Winchesters, some sporting rifles, an assortment of shotguns and revolvers and a practically useless Hotchkiss machine-gun. Their achievements compared with the daring exploits of Vinny Byrne, Jim Slattery, Pat McCrea, Paddy O'Daly and others of the Dublin Brigade. Indeed both brigades had worked together in the attempted assassination of Lord French.

From the end of 1920, while the campaign was at its height, Lloyd George was actually endeavouring through secret intermediaries to open negotiations with Sinn Féin with a view to a settlement. Collins, taking his life in his hands in cycling daily through hold-ups and searches with his papers hidden in socks, sleeping nightly in different houses, found himself — in the interim between Griffith's arrest and de Valera's return — as Acting President of Dáil Éireann, discussing contorted truce offers from Lloyd George. On Christmas Eve de Valera, with the assistance of Collins's agents, arrived secretly in Dublin and was briefed by Collins. That evening Collins had the narrowest of his many escapes from capture.[15]

There had been no let-up by the military and the Black and Tans in raids, arrests and hold-ups, and a gang of Auxiliaries surprised Collins, Tobin, Gearóid O'Sullivan and Rory O'Connor dining in a private room in the Gresham Hotel. A suspicious officer gave prolonged scrutiny to Collins's face, comparing it with a photograph. It was touch and go, but the Auxiliaries eventually departed, having let the greatest capture of their lives slip through their hands.

The proclamation ordering the surrender of arms by 27 December had no effect. There were the several large-scale clashes between the troops and Volunteers on the eastern boundary of Tipperary. On 5 January 1921 the martial law area was extended by proclamation to include Counties Clare, Kilkenny, Waterford and Wexford. Curfew restrictions were rigorously imposed and a system of 'official punishments' — a euphemism for summary execution — came into play. Unfavourable reaction from world opinion, particularly American, against these reprisals was so strong that the British side instructed that they be stopped after about eight months.

More reinforcements were demanded to enforce martial law. The 2nd Battalion King's Royal Rifle Corps arrived in Belfast on 7 December 1920 to relieve the 1st Battalion which had been added to the Irish command in September 1920 and was now being sent to guard the internment camp at Ballykinlar. Later in December the 3rd Battalion Rifle Brigade and the 1st Battalion Gloucestershire Regiment were allotted to Dublin District and the Sixth Division respectively.

At the end of December 1920 and during January 1921 the following battalions arrived:

1st Battalion Royal Warwickshire Regiment, for Sixth Division;
2nd Battalion Suffolk Regiment, for Fifth Division;
2nd Battalion King's Own Yorkshire Light Infantry, for First Division;
1st Battalion Royal Scots Fusiliers, for Fifth Division;
2nd Battalion The Loyal Regiment, for Sixth Division;
2nd Battalion King's Own Scottish Borderers for Sixth Division;
2nd Battalion East Surrey Regiment for Dublin District.

This raised the number of battalions in Ireland to fifty-one, a scale of operation not generally appreciated. They were structured to handle the tactical employment of armoured cars and of armoured tactical lorries (armoured personnel carriers). The organisation of armoured cars had been developed during the latter part of 1920. Originally these armoured cars consisted of sixteen Austins and twenty Jeffrey Quads, with a few Peerless. They were armed with Hotchkiss guns. The Austins were manned by the 5th Armoured Car Company, which consisted of Tank Corps personnel. The Jeffrey Quads and Peerless were manned by infantry crews drawn from local battalions.

During September additional Peerless cars were allotted for the protection of the mail service. The Austins and Jeffrey Quads gradually became derelict owing to lack of spare parts, but Peerless armoured cars were sent from England, and by the beginning of 1921 there were in Ireland fifty-four of these and two Rolls Royce armoured cars. These were eventually increased to seventy Peerless and thirty-four Rolls Royce by the spring of 1921. The cars were distributed to divisions, and by them to brigades as and where considered necessary. They were used to escort patrol lorries or convoys, and for quelling disturbances or taking part in raids for arms.

Tank Corps personnel of the 5th Armoured Car Company took over the manning of Rolls Royce or Peerless as the Austins became derelict, but the crews of the great majority of the cars had still to be provided by infantry or cavalry. The wide dispersion of the cars made organisation, administration and maintenance difficult. Four armoured car company organisations were improvised, one for each division.

During November and December 1920 tactical lorries used by patrols were armoured, rifle-proofed, and subsequently revolver-proofed. By the end of 1920 sets of plates for up to eighty lorries had been supplied. Eventually, practically every lorry and Crossley tender was armoured with either rifle or revolver-proof plates. In large towns such as Dublin or Cork the armouring was of great use, but in country districts, against riflemen, less so. Only a small percentage of them was fitted with rifle-proof plates and the speed of armoured lorries was thereby considerably reduced. Furthermore, lorry patrols had to dismount when attacked: after the first exchanges the armouring had little relevance. The high hopes held out for the performance of these reinforced battalions did not materialise. Aggrieved commanders explained to their remonstrating masters in Whitehall that there was no defined theatre of war, no front line, no 'no man's land', and that the only secure base for any body of troops was within its own barracks walls; and that the main difficulty of offensive action was the lack of an objective. They complained about the absence of martial law all over the country and of the problems of co-ordination arising from the divided control of military and police. They distanced themselves from the out-of-control Auxiliaries, at whose door they laid the responsibility for setting Cork city on fire on 11–12 December 1920.

On the other side flying columns pressed on and paid the price. On 15 February 1921 in an encounter at Mourne Abbey with the Manchester Regiment and Black and Tans eight Volunteers were killed and eight captured. On 20 February at Clonmult, Co. Cork, in a engagement with the Hampshire Regiment, five were killed and the remaining sixteen withdrew into a farmhouse where the whole party was killed or captured. In all thirteen Irish soldiers were killed and eight captured in that action.

During March 1921 hostilities climaxed. On 3 March Col. Cummings, Col. Comdt of the Kerry Brigade, was killed in an ambush between Killarney and Rathmore. On 6 March the Mayor of Limerick, George Clancy, and the ex-Mayor, Michael O'Callaghan, were murdered.

A large column of *Óglaigh an hÉireann* attacked the Essex Regiment on 19 March 1921 near Bandon, Co. Cork. The Crown forces suffered sixteen casualties, killed or wounded; the Irish army had six killed, six captured and eight wounded. Volunteers were also reported to be concentrating in force in Kerry in March 1921 and the British believed that a rising was imminent in that county. Sanction was given for the use of bombs and machine-gun fire from aeroplanes.

By the end of April 1921 more than 3,300 IRA members had been interned. There were now two internment camps in Ballykinlar, one at Bere Island, one at Spike Island and one (later two) at the Curragh. Applications to set up internment camps outside Ireland had been refused. Roads continued to be cut by trenches or blocked by felled trees or improvised walls, and bridges were blown up in many areas. In Dublin bombs were thrown at patrol-carrying lorries. Heavy casualties were suffered by both sides in these actions and the British considered re-imposing curfew in Dublin. They made several important captures of arms, and on 29 April an IRA battalion was surprised and surrounded, resulting in the capture of the battalion staff and forty men, together with some arms.

The military remained convinced that rigorousness and continued enforcement of restrictions produced better results than efforts at conciliation. The Commander-in-Chief stated that he considered the policy of repression would in time wear down the rebels. To be effective he felt that coercion had to be more intense; that the Auxiliaries must be disciplined and be prevented from carrying out unauthorised reprisals and that unity of command should be instituted by reorganising the police force.

Once more industrial troubles in England provided a respite for the increasingly hard-pressed Volunteers. Ten battalions were earmarked to embark for England at short notice to deal with yet another coal strike there between April and July 1921: four from the First Division and two from each of the Fifth and Sixth Divisions and Dublin district. The moves were to be by battleships and were worked out so that within seventy-two hours of the receipt of orders all ten battalions could be ready to embark. On 4 April orders were received that the first two battalions were to proceed to Liverpool. The 1st Battalion Somerset Light Infantry from Belfast and the 2nd Battalion Duke of Wellington's Regiment from Dublin sailed on 6 April. The 2nd Battalion King's Shropshire Light Infantry from the Curragh and the 2nd Battalion King's Own Yorkshire Light Infantry from Derry were at the same time ordered to concentrate at Kingstown (Dun Laoghaire) and Belfast respectively. The 2nd Battalion King's Shropshire Light Infantry sailed on 7 April and the 2nd Battalion King's Own Yorkshire Light Infantry on 9 April. Their ferocious reputation preceded them and their unexpected arrival in Liverpool helped to quieten the miners. All four battalions returned to Ireland between 9 and 11 May to pacify the Irish instead of the miners.

From May onwards the resilient Irish Army maintained offensive momentum by raids on mails, holding up trains conveying military stores, cutting telegraph wires, blocking roads and destroying enemy property and public buildings.

An obsession with large-scale engagements proved costly in the case of the unfortunate attack on the Custom House on 25 May 1921 in which de Valera had a minor involvement.[16] Seventy-five per cent of the men in the operation were 2nd Battalion men under the command of Tom Ennis. The 'Squad' was commanded by Paddy O'Daly and Tom Kehoe with the Active Service Unit under the command of Paddy Flanagan. They were greatly weakened as a result: seven killed; ten wounded; seventy captured. It was the biggest single operation employing the greatest number of men that the army of Ireland had carried out since 1916. It was followed immediately by British negotiations for a truce.

Unofficial executions continued to be carried out in tit-for-tat assassinations. The war was fought out in the streets and in the fields. Landmines were placed on roads and fired mechanically. A musketry party of the Hampshire Regiment was blown up near Youghal, Co. Cork, where seven were killed and nineteen wounded. On 1 May at Kildorrery, Co. Cork the Volunteers lost two killed and five wounded in an attack on a mixed party of the Queen's Royal Regiment, the Green Howards and RIC. On 2 May at Lackelly, Co. Tipperary, an attack by a 200-strong group on Green Howards and RIC resulted in seven killed and a large number wounded. On 3 May in the Partry Mountains near Tourmakeady, Co. Mayo, several were killed in an attack on the Border Regiment and RIC. On 18 May at Kilmacthomas, Co. Waterford, a column was surprised by troops and thirteen Volunteers were captured.

The British responded by organising drives on a large scale over a wide area using cavalry and local infantry units equipped with wireless. The first began on 5 May 1921 in the Mullingar-Tullamore district of the Fifth Division. The second drive in the first three weeks of June was in Co. Longford and Co. Leitrim, also in the Fifth Division area and in Co. Monaghan, in the First Division area. On 6 June a similar operation using aircraft was carried out in Kerry. Undeterred, *Óglaigh na hÉireann* counter-attacked. On 3 June a Royal Army Service Corps repair workshop in Dublin was burned down. Attacks on troop trains intensified. On 24 June a train conveying the Kings Escort of the 10th Hussars from Belfast was derailed by explosives: three soldiers were killed and four injured; fifty-one horses were lost.

Pressure was maintained on all fronts. Six soldiers of the Beds and Herts Light Infantry were killed at Glasdrummon, Co. Leitrim, and at Clonbanin in Co. Cork a colonel and three soldiers were killed. In Co. Kerry thirteen RIC were killed —

nine at Rathmore and four in Clonmore. This was followed by the killing of six more at Carrowkennedy, Co. Mayo. (In the last two actions six of the ten 'British' killed were Irishmen!)

This succession of actions finally brought home forcibly to the British politicians in Westminster that there *was* a war going on in Ireland. The actions of men like Barry similarly brought home to the military that they were up against men who were determined to wage that war with professional expertise learned the hard way on the field of battle. Barry had served with the Mesopotamian Expeditionary Force from 1915 until his demobilisation from the British army in 1919 when he joined the Irish Army. When GHQ decreed in the summer of 1920 that a flying column be started in each brigade area West Cork adopted the idea enthusiastically and developed it. Barry saw at once that guerrilla warfare demanded a special type of training. He paid meticulous attention to detail and exacted uncompromising discipline.[17]

Tom Barry was the outstanding field commander. MacEoin's ambushes at Ballinalee (November 1920) and Clonfin (February 1921) were well executed too, but Barry was the supreme professional soldier: a perfectionist. The behaviour of the Essex Regiment convinced him of the need for counter-terror. (When Essex officer Percival ingloriously surrendered to the Japanese in Singapore in 1941 Barry rubbed in the defeat by sending him a telegram recalling their Cork encounters in 1921.) He methodically had sixteen British agents shot. All his decisions in the field flowed from a calculated, military estimate of the situation. The murders of Volunteers (April-May 1921) by the Essex Regiment were particularly brutal. Gen. Strickland, Cork, the British GOC of the martial law area, ignored written warnings that executions of Volunteers would bring counter-action. Father T.F. Duggan, a Military Chaplain in World War I, who had a good grasp of technical military matters, proposed a rescue of the Volunteers doomed to death. Barry agreed. Attacks were arranged from Innishannon to Castletownbere including a daring assault mounted on Bandon by Barry himself. Only one IRA man (Dan O'Brien) was executed in Cork after 14 May.

In the first six months of 1921 sixteen British agents were shot by the West Cork Brigade. They had been responsible for the deaths of several Volunteers and the arrest and ill-treatment of many more. Either the spies and informers would die or the IRA would be wiped out. By the end of February, twelve were shot dead. Those British agents were either paid spies, unpaid informers or ex-British officers. The unpaid informers came mainly from the wealthier land-owning class and were more dangerous than the paid spies. They were sincere believers in British domination and Irish subjection and in a benevolent feudal despotic way felt that the Irish were better off that way benefiting from in-service jobs. They were armed by the British. Some were shot in their homes, others were intercepted when travelling. Brigade did not seek GHQ sanction and they dared not put all the evidence in writing for fear of capture. But a tight rein was kept on battalions and no spy was executed without a Brigade Order. One obviously working-class paid spy, who gave himself away recovering from a drinking bout, was a Catholic. Another, a large farmer and unpaid informer, was a Protestant.

A man's religion did not matter to Barry. The security of his force was all that counted. A 'retired' Lieutenant-Colonel who was executed had guided in person raiding parties of the Essex Regiment. He had been a great menace. In addition to the sixteen killed many other hostile loyalists fled to Britain. One of the latter was a Protestant minister, head of an Intelligence Group who organised all information collection and transmitted it to the British.

The result of the counter-attacks was a significant drop in Volunteer casualties. Deprived of guidance from their agents the Essex raided blindly but were more careful about murdering prisoners. This was solely because British terror had been met effectively by IRA counter-terror. British propaganda tried to fan the flames of religious intolerance by announcing the religion of an executed agent when he was a Protestant. Although the West Cork Brigade shot in quick succession five Catholics who were British agents, never once did the British use the term Catholic in their announcements. Their plan was to persuade the Protestant community that they would be extirpated under a republican government.

The majority of West Cork Protestants, although their hostility to the campaign was well known, were not interfered with. They were entitled to their opinions. What was demanded of them was that neither they nor Catholics would commit a hostile act against the army in the field or actively aid the British troops or administration with which Dáil Éireann was at war.

Barry extrapolated the following order of battle from a document dated 17 May 1921 signed by Major Gen. Strickland, General Officer Commanding the Sixth Division which stated, *inter alia*, that the following units of British Infantry, Machine-Gun Corps, Royal Field Artillery, Royal Garrison Artillery, Royal Engineer and of the Auxiliary Division were stationed within Co. Cork at that date:

*Infantry:*

The 1st Battalion, The Buffs Regiment; The 1st Battalion, The King's Regiment; The 2nd Battalion, The Hampshires; the 2nd Battalion, The King's Own Scottish Borderers; The 2nd Battalion, The South Stafford Regiment; The 1st Battalion, Essex Regiment; The 1st Battalion, The Manchester Regiment; the 2nd Battalion, The Queen's Own Cameron Highlanders; The 2nd Battalion, The East Lancashire Regiment; The 1st Battalion, The West Surrey Regiment; The 1st Battalion, The Gloucestershire Regiment.

Total strength, 8,800 first-line infantry troops (Major — later Field Marshal — B. L. Montgomery was Brigade Major to the 17th Infantry Brigade in Cork).

*Machine Gun Corps:*

The 1st Battalion Machine Gun Corps, strength 480 officers and men.

*Royal Field Artillery:*

The 2nd Brigade R.F.A., The 7th Brigade R.F.A. Six Batteries. Strength 720 officers and men.

*Royal Garrison Artillery:*

The 31st Fire Command (Queenstown) (Cobh), The 32nd Fire Command (Bere Island). Strength 440 officers and men.

*Royal Engineers:*

The 33rd Company, Royal Engineers. Strength, 240 officers and men.

*Divisional and Brigade Headquarters' Staffs, Transport and Supply Units:*

Strength, 200 officers and men.

*Auxiliary Division:*

J Company, Auxiliary Division (Macroom); L Company, Auxiliary Division (Millstreet); O Company, Auxiliary Division (Dunmanway). Strength, 540 officers and men.

There were also naval forces and twenty-three garrisons of Black and Tans within Co. Cork, totalling 1150 officers and men. Excluding naval personnel there were approximately 12,600 armed British troops, Auxiliaries and Black and Tans in Co. Cork seven weeks before the truce: 8,800 front-line infantry troops; 1150 Black and Tans; 540 Auxiliaries, 2080 machine gun corps, artillery and other units.

Standing against that force were 310 riflemen in the whole of Co. Cork. The only other IRA arms within the county were five machine guns and 350 automatics and revolvers. *Cumann na mBan* was organised in companies and districts corresponding to IRA units. Its help was invaluable. But the greatest asset the Cork Volunteers had was Barry's military genius. Crossbarry was a classic battle.[18]

On 16 March 1921 the brigade flying column of 104 officers and men armed with only forty rounds of ammunition for each rifle moved against 300 enemy troops being sent from Kinsale to Bandon as reinforcements. That operation aborted and the British decided to mount a massive search and sweep operation to seek out and destroy Barry's column, which was made up of seven sections of fourteen men in each, including the Section Commander. A piper accompanied the column. Motorised infantry outnumbering the column by ten to one converged on Crossbarry to take out Barry. With a masterly eye for ground he skilfully deployed his column. He surprised the advancing British convoy, destroyed nine lorries and inflicted heavy casualties.

The piper played martial airs on his warpipes as four of the sections attacked. Within minutes of the opening of the attack Barry had smashed the British encircling lines wide open and then played ducks and drakes with their 'ring of steel'. British corpses were strewn on the Crossbarry road.

This was a soldier-to-soldier encounter and, thanks to Barry, the Irish Army won the day.

His attack on Rosscarbery on 22 March 1921 was also a fine feat of arms which was complimented by Michael Collins. By forced marches and again by making skilful use of terrain the column, after the initial encounter, outwitted British reinforcements of the dreaded Essex and Auxiliaries who were closing in on Rosscarbery from Bandon, Clonakilty and Dunmanway.

The sea also figured in the campaign. Eleven destroyers, three sloops and ten trawlers were used to try to prevent the import of arms. The difficulty of importing arms was very great, though Collins did get some in through secret channels.[19] Small islands in loughs and inland waterways were extensively used for concealing arms and ammunition. Launches to search and sweep those areas were concentrated on the Shannon at Limerick in June 1921, a month after the elections for the Northern and Southern parliaments under the Act of 1920 in which Sinn Féin topped the polls.

One outcome from the election result in the North was the undertaking in June of a reorganisation of the Ulster area. The First Divisional area was abolished and constituted as the 15th Infantry Brigade Area. The Londonderry Infantry Brigade ceased to exist and a new infantry brigade, the 26th (Provisional) Infantry Brigade, was added to Dublin district, to include Counties Monaghan, Cavan and Louth, which were to be transferred from the First Divisional Area. As a preliminary to this, Co. Sligo and the northern portion of Co. Leitrim had already been transferred from the Londonderry Brigade to the 13th Infantry Brigade (Fifth Division) and the remainder of the reorganisation was carried out gradually in stages.

On 10 June the Londonderry Brigade was abolished, its area and troops being absorbed in the 15th Infantry Brigade. On 14 June the Colonel Commandant and staff of the late Londonderry Brigade opened their headquarters at Dundalk as the 26th (Provisional) Infantry Brigade, covering Counties Monaghan, Cavan and Louth. The brigade remained under the GOC First Division until 24 June, when it was transferred to Dublin district; Co. Meath was subsequently added to this brigade.

On 28 June the First Divisional Headquarters returned to Aldershot. From this time, therefore, the 15th Infantry Brigade consisted of the six Ulster counties with Co. Donegal, and came directly under GHQ. All these moves made demands on the Irish Army for increased intelligence. It also had to adjust its dispositions accordingly to counter British movements.

By the end of May 1921 the British government had concluded that as soon as the industrial troubles in England were over it would stamp out once and for all the Irish rebellion before the coming winter. The number of additional units which it reckoned would be available for this extirpation were eighteen to twenty infantry battalions, three cavalry regiments and a proportion of armoured cars. Drastic steps were to be taken to enforce martial law all over Ireland (excluding the six counties of 'Ulster'). A blockade was to be instituted and press censorship imposed. No detachment would number less than a company, which would send out patrols. All movements were to be on foot, accompanied by as little transport as possible. If the rebels took to the hills they were to be left there. Otherwise mobile columns would only move against pinpointed targets.

During June and the beginning of July the extra troops required to carry out the government's policy of drastic action arrived and were allotted as follows:

| | | |
|---|---|---|
| 14 June, | 1st Bn Northumberland Fusiliers | Fifth Division. |
| 15 " | 1st Bn Royal Sussex Regiment | " |
| 16 " | 2nd Bn Royal West Kent Regiment | Dublin District. |
| 17 " | 1st Bn Middlesex Regiment | " |
| 28 " | 1st Bn York and Lancaster Regiment | Sixth Division. |
| 28 " | 1st Bn Sherwood Foresters | " |
| 2 July | 1st Bn West Yorkshire Regiment | " |
| 2 " | 2nd Bn Oxfordshire and Buckinghamshire Light Infantry | " |
| 2 " | 1st Bn Duke of Cornwall's Light Infantry | Dublin District. |
| 2 " | 1st Bn King's Own Yorkshire Light Infantry | Fifth Division. |
| 5 " | 2nd Bn Cheshire Regiment | Sixth Division. |

| | | |
|---|---|---|
| 5 July | 3rd Bn Royal Fusiliers | Sixth Division. |
| 5 " | 1st Bn Highland Light Infantry | " |
| 5 " | 1st Bn Loyal Regiment | Dublin District. |
| 5 " | 1st Regiment Royal Artillery Mounted Rifles | Sixth Division. |
| 6 " | 4th Bn Worcestershire Regiment | Fifth Division. |
| 6 " | 2nd Bn Gordon Highlanders | " |
| 7 " | 1st Bn Seaforth Highlanders | Dublin District. |
| 9 " | 2nd Regiment Royal Artillery Mounted Rifles | Sixth Division. |

The Royal Artillery Mounted Rifles were substituted for cavalry on the basis of one artillery brigade forming one squadron, with four troops each formed from a battery. The following reinforcements were to follow:

One battalion Royal Marine Light Infantry;
One battalion Royal Marine Artillery;
Two companies Tank Corps organised as armoured-car companies;
Additional signal personnel;
Proportion of Royal Engineers;
Proportion of Administrative services.

There would be no half measures this time. Intelligence estimates revealed Sinn Féin's precarious position. The active service units and flying columns were being harried everywhere and internment camps were filling up. De Valera was captured but released for political purposes. The British, without fully realising all its implications[20] were determined to get a military solution to the Irish political problem. They undoubtedly had the capability to win a pyrrhic military victory with saturation terror tactics. Collins, the Director of Intelligence, was painfully aware of the truth of this and all that it involved.

At the height of the struggle figures for the British forces were given as 60,000 regular troops and 15,000 Auxiliaries and Black and Tans in addition to the RIC. (In the British House of Commons on 2 June 1921 Sir Hamar Greenwood, Chief Secretary for Ireland, stated that the total enlisted strength of the Auxiliary Division was 1,498 officers and men.) The nominal strength of the Dublin Brigade was 3,500, of whom not more than 1,000 were armed. Except for the Active Service Unit, the Volunteers could only operate when they could get away from their civilian jobs. Barry gave 310 riflemen as the strength of the field force in the whole of Co. Cork. Collins reckoned that in the whole of Ireland the Irish Army had not more than 3,000 fighting men. In 1920, for example, the armament of C Company, Cavan Brigade was seven revolvers of various types, thirty shotguns and 200 cartridges.

On the other hand, the British found themselves operating in a hostile country. Having found legal procedures too cumbersome to deal effectively with a whole population in rebellion they resorted to using terror as a weapon and to reprisals as a policy. This, together with the bad reputation of the auxiliary policemen, proved counter-productive.

Martial law, however, did force the Volunteers to conceal their arms in dumps when not in use and a good many of these were discovered. Arms were also lost in the course of a series of heavy attacks on bodies of troops during January, February and March 1921. The Irish inflicted heavy casualties but they suffered still more severely themselves. The enemy's development and organisation of intelligence in Ireland in 1920–21[21] was paying off. Also by the end of June and the beginning of July another eighteen battalions had arrived in the country with the mission of enforcing the drastic action policy.

In British eyes the Volunteers were thugs and terrorists — not freedom fighters. They dubbed the May election a 'revolver election', meaning that it was as much as anyone's life was worth to vote against Sinn Féin. The wonder was that the Irish Army achieved so much. It wrought prodigious feats in this sprawling, convoluted, unconventional war.

Intelligence had been its secret weapon. Masterminded by Collins's genius, the Irish outsmarted the British. The silencing of the RIC was critical. The time had been opportune as during the Chief Secretaryship of Birrell the secret service had practically ceased to exist. Sinn Féin used the opportunity to organise and plan in comparative security. The mails were raided and papers seized. A 'mole' in the Central Telegraph Office supplied copies of classified telegrams to Liam Tobin, Assistant Director of Intelligence. They were all addressed to RIC District Inspectors and contained information on impending raids and contemplated arrests. As the Volunteers had the key words decoding was no problem; the key word changed once a month but in notifying the change the key word was always telegraphed in the existing code. This compensated to some extent for the Irish Army's lack of equipment and for deficiencies in organisation.

Although they were organised on paper by counties at first, it was the status of an objective that dictated on the day the requisite organisation for a particular task. Military or police barracks were definite objectives. In the country railway bridges, stretches of road or river crossings were suitable objectives. The support of the people made this inconvenience acceptable. Local organisations were then tailored to meet specific requirements as they arose. A reasonably reliable localised intelligence system was built up, but incessant raids hampered staff work, which at best was rudimentary. Armament varied enormously, and weapon training presented difficulties. It was hard to organise arms dumps or to instruct men adequately on the assortment of weapons they had laid hands on. Ernie O'Malley, when serving as a staff captain with headquarters, wrote:[22]

> Few knew the mechanism of the collection of weapons to be found within one of our Brigade areas. British long and short Lee-Enfields, police carbines, Lee-Metfords, single shot Martini-Henris, Sniders, Remingtons, Winchesters, German, Turkish or Spanish Mausers, French Lebels, American Springfields, Japanese patterns, Austrian Steyers and Mannlichers, old flint muskets, muzzle-loading Queen Annes. Revolvers: the Webley, Colt, Smith and Wesson, Harrison Richardson, bulldog patterns. Automatics: the Naval Webley-Scott, Colt, Browning, German Mauser or Parabellum, Steyer. Machine-guns were rare: Parabellum, Vickers and the German Spandau, the French Hotchkiss, the Lewis gun. There was gunpowder, gelignite, dynamite, blasting powder and odd slabs of guncotton. All these had been bought, captured in action or taken in

> raids on private houses. It was impossible to extract a reliable list of names, arms and stuff from a brigade QM. Companies were afraid that battalion wanted to distribute some of their guns to other companies; the battalion was afraid the brigade would transfer stuff to other battalions. The brigade always made the poor mouth to GHQ to extract more arms. Short of being a very competent fortune teller I could not assess a brigade's armament.

Without standard weaponry, collective training and concentration of force it was unlikely that guerilla warfare, no matter how skilfully waged, could achieve military victory in the field. The limited aim of making the country ungovernable, and the cost of holding it prohibitive, was achieved. British public opinion, sensitive to American public opinion, reacted against the unethical conduct of the Black and Tans.

No one loved the Black and Tans. Their Commanding Officer could not abide them: Brig. Gen. Crozier, a former CO of the 9th Royal Irish Rifles Battalion, resigned in disgust towards the end of 1920. In India in the summer of 1920 the Connaught Rangers[23] mutinied when they received accounts of The Tans' atrocities. Known as Ireland's 'Devil's Own', the Rangers were among the finest soldiers in the world with outstanding records on many fields of battle, but they 'volunteered for the guardroom' in protest against the terror practised against their own people back home. On 2 November 1920 the leader of the revolt, Number 35252 Private James Joseph Daly of the 1st Battalion and from Tyrellspass, Co. Westmeath was executed by firing squad. Thirteen others had their death sentences commuted to penal servitude for life. Varying sentences were passed on approximately 340, sixty of them long periods of penal servitude. Daly died a hero's death. The writing was on the international wall for the tactics of terror. The time had come for a fresh approach, but it took another eight months of bloodshed to achieve it.

At the opening of the Northern Ireland Parliament in Belfast on 22 June 1921 King George V made an emotional appeal for reconciliation. After more than two years of bitter bloodshed peace-feelers shakily pointed to the possibility of a compromise, although the unionists, backed by the British, rejected out of hand a united Ireland solution. They drove the point home by reacting with indiscriminate ferocity against their 'Fenian' fellow citizens.

The portents for co-existence on the island of Ireland were less than promising but war weariness, particularly among the civilian population, dictated that the time had come to call a halt. The additional reinforcements had not yet arrived from Britain so their dispatch was cancelled. The plan to get the launches concentrated on the Shannon was set aside.

The hands of the military were stayed for the moment from their policy of drastic action. On the Irish side *post-hoc* protestations of readiness 'to go another round with England'[24] were neither representative nor realistic. A 'no man's land' was now opening up between the ideal and the possible. Some who had been inactive during the war now became verbal and uncompromising.

On 8 July after discussions the Commander-in-Chief and de Valera agreed truce terms. GHQ telegraphed them to divisions that afternoon. The Commander-in-Chief embodied them in a second letter to Lord Midleton. His text ran:

> Mr De Valera having decided to accept the Prime Minister's invitation to confer with him in London, is issuing instructions to his supporters —
> (*a*) To cease all attacks on Crown forces and civilians.
> (*b*) To prohibit the use of arms.
> (*c*) To cease military manoeuvres of all kinds.
> (*d*) To abstain from interference with public or private property.
> (*e*) To discountenance and prevent any action likely to cause disturbance of the peace which might necessitate military interference.
>
> In order to co-operate in providing an atmosphere in which peaceful discussions may be possible, the Government had directed that —
>
> (*a*) All raids and searches by military or police shall cease.
> (*b*) Military activity shall be restricted to the support of the police in their normal civil duties.
> (*c*) Curfew restrictions shall be removed.
> (*d*) The despatch of reinforcements from England shall be suspended.

(*e*) The police functions in Dublin to be carried out by the DMP.

In order to give the necessary time for these instructions to reach all concerned, the date from which they shall come into force has been fixed at 12 noon, Monday 11 July 1921.

The *Irish Bulletin*[25] published the following slightly different version from de Valera. His reference to the 'GHQ Communiqué' as a 'draft' upset the British. He wrote:

On behalf of the British Army it is agreed as follows:

(1) No incoming troops, RIC, and auxiliary police and munitions, and no movements for military purposes of troops and munitions, except maintenance drafts.
(2) No provocative display of forces, armed or unarmed.
(3) It is understood that all provisions of the truce apply to Martial Law area equally with the rest of Ireland.
(4) No pursuit of Irish officers or men or war material or military stores.
(5) No secret agents noting descriptions or movements, and no interference with the movements of Irish persons, military or civil, and no attempt to discover the haunts or habits of Irish officers and men. (Note — This supposes the abandonment of curfew restrictions.)
(6) No pursuit or observance of lines of communication or connection.
(7) No pursuit of messengers. (Note — There are other details connected with Courts Martial, motor permits, and ROIR [Restoration of Order in Ireland Regulations] to be agreed to later.)

On behalf of the Irish Army it is agreed

(*a*) Attacks on Crown forces and civilians to cease.
(*b*) No provocative display of forces, armed or unarmed.
(*c*) No interference with Government or private property.
(*d*) To discountenance and prevent any action likely to cause disturbance of the peace which might necessitate military interference.

To explain the discrepancies between the two versions the following circular was hurriedly issued to the troops by the Commander-in-Chief:

> In order to avoid any possible misconstruction of the terms referred to in GHQ official statements and those issued as a supplement to the *Irish Bulletin* it is notified for information that the wording of the GHQ official statement is taken from the letter written by G.O.C-in-C. to Lord Midleton (and agreed to in principle by Mr De Valera), and is in no sense a draft. The wording as issued in the *Irish Bulletin* is their interpretation of the same terms issued after discussion at GHQ in a form more acceptable to Mr De Valera's adherents. The spirit of the two documents is identical.

A copy of this circular was sent to Eamonn Duggan but at the request of Mr Cope, Assistant Under Secretary, who took exception to the wording, it was not issued to the press. It had been agreed that Duggan would represent de Valera for communication with GHQ and that Brigade and Division liaison officers would also be appointed.

The truce came into operation on 11 July 1921 as a preliminary to negotiations which would begin an unenthusiastic search for controversial peace proposals. More than half the deputies of Dáil Éireann were in prison or internment camps at the time of the truce. The British announced that they would all be released at once with the exception of Gen. Seán MacEoin. They maintained that he was awaiting hanging for murder and that the law had to take its course. At the next meeting of the Dáil Collins insisted that there would be no further negotiations until MacEoin was released. He was released. (In a previous attempt to rescue him from Mountjoy in 1921 Joe Leonard and Pat McCrea entered the prison in a hijacked armoured car disguised as a British officers.)

The British military continued working on their contingency plans for the employment of recently arrived troops. Not without reason, there was a good deal of pessimism on both sides regarding the eventual outcome. However, for the delicately poised present, police and military operations practically ceased on 11 July 1921. In the period from 1 April 1920 the British military casualties were:

Killed: forty-three officers and 113 other ranks
Wounded: thirty-five officers and 307 other ranks.

Between 1 January 1919 and 11 July 1922 the police lost 405 killed and 682 wounded.

Some 500 Irish casualties are listed. These are not categorised. The 3rd Tipperary Brigade casualty list shows that in that brigade alone four Brigade, eleven Battalion and sixty-seven Company Officers gave their lives in the fight for Irish freedom, now properly called the War of Independence.

3

# The Civil War (1922-3)

The British military resented allegations that they had come off worst in the field. They were convinced that the drastic measures in train would soon settle matters once and for all. The coal strike in Britain was over and reinforcements were pouring in. Martial law was to be imposed on the twenty-six counties. The truce was only a hiccup in their reckoning.

Gen. Mulcahy conceded the Irish Army's inability to drive out the Crown forces. The best they could do, he said, was to take a moderately sized police barracks. He did not mention Crossbarry. Although GHQ was notoriously out of touch with its country units, it is significant that Tom Barry did not believe either that military victory was attainable.[1]

Collins and Mulcahy had no idea that the struggle was coming to an end. Collins remained wary of British ruses to wean the people away from the army. He did not share de Valera's notions about belligerent rights. He felt that the British, with their superior combat power, would welcome clashes. He doubted the country's capability to bear belligerent responsibilities.[2] The British wavered. On the one hand they acknowledged that a solution of the Irish problem and 'the pacification of Irishmen' was not, and never could be, the task of soldiers: that it was a political problem and that no military operations could bring it about. On the other hand it was claimed that the troops could reduce the rebels to impotence, thereby creating a situation amenable to the imposition of a political solution. Under the truce conditions, however, their hands were tied, they felt powerless to suppress 'illegalities' (and regarded the functioning of the Sinn Féin courts as such). All they could do was to aid the civil power. It was beyond their grasp to take in that while the 1916 Rising was an assertion in arms by a highly motivated minority, the War of Independence was a stand by a lawful government democratically elected by a large majority of the people.

The 1918 General Election had mandated the establishment of an independent Irish Parliament on Irish soil. *Óglaigh na hÉireann* gave allegiance in 1920 to the lawfully constituted government elected by the people.[3] It had previously been controlled by an executive[4] which now dissolved itself in order to remove ambiguity as to the Dáil's authority. The Dáil in turn clarified that England and Ireland were at war and that *Óglaigh na hÉireann* was the national army of defence, justified in treating the armed forces of the enemy exactly as any national army would treat invaders. Colonial hangovers clouded perception of that fundamental right.[5]

Gen. Macready's arrival at the Mansion House in uniform on 8 July 1921 to clarify the proposed truce terms was the first sign of official British recognition for *Óglaigh na hÉireann.* The Irish Army, in accordance with its code of chivalry enshrined in the 1916 Proclamation, treated him courteously in spite of his professed loathing for Ireland and its people and a pistol bulging provocatively out of his tunic pocket. A long-sought objective[6] was achieved with his acknowledgment of the appointments of Eamonn Duggan and Robert Barton as liaison officers for truce purposes between the Irish and the British armies. The following April, when considering reinvasion, the British confirmed that recognition would be accorded to persons in uniform belonging to armed forces of the Republic. They would not, however, admit their rights to recognition by other nations.[7]

Collins and Mulcahy had doubts about the truce lasting. They emphasised that the breathing space must be used to improve organisation, training and public relations. Guerilla forces had to depend on help, voluntary or otherwise, from civilians in their areas. No one knew better than Collins how volatile that support was, even though many times during the cold winter of 1920 people left their warm beds for the tired men of the flying column. But while he was keenly conscious of the difficulties of resuming the armed struggle with any prospect of success, he felt that drilling, training and recruiting could both influence public opinion and prepare for contingencies. He knew that the people were sick and tired of war, even though they continued to provide 'safe houses'. As a last resort he advised dragging out negotiations so as to be able to take advantage of the long winter evenings for a renewed guerilla campaign. Gen. Michael Brennan, Officer Commanding the First Western Division, was certain that hostilities would resume and set about procuring arms and ammunition.[8]

Following the truce most IRA units went into training in summer camps. Those on holiday or unemployed spent all their time there. Training was programmed for 7.30 a.m. (5 a.m. on weekends) and generally went on until 7 p.m.[9] Macready complained that advantage was taken of the truce to transform 'a disorganised rabble' into a 'well-disciplined, well-organised and well-armed force'.[10] About 100,000 volunteers were on the rolls at the time, some of whom had seen active service in France.[11] In addition many new recruits ('trucileers') now flocked in from hitherto inactive brigades. They were restive for immediate action. Referring to their previous inactivity, Collins's caustic comment was that they had arrears to make up.[12]

De Valera and Lloyd George met in London on 12 July 1921 to fence for a peace formula. The British Cabinet took an immovable stand on two conditions: one, that Ireland remain in the empire; two, that there would be no coercion of Northern Ireland.[13] On 21 July de Valera returned empty handed to Dublin. He acknowledged that he was a negotiating novice confronting an acknowledged master of diplomatic wiles.[14] Fruitless dialectical exchanges ensued. Eventually on 11 October Lloyd George invited the Irish side to a conference in London. De Valera elected not to go. He argued that his place was at home holding the Sinn Féin coalition together.[15] He wanted to show the British that they were dealing with a united determined people. The Army, he further maintained, needed strengthening and contingency planning. He was conscious, too, of the difficulties involved in resuming hostilities. Like Collins, he knew that British intelligence had used the truce breathing space to become better informed.[16]

His decision to stay at home brought forward the names of Griffith and Collins to attend instead. He had his doubts about their republican credentials so he included a strong republican,[17] Robert Barton, in the delegation to keep an eye on them. He added in support Barton's cousin, Erskine Childers, as secretary, and two lawyers: Eamonn Duggan to Collins's side; George Gavan Duffy to Barton's, satisfying himself that this provided 'an adequate balance'. Algebraic balancing, however, was not the requirement; proper briefing to present a united front to Lloyd George was the crying need.

Collins baulked at going. He suspected de Valera of setting a trap for himself and Griffith,[18] but de Valera dismissed this. The delegation was invested with ambiguous plenipotentiary powers, being restricted from signing a treaty without referring it back to Dublin. That ploy to exercise remote control from Dublin failed to fool Lloyd George. In any case, the delegates were not readily disposed to disrobe themselves of their plenipotentiary status. They were given instructions[19] but received no written mission to analyse, no Cabinet guidance as to what concessions, if any, might be made. Lloyd George exploited the delegation's dilemmas and played on their self-esteem as plenipotentiaries. In the small hours of the morning on 6 December 1921 he delivered his ultimatum of 'immediate and terrible war' and induced the unsettled Irishmen to sign a treaty without referring it back to Dublin.[20] The delegation believed that the terms they had got were the best available; that there was no alternative; that to reject them meant a renewal of the war; that the promised boundary commission would secure the ending of partition. Lloyd George had lulled the Irish side into believing that a revision of the boundary would render Northern Ireland unviable as a political entity. At the same time he convinced the unionists that it would copperfasten their ascendancy position.[21]

The Treaty was signed at 2.30 a.m. on Tuesday 6 December 1921. Northern Ireland was specifically safeguarded. A restyled Ireland, 'the Irish Free State', became, like Canada, a self-governing dominion of the empire. An oath of allegiance to the Crown had to be taken by members of Dáil Éireann. Harbour defence was to remain in charge of British care and maintenance parities. Coastal defence forts in Berehaven, Cobh and Lough Swilly were to remain in British hands.

The signing of the Treaty brought to the surface deep-seated differences in Sinn Féin. On 7 January 1922 the Dáil narrowly ratified the Treaty by sixty-four votes to fifty-seven. Following that decision the executive of *Cumann na mBan* by twenty-four votes to two rejected the Treaty — 'the Furies', P.S. O'Hegarty dubbed them distastefully. A rival organisation to *Cumann na mBan*, The Society of Freedom, sprang up as pro-Treaty wives in retort rallied round their husbands.

The debate divided the country and split the army, which had not yet become accustomed to subordinating itself to any civil authority.[22] Ironically, Collins had himself to blame for that wayward streak in the Forces.

As Director of Intelligence he was nominally subordinate to Brugha, the Minister for Defence.[23] As Minister for Finance, however, he was more than Brugha's equal. Inevitable clashes provoked a fateful vendetta between the two. Collins was also President of the Supreme Council of the IRB. He felt superior to Brugha, who in turn resented him. He foiled Brugha's efforts to assert full Dáil control over the army.[24] The diminutive minister in return resented the hero-worship accorded to the flamboyant 'Big Fellow'. In his opinion, Collins was a bluffer, a braggart without substance.

Compounding such personal hatreds, many patriotic Irishmen were genuinely deeply dissatisfied with the terms of the Treaty. When it was signed, therefore, it provided a pretext for floodgates of antagonisms and animosities to burst open. A call for a Convention on 12 January was an outward manifestation of endemic dissidence. One aim was to revert the army to executive direction, free from the constraints of Dáil control.

Mulcahy was placatory to begin with, reassuring the Dáil (Gen. MacEoin privately dissenting) that the army would continue to be the army of the Irish Republic.[25] Both sides wanted the army intact on their sides and took pains to curry favour with it. At the end of the Treaty debates Brugha had promised the Dáil that army discipline would be maintained.[26] De Valera affirmed that his professed anxiety had been to ensure that the split in the country would not adversely affect the army.[27] He urged the HQ staff and the divisional commandants to give the same loyalty to Mulcahy as they had given to Brugha.[28] He stressed that the army was an instrument of civil government which must remain subject to the Dáil. His rhetoric, however, was open to a different interpretation.

The majority of GHQ officers complied with the Collins-inspired IRB orders to support the Treaty.[29] The First and Second Southern Divisions under Lynch and O'Malley rejected it. O'Malley also repudiated the Dáil.[30] Then at the end of March the executive appointed by the proscribed Convention refused to accept the authority of the Minister of Defence and the Chief of Staff.[31] That finally convinced Griffith that the Dáil must have control of the army. He disapproved of Collins's frenetic efforts to avoid splitting it. From the time of the Treaty debates he became certain that Civil War was unavoidable and that the best thing to do was to get it over and done with as quickly as possible.

On 14 January 1922 a Provisional Government was brought into being to administer the twenty-six counties in the interregnum before the coming into existence of the Irish Free State on 6 December 1922. This forked the flow of authority, in effect neutering the nominal Dáil. Moreover the British evacuation had left in its wake a state of chaos:[32] no regular police force; no system of justice: no security; trade and commerce at a standstill: a divided country; a split army.

Furthermore financial policy had yet to be formulated. Changes in banking and finance had not been envisaged. The Bank of Ireland[33] was slow to respond to a request to act as the new government's financial agents and to accommodate £1m. credit. It failed to comprehend the conservative nature in financial matters of the political revolutionaries and was inhibited — in spite of more optimistic noises from the Treasury on the financial prospects of the new state — by the British government's reluctance to guarantee any loans they might make to the Irish government.

Notwithstanding all that, that Provisional Government decided to press on with implementing the terms of the Treaty. That meant confrontation and conflict. This was the atmosphere in which the uniformed regular army of the new Irish Free State (*Saorstát na hÉireann*) began to be formed. The extremely equivocal position of the hundred thousand or so Volunteers on the rolls put paid to a proposition for the orderly evolution of a 4,000- to 12,000-strong[34] regular national army, demobilising those who were surplus to requirements.[35] As things turned out, the first full-time regular unit of the new Irish army was formed from members of the Active Service Unit (ASU) of the Dublin Brigade (Guards) who had an illustrious combat record in the War of Independence. In 1919 Paddy O'Daly started with only eight men. A year later its strength increased to twelve. Eventually it consisted of about fifty picked men on a full-time paid basis. They worked in co-operation with the Collins 'Squad' (nick-named the 'Twelve Apostles') and with his intelligence personnel. They took their orders direct from Collins and not from Volunteer Headquarters.

After the truce the ASU and the 'Squad' shared camps in Glenasmole (South Dublin: mostly 3rd and 4th Battalions) and Kilmore (mostly North Dublin, 1st and 2nd Battalions). Towards the end of January 1922 the regrouped Active Service Unit assembled in Celbridge for fitting out.[36] This was the beginning of the Regular Army as we know it today.[37] They all had pre-truce active IRA service.

Properly uniformed and equipped, the ASU, commanded by Capt. Paddy O'Daly, marched through Dublin[38] past the City Hall to take over Beggars Bush Barracks from the infamous Auxiliaries. The salute at the City Hall (where Seán MacEoin had been sentenced to be hanged in 1921) was taken by Michael Collins. Both he and all the men marching past had borne the brunt of the fighting in the struggle for freedom, and had come a long way together. It was an emotional moment. There were some tears on the stand. The two lieutenants in the company were Joe Leonard and Paddy O'Connor, both of whom became colonels shortly afterwards. O'Daly later became a major general and GOC Kerry Command as the army rapidly expanded. By April 1922 3,500 had enlisted.[39] The expansion of the active service unit into the future National Army was well under way. The Guards went into the 'Bush' as a company in February. In March they were a battalion with O'Daly still in command; in May they became a brigade and he was promoted to brigadier. All this, however, was not happening without serious dissent.

The anti-treaty divide in *Óglaigh na hÉireann* repudiated the Treaty and all it stood for. Their position was that they had taken an oath to the Republic and would resist any move to disestablish it.

In February Ernie O'Malley's anti-treaty Southern Division raided Clonmel Barracks and captured a large quantity of arms and ammunition.[40] In March rival forces clashed in Kilkenny, but a detachment of the Dublin Guards (as the former Active Service Unit was now called) quickly restored order. On 29 March the 1st Brigade (Cork City), First Southern Division in a daring coup hijacked the admiralty vessel, *Upnor*,[41] and captured its substantial arms and ammunition cargo destined for Woolwich Arsenal. Around this time the pro-treaty Beggars Bush Force received 2,000 Lee-Enfield rifles and a considerable amount of ammunition from the British.

On 15 March 1922 de Valera formed a new party, *Cumann na Poblachta* to provide a constitutional base from which to resist the Treaty. It made little impact but it did distance him from his earlier fighting talk. He had been outraged when the *Irish Independent* misinterpreted his 'wade through Irish blood' speech as an incitement.[42] He said he had meant it as a warning, but his explanation made no difference to the anti-treaty military wing. They were indifferent to any views of his.[43] As in the previous guerilla campaign he exercised no influence on the conduct of battle. Rory O'Connor publicly demonstrated his indifference and embarrassed de Valera in his own surroundings by rejecting the Dáil's authority. De Valera demurred but stopped short of denunciation.[44]

Not all sections of the post-truce *Óglaigh na hÉireann* organisation had such choppy baptisms. Capt. (later Major Gen.) James Lillis,[45] as adjutant of the Independent Carlow Brigade, saw nothing at the beginning of 1922 to signify to him that Civil War was either imminent or inevitable. On 22 January Capt. Seán McBride[46] came down from GHQ to his Duckett's Grove (Carlow) encampment in uniform (presumably Volunteer) to monitor a local court-martial. On 9 February Lillis took over Carlow Barracks from Capt. Dorman Smith,[47] the Adjutant of the 5th Northumberland Fusiliers. There was nothing unusual to report.

Portlaoise Military Barracks was handed over initially by a British officer to a Volunteer staff officer of the Third Southern Division. Shortly afterwards, around 10–12 February, a contingent of local Volunteers, members of the 1st Battalion, Leix Brigade, numbering about twenty men and two or three officers, marched in to occupy the barracks. Some of these continued to serve, while others were allowed home. A Signal Cadet unit under Col. Comdt (later Major Gen.) P.A. Mulcahy (brother of Dick) then took over and were in occupation during March and April. Later on a detachment of Beggars Bush troops arrived as a matter of routine.[48]

This semblance of routine in some places disguised the reality that the army was bitterly split into pro-treaty and anti-treaty factions. The soldiers — Collins and Mulcahy (pro-treaty), and Lynch (anti-treaty) — left no stone unturned in searching for a formula to bring both sides together. In contrast Griffith and O'Higgins[49] remained unmoved and hawkish. They had not been totally immersed in *Óglaigh na hÉireann*'s *esprit de corps*.

On the other side, the Convention on 26 March threw the split into relief, with its abandonment of all authority except that deriving from its own executive. Members of the army were now forced to take a stand. 'Which way is Mick [Collins] going'[50] was the after-Mass query which gave many their answer. The slogans on walls read 'Collins stood by us: we'll stand by him'.

The opposing sides called each other names and one cast doubts on the other's republican parentage. Neither side paid any attention to what the other was saying. The British for their part made little or no distinction between them even when handing over posts and equipment: they were all 'Shinners' to them. Many who took opposing sides afterwards admitted that they could as easily have gone one way as the other. It was force of circumstances at the time, a flick of a coin.

On 18 February in Limerick Liam Forde, the mid-Limerick Brigade Commander, on the eve of taking over from the British for the Provisional Government, suddenly switched allegiance, renouncing GHQ. It (GHQ), estimating Limerick to be key terrain, reacted quickly, detailing Michael Brennan,[51] Commander of the First Western Division (largely composed of Clare and Galway units), to forestall him.

With great skill, deceiving his opponents as to his actual combat power by recycling the same set of rifles to arm successively arriving detachments at the Longpavement Station just outside Limerick, Brennan accomplished his mission. (It had been a toss-up beforehand which side he took. Personalities such as the Barretts rather than principles influenced his decision.) His success now enabled mediation to take matters further and avoid bloodshed. The outcome seemed to augur well for avoiding an army split.

As further evidence of this trend Frank Aiken was in Portobello (Cathal Brugha) Barracks in late April during a uniform-measuring session. Wellington (Griffith) Barracks had been taken over on 22 April as the pro-treaty HQ Second Eastern Division, and in the middle of the square there stood Dan Breen (anti-treaty) and Paddy Daly (pro-treaty) having a chat. Someone, however, did take a pot shot at them before they finished, as a sign of disaffection with the Treaty.[52] Desmond Fitzgerald, on the other hand, moved about freely.[53]

Early in May there were clashes again in Kilkenny but, though there was fierce fighting for Ormond Castle and a profligate expenditure of ammunition, casualties were minimal. Old comrades were loath to kill each other. A detachment of the Dublin Guards (the ASU) was again hurried there to restore order, which they did.

However, some other recurring armed clashes sounded ominous. Nevertheless de Valera was taken aback when on 13 April Rory O'Connor occupied the Four Courts,[54] the Masonic Hall (Parnell Square) the Ballast Office (Westmoreland St), Moran's Hotel (Talbot St) and Kilmainham Jail. O'Connor had no time for any politicians, including de Valera. Collins, on the other hand, he respected as a fellow soldier. 'The Big Fellow' in turn was prepared to go to any extremes to find a basis for reunification of the army, and to that end went so far as to enter into an unworkable pact with de Valera which imperilled the Treaty position and alarmed the British.[55] He rebuked Churchill for lax security the previous February, when the latter complained about the anti-treaty raid on British-occupied Clonmel.

But Griffith was infuriated when Collins stalled once more on taking action to dislodge the Four Courts garrison. It looked as though he (Collins) had more in common with O'Connor than he had with either Griffith or de Valera. The North provided the common ground. The pogroms in Belfast preyed on Collins's mind.

He exchanged the rifles which had been given by the British to the Beggars Bush force for the anti-treaty ones in the Four Courts and transshipped them to the North.[56] This exchange ensured that these weapons, if captured by the British, could not be traced back to him. He was determined to build up the Irish Army north and south in order to negotiate from a position of strength. The guerilla warfare genius had not suddenly become a committed constitutionalist. As far as he was concerned the Treaty was a stepping stone to a Republic — a freedom to achieve freedom: nothing more.

O'Connor's position was that the executive was now the sole authority, and Collins seems to have treated that indulgently enough even when they raided banks.[57] (On 1 and 2 May 1922 twenty-six banks were raided: bank losses were £156,392 12s.6d.). One of his disciples, however, Lt Vinny Byrne of 'Bloody Sunday' fame, with great presence of mind and bravery quelled an attempt by the Four Courts garrison to hijack the guard in the Bank of Ireland. He was promoted in the field to captain. Byrne was a born soldier who knew he was every bit as republican as his opponents. (He left after the mutiny in 1924 because the army was not republican enough for him.)

The British grew increasingly uneasy at the way the situation was developing. Apart from the occupation of the Four Courts, large areas in the south and west appeared to be occupied by anti-treaty forces, and there were even clashes between pro-treaty forces and British troops in the Belleek and Pettigo areas. Contingency plans for reoccupation were drawn up.[58]

The assassination of Field Marshal Sir Henry Wilson[59] on 22 June 1922 by Comdt Reginald Dunne and Volunteer Joseph Sullivan was the last straw. Wilson had been sentenced to death in his absence by an IRA court. If the British knew that Collins had ordered Wilson's death they did not let on. It suited them to blame the Four Courts garrison and to give Lloyd George and Churchill an opportunity to warn Griffith and Collins that if the occupation of the Four Courts was not ended the British government would regard the Treaty as having been violated. Macready was summoned to Downing Street to discuss his capability to attack and capture the Four Courts on his own. In the North No. 2 Squadron RAF was sent to Aldergrove, outside Belfast. A cruiser was sent to Derry, a destroyer to Belfast. Churchill offered Collins the RAF, sporting Free State colours, to bomb the Four Courts.[60]

Collins's first reaction was to let the British 'do their own dirty work'. But a combination of circumstances took matters out of his hands. The Four Courts garrison stepped up its provocation. It raided a garage in Baggot St (Dublin) to commandeer transport for the North.[61] It kidnapped the GOC Regular Troops, 'Ginger' O'Connell. Griffith did not need British pressure to act, his patience had run out. The time had come, and an attack was now inevitable. Up to that, while there was no realistic chance of a pact-begotten coalition, hopes had not yet been abandoned for army unification, and a further conference between the two sides had been arranged.

In the meantime the pro-treaty forces lost no opportunity to make an impression. Seán MacEoin's wedding to Mary Cooney[62] in Longford on 22 June was made the occasion of military display. Troops under Comdt Gen. Tony Lawlor lined the streets and were played through by the Athlone IRA band. A guard of honour under Comdt James Conway and Comdt Seán Duffy was posted outside the Cathedral. It consisted of thirty members of Gen. MacEoin's own North Longford flying column, carrying rifles and revolvers and attired in trench coats just as they were in the days of the Black and Tans. The passage to the Cathedral was lined by detachments from the First Eastern Division Mullingar under Lt J. Mooney and the Third Midland Division under Lt Nicoll. Outside were the *Garda an Dorais*, composed of IRA artillerymen from Athlone and officers and men from every barracks in Longford and the surrounding counties. Arthur Griffith and Michael Collins arrived and were cordially greeted by the crowd, the soldiers presenting arms.

Gen. O'Duffy, Chief of Staff, was the best man. Mrs McGrath,[63] mother of RIC District Inspector McGrath in connection with whose death Major Gen. MacEoin had been sentenced to be hanged, sent a present accompanied by a very touching letter wishing him and Mrs MacEoin every happiness and good luck. Buglers blew a fanfare as the couple left for their honeymoon in Donegal (into the thick of the Civil War shooting as it happened).

On 25 June the Wolfe Tone anniversary march-past at Bodenstown, near Naas, Co. Kildare presented the pro-treaty forces with another stage on which to flex muscles. On the parade were motor-cycle combinations equipped with wireless outfits and operators armed with Thompson sub-machine guns. Combat power rather than ceremonial was the message. Political processes were not producing the required results.

The publication of the Constitution on polling day,[64] 16 June, made matters worse and precipitated a further split. Tom Barry's proposal to serve seventy-two hours' notice on Gen. Macready (whose forces were still in part of the country) terminating the Treaty was opposed by Brugha and Lynch, who stalked out of the meeting and set up a rival HQ across the river from the Four Courts in the Clarence Hotel. Barry's purpose was to bring the Beggars Bush force back into a common front.

Only the charismatic Collins could have done that, but he had made up his mind that the public would not support 'going another round with Britain'. The British themselves appreciated that a preemptive attack by them on the Four Courts was on. The Provisional Government saved them the trouble. Griffith reckoned that they were now strong enough to impose the government's will. The split in the anti-treaty side had been patched up. Lynch resumed his role as Chief of Staff. His ambiguous attitude secured him a safe passage south from the pro-treaty forces. The sides raggedly lined out accordingly.

The Four Courts was surrounded by troops under the command of Brig. Paddy O'Daly. At midnight on 27 June he demanded the release of O'Connell and the evacuation of the building. At 3.40 a.m. Comdt Gen. Tom Ennis of the Eastern Division sent in a note to the same effect. The garrison did not comply and shortly after 4 a.m. the guns opened up. The Civil War[65] had begun in earnest.

It turned out to be an untidy war without a clear-cut beginning or a definitive end. The fighting was episodic and erratic. Hostilities broke out in Dublin, spilled down to Waterford via Blessington and fumbled westward towards Cork. Interspersed were a few daring imaginative sea landings in Cork, Fenit (Co. Kerry), Tarbert (Co. Kerry) and Westport (Co. Mayo), and disjointed operations in the midlands and west. Neither in this campaign nor until late in the War of Independence were there significant actions in the North.

Neither side had prepared properly for war; only the British gave contingency planning a thought.[66] Their idea was to proclaim martial law; attack a republican government and seize dissidents, irrespective of the view of the Provisional Government, and they had that capability. Two destroyers were ordered into the river Liffey. The reestablishment of a Pale around Dublin prior to reconquest was in Churchill's mind.[67]

In the event a lower profile sufficed. 'War by the Irish on the Irish' gratified Birkenhead.[68] The two dedicated *Óglaigh na hÉireann* members, Lynch and Collins, tragically found themselves on opposing sides, and both were to be killed in action.

The two sides of the same coin continued to protest that only they were the true IRA. The public, depending on their allegiances, simply labelled them 'National', 'Free State' or 'Regular' on the one hand as against 'Republicans', 'Diehards' or 'Irregulars' on the other. A common front against the British was now out of the question. The problem of the North no longer dominated.

The Four Courts garrison of 180 men under Comdt Patrick O'Brien were drawn from the 1st and 2nd Battalions of the Dublin Brigade. The members of the army executive present, including O'Malley, Mellowes, McKelvey and O'Connor, did not interfere in the battle although they had ordered the occupation and issued a proclamation.

De Valera supported the proclamation but not the occupation. He then rejoined his old Battalion (the 3rd) as a private and was attached to Battalion Headquarters in Hammam

Hotel, O'Connell St. He got no promotion. The following month, during the battle for Clonmel, Seán Moylan, Director of Operations, made him a nominal assistant. Oscar Traynor, Officer Commanding the Independent Dublin No. 1 Brigade, gave the orders in Dublin, though he had disagreed with the occupation of the Four Courts. He saw it as replicating the 1916 failure. Full-scale guerilla warfare was what he advocated.

The attacking pro-treaty troops had little or no training. The venerable artillery (18-pounders) procured from the British military turned out, under the control of Gen. Emmet Dalton, to be their most crucial asset. Direct fire was employed. No sight clinometers were used: 'they just looked through the bore and never missed'.[69] The building caught fire. A huge explosion destroyed the Public Records Office with its irreplaceable historical documents dating back to 1174.[70] After hand-to-hand fighting the garrison (down to 140) threw their arms in the fire and surrendered as ordered by Traynor.

He had set up a triangle of strong points in the city centre: Moran's Hotel (Talbot St); Barry's Hotel (Great Denmark St); Nelson Pillar. His intention had been to summon reinforcements from the country, take the investing pro-treaty troops from the rear and fight his way through to relieve the beleagured garrison. When that failed to materialise he ordered the Four Courts garrison to surrender in order to leave him free to wage a guerilla campaign. The executive inside did not countermand his orders.

After the fall of the Four Courts the Provisional Government forces threw a cordon around Traynor's poorly deployed elements. Using fire and movement, involving the employment of single gun artillery, armoured cars, mounted infantry and foot soldiers, they infiltrated Traynor's position. By the Monday evening Parnell Square, Talbot St and the western side of O'Connell St had fallen. Next morning Gardiner St and Marlboro St fell. The east of O'Connell St was ablaze, engulfing Brugha in the Hammam Hotel. Traynor for the second time in a week had to order surrender. De Valera escaped. Brugha died fighting bravely, gun in hand. After eight days of confused street fighting the pro-treatyites had come out on top.

The government now got an overwhelming response to its well-timed 'Call to Arms'. Recruitment proceeded at the rate of 1,000 a day until a strength of 60,000 was reached. General Headquarters staff of the Volunteer organisation was instructed to place its entire establishment on an active service basis. Officers commanding local units appealed to all Volunteers to accept six months' permanent service. Others who wished to join could do so through the local Irish Volunteer organisation. The government confidently looked to the Irish Volunteers for support.

Collins, who was head of the Provisional Government established by the Treaty, did not enter the Regular Army until the start of the Civil War. He then became Commander-in-Chief with full General's rank and had his office in Portobello (Cathal Brugha) Barracks (beside the present School of Music buildings). He lived in a single room in the officers' mess. Richard Mulcahy, Minister for Defence, who was married with a young family, took over Lissenfield — the British GOC's house[71] — beside the Barracks.

Ad hoc command organisations developed rapidly. General order No. 1 signed by Mulcahy on 5 July 1922 roughly created the following '*District Commands*':

(1) Eastern District Command, commanded by General O'Duffy: 2nd, 3rd, 4th, and 5th Northern Divisions; 1st and 2nd Eastern Divisions; Carlow Brigade; North Wexford Brigade; South Wexford Brigade.
(2) Western District Command commanded by Major Gen. McKeon: 1st Northern Division; 2nd, 3rd, 4th Western Division.
(3) Southern District Command, commanded by Lt Gen. O'Connell: 1st, 2nd, and 3rd Southern Divisions; 1st Western Division.

By the 28 July the names of the commands were: Eastern; South Western; Curragh; 2nd Southern; Western; 1st Northern. By the end of August it was proposed that the South Western Command be subdivided into two, Cork and Limerick. In the event it became Cork and Kerry. The commands, now numbering eight, were shaping as follows:[72]

| | | |
|---|---|---|
| Eastern | GOC Daniel Hogan | HQ Griffith Barracks |
| Cork | GOC Emmet Dalton | HQ Cork |
| Kerry | GOC WR Murphy | HQ Tralee |
| South Western | GOC Michael Brennan | HQ Limerick |
| Western | GOC Sean McKeon | HQ Athlone |
| Northern | GOC Joseph Sweeney | HQ Stranorlar |
| Waterford | GOC J.T. Prout | HQ Kilkenny |
| 3rd Southern | GOC P.A. Mulcahy | HQ Roscrea |

The anti-treaty forces were perforce even more haphazardly organised, retaining, where appropriate, pre-truce territorial designations.[73]

Units were not yet formally established, since the novice army had to fight a war as part of its initial training, but broadly speaking, the national army was organised into commands, brigades, battalions and companies, under a Commander-in-Chief assisted by a General Headquarters staff. Each command area was in the charge of a GOC, usually a Major General. Each brigade area was in the charge of a Brigadier or Colonel, while battalions were commanded by Commandants and companies by Captains. General Headquarters comprised the Departments of the Commander-in-Chief, Chief of Staff, Adjutant-General, Quartermaster-General and Director of Intelligence, Director of Organisation. Organisation of some kind was essential, as the only instrument at the immediate disposal of the government to maintain law and order and to protect life and property was the National Army. It was crucial to maintain it as an organised disciplined force to uphold the law and to wage war. That was a big demand. Both sides were inexperienced in conventional warfare.

On the day the Four Courts was attacked (28 June) the anti-treaty South Dublin Brigade, which included Wicklow units under Comdt Andrew McDonnell and the mid-Kildare Brigade under Comdt Paddy Brennan, was ordered to concentrate in Blessington, prepared to move on Dublin. A pre-emptive pro-treaty attack disrupted those plans, so by 2 July Traynor found himself encircled with no sign of the expected reinforcements from Blessington. Time and space, lack of communications and transport, absence of effective unity of command and overall, grasp of the situation and, above all, particularism, ruled out the prospect of reinforcements being sent from the First Southern Division in Cork and Kerry.

O'Malley took command of the dislocated anti-treaty forces in the Blessington area and redeployed them as best he could to occupy a defensive position, cutting the routes leading south from Dublin. At his disposal were:

The South Dublin Brigade (150–200 strong), under Comdt Andrew McDonnell;
Elements of the Kildare Brigade under Comdt Paddy Brennan;
Elements of the Tipperary Brigade under Comdt Michael Sheehan.

Their armament was nondescript. The irony was that the rifles of the Kildare Brigade had been shipped north by Collins via Beggars Bush and had not been replaced.

A series of defensive points was set up. Elements of the 6th Battalion, Kildare Brigade went to Ballymore Eustace to dominate the Naas and Dublin approaches. They were reinforced by elements of the Tipperary Brigade. By Tuesday 4 July a rag-tag 'line' stretched from Blessington to the Meath border. Blessington, Brittas and Kilbride were physically occupied, with headquarters in Blessington.

The pro-treaty forces converged on Blessington on three axes: deployed units of the Curragh Brigade under Comdt Bishop marched from the south and east through Carlow and Wicklow; units of the Dublin Brigade under Comdt Heaslip drove south and then eastwards across the Dublin mountains; elements from the west under Comdt McNulty swung on Blessington through the Wicklow mountains. Barra O'Briain made a critical cut off forced march across country from the Curragh. The force totalled 500 and the advance guards were made up of infantry combat teams which included armoured cars. On contact hand-to-hand fighting developed. By Thursday 6 July Bishop had deployed artillery and armour for a final assault on Blessington from a start line about 800 yards away. McNulty was delayed crossing the mountains so the ring around the town was not closed and the defenders withdrew through the gap. Only a token garrison was left in

Baltinglass as the anti-treaty forces dispersed south-eastwards into the mountains.

A reluctance to shoot to kill was still evident. Two brothers, Rob and Johnny Goodwin from Stillorgan, fought on different sides in Blessington. One of them said that although there was 'more ammunition fired there than at the Somme no one was hurt'.

The battle of Limerick which followed was one of the major turning points in the war. The previous March civil war had been narrowly averted there. Shoot-to-kill reservations were now wearing thinner. A temporary truce signed on 7 July between 'the Executive Forces, Irish Republican Army' and 'First Western Division and the Fourth Southern Division, Dáil forces, Irish Republican Army', was broken before 'the ink wherewith 'twas writ could dry'.[74]

An intriguing factor worked in the pro-treatyites favour at this juncture. It finally dawned on the Bank of Ireland that the Provisional Government was all that stood between the country and anarchy and it loosened its purse strings accordingly. Unpaid troops had been getting very disaffected. Comdt Pat King and Capt. Martin Bell drew the cash from the Bank and toured the country, paying troops in the thick of the fighting. It was in the nick of time as there had been ominous rumours that the Regulars would help themselves even if this meant changing sides. The Bank of Ireland, Comdt King and Capt. Bell saved the day.

The anti-treaty forces in Limerick concentrated mainly in the Upper O'Connell St area of the city and in the docks. The pro-treaty side held the area east of William St and opened fire from the barracks there. The fall of Limerick would open the way for a sweep into Kerry and North Cork, into the heartlands of the 'Munster Republic' which Lynch was trying to set up behind the Limerick-Clonmel-Waterford line. Raids, sorties and house-to-house fighting developed in Limerick. On 19 July, forced by artillery fire to evacuate the Strand Barracks, King John's Castle and the Ordnance Barracks in Musgrave St, the retreating anti-treatyites fought a well-conducted rearguard action, making good use of covering machine-gun fire. Blowing bridges and erecting road blocks with felled trees, they withdrew to a defensive position in the Kilmallock-Bruree area. Barracks and other occupied posts were all burnt on evacuation.

Traversing the bocage-type terrain around Kilmallock proved difficult for the raw pro-treaty troops untrained in field craft. In addition, their commander, Major Gen. Murphy, encrusted in his trench-warfare experience (he had commanded a British Army Brigade in France), was painfully ponderous. He inched along, relying on his map, ordering his green troops to dig in the minute they came under sniper fire. He had Lucas-like reflexes.[75] By contrast, leadership in the opposing forces was of a high calibre: Liam Deasy, Divisional Commander; Seán Moylan, Director of Operations; Moss Twomey, General Staff Officer. Vice-Brigadier John Joe Sheehy's handling of Humphrey Murphy's combat-ready Kerry No. 1 Brigade was outstanding.

It took the old reliable 18-pounder covering the fire and the dash of the crack Dublin Guards under Comdt. Tom Flood[76] to penetrate the defence. Over 2,000 troops took part in the attack on Kilmallock which was occupied at 4 a.m. on Saturday 5 August after a fierce fire fight between the pro-treaty troops in Ashill Towers and anti-treaty troops in the Workhouse, which again they burned down as they evacuated. The Kerrymen, covered by the Corkmen, withdrew to meet the sea landings in their own backyard in Fenit on 2 August. Armoured cars (notably 'Danny Boy', later changed to 'Tom Keogh') played a significant part in the victories in Limerick City, Kilmallock, Bruree, Patrickswell, Adare, Rathkeale, Newcastle West, Abbeyfeale and later at Kilworth, Killorglin, Castlemaine, Tralee and Killarney.

Around the same period (18 July) the other end of the anti-treaty line at Waterford came under attack. It was defended by a force of 300 men, elements of the 1st Cork Brigade, all under Col. Comdt Pax Whelan now O/C Waterford Brigade and member of the executive (in January 1919 he had been O/C West Waterford Brigade). They were armed with rifles, Lewis guns and Thompson sub-machine guns. They sported pro-treaty uniforms with civilian caps. Cars, provisions, clothing and wireless equipment from ships in port were commandeered. The bridge across the river Suir was raised and the principal buildings were occupied.

The attacking Second Southern Division (700 troops, many of whom had fought at Dublin and Blessington) were under the command of Col. Comdt Prout in Kilkenny. His subordinates were Comdt Heaslip and Comdt Paul. Paul had also served in France and had commanded an East Waterford IRA Battalion during the War of Independence. He knew the area backwards. The troops came from Counties Waterford, Wexford, Kilkenny and Tipperary and also had good local knowledge. An advantageous road network fanned southward. The aim was to take Waterford, roll up the line of the 'Munster Republic' north through Carrick and Clonmel and there to link up with the forces moving south from the Thurles-Cashel-Roscrea area.

Using civilian transport and horses the group left Kilkenny. On 18 July after pausing at Kilmacon for General Absolution the horse transport was dispensed with and three columns were formed. The 18-pounder was attached to a Crossley lorry. By darkness small pro-treaty parties had reached the railway line, 400 men had advanced over open ground unopposed until they came under fire from an outpost at Bilberry Rock at 6.45 p.m. Closer to Mount Misery that fire intensified and they took cover on a reverse slope. A left flanking attack was then decided on. That involved a river crossing and required covering fire.

At dawn next morning (19 July) the 18-pounder was brought across the golf course and placed on a rock overlooking the city. Although harassed by machine-gun and rifle fire, effective single gun high explosive and shrapnel shoots over open sights at ranges of 1,200 to 2,500 yards were carried out. No incendiary shells were used. Paul's own house was hit.[77] Thirty-six shells were fired. The infantry barracks were badly damaged. Five shells hit the jail but only the roof was damaged.

To add to Whelan's troubles a planned anti-treaty flank counter-attack went wrong. Three of their columns — 150 men from Cork under Jim Hurley, Tipperary under Michael Sheehan and Kilkenny under Andrew Kennedy — concentrated under the command of Comdt Gen. Dinny Lacey at Mullinavat to attack the right flank of Prout's advance. Dan Breen's reserve of 100 was located ten miles to the north to protect the rear and keep the right flank open. Sheehan attacked prematurely. Surprise was lost, wrong conclusions drawn. A fresh mission was hastily given to withdraw to Carrick-on-Suir and from there to hem in and harass the enemy.

The following night under cover of darkness a group of 100, commanded by Capt. Ned O'Brien, a veteran local IRA fighter, and Capt. Dominic Mackey, crossed the river to attack the anti-treaty right flank. The defence was completely surprised. There was no protective screen, no outposts. Troops under Capt. Mackey worked down the bank, dodging a patrol, with the objectives of seizing the building overlooking the quay and of lowering the bridge. They were virtually unopposed. They surprised the Irregulars on the quays, rushed the County Club, the Adelphi Hotel and the Imperial Hotel which was flying the Red Cross (unjustifiably the attackers maintained). They gained their foothold and set up headquarters in the Imperial Hotel. Advancing along the quay they gradually established domination of the city, leaving only two important strongholds — the post office basement and the Granville Hotel — to the Irregulars. Around 5 p.m. on Thursday 20 July the pro-treaty 18-pounder was brought into position on the railway lines and gave covering fire to the Infantry to enable them to capture the post office and other prominent buildings.

By Friday 21 July the only resistance left was sniping from the jail, Ballybrickin, Barrack St, the Protestant Cathedral and a few other isolated posts. The jail was the only significant defensive position left: fifteen men were holding out there. The 18-pounder was brought along the railway to fire on the bridge. A Lancia armoured car was detailed to give covering fire. Sgt Howlett with great bravery mounted a Lewis gun, stood up in the car and gave the necessary covering fire, still firing as he was riddled with bullets. Five shells again landed on the jail and this time the order was given to evacuate. Looters at once descended on the place and everything portable was stolen.

The anti-treaty troops were now retreating to Carrick and Dungarvan. There had been little support for them in John Redmond's old stamping ground. The Corkmen, 'foreigners' to the locals, were particularly unpopular. Security was honoured more in the breach than in the observance. No one demonstrated an eye for ground: Mount Misery was inexplicably neglected. There was not even a pretence at perimeter defence. The anti-treaty officers were untrained and inexperienced. They had no artillery. They had, however, made provision for a hospital and for radio communications.

At 9 p.m. on Friday 21 July the pro-treaty troops lowered the bridge to volleys and cheers. A significant victory in arms had been won. The line of the 'Munster Republic' was now turned at both flanks.

The pro-treaty side were now benefiting from the advantage of having some semblance of centralised command and overall direction. On 13 July an Army Council was set up composed of Collins, Commander-in-Chief, Mulcahy, Chief of Staff and Minister for Defence, and O'Duffy, Assistant Chief of Staff. Related command appointments were made.[78]

On 15 July the anti-treaty HQ moved to Fermoy. Prospects of a military victory for them were now non-existent. Guerilla warfare was the only course left.[79] That was not immediately apparent to them, however. They did not have any overall strategy and fought on blindly.

Three columns of 'Irregulars' — two from the First Southern Division (one Cork, one Kerry) and one Tipperary column — counter-attacked preemptively in Thurles and Golden to protect Tipperary town; they were repulsed. The attack lacked co-ordination. Again, there was no unity of command.

The defending 500-strong pro-treaty troops were mostly local volunteers from the Thurles, Templemore and Gould's Cross areas stiffened up by units of the ubiquitous combat-crafty Dublin Guards. They pushed on to Tipperary town by two routes on 29 July. Approaches to the town were mined and buildings were fortified and sandbagged. After bitter house-to-house fighting by the Dubliners and an encircling movement towards Bansha by the Tipperary men, the town was evacuated by the anti-treatyites, who then retreated to the Glen of Aherlow to continue the fight from there.

A detachment of Dublin Guards under Comdt O'Connor and a detachment of Tipperary troops under Comdt Ryan attacked the village of Golden at 7.30 p.m. on Friday 27 July. Twenty-four Irregulars were taken prisoner; two were killed. A Lewis gun, thousands of rounds of .303 ammunition and a Lancia car were captured. At 5 p.m. on Sunday they attacked Tipperary town and by the midday on the following day — 30 July — the whole town was in the hands of the troops. Their casualties were four killed and three wounded. There were several unexploded mines in the town. Before retirement the Irregulars burned part of the barracks and completely destroyed Cleeve's factory. The line was now penetrated in the centre as well as being turned at both flanks.

Clonmel was isolated. Only Carrick-on-Suir stood between it and Prout's force advancing from Waterford. Dinny Lacey had been ordered to hold Carrick-on-Suir and maintain it as a reserve base for transport and communications. At his disposal were (eventually) four columns of Tipperary men and three companies, including Dan Breen's at Kilmagonny. He organised a defence against Prout along the line between Cregg and Three Bridges. He ordered the permanent destruction of roads, railways and bridges in the area. This further alienated the civilian population, already aggravated by the cavalier system of requisitioning in the town where food was running short.

Prout's advance was held up at Piltown on 1 August, and he was lucky to survive an attack on his rear from Fiddown Bridge. The anti-treaty side failed to commit its reserve at a crucial moment. Once again the 18-pounder proved its value, neutralising dug-in anti-treaty forces at Killooney House. Artillery and machine-gun fire broke up a counter-attack on the right flank. On 3 August the pro-treaty forces entered Carrick-on-Suir; harassed by sniper fire they prepared to move on Clonmel. Three days later they captured it.

The attacking force left Carrick on 8 August in column-of-route along the northern secondary roads on the Ballyreale-Ballypatrick-Kilcash Castle axis. The heavily defended main road up the middle was avoided. A series of hotly contested fire and movement engagements followed, with both sides making excellent use of terrain. Eventually the anti-treatyites were forced back into the town, leaving snipers behind to impose maximum delay. A vigorous rearguard action was fought before evacuation. On 10 August the pro-treaty forces occupied Clonmel. Next day Lynch and his staff burned their headquarters in Fermoy Barracks and took to the hills.

Nothing seemed to have gone right for the anti-treaty forces, and in general they paid the price for their lack of an overall mission and offensive action. They did have some bright ideas but they were unable to execute them. They planned to capture Baldonnel aerodrome with its aircraft and to bomb Leinster House from the air. The members of the government were confined to Leinster House under heavy guard. Three times the elements detailed for the attack failed to rendezvous and three times the attack had to be called off. This was demoralising. The Dublin detail were intercepted and captured as they left the capital. Local Meath detachments were captured as they tried to destroy a bridge at Shackleton's Mill.

A second plan to isolate Dublin by severing lines of communications and blowing bridges was disrupted when Col. Hugo McNeill captured their battle plans a couple of days prior to the operation scheduled for Saturday 5 August. The forewarned pro-treaty forces lay in wait and took 200 prisoners. A belated offensive action against pro-treaty positions in the Dublin areas of Finglas, Phibsborough, Drumcondra and Harcourt St fizzled out. The writing was on the wall.

The first phase of the conflict in which anti-treaty forces attempted to maintain their hold upon towns and districts was coming to an end. Whenever they vacated such a position they destroyed it by fire and explosives to prevent government troops using it.[80] To hamper troop movements railway bridges were blown up, rails lifted and stations destroyed: roads were cratered and bridges and viaducts destroyed. There was much mindless destruction of public and private property. There were still confrontations between opposing forces of some strength but the struggle degenerated into bitter guerilla warfare following the pattern of the Black and Tan conflict. The conventional side of the war was over though there was bitter fighting still to come, particularly in Kerry.

In August 1922 the Provisional Government prescribed that the following declaration should be made as a condition of employment by all civilian employees paid out of public funds:

> 'I declare that I have not taken part with or aided or abetted in any way whatsoever the forces in revolt against the Irish Provisional Government and I promise to be faithful to that Government and to give no aid or support of any kind to those who are engaged in conflict against the authority of that Government.'

Imaginative sea landings accelerated the pro-treatyites successes in the conventional sphere. The landing of reinforcements by sea at Westport[81] clinched the takeover of Mayo; Castlebar was occupied on 25 July and Ballina was taken three days later by a column from MacEoin's division commanded by Col. Tony Lawlor. It had swept westward from Athlone practically unopposed.

The landing at Fenit[82], the port of Tralee, by four companies of the Dublin Guards under the command of Gen. Paddy O'Daly on 2 August (three days before the capture of Kilmallock) had a chain reaction. Not only did it envelop the rear of the Cork-Kerry anti-treaty redoubt, it also had the effect of drawing off the cream of the redoubtable fighting men from the critical battle for Kilmallock, leaving the axis ahead clear for the pro-treaty forces to advance.

The mines in Fenit harbour were defused but the fighting in Tralee was bloody. Ballymullen Barracks was set on fire before the town was evacuated. After Lynch had retreated from Limerick another force from Kilkee (Co. Clare) landed on 3 August at Tarbert under Gen. Michael Hogan.[83] He drove on to Listowel and joined O'Daly in Tralee. He took command of the northern half of the county; O'Daly the southern.

In neighbouring Limerick Brig. James Slattery (again making critical use of an 18-pounder) captured Newcastlewest and Rathkeale. On 5 August the anti-treaty Brigade back from Kilmallock assembled at Farranfore to prepare to counter-attack. However by 15 August most of the north Kerry towns had fallen to the pro-treaty forces. The rugged terrain of south Kerry and civilian support enabled the anti-treaty forces to hold out longer there.

Dublin men with a sprinkling of Northerners made up the bulk of the pro-treaty forces in Kerry: in Tralee the 27th Battalion; in Killarney the 6th; the 9th in Cahirciveen; the 17th in Kenmare and the 19th in Castleisland. They did not have proper basic training, which made the enforcement of discipline difficult. The GOC, Major Gen. Paddy O'Daly, though he had a lot of combat experience (he was the captain who took over the 'Bush' from the Auxiliaries a few short months previously), was comparatively inexperienced for this level of command in unconventional operations.[84]

On 22 August 1922 Michael Collins, the outstanding personality of the generation that founded the modern Irish State, was killed in an ambush in Béal na mBláth near Bandon, Co. Cork.[85] He died in a firing position, firmly gripping his rifle across which his head rested. The nation and the army mourned the passing in his prime (he was aged thirty-one) of its most loved leader. A thousand Republican prisoners in Kilmainham Jail spontaneously knelt down and said the rosary for the repose of his soul when they heard of his death.[86] Collins's contribution to the attainment of national independence was unrivalled. Like Griffith, Collins was a man of no property. He gave his all for his country. He became the most wanted man in Ireland when the British put £10,000 on his head, dead or alive. He wore no disguise and cycled openly through Dublin. The enemy had no proper description of him and though hundreds knew him none betrayed him. He was an ebullient, friendly, laughing, boyish, emotional patriot of extraordinary talents and charisma.

He was succeeded by the Chief of the General Staff, Gen. Richard Mulcahy, who immediately sent a message to the men of the army calling for calm discipline and no reprisals. In a move to enforce this direction (though Mulcahy dragged his feet here in moving against an old battle-scarred comrade), Major Gen. Paddy O'Daly was later removed from his command on 4 October 1922, following investigations into reports of ill-treatment of prisoners.

Gen. Murphy was given command of Kerry and west Cork and characteristically requisitioned strong reinforcements of transport, armoured cars and artillery for heavy-handed search-and-sweep operations. The elusive guerillas operating in safe countryside never presented him with a lucrative target. Columns consisted of thirty-five men broken down into self-sufficient squads of six. Machine-gunners, signallers, engineers were included. Using the tactics proven against the British, supply lines and communications were ambushed. Movement between towns was hazardous. This angered the general public; frustrations grew; outrages followed.

The worst of these happened at Ballyseedy Cross, near Tralee. A tree had been felled by the Irregulars to make a road block and a trap mine was laid so that any attempt to clear the road would explode it. It killed three officers and two soldiers. As a reprisal nine prisoners were tied to the same tree and eight of them were blown to pieces by a similar mine. The ninth (Stephen Fuller, afterwards a Fianna Fáil TD) by some fluke was blown free and lived to tell the tale. The vendetta about the state of discipline in the army between O'Higgins and Mulcahy was exacerbated.

The most daring of the sea landings took place at Youghal, Union Hall and Passage West on 8 August. Once more Dublin troops under the command of Gen. Emmet Dalton and Gen. Tom Ennis were in the vanguard. They had embarked the day before from the North Wall Dublin on the *Arvonia* and the *Lady Wicklow.* Cork was controlled by anti-treatyites. British warships dominated the harbour and British soldiers were in possession of the forts: Spike Island, Haulbowline, Carlisle, Camden and Templebreedy. Mines had been laid by the anti-treatyites to fool British intelligence, thought by the Irregulars to be in league with the pro-treatyites.

With great coolness — although none of them had previous seafaring experience and there was enough melodrama aboard (in pressing a pilot into service at gunpoint) to satisfy a Hollywood film director — they steamed up the river Lee around midnight on 8 August and brought off total surprise with the landings. The deception measures to indicate that the attack would come overland from the north had worked.

The advance towards Cork from Passage via Rochestown led to bloody encounters in which both sides showed great bravery and resource. The battle for Rochestown raged all day on Wednesday 9 August. Defence posts held up the advance until a decision was taken to evacuate Cork and set fire to its Victoria (Collins) Barracks.[87] On entering the city Gen. Dalton proclaimed the intention of the national army to restore normal life as quickly as possible. The anti-treatyites moved to the mountains of west Cork and Kerry to resume guerilla action in liaison with their Kerry comrades. Cork, the capital of the 'Munster Republic', was now in pro-treaty hands. Disjointed actions which had occurred more by jolt than by deliberation somehow seemed to be slipping into place.

Enniscorthy had fallen on 7 July, followed the next day by Nenagh; Abbeyleix was already captured. By mid-July Galway city was in pro-treaty hands (the anti-treatyites still dominating the surrounding countryside). In Sligo the fortunes of war favoured the pro-treatyites while in Roscommon — apart from a spirited encounter in Boyle — republican opposition was limp. The Westport sea landings had led to the easy occupation of Castlebar and Ballina and the collapse of the Western stronghold.

The terrain made Donegal a tougher nut to crack, but eventually the superior pro-treaty war machine ground down resistance. The commander of the Irregular Second Northern Division, Kerryman Comdt Gen. Charles Daly, Brig. Seán Larkin and two lieutenants, Daniel Enright and Timothy O'Sullivan, were taken prisoner and held for eight months before being shot by firing squad — just two months before the ceasefire.

The North was as confused as the rest of the country. Frank Aiken's Fourth Northern Division, with under command the 1st Northern Brigade, remained neutral initially. They had the particular Six-County situation to contend with also. In March 1922 cross-border roads were barricaded and trenched and local people were prevented by the Northern police from removing them. Trains were derailed and carriages set on fire. The Special Constabulary was running riot and widely intimidating nationalists. On 26 May 1922 they raided and looted Gallagher's pub at Flurry Bridge, Co. Louth, south of the border. Troops from the military barracks in Dundalk and from Dungooly camp, as well as British army reinforcements from Newry, were involved. The Fourth Northern Division identified with the forces of the Provisional Government. Emotively too, the 'Specials' had crossed the border to arrest five girls from Bessbrook. Gen. Frank Aiken demanded their release as one of the conditions for the cessation of hostilities. It was a serious incident, confusing to potential Civil War adversaries. In that situation their common enemy was clear.

But it was more complex than that. In the previous March-April delegates from the 1st Brigade participated in the banned Army Convention in spite of a decision by the Fourth Northern Division not to take part. This brigade had two battalions in Armagh and two in north Louth. The two north of the border abided by the Division decision; the two on the southern side followed the executive. However, the latter were included in the active service unit of sixty men under Brig. McKenna for operations in the Six Counties, and the military barracks was used as a depot for weapons received on Collins's instructions for distribution into the Six Counties. Following an incident involving the capture and escape of Brig. McKenna and Frank Aiken's intention to mediate and take responsibility for him, the Fourth Northern Division decided to adopt a neutral position, to make every effort to secure a cessation of hostilities and to call off attacks on the Six Counties. As against that in July 1922 the Provisional Government forces disbanded the 'North Louth Police' which had been formed to protect Protestant families. Aiken went to Mulcahy, the Minister for Defence, to persuade him to call a truce. He travelled south to Liam Lynch, Chief of Staff of the 'executive' forces with a similar plea. He failed and returned to Dundalk. In the interim Gen. Eoin O'Duffy, now Assistant Chief of Staff, Government forces, formerly O/C Fifth Northern Division, prevailed on Aiken's second-in-command to occupy the Police Barracks in Dundalk held by executive supporters.[88] On the one hand desertions were taking place from the Division to the government side, on the other hand arms were dumped at Soldiers Point, Dundalk, as a precaution against a move by the government forces on Dundalk.[89] On 16 July the pro-treaty Fifth Northern Division stole a march on them and captured Dundalk

Barracks, imprisoning Aiken and his men. On 27 July mines breached the jail walls, enabling Aiken and a hundred of his men to break out. Using mines again and large amounts of explosives to good effect he (Aiken) recaptured the barracks on 14 August, seizing 400 rifles, machine-guns, grenades, ammunition and one 18-pounder piece (which they spiked). They in turn were ousted in lively actions by two encircling pro-treaty Divisions under Gen. Dan Hogan and Col. Hugo McNeill (who used aircraft in his attack). By the end of July the anti-treatyites were abandoning towns and firing buildings before they evacuated. By the middle of August they no longer held any town. De Valera was snubbed by Lynch when he proposed surrender.[90] Hostilities dragged on.

On 12 October 1922 Col. Comdt P.A. Mulcahy O/C 3rd Southern Command reported to the Chief of Staff that the morale of all ranks was 'splendid' and that where he found slackness he had shifted officers and interchanged garrisons. He set up a Command Training Depot in Kilcormac to give a hard three-week course in column work, patrol duties, rounding up operations etc. Part of the training would be along the banks of the canal to keep a constant watch on canal boats between Rahan and Ferbane. He identified the Rahan-Fallagh area as one of the centres of the 'canal robber gang'. He complained of the shortage of uniforms, greatcoats, machine-guns and hand grenades, and looked for 200 more rifles to equip the remaining unarmed troops in the area. There were still roving bands of Irregulars in his area but he reckoned that harassment immobilised them. Four main columns operated in the area and in addition each post had its own 'little column'. He said that information, even in hostile areas, was now coming in more frequently and that the troops were well supported by the civil population.[91]

There were ambushes of small parties of motorised troops, individual killings said to be 'executions' and widespread seizure and wanton destruction of property by the anti-treaty side. There were wholesale arrests, dubious methods of interrogation of prisoners and many acts of indiscipline, including mirror individual killings thought to be 'unofficial executions' by the Provisional Government forces. There were insistent calls (mainly from Ernest Blythe, Minister for

Local Government) for the introduction of military courts on the one hand; on the other there was great concern within the government about the state of discipline in the army. The loss of its two leaders within two months of the start of the Civil War had thrown the Provisional Government out of gear: broken-hearted Griffith had died on 12 August, and ten days later Michael Collins was killed in action.

Gen. Mulcahy had asked the Dáil for Emergency Powers and on 27 September had been granted them by the Army (Special Powers) resolution. *General Regulations as to Discipline* were to come into force at such time as the Army Council should determine and announce by proclamation. By order of the government dated 28 September the Army Council had been constituted as follows: Richard Mulcahy, Commander-in-Chief, and Seán McMahon, Chief of Staff, both with the rank of General; and Gearóid O'Sullivan, Joseph McGrath and Diarmuid O'Hegarty to be respectively Adjutant General, Director of Intelligence, and Director of Organisation, with the rank of Major General.

On 3 October a government proclamation offered an amnesty to all of those in arms against the State provided they surrendered their arms on or before 15 October. The Army Council issued a similar proclamation. On 15 October military courts with powers to inflict the death penalty were set up. A vicious circle of executions and reprisals followed.

Now that the anti-treaty side had demonstrably lost the conventional war de Valera's lone voice that the war had a political as well as a military aspect finally got a hearing. In October 1922 a government was set up under his presidency which claimed to represent the legitimate authority of the republic.[92] On 8 November a proclamation under the signatures of de Valera and Stack, as members of a reconstituted republican government, was published, declaring the Provisional Government to be illegal. But the tide was running against them by that stage and, more importantly, they were being held down on all sides by the growing combat efficiency of the pro-treaty forces. Military courts were another nail in the coffin.

Command O/Cs determined who came up before the military courts. In the Kerry Command Matthew Moroney,

Thomas Divane, Cornelius Casey and Dermot O'Connor were sentenced to death. Gen. Murphy was responsible for providing for the execution of the sentences. Whether in a backlash from Ballyseedy or not, he procrastinated and no execution ever took place. On 5 November Ernie O'Malley, Assistant Chief of Staff of the anti-treaty forces, was captured in a shoot-out (a soldier was shot dead) at 36 Ailesbury Rd, Dublin, the home of Mrs Humphreys, a sister of The O'Rahilly who was killed in 1916. He was wounded, and hospitalised: when his condition improved the question of his trial by military court arose. Regulation 83 of *General Regulations as to Discipline* laid down that no accused person could be tried by court-martial unless certified to be physically able and fit to stand trial. Military courts were instructed to have due regard for these procedures as far as possible. The Army Medical Service Authority (under Comdt Matt O'Connor) repeatedly delayed the requisite certificate, and O'Malley, who had an outstanding pre-truce national record, was never tried. Others were not so lucky.

On 8 November four young men (all under twenty-two), Peter Cassidy, John Gaffney (Third Battalion IRA) James Fisher and Richard Twohig (Second Battalion) were sentenced to death by the second military court in Griffith Barracks. Next day troops on parade in the barracks came under rifle and machine-gun fire from the roofs of the houses on the far side of the canal at the rear of the barracks. One soldier and two civilians were killed: seventeen soldiers were wounded. It was indignantly recalled that during the fight against the British a similar plan was turned down for being 'too dirty'.

The sentences on Cassidy and the others were carried out in Kilmainham Jail on 17 November. The firing party and the officer-in-charge were young and raw. Three of the young men to be executed were killed instantly. It took the ritual *coup de grace* revolver shot to despatch the fourth. A prove-officer stood by to put out of pain anyone not already dead.

On 10 November night attacks of sustained rifle and machine-gun fire were again made on Griffith and Portobello (Cathal Brugha) Barracks. Next morning Erskine Childers was arrested.[93]

Childers, a somewhat effete Director of Propaganda and Publicity, had been ridiculously demonised by the pro-treatyites: every blown-up culvert was attributed to his evil genius. The idea of an Englishman interfering in Irish affairs maddened them. The truth was that both de Valera and Childers had been ostracised by the scornful republican fighting generals. They were given no military standing whatsoever.

On his way back to Dublin to act as secretary to the reconstituted republican government, Childers stayed the night of 10 November with his cousin, Robert Barton, in Annamoe, Co. Wicklow. In the early morning a small party of troops seized him as he drew a small automatic pistol, which, however, he did not fire as the ladies present would have been endangered by an exchange of shots. He was put in the guard room in Portobello Barracks and, to their discredit, subjected to some rough treatment by a a few officers. He was charged and tried by military court on 16 November for the offence of possession, without lawful authority, of an automatic pistol[94] (a present from Michael Collins). He was sentenced to death and executed by firing squad at Beggars Bush Barracks on the morning of Friday 24 November. It was too dark to proceed at the appointed hour so Childers had to wait until there was sufficient light. He smoked and chatted with the firing party, disclaimed any feeling of ill-will against anyone and died most bravely.

The next trial by military court took place in Griffith Barracks where three men, Joseph Spooner, Patrick Farrelly and John Murphy, together with a young UCD student, Séamus Mallin, were charged with attacking a lorry containing government troops with bombs and revolver fire in the South Circular Road. The only charge against Mallin was possession of a revolver without lawful authority. On 30 November Spooner, Farrelly and Murphy were executed. Mallin's sentence was commuted to penal servitude for life.

On 27 November the Chief of Staff of the anti-treaty forces in a letter addressed to the 'Speaker of the Provisional Parliament of Southern Ireland' had referred to the many crimes committed against prisoners by its members and its armed forces and went on:

> Finally you are now pretending to try IRA prisoners before your make-believe courts. You have already done to death five after such mock ceremonials. You now presume to murder and transport the soldiers who had brought Ireland victory when you, traitors, surrendered the Republic twelve months ago.
>
> Next to the members of your 'Provisional Government' every member of your body who voted for this resolution by which you pretend to make legal the murder of soldiers, is equally guilty. We therefore give you and each member of your body due notice that unless your army recognises the rules of warfare in the future we shall adopt very drastic measures to protect our forces.

Shortly afterwards Thomas Derrig, Adjutant General of the anti-treaty forces, signed an order for the 'execution' of all members of the Provisional Government, all members of the Dáil who had voted for the Army (Special Powers) Resolution and of Command Legal Officers. With effect from 6 December 1922 the Irish Free State (otherwise called *Saorstát Éireann*) came into being. The last of the British forces then left Dublin and in accordance with a proviso in the 1921 Treaty they handed over the Royal (Collins) Barracks; Marlborough (McKee) Barracks and GHQ, Parkgate. Derrig's order[95] was translated into action on 7 December when Brig. Gen. Seán Hales, TD was shot dead leaving the Ormond Hotel on his way to the Dáil. His companion, Pádraig Ó Máille, Deputy Speaker, who had also voted for the Army (Special Powers) Resolution was seriously wounded. Seán Hales and his brother, Tom, had been to the forefront in the fight against the British in the west Cork area: they took opposite sides in the Civil War.

The Army Council next decided to set up a system of military committees — a sort of drumhead courts-martial — to deal summarily with persons arrested in possession of arms, ammunition or explosives. A proclamation dated 7 December was issued to that effect. The following evening the papers carried this announcement:

> The execution took place this morning at Mountjoy Goal of the following persons taken in arms against the Irish

> Government: Rory O'Connor, Liam Mellowes, Joseph McKelvey, and Richard Barrett, as a reprisal for the assassination on his way to the Dáil on the 7 December of Brigadier Seán Hales and as a solemn warning to those associated with them who are engaged in a conspiracy of assassination against the representatives of the Irish People.

O'Connor had been Kevin O'Higgins's best man. GHQ feeling was that the reprisal executions of those members of the Four Courts executive were not merely the most justly deserved of all the executions but also the most justifiable. 'Murder, foul and despicable and nothing else' was the *New York Nation's* comment.[96] There were no further assassinations of Dáil deputies but destruction of the property of government-linked persons intensified.

On 10 December pro-treaty TD Seán McGarry's[97] child lost his life when the family home in Philipsburgh Avenue was set on fire as part of the campaign. Five Irregulars captured in Leixlip were discovered to be deserters from the National Army and were shot. On 20 December seven men were shot following an investigation by the military committee for unlawful possession of rifles, ammunition, bombs and explosives. On the same day the Dublin-Belfast mail train was hijacked, set on fire and sent on a collision course with a train carrying government troops and military stores. An 'unofficial execution' by government forces of a man called Francis Lalor took place. Two men, John Murphy and John Phelan, sentenced by a military court in Kilkenny, were executed on 29 December. The New Year brought little justification for optimism for a return to law and order. The QMG's branch organised its priorities and issued an instruction on 2 December 1922 on the prevention of the waste of food and the correct method of obtaining supplies.

On 20 January 1923 the Army Council issued a proclamation making an order to extend the jurisdiction of the military courts and to include a number of additional offences. The new Civic Guards were being gingerly filtered out but on 11 January one of their stations was blown up. The destruction of property went on: Senator Bagwell's county residence in Clonmel was gutted; Sir Horace Plunkett's mansion, Kilteragh at Leopardstown, was destroyed; so was President Cosgrave's house. County council meetings were disrupted. Senator Oliver Gogarty was kidnapped.

On 18 January Liam Deasy,[98] the Irregular Chief of Staff, was captured while carrying arms. His life was spared when he agreed to make an appeal to his colleagues for unconditional surrender. It brought a curt refusal from Liam Lynch. There was no response to a further offer of an amnesty issued by Mulcahy on 8 February. On 11 February Kevin O'Higgins's father was shot dead in his home in Co. Laois in the presence of his wife and daughter. In mid-February Dinny Lacey, the renowned Irregular leader, was killed in action. In March Con Moloney, who had succeeded Liam Deasy as Deputy Chief of Staff, was wounded and taken prisoner.

Bit by bit the Regular Army was gaining the upper hand. During the fighting its strength reached 55,000: sixty-five infantry battalions and many of the existing corps were formed. However as Lt Gen. Collins-Powell later commented: 'it would be wrong to accept the neat idea that the organisation went smoothly. The civil war disrupted many plans and the growth of the army was quite haphazard in 1922–23.' Nevertheless much was falling into place, almost of its own accord. On 1 March locations of Headquarters and of Infantry Battalions were gazetted (Appendix 3).

Impressive St Patrick's Day parades were[99] held. Gen. Mulcahy reminded the troops of the 13th Infantry Battalion in Collins Barracks, Dublin, of how far they had come in just one short year 'from one small home in Beggars Bush', little knowing then the trials and tribulations that lay in store for them. He recalled that other St Patrick's Day in 1916 when the Irish army, then only three years old, fixed the small number of bayonets they had, thereby serving notice on the invader. He hoisted the flag blessed by the chaplain, Father Pigott,[100] at Parkgate St and went on to the refurbished Curragh Camp to take the salute there from a march past in review formation. He reminded that parade of the lessons of faith and courage embodied in the flag which had been unfurled by men like Pearse and had come through the fires of 1916. There was no danger or difficulty, he said, that, with the people, they could not take over their country safely. At the Cork parade a tricolour from France was presented as a token of affection and esteem. There were strong historic ties between Ireland and France, the second home of the Wild Geese.

Adjutants' and Company Commanders' courses commenced on 9 February 1923; there was talk of a university of the army. Eoin MacNeill, author of the call to arms that led to the 1916 Rising, exhorted the soldiers to look their own height.[101] He pointed out that, since Sarsfield left, the Irish soldier had become a name of honour in many armies and in many lands: the time had now come to show what he could do in his own land, in Ireland's army. In April 1923, while the Civil War was still on, Company Commanders', Machine-gun, NCOs' and Cooks' courses took place in the Curragh. In November an Army School of Instruction was established. The whole outlook was positive. There was a determination to shake off the shackles of British subjection. An army delegation to France in July got a warm welcome from French Army Chiefs.[102]

On 26 June an imposing march past took place at Wolfe Tone's grave in Bodenstown. On 13 August the first anniversary of the death of Arthur Griffith was commemorated by unveiling a cenotaph in Leinster Lawn, sounding the Last Post, firing an artillery salute in the Phoenix Park and a fly past ('circling sombrely') of four aeroplanes. On 22 August Collins and Griffith were both commemorated with a massive victory parade — *Bóthar Buadha* — of Infantry, Cavalry, Artillery and Special services in the Fifteen Acres in the Phoenix Park.[103] An air squadron landed on the parade ground from Baldonnel. Bugles were sounded and an artillery salute fired. It marked the apotheosis of the wartime army. Similar parades were held in Cork and elsewhere.

Social life quickened. On 21 April 1923 the Commander-in-Chief Gen. Mulcahy and President Cosgrave attended the first dance held in Collins Barracks (Dublin)[104] since the take-over. Clarke Barry, a fashionable Cork band, provided the dance music; bands of the 13th and 57th Battalions, the incidental music.

The orderlies of GHQ had held a sociable dance in a St Stephen's Green venue on 15 March 1923, while Warrant Officers and Sergeants of the 54th Infantry Garrison

Battalion similarly disported themselves in Newbridge. Gen. Mulcahy felt that if army bands would tour the country playing classical music it would speed up a return to normality. The new Army School of Music was active from March 1923 (see p.110).

Interest in the Irish language, interrupted by the hostilities, was renewed in the summer of 1923 and army classes were formed. Great enthusiasm was manifested. *Fáinne na nÓglach* was formed on 2 August to foster the use of Irish in the army.[105] Pádraic Ó Conaire had written *Tír an tSíor* for *An tÓglach* on 24 March.

Enthusiasm for sport went hand in hand with this activity. On 29 April 1923 the first convention of the newly formed Army Athletic Association was held at GHQ (then in Portobello Barracks) which put the emphasis on encouraging native games. Father Pigott's proposal that golf and tennis be discontinued as official army games was lost (Lt Niall Harrington had been previously arrested for playing golf!). Top officials of the association had to be Irish speakers. President of the Army Golfing Society[106] was the Chief of Staff; Vice-President, the Adjutant General; Captain, Major Gen. O'Daly, GOC Kerry and Vice-Captain, Major Gen. Davitt, the Judge Advocate General. As a social sign of the times army members were now admitted to *some* (not all!) civilian golf clubs.

Physical restoration also went on apace. The Works Corps[107] did good work repairing Wexford Bridge and constructing an aerodrome. The Railway Protection, Repair and Maintenance Corps[108] too (O/C Major Gen. Russell) performed worthwhile jobs of bridge repairing and maintaining the railway services. The Salvage Corps[109] (O/C Col. Michael McCormack) overcame formidable difficulties. Its most remarkable achievement was in the Glen of Imaal — where the Irregulars had wintered in 1922. The British had had two large camps there, artillery at Coolmooney camp and cavalry at Leitrim barracks. Together these camps accommodated 2,500 men, 500 horses and three batteries of 18-pounders. Over roads which were more like the beds of mountain streams the Salvage Corps brought material to the hangars in Tallaght Aerodrome, its dump in Leinster. They also explored with good results not just the deserted camps of the British but the ruins of barracks in Limerick, Tipperary and elsewhere. On 27 April 1923 the Commander-in-Chief mentioned that the men in the army should be used for construction before being demobbed.[110] There was lot of work to be done and civilian life with chronic unemployment was in a state of disruption. The Army Corps of Engineers[111] prepared schemes for new work and vetted ones initiated by Commands now subdivided into districts serviced by an Engineer Officer with technical staff and essential stores. Also the Coastal and Marine service got under way.

The national army was a new fact of life. Commands were restructured in 1923; instead of eight there were now nine: Dublin, Athlone, Donegal, Claremorris, Limerick, Kerry, Cork, Waterford and the Curragh (Appendix 2). Their GOCs were respectively: Dan Hogan, McKeon, Sweeney, Michael Hogan, Brennan, O'Daly, Reynolds, Prout and Peadar MacMahon. W.R.E. Murphy had been appointed Chief Commissioner of the Dublin Metropolitan Police after a brief period as Director of Training (the DMP was an independent police force until 1925). O'Daly resumed the Kerry Command. Emmet Dalton, disagreeing with the imposition of death sentences, resigned to become Clerk of the Senate. (He had the nickname 'Ginchy' from his outstanding bravery in the First World War.) David Reynolds replaced him. Eastern Command HQ went over to Collins Barracks. General Headquarters was transferred from Portobello Barracks to Parkgate in the spring of 1923. A professional profile was emerging. The dissaffection of *Cumann na mBan* was regrettable but on the other hand corps and services were coming into being.

The Air Corps[112] sprung up seemingly spontaneously in 1922. (Major-Gen. W.J. McSweeney was the first CO). The first Corps aeroplane landed in Baldonnel that summer, but the Corps soon became equipped with three Bristol fighters, two Avro Instructional Machines, one Martinsyde Passenger and a single seater Scout-SE5, operating from Baldonnel and Fermoy. In a brief twelve months it blossomed in size and efficiency while remaining intensely nationalist. No foreign games were permitted and every soldier had to attend an Irish class for one hour each day. On 20 December 1922 young officers from other units were invited to transfer to the Air Corps. By the end of 1923 the school of aeronautics had six out of sixteen pupils flying solo. During 1923 the Flight at Fermoy continued patrols of the Cork and Kerry mountains and 75 per cent of the aerodrome was rebuilt. The seeds for the development of other corps and services were also planted with a true professional instinct.

Initially the artillery [113] handed over by the British (five Mk 1 and four Mk II 18-pounders) was scattered throughout the various military barracks. On 23 March 1923 it was grouped in Clancy Barracks, Islandbridge. At that point the Corps consisted of eleven officers, sixty-two other ranks, ten horses and nine guns. On 23 May thirteen officers sat for the entry examination to the corps: three were successful. On 5 June the man born to be Director, Col. Patrick Mulcahy, O/C Regiment No. 2 Inspection Staff (Athlone Command), was promoted O/C.

The 'freelance' armoured cars (Rolls Royce, Peerless and Lancia) were formally reined in on 14 September 1922 under Capt. Joe Hyland as O/C Armoured Car Corps to constitute the Cavalry Corps.[114] The Armoured Car Corps was involved in almost every action. Some of its vehicles were even fitted with railway wheels and used by the Railway Protection Corps for patrolling.

The Army Medical Service[115] was established in April 1922. With the setting up of the permanent army *Cumann na mBan*'s 1916 tradition of providing medical services was carried on and the Army Medical Corps was divided into field and hospital services. The distinction of being the first female officer went to Dr Brigid Lyons Thornton. She had served in the Four Courts in 1916 and was used by Collins in 1921 in an unsuccessful effort to rescue from Mountjoy Jail Gen. Sean MacEoin who was then awaiting execution. The Army Nursing Service was inaugurated under the Medical Service in 1922. The first Director of the Medical Service, Major Gen. F.J. Morrin, was gazetted in the Adjutant General's Branch in May 1923. The Service at its wartime maximum comprised 110 whole-time medical officers, 200 part-time medical officers and 500 NCOs and men. It contained two whole-time senior surgeons with a fluctuating number of junior surgeons plus two senior consultants.

The Independent Signal Corps,[116] formed in March 1923, also had its roots in 1916. During the Rising a field wireless station was operated from the GPO. Signals played a critical part in the Civil War. Of sixty-three stations set up, linking every unit by wireless, only one was captured by the Irregulars. Col. Archer was O/C the Independent Corps of Signals; Capt. Neligan, Chief Wireless Inspector; Comdt Smyth, Second in Command and Capt. Egan, Chief Technical Officer. They promptly realised the value of wireless. In June 1923 the title was changed to Army Signal Corps.

The Military Police Corps[117] was established under the special authority of Section 75A of the Defence Forces Temporary Provisions Act, 1923, and provided for a Provost Marshal and Assistants. During the period of 1922 prior to hostilities suitable men were enrolled as Military Policemen to assist in taking over the barracks from the British. There were mixed opinions about the republican policemen in existence prior to that. On the outbreak of the Civil War the strength was increased to sixty; by the following December it was fifty. In February 1923 the Military Police Corps was formed and selected men from all units were transferred to it. Companies were drafted to each command under a Captain Assistant Provost Marshal. By May 1923 the strength of the corps was up to 1,500.

In October 1922, in conjunction with Dr J.T. Larchet, it was decided to proceed with setting up an Army School of Music[118] and agreed that 'flat pitch' be introduced. In March 1923 Fritz Brase, a well-known figure in German music, was recruited. With his assistant, Capt. Christian Sauerzweig, he went to the Curragh to inaugurate the school, which became a great morale-booster.

The first Regular Army Corps of Engineering[119] was also created in 1923. It subsumed the earlier Works Corps, Railway Maintenance Corps and Salvage Corps. Major Gen. C.F. Russell was CO; Major T.C. Courtney, Second in Command. Its immediate forerunner had been the 5th Battalion Dublin Brigade IRA, composed exclusively of engineers, which gave distinguished service in the War of Independence.

Chaplains had been appointed. The first chaplain to the Donegal Command, Dr McNeely, was appointed Bishop of

Rephoe in 1923.[120] He had been a chaplain in the British Army until 1919. In June 1922 chaplains were attached to the Forces at the requests of local commanders. In November 1922 a Defence Order readjusted this to twenty-seven whole-time chaplains in charge. In January 1923 a Command Chaplain supervised the work of each command. A report from the chaplains indicated that promiscuity was a bigger problem than drink among the men.

Recruitment and discipline in the young improvised army was the responsibility of the Adjutant General's Branch. The Quartermaster General's Department[121] was divided into four corps: Ordnance, Supply,[122] Transport, Pay.[123]

The provision of Ordnance[124] equipment went back to 1913. In 1916 simple but effective grenades were made. They were of two types: one was fired by a short length of fuse; the other contained a simple percussion mechanism. In the Anglo-Irish War a Munitions Branch and a Chemical Branch were set up in Parnell St, Luke St, Crown Alley and Vicar St (Percy Place). The corps was first established as a separate unit on 15 May 1922 under QMG's Staff Routine Order No 8. Col. Comdt Seán Quinn was the first Chief Ordnance Officer.

After the disbandment of the Coastal Infantry the Coastal and Marine Service was set up[125] consisting of Coast Patrol Boats and the Marine Investigation Department which watched the coast from Narrow Water in Carlingford Lough, round by the east, south and west coasts to Moville in Lough Swilly. The outcome of the shooting war was only a question of time.

On 11 April Liam Lynch, the Irregular Chief of Staff was captured in a fight in the Knockmealdown Mountains.[126] He was badly wounded and died that evening. He had ordered his men to leave him as they were carrying important dispatches which had to be got through. He was an idealist and in contrast with his earlier effort to prevent a split in *Óglaigh na hÉireann* he was now charged with intractability and with prolonging the struggle long after most leaders had recognised its futility. However, in his possession was a paper for de Valera's signature ordering an immediate cessation of hostilities and requesting that weapons be handed into secret dumps pending elections. Frank Aiken succeeded Lynch as Chief of Staff and continued negotiations on his predecessor's peace proposals.

Lynch's opposite number and great friend Michael Collins had predeceased him, like Lynch dying a soldier's death on the battlefield. They had a great respect and love for one another. The bonds of the old *Óglaigh na hÉireann* were 'hoops of steel' that not even a Civil War could fully sunder.

On 14 April 1923 a dramatic encounter occurred when a party of Irregulars were secreted in the caves of Clashmaelcon [127] in north Kerry. An Officer and a Volunteer lost their lives before their surrender after holding out for three days. Three of the Irregulars (including the leader 'Aeroplane' Lyons) were drowned. One of the three who surrendered was an Englishman, a deserter from the British army.

On 27 April de Valera and Aiken published peace proposals. The government, however, would not budge on two principles: one, that all political questions must be determined by the majority vote of the people's elected representatives; two, that all arms should be under control of the executive government responsible to the people through their elected representatives. They insisted that all arms would have to be surrendered.

The outcome was inconclusive. A general order to cease fire and dump all arms was eventually issued by Aiken and de Valera on 24 May. On that same day the last significant military action took place when troops operating from Clifden and Ballinrobe captured the entire HQ Staff of the anti-treaty Fourth Western Division together with fifty-eight rifles, 500 bombs, six cwt of explosives and a large quantity of ammunition. De Valera said that military victory must be allowed to rest for the moment with those who destroyed the republic.[128] The war was over but warlike activity spluttered on. Noel Lemass (anti-treaty) was kidnapped on 3 July. His body was found in the Dublin mountains on 12 October.[129]

The last executions took place on 30 May when Michael Murphy and Joseph O'Rourke were shot for the armed robbery on 24 May of the Munster and Leinster Bank in Athenry.[130] This brought the government execution tally to seventy-nine,[131] almost twice as many as the British had executed from 1916 to 1921. The Irregulars executed fifty-three. Twelve thousand republican prisoners were taken. Six hundred pro-treatyites had been killed in action during July and August. The total fatal casualties on both sides came to 4,000.

*Óglaigh na hÉireann* had had its baptism of fire in 1916. It was forged further in the War of Independence. It had now come through the most testing crucible of all: a civil war. It had never known what it was like to be a peacetime army subordinate to a democratically elected government and subscribing to the principle of the primacy of politics. It would have to learn. The Defence Forces Temporary Provisions Act 1923 put it on a statutory footing under the law. For the first time in seven and a half centuries Ireland was now to have a regular peacetime army.

# 4

## The Army Legalised (1922-4)

The anti-treatyites regarded the Provisional Government as illegitimate.[1] They did not accept that it was the proper constitutional successor to the Second Dáil which was supposed to reassemble prior to its dissolution on 30 June 1922. The bombardment of the Four Courts rendered irrelevant such fine points. It also put a stop to Collins's flirtations with the Four Courts garrison and to his gun-running adventures to the North. Griffith with his other Cabinet colleagues saw that a military victory would have to be achieved first if they were to govern the country.

The republican side reacted correspondingly. It took defeat in the field to convince them of the validity of de Valera's insistence that the war had a political as well as a military aspect.[2] They came around eventually to setting up an Emergency Government[3] in October 1922 claiming to represent the legitimate authority of the republic. It did not attract popular support: the people longed for peace. The bishops denounced it on 12 November 1922 for carrying on 'what they call a war, but which in the absence of any legitimate authority to justify it is morally a system of murder and assassination of the National Forces'.[4] De Valera protested that the bishops' pastoral lacked charity, objectivity and accuracy.

For its part the Provisional Government maintained that not only had it the right but that it also had the duty to protect the citizens' fundamental rights to property and to freedom of speech. It saw the occupation of the Four Courts by the republican executive as an unlawful usurpation of power that had to be put down. In republican eyes they had no legal rights to do so. The Provisional Government's resort to ever more draconian methods as time went on confirmed that conviction. After the expiry of the government amnesty on 15 October 1922 belligerent rights, hitherto accorded to the anti-treaty forces, were withdrawn. Language reminiscent of the Black and Tan times was used to castigate the Irregulars; they wore no uniforms nor recognisable emblems; they did not carry arms openly; their targets were civilians. There was no consensus on what constituted the rule of law.

The course the War of Independence had taken made it impossible for the new State to absorb the RIC in the same way as it had the unarmed Dublin Metropolitan Police, and so the RIC were disbanded. Outside Dublin there was no police force at all. The republican police had lost whatever effectiveness they had had with the outbreak of the Civil War. The Civic Guards had been launched in the RDS Ballsbridge in February 1922 under its first commissioner, Michael Staines. It then moved to the Artillery Barracks, Kildare where a mutiny took place in May and June 1922.[5] Some original members left the Force; others either went to the Irregulars or rejoined their old Regular Army units. Thereafter, apart from self-protection, the only security available was such as the prevailing military forces might afford. That depended largely on the personality of the local commander.

No local courts were functioning. The Courts of Petty Sessions and Quarter Session had been supplanted by the republican Parish and District Courts, but in June 1922 the then Minister for Home Affairs, Eamonn Duggan, withdrew the authority of these courts and they ceased to function. The 'British courts', as they were then known, had been functioning in the King's Inns since the seizure of the Four Courts. The whole machinery of the administration of justice had been transferred by the terms of the Treaty to the Provisional Government. The problem was to make it work in a disaffected environment. To make matters worse, indiscipline was rife in the army. Collins, as Commander-in-Chief, was greatly concerned. He decided to appoint a Judge Advocate General to the Force, and Cahir Davitt[6] was chosen. He was under no illusions about the magnitude of the task of introducing and implementing a code of discipline for the National Forces. It was proposed to establish a legal section in the Adjutant General's branch responsible for the conduct of courts-martial and the general administration of military law. Military courts were not presaged at that point.

On 15 August (his 28th birthday), Davitt reported to the Assistant Adjutant General, Kevin O'Higgins[7], who was then lending his services to the army. O'Higgins had been Assistant Minister for Local Government and later Minister for Economic Affairs in the Republican Government. He brought Davitt to Collins: the Adjutant General, Gearóid O'Sullivan, was in attendance. A Youghal solicitor, George Pope Hodnett, who had served throughout the 1914–18 war and reached the rank of major, was also present. Davitt recalled being very impressed by Collins. He remembered him as a powerfully built handsome young man in his early thirties with a mass of dark hair, compelling eyes and a markedly determined-looking mouth and jaw. He was wearing a crumpled general's uniform which badly needed pressing, sat uncomfortably at his desk, squirming the while and complaining of rheumatism.[8] He tersely ordered Davitt to take over the legal section of the Adjutant General's office with Hodnett as his second-in-command. (He had already conveyed his anxieties about the state of discipline in the army to Hodnett.) He told them to start at once; without delay they were to draw up a code of discipline for the army as well as rules of procedure for courts-martial. An office was provided in Portobello (Cathal Brugha) Barracks and they were to recruit their own staff. He also told them to get into uniform as quickly as possible. On Hodnett's advice Davitt at once purchased in Easons the British Army *Manual of Military Law* and they got down to work.

At that time the main area of military operations was in the south west. Gen. Murphy (ex-British army) was in command in Kerry under Gen. O'Duffy whose HQ was in Limerick. Kingsmill Moore[9] (later a Judge of the Supreme Court, then ex-RAF officer and a kind of a war correspondent for the *Irish Times*) was asked by Murphy to draft charge sheets and court-martial procedures in order to give some semblance of formality to trials.

It now fell to Davitt to deal with the outcrop of these *ad hoc* arrangements. In one case a soldier had been charged with highly 'righteous [sic] conduct in that he threatened to shoot his superior officer with a machine-gun'. In another case a civilian employee who stole a pair of trousers belonging to Col. James Hogan (later Professor of History at UCC) was sentenced to three years' penal servitude with twelve strokes of the cat at the end of every three months of the first year of his sentence. Davitt approached the Adjutant General to have such sentences nullified. He started to draft a code of discipline as a matter of urgency. In the meantime martial law, which in effect meant the will of the Commander-in-Chief, was going to be the only effective law. It was also obvious that the legal basis for the existence of the national army was a matter of some doubt and that most of its operations and activities would eventually have to receive *ex-post facto* recognition and legislative sanction by means of an Act of Indemnity.

Davitt planned to attach to the headquarters staff of each command a legally qualified legal officer with appropriate subordinates and support staff. He would attach a legally qualified Chief Legal Officer to GHQ as part of the Adjutant General's branch.

The untimely death of Collins allowed Davitt to disregard his order to get into uniform. He convinced himself that, since his duties were mainly judicial in character, the Judge Advocate General should be independent and not be obliged to take orders from anyone. He therefore retained his civilian status and took on duties of an advisory and supervisory nature only. He made Hodnett, who had military rank as an officer on the Adjutant General's staff, responsible, under his supervision, for the direction of the legal staff and for the administration of military law generally in the army. He incorporated these concepts in his draft of the disciplinary code.

He also consulted Paddy McGilligan,[10] a barrister, who lent him the texts of the disciplinary codes of the French and US armies, together with a collection of opinions given by the US Judge Advocate General. But in the main the draft regulations were adapted and modified from the British *Manual of Military Law* with some borrowings from other systems and a few original ideas of his own. The draft eventually came into operation as *The General Regulations as to Discipline.*

In Davitt's own words, these regulations comprised a preliminary section, ten parts sub-divided into one hundred clauses, and two appendices. The preliminary section contained certain definitions and a general provision that every person subject to military law who committed an offence specified in Part I should on trial and conviction by court-martial be liable to suffer such punishment as was specifically provided therefor in Parts II and III. Part I contained in fourteen separate clauses a list of seventy-four military offences set out under headings such as *Offences in relation to Military Service, Mutiny and Insubordination, Desertion and Absence without Leave, Disgraceful Conduct, Drunkeness, Offences in relation to Property* and so on. In addition to every type of military offence they included all offences against the ordinary criminal law as to person and property. Parts II and III provided for appropriate punishments, ranging downwards from death and penal servitude to reprimand. (Flogging was not included!) Part IV provided for the arrest and detention of military offenders; Part V for the investigation of charges and their summary disposal in certain cases by Commanding Officers; Part VI for the constitution and convening of courts-martial, their jurisdiction and procedure; Part VII for the confirmation of their findings and sentences by confirming officers; and Part VIII for the execution of sentences. Part IX contained certain supplementary provisions as to courts-martial, while Part X, under the title *Miscellaneous*, included provisions as to the organisation of the legal staff, the duties of the Judge Advocate General, the legal officers and the legal staff generally, together with two appendices of *Forms*.

The duty of the command legal officer was to advise the GOC Command on all matters of military law and generally on all court-martial matters; to direct and generally to supervise the administration of military law in the command area; and to provide for the attendance of a legal officer at every local court-martial held in the area. The duty of a legal officer at a court-martial was to act as Judge Advocate; to ensure, as far as legal advice could do so, that the trial was fairly and properly conducted in accordance with the regulations; to sum up the evidence for the assistance of the court, and generally to render whatever legal advice or assistance should be required. The duties of the Chief Legal Officer were laid down. The additional duties of the Judge Advocate General were to advise the Commander-in-Chief and the Army Council on all matters of military law and generally on all court-martial matters; to advise the confirming officers on the confirmation or otherwise of court-martial findings and sentences, and, after confirmation or otherwise, to preserve the proceedings of all courts-martial.

It took Davitt several weeks to complete the draft of the *General Regulations.* They were then made by the Minister for Defence to be promulgated as a General Order by the Commander-in-Chief. They came into force on 1 November 1922. Instantly the legal section was inundated with requests for guidance and clarification. Support staff had to be recruited. Louis Carrig[11] was taken on and proved to be a cornerstone. The legal staff officers enlisted were John Donovan[12], Charlie Casey[13] and Thomas J. Coyne.[14] They had all held commissions in either the British army or the Royal Air Force and had seen extensive active service in France. It was inevitable that British army methods would predominate. Even the defendants at courts-martial were affronted if British army 'spit and polish' was lacking.[15]

There were many teething problems. A civilian clerk named McGuinness was remanded for court-martial even though he was not a serving soldier. The President of the court-martial, Col. Byrne, got himself relieved of that job by visiting the guard room the night before and threatening to shoot McGuinness, who next day duly objected to Col. Byrne as President. The court had to be reconstituted and the trial then went ahead. McGuinness, the civilian, was found guilty by the court-martial and sentenced to death, commuted to penal servitude for life. He was not released until the granting of a general amnesty in 1924.[16]

The additional establishment of military courts in October 1922 further complicated Davitt's tasks and necessitated more hurried recruitment of properly qualified staff to man them. From a list of names supplied by Kevin O'Higgins he made the following legal appointments:[17] Charles Wyse Power to Cork; Henry Conner (with William Cahill as assistant) to

Limerick; Trant McCarthy to Kerry; John J. Hearne (with J.J. Bergin as assistant) to Athlone; William T. McMenamin to Stranorlar; Joseph T. Mooney (with Fred Lidwell as assistant) to Kilkenny; Joseph Reidy to Roscrea. The appointees all held the rank of Commandant and, anomalously, received a salary of £800 p.a. Donovan, Casey and Coyne were to remain in GHQ as Lieutenant Commandants with salaries of £400 p.a. Davitt still received his judicial salary of £750 p.a.; Hodnett £600 p.a. It seemed to have been *déclassé* for legal men on enlistment to mention remuneration as part of their conditions of service. When the army was at its peak figure of 50,000 to 60,000, the sanctioned legal staff numbered forty to fifty.

Davitt also speedily completed on instructions a draft of *General Regulations as to the Trial of Civilians by Military Courts* and it was issued as a General Order on 2 October 1922. It provided for the establishment of the proposed military courts, their constitution, jurisdiction and procedure and for the trial of persons charged with specified offences ranging from attacks on the National Forces to looting and possession of firearms. Punishments were death, penal servitude, imprisonment, deportation, internment and fine. The court determined its own procedure, having regard to procedures provided in *General Regulations to Discipline.* Government proclamations were supported by Orders issued to the same effect by the Army Council.

In August 1923 the following three acts were passed, reflecting the legislature's perception that a state of war and armed insurrection no longer existed: the Public Safety Act which provided for the arrest and detention without trial of suspected offenders; the Indemnity Act which sanctioned actions taken to suppress the insurrection; and the Defence Forces Temporary Provisions Act. Capt. Richard N. Cooke SC[18] put these rapid developments in context:

> It is necessary to go back before the Treaty and to take notice of the state of affairs immediately before the First World War to place this matter in its context.
>
> Under the original Home Rule Act, that is to say the Government of Ireland Act 1914, which was initially

Eamon de Valera, 1916

A group of Irish Volunteers, 1914–15

Griffith and Collins with IRA Guard of Honour at Sean MacEoin's wedding, June 1922

Tom Barry
in later life

Ceremonial Parade at Griffith Barracks, 1923

Col. Fritz Brase (*seated, second left*) with Richard Mulcahy, 1923

Eoin O'Duffy and Michael Brennan

Kohl, von Hunefeld and Fitzmaurice in New York following their transatlantic crossing, 1928

Volunteer Officers Matt Feehan and Vivion de Valera

Col. Tom McNally, Lt Gen. Dan McKenna (chief of staff), Thomas Derrig and Maj. Gen. Hugo MacNeill at an Army Sports Day during the 1930s

An 18-pounder gun team in action, May 1930

An 18-pounder mechanised gun team in training, May 1939

A 25-pounder Battery in training, 1940s

suspended for the duration of the war which broke out in 1914 and ultimately repealed by the Government of Ireland Act 1920, the Irish Parliament thereby instituted was expressly forbidden to have anything to do with the formation of an army. Section 2 of the 1914 Act says that the Irish Parliament shall not have power to make laws in respect of the following matters in particular, or any of them, namely — and then there follows a series of paragraphs, the third of which reads as follows:

> The Navy, the Army, the Territorial Force or any other naval or territorial force, or the defence of the realm or any other naval or military matter;

In other words, the new home rule government of Ireland had no power to raise or regulate an armed force.

Similarly, the Parliament of Southern Ireland and the Parliament of Northern Ireland were deprived by the Government of Ireland Act 1920 of power to make laws in respect of —

> (3) the navy, the army, the air force, the territorial force, or any other naval, military or air force, or the defence of the realm or any other naval, military or air force matter . . . etc.

The Treaty of 1921 was signed on 6 December 1921 and Article 8 of the Treaty provides as follows:

> 8. With a view to securing the observance of the principal and international limitation of armaments, if the government of the Irish Free State establishes and maintains a military defence force, the establishment thereof shall not exceed in size such proportion of the military establishments maintained in Great Britain as that which the population of Ireland bears to the population of Great Britain.

Thc right, therefore, of the new State to raise its own defence force was conceded as a necessary condition of the signing of the Treaty itself. It had not been conceded in either the 1914 or the 1920 'Home Rule' Acts.

Article 46 of the Constitution of 1922 provided that the *Oireachtas* should have the exclusive right to regulate the raising and maintaining of such armed forces as are mentioned in the Schedule to the Treaty in the territory of the Irish Free State (*Saorstát Éireann*) and that every such force should be subject to the control of the *Oireachtas.*

The Defence Forces (Temporary Provisions) Act, 1923 was passed on the 3 August 1923. In the fourth recital introducing the act it says that it is a matter of urgent necessity to provide a code of laws and regulations for the enforcement of military discipline in the existing armed forces of *Saorstát Éireann* and such other armed forces as may be raised under the act.

Section 4 of the act says that it shall be lawful for the Executive Council to raise and maintain an armed force to be called *Óglaigh na hÉireann* (hereinafter referred to as the Forces) consisting of such number of officers, non-commissioned officers and men as may from time to time be provided by the *Oireachtas.*

Section 22 of the 1923 act provides that the Forces shall be established as from a date to be fixed by Proclamation of the Executive Council in the *Iris Oifigiúil.* One would have expected that such a proclamation would have been made forthwith but while I have discovered an Order of Executive Council entitled Council of Defence (Constitution) Order, 1923, (No. 11 of 1923) which would appear to have been made on 28 August 1923, I have not yet found any Order for the establishment of the Force hereinbefore referred to until 1924.

The particular Order is entitled 'The Defence Forces (Temporary Provisions) Acts, 1923 and 1924, The Defence Forces (Establishment) Order, 1924 (No. 11 of 1924)' and it says that the Executive Council in exercise of the power in that behalf conferred on them by Section 22 of the Defence Forces (Temporary Provisions) Act, 1923, proclaim an order that the Forces shall be established as from 1st day of October, 1924. The Order is dated 27th day of September, 1924.

I enclose copies of each of those Orders and of the

Order of 1927 whereby the Reserve was established, which you may find of interest.

You will notice that in the preamble to the Order setting up the Council of Defence it says that the Commander-in-Chief of, and all executive and administrative powers in relation to, the National Forces (including the power to delegate authority to such persons as shall be thought fit) shall be vested in the Executive Council . . . . Throughout the Order the Forces are referred to as the National Forces and it seems a strong probability that this is where the term which you heard me use years ago 'National Army' originated.

I should perhaps have drawn your attention earlier to the provisions of Part 4 of the 1923 act. These are entitled 'Transitory Provisions'. The effects of the provisions are to provide that the armed forces of the State, as they were constituted and existed, should be deemed to be the armed forces to be raised under Article 46 of the Constitution and that the maintenance of such forces was thereby declared to be legal; that the organisation of the National Forces should be as at present existing subject to the power of the Minister to make such changes therein as he might deem necessary; that all Orders and Regulations then in force in the National Forces should continue to be in full force and effect and generally speaking to adopt the then existing force to the force which was now being legally constituted by the provisions of the Act of 1923.

Col. James Flynn recalled[19]

The Defence Forces (Temporary Provisions) Act, 1923 q.v., is the legal instrument providing for 'the establishment' of the Forces (and the Reserve). It had effect from 3 August 1923, and was the authority for the future existence of the Defence Forces. It was renewed annually by the *Oireachtas*, with current necessary amendments.

This act also regularised the position of all previous National Forces, including those of The Provisional Govt 1922 and also of the Civil War period. It established the continuity of all these forces from the beginning as

> having been the Regular Army, by the provisions of its early sections (or Parts) and 'definitions'. I think, but I am not sure, those particular provisions may have mentioned dates relating to some of these earlier forces. I have not got a copy of the 1923 act to refer to now, and am relying on memory — a not always reliable agent. But I seem to recall that the 31 January '22 was mentioned in connection with what I may call 'the Beggars Bush' force. No doubt you will be able to check that point by referring to the act.
>
> The Army that existed before 3 August 1923, did so under authority derived from an article of the 1922 'Constitution Act' and 'enabling Regulations' entitled 'Defence Orders' which, inter alia, promulgated the Disciplinary Code, and the Administrative and other regulations as necessary.

The Army Council's Order of 18 January 1923 had included murder among the additional offences which could be dealt with by either military court or committee. But the latter could only deal with this offence if the offender were caught red-handed and there were a real issue to be tried. A man named Martin Byrne was recommended the death sentence by a committee when he was charged with the murder of Dr O'Higgins. The Army Council approved. Davitt felt that this case should not have been dealt with by committee and finally managed to persuade the Adjutant General to refer the case to a military court where Byrne was ultimately acquitted: correctly so, Col. M.J. Costello, Director of Intelligence, pronounced, on examining the file a year later.

However, legally enshrining regulations did not automatically ensure the imposition of good order and military discipline. No disciplinary action had been taken against those responsible for the Ballyseedy outrage in March 1923 (see chapter 3). Nevertheless progress was made by the legal staff in connection with courts-martial and the legal aspects of the administration of the disciplinary code. That work eventually bore fruit in correcting the failure to bring certain military offenders to justice and in redressing a tendency of courts-martial to be over-strict with soldiers but too lenient with officers. Failure to bring to book those responsible for the Ballyseedy affair, and the several 'unofficial executions', rested with Commanding Officers and the Military Police. Command legal officers were enjoined to impress on their GOCs the importance of a strict but impartial enforcement of military law.

Nearer home Davitt had his disciplinary problems. His disregard of Collins's order to get into uniform rebounded on him since, having no military rank, he had no authority to give orders. A clash with Power[20] made him change his mind. On 13 June 1923 he entered the army as a Major General[21] and settled in to routine military duties.

Still no one had been made accountable for the 'unofficial executions' by government forces. A dental student, Bonfield, two men called Kernan and Breslin and later a man called Hogan had been murdered in April 1923. The conspiracy of silence was maintained against a background of a string of provocations by the Irregulars: the burning of the court house and the looting of the shops in Dromahair, Co. Leitrim; the murder of two kidnapped officers, Lt Cruise and Lt Kennedy; the kidnapping of Civic Guards in Sligo; the burning of the Presbyterian Church in Duncannon, Co. Wexford; the blowing up of a railway carriage in Dublin; an attack on Headford Military Barracks; the burnings of Sir John Dillon's house at Leamullen, Co.Meath, the house of the Sub-Sheriff Robert Thorp near Bagnalstown and Tubberdaly House, the residence of Beaumont Nesbitt, and three other mansions; the burning and looting of a train on the Midland Great Western Line; the wrecking of the Lee drapery premises; an army officer shot dead in a street in Cork and a soldier similarly in Ennis. Davitt would not countenance for one moment a suggestion that these outrages constituted extenuating circumstances justifying 'unofficial executions'. On the other hand, he strongly disagreed with the minority view which looked on official executions as murders. That view maintained that the Treaty should never have been made and that the Irish delegates had no right to sign it; that the Dáil had no right to approve it or to appoint the Provisional Government to implement its provisions and to govern; that the only legitimate legislative power lay with the minority of Dáil deputies who voted against the Treaty; that the only legitimate executive authority was vested in the anti-treaty section of the Volunteers and later in the reconstituted republican government appointed by the Dáil minority.

Majorities had emerged mandating opposite opinions which rejected by implication a resumption of a bitter struggle with the British. Davitt consequently regarded the infant Provisional Government as being the *de jure* as well as the *de facto* government of the State. De Valera's political genius (later to stand the country in such good stead) was lost on him. He believed the government had every right to use military force as well as all other legitimate means including the taking of human life if necessary,[22] but that this right could only be exercised under the strict rule of law with the Defence Forces — subject to good order and military discipline — as an instrument of democratic government. Good order and military discipline was the rub.

The following incident was indicative of the standards prevailing in some sections. On the cessation of hostilities a dozen or so soldiers took out a lorry without permission and went on a drinking excursion. One of the delinquents giving evidence at the subsequent court-martial said that during the course of the expedition he saw nothing happen that was in any way irregular 'beyond the looting of the tents on Killiney strand and the burning of Killiney Castle'! Another case concerned an assault on the two daughters of a Kerry doctor on the grounds that they had been friendly with members of the British Crown Forces (another version centres around unrequited love and jilting). The girls were beaten with the cross straps of Sam Browne belts and dirty oil was poured over their heads. The police implicated three officers from the HQ of the Kerry Command. (A certain amount of ill-feeling had developed between the guards and the army because of a cooling of relations between the Departments of Defence and Justice.) A Court of Inquiry, presided over by John Hearne, sat in Tralee to investigate the 'Kenmare incident'. Its 'whitewash' outcome added fuel to the fire in the vendetta between O'Higgins and Mulcahy regarding the state of discipline in the army. In spite of O'Higgins's bitter vehemence there was no court-martial. Davitt for his part was quite satisfied that a *prima facie* case did exist. However, Mulcahy's loyalty to Paddy O'Daly, the Kerry GOC, led him to believe otherwise. The advice of Hugh Kennedy, law advisor to the Provisional Government, was sought. His advice coincided with Mulcahy's disposition; O'Higgins was livid, Davitt dismayed.

Meanwhile during the summer months Gerald McCarthy[23] laboured in drafting the 246 sections and nine schedules which became the Defence Forces (Temporary Provisions) Act 1923 and which occupies 253 pages of the volume of statutes for the year. It was based largely on the British Army (Annual) Act and their Reserve Forces Act of 1889 with some amendments, making some use where appropriate of the legislation providing for the establishment and maintenance of the military forces of Canada, Australia and South Africa. It was enacted for a year only and would then expire unless renewed.

In the Dáil Mulcahy recommended the measure somewhat cursorily. There was little debate. The few members who did speak seemed not to have read the bill. Johnson, the leader of the Labour Opposition, deprecated the class distinction preserved in the terms 'Officer' and 'Private Soldier' without, however, suggesting how they could be dispensed with. The Second Reading took less than an hour. The bill passed through Dáil and Senate without amendment and became law on 23 August 1923. It was re-enacted yearly until replaced by fresh legislation in 1954.

From the time they joined up the legal people kept themselves to themselves. There was an atmosphere of antagonism, if not downright hostility, on the part of some officers towards them and the Medical Services and towards the Adjutant General's branch as a whole, of which these sections formed parts. This may have had something to do with the fact that these officers enjoyed higher salaries than line officers and many of them had held commissions in the British forces.

For the last quarter of 1922 the legal officers remained mostly confined to barracks and sought relaxation in playing cards in a common room, occasionally meeting friends in the officers mess and taking the odd trip for supper to the Shelbourne Hotel. Apart from meal times they did not unduly frequent the mess. In that way they avoided being witnesses to the odd intemperate outburst or bizarre incident.

One such incident is related to Collins's escorting armoured car at Béal na mBláth. The machine-gun in this car jammed very shortly after opening fire and did not come into action again. The machine-gunner, a soldier named John McPeake, deserted some weeks later to the Irregulars, taking the armoured car with him. A 'flying squad' of officers left Portobello (Cathal Brugha) Barracks in search of him and the car. Having accomplished the mission they returned in triumph and adjourned to the mess to celebrate. In the course of the celebrations, which went on until the small hours of the morning, an officer was carelessly handling an automatic pistol when it was accidentally discharged, mortally wounding a mess waiter known as Bob. The chaplain, Father Concannon, was sent for and Bob was assured that everything would be all right now as Father Concannon was there to hear his confession. Barely able to talk, Bob managed to croak, 'Tell Father Concannon to go and f. . . himself. I'm a Protestant'.

McPeake was charged with the larceny of the armoured car and was sentenced to four years' penal servitude.[24] Some years later when he was convicted by Liverpool magistrates on some other offence he chose jail in England in preference to deportation to Ireland where, he assured the magistrate, his life would not be safe.

After the war movement around the country became easier. Social intercourse became less inhibited. Early in 1923 Eastern Command HQ had transferred to Collins Barracks, and the dormitory and the common room for the legal staff were broken up. Davitt, Sheehy, Kenny, McCarthy and Casey all resumed recreational activities and spent pleasant week-ends playing golf by day and poker by night with Army Medical Services comrades in the Curragh Camp; Matt O'Connor, Sam Doyle, Tom Higgins, Frank Morrin and Vesty Boland were among the medics. The legal men discovered a hard tennis court in Parkgate and put it to good use. Normalcy was slowly establishing itself.

Things had improved by the late summer of 1923 to the extent that Army Championship Competitions were held in athletics, boxing (with Tancy Lee, the Lonsdale Belt holder as instructor), football, hurling and golf as well as other sports. It provided an occasion for Davitt to receive (apart from Michael Collins's original direction to him) a direct order from a military superior. He was detailed by Gen. Mulcahy to accept presentation of a cup for a tennis tournament which he had not won. Due to a slip-up the tournament was not held but Gen. Mulcahy did not want to disappoint the presenter of a valuable silver cup, Senator (and retired British Army Colonel) Hutchinson-Poe, who was actually on the ground expecting to see his cup presented. Davitt did as he was told.

In October 1923 Davitt and Joe Kenny took a break in Paris. There they ran into Jim Doyle and Major Gen. Tom Cullen. Doyle had been manager of the Gresham Hotel which had been destroyed in the course of the fighting in Dublin following the attack on the Four Courts. He was then major-domo to the Governor General with the title of Controller of the Household. Cullen was one of the two senior ADCs to the Governor General (the other being Major Gen. Liam Tobin). Kenny and Davitt returned to routine duties at the Dublin Command HQ and GHQ respectively, exhausted rather than refreshed by their period of leave. They were quite oblivious of the rumblings beneath the surface which culminated in a series of actions amounting to mutiny by a number of officers, among whom were Cullen and Tobin. Nothing in Paris had given Davitt any inkling that anything untoward was afoot.

Some of those officers had had very close associations with Collins; several had been members of the Dublin Volunteers Active Service Unit, which had been in close combat with the British crown forces in carrying out street ambushes and other hazardous actions, and who had borne the brunt of the fighting. Some of them had been in Joe McGrath's Intelligence Branch and were a law unto themselves, not amenable to ordinary discipline. After the Civil War they were dissatisfied with their appointments and disappointed with their diminished status. They protested that the government was not interpreting the Treaty in accordance with Collins's stepping-stone theory.[25] They formed their own organisation in the army, the 'Old IRA' group, in order to get control of the army and use it to achieve political and personal objectives. They contemplated using it as an instrument to impose their will on the government. Their political acumen did not match their undoubted wartime intrepidity.

They presupposed that the army would be officered by a like-minded Officer Corps. They strongly disapproved of officers who had held commissions in the British army and they told the Minister for Defence that they wanted a say with regard to demobilisation. They were determined to ensure that whoever else went their men would remain.

To complicate matters further there was another organisation within the army, the IRB. It had been dormant since the Treaty but the QMG, Seán O'Muirthile, had reorganised it under the Army Council to prevent it falling into the hands of the Irregulars. No members of the Old IRA were permitted to participate. Antagonisms were mutual. These were exacerbated by the proposal to reduce the May 1923 strength of 55,000 to 31,300 by January 1924. Short service contracts facilitated the smooth demobilisation of the NCOs and men. The officers presented a trickier problem. Three categories were listed for dismissal: (*a*) unsuitable officers (*b*) post-truce officers who had no special qualifications and (*c*) pre-truce officers who were surplus to requirements. Feelings boiled over when in September 1923 a Defence Order was issued providing advance notice of the demobilisation of officers.[26] In Collins Barracks, Dublin, a portrait of Michael Collins was smashed and burned in the square as a protest by some disgruntled officers.[27] As they presented it, the wrong men were being kept on while they, who in their own minds had done all the fighting, were getting their tickets. They formed an Old IRA Organisation: IRAO.

Demobilisation represented a knotty problem. A new scheme of army reorganisation was in progress (see Chapter 5), which provided for a Force of 1,300 officers with 18,000 men. This meant a drastic reduction from the army's maximum strength, involving the immediate demobilisation of around 2,000 officers and 27,000 men. It involved reductions in rank for a number of officers, including incidentally Davitt to Colonel and Hodnett to Major. Many officers bitterly resented being demobilised and a number of them at the Curragh refused to accept their demobilisation papers. They were charged with insubordination, convicted by court-martial and sentenced to dismissal. Due to a technical slip-up in the proceedings, the Adjutant General was unable to confirm the sentence and consequently ordered a new trial. Meanwhile the insubordinate Curragh officers yielded to persuasion. For the most part they were allowed to accept their demobilisation papers and depart quietly from the army. That decision seemed to allow the insubordinate officers to 'get away with it' and was later judged to have been prejudical to good order and military discipline. The tensions between the two rival organisations (Old IRA and IRB) within the army mounted.

Matters came to a head on 6 March 1924 when Major Gen. Liam Tobin and Col. Charles Dalton delivered an ultimatum to the government on behalf of the Old IRA group of officers. (Tobin was aide-de-camp to the Governor General; his brother Nicholas, had been killed in the Civil War. Dalton was a brother of Gen. Emmet Dalton, now Clerk to the Senate.) They demanded an immediate conference with the government to 'discuss the interpretation of the Treaty on the following conditions: (1) Removal of the Army Council; (2) Immediate suspension of demobilisation'. The government reacted sharply to this effrontery. It ordered the immediate arrest of Tobin and Dalton who, however, managed to evade apprehension. On the following day 900 officers were demobilised and accepted their papers without protest. Certain officers who had not been demobilised proceeded to leave the army in an irregular manner. Two deserted from Gormanston Camp, taking with them a Crossley tender and a quantity of rifles, ammunition and equipment; three decamped from Baldonnel with another Crossley and three Lewis machine-guns; two more deserted in similar circumstances from Roscommon; while twenty-five men deserted at Templemore, taking to the hills with arms and ammunition. A senior officer from GHQ was denied admission to Templemore Barracks. Armoured cars from Dublin recovered twenty-nine rifles. The mutinous Battalion (36th) was transferred to Command HQ while a new garrison, a Company of the 7th

Battalion, quickly restored order there. An officer absconded and a quantity of ammunition also went missing in Tullamore. In all, over fifty officers had made off with arms and ammunition and forty-nine others, including three major generals and five colonels, had resigned. Some officers tendered their resignations as a formal protest against their view that freedom fighters were demobilised while ex-British officers and soldiers were retained.[28] This allegation was based on myth: only 157 technical officers were so retained. Personality clashes, particularism, losses of position, power and prestige at a time of high unemployment outside were the main factors causing the dissatisfaction. On Monday 10 March 1924 the newspapers headlined[29] a mutiny in the Free State Army in Dublin, Tipperary, Mayo and Roscommon led by Major Gen. Liam Tobin and Col. Charles Dalton. Both of them had been demoted: Dalton to Commandant, Tobin to Adjutant of Baldonnel Aerodrome, and they felt that they had been unfairly treated. The army was reduced by 66 per cent: 900 officers were demobilised.

The government reacted angrily to the challenge to its authority: 'it is an outrageous departure from the spirit of the army. It will not be tolerated, particularly will it not be tolerated by the officers and men of the army who cherish its honour.'[30] The latter were particularly annoyed at the pro-British smear of the mutineers. Their national records were second to none, and in any case the retention statistics were wrong.

The mutineers might have been on firmer ground if they persisted with accusations against the apparent departure from the pragmatic but aggressive policies of Collins instead of making a protest without substance against the demobilisation of old IRA men while ex-British officers were retained.

After the Treaty was signed Collins had impressed on the nationalists in the North that they had no intention of accepting Partition even if it meant smashing the Treaty. In February 1922 he advised them to ignore the authority of the Northern Local Government Board and undertook to pay teachers there their full salary whether dismissed or not. O'Duffy, authorised by Collins and Mulcahy, started operations against the 'Specials' and captured a few barracks. This brought a swift and terrible retribution on the defenceless Catholic community: several families were wiped out. In May O'Duffy undertook to provide a barracks for men of the Second Northern Division in order to train them for an invasion of Northern Ireland in the late summer. (This explains Collins's flirtation with the Four Courts garrison.) But by July the Free State Government had its hands full with a civil war and they cancelled activities in the North. However, Keane (Pearse) Barracks was to be provided in the Curragh for those who had to leave the North, where they would be trained under their own officers for exclusively Six County operations. The organisation was to remain the same, but this changed on 17 August 1922 when it became clear that the objective was to absorb all units into the national army and sever the Northern connection. This departure gave rise to more grievances and more splits. Some joined the national army (among them the Deputy Divisional O/C, Daniel McKenna). The remainder were disbanded on 31 March 1923. Posts in his area on the Southern side of the border had been handed over to Comdt Sweeney.

The Northern officers felt that they had been misled and that uncalled-for tactics had achieved nothing other than the wholesale wiping-out of Catholic areas (Appendix 4). Whether as a sop or not they were allowed to retain the ranks they had brought in from the Volunteers. This gave them an enduring head start in subsequent races for promotion. They constituted another grievance to the mutineers, who also believed that nothing very much had been done in the North during the War of Independence. The Northern government, assisted by the British, interned 600. Fifty thousand had left the area. This pained Collins but he had more than enough to do by that time. He remained throughout practical, pragmatic and down to earth.

The Dáil and the British alike were disquieted at the mutiny, and grave apprehension was awakened in Northern Ireland 'especially as those appointed to the higher positions in the Free State Army are men — for the most part very young men — who are notorious for their hostility to Northern Ireland'.[31] They saw Joe McGrath's motives in resigning as indicating a wish to place himself outside the current government as he did not think that it (the government) would last long. Mulcahy had at this time ceased to be Commander-in-Chief although he was still Minister for Defence. Eoin O'Duffy had left the army in 1922 to become Chief Commissioner of the Civic Guards. The government now recalled him to the army with the rank of General and appointed him GOC the Defence Forces. It gave him authority and control over the administrative departments at GHQ. He was made Inspector General as well, with the intention that he should intervene between the Minister for Defence and the Council. His mission was to restore order.

On receipt by the government of Tobin's and Dalton's ultimatum McGrath had resigned his position as Minister for Industry and Commerce not, as he explained, because he had any sympathy with these officers but as a protest against what he called the muddling of the Department of Defence which, in his opinion, had led to the situation that had developed. On 4 March President Cosgrave stated in the Dáil that the government would hold an enquiry. Tobin and Dalton expressed satisfaction at this.

McGrath was to be the intermediary between the government and the Old IRA group, and on 17 March Cosgrave wrote to him saying that if all officers who had deserted, or were absent from their duties without leave, returned and submitted to arrest, restoring whatever military property they had unlawfully taken away, they would be released on parole pending the result of the proposed enquiry.

Notwithstanding this, a party of troops under Major Gen. McNeill raided an Old IRA meeting in Devlin's pub in Parnell St.[32] After some parleying and an exchange of shots McGrath intervened and conferred with the officers in Devlin's. Ten submitted to arrest; the others escaped.

The Cabinet was displeased at this turn of events, and called for the resignations of three members of the Army Council. O'Sullivan and O'Muirthile then sought legal advice from Davitt. They told him that they had discussed the matter with the Chief of Staff and that he was disposed to refuse to resign. Davitt told them that there was no point whatever in refusing their resignations; that if they did not resign they would be dismissed; that a refusal would place them almost in the same category as the officers who had refused to accept demobilisation, and would have a very bad effect on discipline and on public opinion towards the army. They decided to tender their resignations, which were accepted. MacMahon refused to resign and was dismissed. Though relieved of their positions they all retained their ranks. Mulcahy, on learning of the request for their resignations, resigned his position as Minister for Defence.

The government's action seemed to condone mutiny and to penalise unfairly the Army Council. O'Higgins subsequently explained that the raid on Devlin's, directed by Mulcahy in consultation with O'Sullivan, had cut directly across government policy as outlined in Cosgrave's letter to McGrath on 17 March. Mulcahy's information was that a *coup d'état* and a kidnap of Cabinet ministers was planned. The raid was made without reference to either Gen. O'Duffy or to the Executive Council. The Government's demand for the resignations of MacMahon, O'Sullivan and O'Muirthile was not, it said, simply because of the raid but because it did not feel that the officers ordering the raid were the best people to handle the mutiny. O'Higgins used the occasion to denigrate Mulcahy, revealing in the process an unlikeable personal animus and opportunism.

The army took the matter in its stride. The mutiny was confined exclusively to a small proportion of senior officers who were eventually allowed to resign. The provision of £170,000 for supplementary grants for officers with pre-truce service was seen by some as a sop to the mutineers. (Fianna Fáil were later to extend this scheme to anti-treaty officers.) McGilligan succeeded McGrath as Minister for Industry and Commerce; Peadar MacMahon succeeded his namesake as Chief of Staff; Hugo McNeill became Adjutant General; and Felix Cronin QMG. An Army Enquiry Committee was set up to 'enquire into the facts and matters which have caused or led up to the indiscipline and mutinous or insubordinate conduct lately manifested in the Army'. It consisted of James Creed Meredith as Chairman, McGilligan, Gerald Fitzgibbon KC, Capt. Bryan Cooper (who had held the same rank in the British Army) and Denis Gorey. All except Meredith were members of the Dáil. They were appointed on 3 April, held forty-one sittings commencing on 7 April, examined twenty-seven witnesses, and made their report on 7 June.

Mulcahy, MacMahon, O'Sullivan, and O'Muirthile were in the position of defendants and were represented by Counsel; Mulcahy by Martin Maguire and the other three by Cecil Lavery. Davitt was called to give evidence. One of the queries put to him which he left unanswered was:

> Are you aware of any instances in which manifest zeal in the matter of investigating or endeavouring to secure the punishment of offences against discipline was followed by the removal from one area to another of the person manifesting such zeal or by any prejudicial action, against such individual? If so give particulars.

When pressed for a reply Davitt answered that the only instance of which he was aware was that of Gen. MacMahon, Gen. O'Sullivan and Gen. O'Muirthile, who were relieved of their posts for arresting a number of mutinous officers. Meredith and McGilligan were not amused. The other three burst out laughing. He was also questioned on the so-called 'Kenmare incident' (see p.126) and later stated that the Court of Enquiry felt that Kennedy's advice on the matter was incomprehensible.

The Committee found the facts of the mutiny as outlined above.[33] They found that the discipline in the army was fairly satisfactory and had shown steady improvement from the days of its formation. It found that 'Secret Societies, factions and political organisations' in the army did affect discipline among officers especially by undermining their confidence in the impartiality of their superiors. The following paragraphs 26 and 27 of the findings were particularly noteworthy:

> 26. It was suggested that the late Adjutant General condoned or connived at insubordination by failing to punish it in the case of highly placed officers. The principal instance was the Kenmare case. In dealing with that the Adjutant General strictly followed the advice of his legal adviser, the Judge Advocate General. He put the case in train for a court-martial, and he was no party to dropping the proceedings. . . .

> 27. Gen. Mulcahy accepted full responsibility for the decision to drop the Kenmare case. In our opinion this was a grave error of judgment on his part. It did not contribute to the mutiny, but it did militate against discipline generally by encouraging suspicion in the minds of officers and others that the Army Authorities were disposed to hush up charges against persons in high authority.

There were numerous other findings. Davitt wondered who could have suggested that the Adjutant General had condoned or connived at insubordination, especially in the Kenmare case. The Courts of Justice Act had become law on 12 April 1924, and Davitt decided that he wished to return to the bar. He felt that there was no future in the army for him. (He had joined as a Major General!) He was allowed to resign his commission and retain his position of Judge Advocate General on a part-time basis. He returned to the bar generously subsidised. His work as part-time Judge Advocate General over the next two years was of a routine nature and not very onerous. He was appointed temporary Judge in November 1926 and resigned as Judge Advocate General, having accomplished the mission given to him by Collins to draw up a code of discipline for the army as well as rules of procedure for courts-martial. The Civil War was at its height and the country was in a state of chaos in August 1922 when he addressed the problem of the government's concern about the state of discipline in their military forces. The national army[34] had been and was being recruited in haste from diverse elements to meet an emergency. The anti-treaty forces had adopted guerilla tactics. He realised that the task of conducting military courts would also fall within his province. His *Trial of Civilians by Military Courts*, dated 22 October 1922, changed the course of judicial procedures, and his *General Regulations as to Discipline*, dated 21 November 1922, was a milestone in providing a disciplinary code for the Force. He contributed significantly to the legalisation and governing of the army.

Another most significant milestone was the steadiness, professionalism and discipline displayed by the bulk of *Óglaigh na hÉireann* during the crises. It was an affirmation of constitutional rule, relating the roles of the soldier and the State.

# 5

## Fluctuations and Adjustments (1923–39)

The machine hastily put together to meet the Civil War crisis was crude because of its precocious growth and defective because of its limited purpose. In 1923 reductions in strength and reorganisation were imperative. The ill-defined small-group combat units variously commanded were to be replaced by a more appropriate structure based on more rigid Regular Army lines. The hallowed title, *Óglaigh na hÉireann*,[1] had persisted and was reaffirmed. To the present day it remains the proprietory statutory title of the Defence Forces (Defence Act of 1954).

The pre-truce Volunteer system was based almost exclusively on a territorial organisation which was incompatible with Regular Army concepts. Reorganisation was based on the establishment of battalions, though for administrative purposes a certain territorial basis was retained for brigades and commands.

The quashing of the mutiny in 1924 set the seal on the transition from a revolutionary military organisation which had successfully conducted a guerilla campaign and survived a bitter Civil War, to a disciplined Regular National Army, subject to constitutional rule and subordinate to the government. The mutineers had lost touch with this progression.

The raising, equipping, training and maintaining an army of 44,000 men in twelve months under active service conditions had been a stupendous feat. It was no wonder that in some cases discipline was loose and morale low. In the stress and need of the moment many undesirables were enrolled ('mostly the dregs of British post-war mobilisation' according to an internal army report of the period). Pre-truce men maintained the old *Óglaigh na hÉireann* ethos and esprit. They reckoned that they were as republican as the next and they had combat records to prove it.

Routine orders in Mullingar in June 1922 were headed 'Columb IRA Barracks'. The present 3rd Infantry Battalion was formed on 1 April 1924 at Sligo, then 35th Battalion HQ, from the amalgamation of the old 3rd and 35th Infantry Battalions. Comdt Edward McBrearty, O/C 35th Battalion, who was appointed O/C, had previously been Lt Comdt First Northern Division. The new battalion was made up mostly of Donegal and Derry men, all of whom had been pre-truce soldiers of *Óglaigh na hÉireann.* In the Civil War they had fought in Donegal, Leitrim and Sligo, attacking and capturing Irregular positions in the Donegal mountains, Belleek, Pettigo, Inch Fort, Glenveigh Castle and Finner Camp. They restored order in north Leitrim and north Roscommon after their transfer to Boyle. They asserted their republican status. After the mutineers had labelled themselves 'Old IRA', however, the matter of title became more muted; but many Regulars insisted that the name IRA was theirs by right. Many continued to mutter that the greatest mistake they ever made was to open up recruiting to the trucileers in 1921. The Active Service Unit (ASU) almost to a man had sided with Collins (Paddy Rigney and Ned Byrne were two who did not), though some of them later led the abortive 1924 mutiny.

When the IRA became merged in the national army[2] Gen. Mulcahy was appointed Minister for Defence, and on the death of Gen. Collins he became Commander-in-Chief. He had taken a prominent part in the battle of Ashbourne in Easter Week 1916. In a letter to the troops dated 20 February 1923[3] he complimented them on making a good job of the army. He posed questions as to what an army meant for the country, what the country wanted it for, what it could effect for the people and their character. The army at that time was sometimes referred to as Regular troops of the IRA.[4] Upon reorganisation in 1923 all the top jobs went to those who had pre-truce IRA active service.

Gen. Sean Mac Mahon,[5] the Chief of Staff since September 1922, was out in 1916, fighting with his men in Ringsend and taking part in the stand made at Boland's Mill. As QMG during the Anglo-Irish war he distributed arms and supplies throughout the country. On the formation of the Regular Army in February 1922 he procured equipment, armament and supplies for the new force. Mulcahy called him 'the army's first real Chief of Staff'. The Adjutant General was Lt Gen. Gearóid Ó Súilleabháin.[6] An honours graduate in Celtic Studies (1913) and Irish language teacher he fought side by side with Seán MacDermott in the GPO in 1916. He was closely associated with Collins during the Anglo-Irish war. Lt Gen. Seán O'Muirthile[7] was the Quartermaster General. A Gaelic League enthusiast, a short time before Easter 1916 he was sent to Limerick to prepare the area to receive arms. These were to be passed through Kerry to signify that the Rising was really on. The Director of Intelligence was Lt Gen. Diarmuid O' Hegarty.[8] Well known in Irish-Ireland circles he fought as Second Lieutenant in F Company 1st Battalion in Church St during the 1916 fighting in Dublin. In 1919 he became Secretary to the Dáil. After the truce he retired to civilian life but when hostilities broke out he took up a position as Governor in Mountjoy Prison. However, he soon returned to politics and was succeeded by Major Gen. Seamus Hogan, a brother of the Minister for Agriculture and of the GOC Claremorris Command. Prior to joining the army he was Professor of History in University College, Cork. He served with the East Clare column during the War of Independence, and retired in 1923 after four years' active service.

The credentials of the GOCs were likewise irrefutable. Major Gen. Daniel Hogan[9] had been in charge of the famous Co. Monaghan Flying Column, taking part in many notable operations including the attack on Ballytrain RIC Barracks (with Gen. O'Duffy), one of the first barracks to be attacked. His brother Michael was captain of the Tipperary team who had been shot dead in Croke Park on Bloody Sunday. Major Gen. Reynolds[10] (Cork) saw service all over the south and west and before the truce was organiser in Galway. Major Gen. Michael Brennan[11] was a brilliant soldier who later became a crucial Chief of Staff from 1931 to 1940. His quick thinking in the Civil War saved Limerick for the Treaty forces. He was interned prior to Easter 1916. The very first RIC barracks to fall — Newmarket-on-Fergus — fell to him and five Volunteers. Major Gen. Paddy O'Daly (Kerry)[12] had an extraordinary combat record. In 1916 he took the Magazine Fort and held the Four Courts. He started the Dublin Guards and in 1919 captured an armoured car from the British. With the Dublin Guards he took part in the destruction of the Customs House in 1921. Under his leadership the Guards amalgamated with the active service unit (ASU) to constitute the embryonic Regular Army which made its first public appearance in uniform in February 1922 take over Beggars Bush Barracks from the 'Auxiliaries' (see Chapter 3). He was in charge of the attack launched on the Four Courts on 29 June 1922 and on 2 August with four companies of the Guards he landed in Fenit, Co. Kerry. He made a critical if controversial contribution towards military victory in the Civil War. Major Gen. Séan MacEoin (Athlone) was the legendary freedom fighter, the 'Blacksmith of Ballinalee'.[13] A Tipperary man (Dundrum) with Kilmallock connections, Major Gen. John T. Prout[14] (Waterford Command) came from the famous US 'Fighting 69th Division' (forever linked with 'Meagher of the Sword'). The French had awarded him the *Croix de Guerre* for gallantry in the First World War. He had been instructor and intelligence officer in the pre-truce 3rd Tipperary IRA Brigade. In the Civil War he took Waterford after a three-day siege and Carrick-on-Suir after two. Major Gen. Michael Hogan (Claremorris)[15] was a member of Tom Barry's column and had organised the raids on Windsor and Chelsea Barracks. He joined O'Daly in Kerry and operated all over Limerick and north Cork. Major Gen. Joseph A. Sweeney (Donegal)[16] fought in the GPO in 1916 under Pearse. He started two Flying Columns which he commanded himself. Many of his old column men now held commissions: all his officers had served as Volunteers. Major Gen. Peadar MacMahon[17] (Curragh) joined up in the Rotunda in 1913 and saw action in the thick of the 1916 fighting as a section commander in Stephen's Green, College of Surgeons and finally in Jacobs. The Chief Pay and Accounts Officer, Col. Eamon Morcan, too had pre-truce service. The leadership of the evolving army had good national records.

The national army was the big new fact of life: the centre of activity. The Commander-in-Chief appealed to all ranks to subscribe to the national loan to get the country back on its feet. He had said that the men in the army should be used for reconstruction before they were demobilised.[18] The country was largely undeveloped, and roads, for example, were crying out for attention.

It looked as if a transition to constructive peacetime soldiering was coming to fruition. There was a general tightening-up of discipline; identity cards were insisted on. Leakage of information (especially via 'girls and youths') was admonished. To emphasise a return to peace time, walking sticks for officers of approved design were issued on 5 June 1923.

Despite an early official announcement, demobilisation seemed a far cry away — something that might happen to others — and it came as a shock then when well-known senior and junior officers first found out that they had been demobilised when they read it in the newspapers. Old units disappeared. It was the old story, the soldiers complained: when the rifles ceased to crackle the army became nobody's child. An unsettled period of fluctuations and adjustments followed. It would be a mistake to imagine that things fell tidily and serenely into place. There was no evidence of an overall plan.

On 31 July 1924 reorganisation was set in train (Orders No. 3, Defence Forces (Organisation) Order 1924). For the purposes of decentralisation *Saorstát Éireann* was now divided into the following Military Districts which were designated as *Commands* (Appendixes 2 and 3):

(*a*) The Western Command;
(*b*) Southern Command;
(*c*) Eastern Command;
(*d*) The Curragh Training Camp

No. 1 Brigade with headquarters in Ballyshannon covered the northern half of the Western Command; No. 2 Brigade with headquarters in Athlone covered the rest. In the Southern Command No. 3 Brigade was based in Cork, No. 4 in Limerick. In the east No. 5 was in Kilkenny, No. 6 Dublin northward and No. 7 Dublin southward. Generally each brigade had three battalions and a unit each of the support arms. Combat grouping was flexible.

It was laid down that the Forces should consist of the following formations: the military branches of the Department of Defence: headquarters of commands, headquarters of brigade areas and headquarters of brigades; the Curragh Training Camp; the Infantry Arm; the Armoured Car Corps; the Artillery Corps; the Army Corps of Engineers; the Army Air Corps; the Army Medical Services; the Military Police Corps; the Army Signal Corps; the Army Transport Corps; Barrack Staffs; the Army School of Music and the Irish Military College. An order was laid down for the Corps. The Infantry was confirmed in precedence and organised into twenty-seven battalions, a drop of thirty-eight from the Civil War period. In the following years it went down and down until in 1930 there were only five.

Each of the following formations was declared a Corps for the purposes of the Act with precedence in the following order:

(*a*) The Infantry Arm;
(*b*) The Armoured Car Corps;
(*c*) The Artillery Corps;
(*d*) The Army Corps of Engineers;
(*e*) The Army Air Corps;
(*f*) The Army Medical Services;
(*g*) The Military Police Corps:
(*h*) The Army Signal Corps;
(*i*) The Transport Corps

In October 1924 the QMG's branch had a Supplies and Ordnance Sub-department in Islandbridge (Clancy Barracks) with an Ordnance Section in each command. In September 1931 these were named the Army Ordnance Service. The name 'Corps' was applied to the combat arms: Infantry, Artillery, Air, Armoured Cars, Engineers, and Signals: 'Service' was applied to administrative elements serving the fighting units, for example, Supply and Transport, Military Police, Ordnance and Medical. (Since May 1942, however, they have been entitled 'Corps').

On 1 October 1923 there were three types of armoured cars in service, scattered throughout the country with a weak system of central control at the Portobello Barracks

HQ. Each of the eight commands had a quota. Spasmodic disturbances in the wake of the Civil War precluded concentration. The 1924 reorganisation allotted one company (eight cars) to each of the four new Commands with a Corps HQ in the Curragh. A large number of surplus converted Lancias were withdrawn. Corps training from June 1924 to the autumn manoeuvres was elementary due to depletion of trained personnel. Collective training remedied this situation to some extent, and an intensive cycle of mechanical and gunnery training, concluding on 1 September 1927, advanced the development of the Corps to include tanks.

On 17 June 1924 the Artillery Corps was reorganised. The following January No. 2 Battery was formed and the Corps transferred from McKee Barracks, Dublin, to the Artillery (McGee) Barracks, Kildare, where it found a permanent home. The first firing practices commenced on 1 September 1925. On 9 April 1926 Col. McGovern, Director of Training, and Col. O Carroll, Director No. 2 Bureau, recommended that guns be painted grey instead of pillar-box green. Pragmatism and the pursuit of excellence became the hallmarks.

Formidable tasks of care and maintenance and provision of a skilled force to deal with any natural emergency faced the newly formed Army Corps of Engineers. Neglect by the British, burning by the Irregulars, vandalism from the Regulars (arising from overcrowding in 1922 and 1923 with comparatively undisciplined troops) had left all barracks and posts in a bad state of repair. On reorganisation in 1925–6 it was laid down that Engineer policy should now embrace (*a*) maintenance of military property and (*b*) the establishment of a Field Engineering service. This departure involved the additional employment of civilian tradesmen. Provision was made for formation of the different Engineer companies — Mining, Bridging, Communication, etc. — into a battalion.

In the Air Corps the mutiny (during which thirteen officers resigned) upset them momentarily, but quickly afterwards the mechanical side was organised, aerial photography started and a repair workshop opened. By 1926 there were regular training schemes for pupil officers, cadets and mechanics. On 19 February 1926 creditable rescue operations were carried out on the *Cardigan Castle*, wrecked off Clifden

Bay. A new organisation aimed at (*a*) training a sufficient numbers of pilots and mechanics to man proposed peacetime Coast Defence and Army Co-operation Units and (*b*) — something that seems to have been inexplicably lost sight of in recent times — the creation of a reserve of pilots and mechanics capable of filling appointments in future civil aviation concerns. Experimental work in that sphere was carried out by personnel of the Air Corps. Provision was made for participation in a Meteorological Service and for co-operation with the Ministry of Fisheries.

Recognition came in April 1928 when Col. J.C. Fitzmaurice, Officer Commanding the Air Corps, piloted with the Germans, Baron von Hunefeld and Capt. Koehl, the first epic east to west flight across the Atlantic. On July 1926 the strength of the Air Corps was materially strengthened by the acquisition of four Moths from England.

In 1923 the organisation of the Army Medical Service was fluid and medical units non-existent. In 1924 a Training Depot was opened and in 1925 the Corps was organised into companies, sections and squads. Wound and Military Service Pension claims eased off in 1926, allowing concentration on preventative medicine with the following remedial results.

| *Cases reported* | *1923* | *Rate per 1000 men* | *1926* | *Rate per 1000 men* |
|---|---|---|---|---|
| Lice | 51,138 | 1,278 | 2,139 | 178 |
| Scabies | 2,038 | 51 | 148 | 12 |
| Venereal | 638 | 16 | 160 | 11 |
| Other preventable diseases | 1,250 | 31 | 357 | 28 |
| Total: | 55,064 | | 2,804 | |

In the Military Police Corps in April 1924 a thousand men had left in the general demobilisation, leaving the strength at 385. This was increased to 500 a short time afterwards and provision was made for an HQ, five companies and Military Detention Barracks at Arbour Hill, Dublin; Curragh Camp; Cork and Athlone. The strength remained at 500 until 1928; by 1931 it was down to 210.

The 1924 organisation provided the Army Corps of Signals with an HQ, and a Headquarters Company and a Command Company for each of the three commands and for the Curragh Training Camp. Horsed cable detachments became a feature in the late twenties.

At the time of the General Election of 1923 the transport services of the army were administered by the QMG and did not function as a Corps. The reorganisation of July 1924 resulted in the formation of the Army Transport Corps to control and administer all army transport, mechanical and horse, and to control railway and sea transport when employed. In 1926 the prestigious army Showjumping Team was added.

The No. 1 Army Band under 'Fitz Brassy',[19] as he was popularly known, had quickly made a name for itself which was beneficial for the army's image with the public. On 13 October 1923 a concert by the band in the Theatre Royal, Dublin, was highly popular, and on 20 November the Army School of Music was established in Beggars Bush Barracks with Comdt J. Coughlan in charge of administration. All brass bands and pipe bands were transferred to the school by 1 January 1924 (but the Artillery Corps held on to its own unofficial band 'to brighten up the dreary evenings', as they put it). Four complete army bands were formed. No. 2 Band was allotted to the Southern Command, No. 3 was stationed at the Curragh, No. 4 was a training unit initially destined for the Western Command. A fifth band was to be formed as a reserve and No. 1 Band was also recognised as the band of the Eastern Command for military purposes. In addition to the brass bands, six pipe bands were formed and allotted to selected battalions. Three massed bands helped make the 1927 Military Tattoo a great success. In the 1929 Tattoo thirty buglers were added and in the 1935 Tattoo there were four army bands, five pipe bands as well as massed fanfare trumpets and drums. Three bands competed in the 1929 Tailteann Games, winning first, second and third prizes.

In November 1923 a Head Chaplain was appointed by the Hierarchy.[20] The Army School of Instruction gave rise to Musketry Schools.[21] The 1923 DFTP Act provided for the establishment of the Irish Military College, but the return of a military mission to the US in 1926–7 was awaited before proceeding. A new battalion was formed on 16 March 1924, in which the officers would all be 'natural' Irish speakers. All battalion commanders were commandants at that period, and NCOs who had passed tests were gazetted. The army was at last settling down.

Notwithstanding this emerging professionalism and the army's combat record in three campaigns, the Department of Finance (which owed its existence to the army) laid down that the army was not professional enough to merit full pay (Order No. 7, 30 September 1924). It is arguable whether it ever subsequently changed its mind. It promised, however, to review the pay position after 31 March 1925. It was true that the tremendous achievement of putting the improvised army of the new State in the field under active service conditions had been implemented by amateurs. Approximately 90 per cent of the officers and 50 per cent of the men had never served in any Regular Army.

Infantry naturally took pride of place. The men of 1916 and the freedom fighters of 1917–21 had been basically infantrymen. On 24 January 1923 the mass of troops throughout the country were organised into Infantry battalions numbering one to fifty-eight together with three Garrison and seven Reserve battalions (Appendix 3). The following November the 19th, 26th, 41st, 53rd, 60th, 64th and 65th Battalions were disbanded.

However, the emergence since 1923 of Corps and Services from being mere casual adjuncts to the Infantry Arm to having their own distinct co-ordinated status indicated a progress in peacetime professionalism which was lost on Finance. The promised pay review resulted in a reduction for the private soldier. There was an upward revision of Medical Officers' pay with effect from 10 July 1925 but a downward revision with effect from 14 October 1926 for the private soldier, who was unrealistically expected to perform the duties of the next higher rank in an emergency.

The General Staff pleaded for a defence policy, or at least the outline of one. Stung by the pay assessment it pointed out that policy since the foundation of the army had been simply the establishment of forces for the suppression of

Irregulars and the education of officers and men in the basics of their profession. That was no longer good enough, and in the absence of any proper policy it was impossible to organise and equip the Forces to any useful purpose.

On 22 July 1925 the Minister for Defence (Peadar Ó hAodha) submitted the Chief of Staff's (Lt Gen. Peadar MacMahon) memorandum to the Executive Council, stressing the urgent need for the army to have the outlines of the government's defence policy. Acknowledging that the military should appreciate political and economic factors, the memorandum emphasised that in return the government must appreciate the military factors. Fundamentally the army wanted some idea of the nature of the aggression to be anticipated and the identity of potential aggressors against whom they must defend the country. They felt they could handle threats to internal security from any of the following sources:

(*a*) serious disturbance in the north east;
(*b*) An outbreak by the Irregulars;
(*c*) A serious riot or disturbance by any body such as the association of ex-army men; the Communists, etc.

The memo dealt with various factors affecting defence problems. It was wary of the British but sensitive to her need for flank protection. It advocated the adroit use of propaganda and diplomacy to curb 'England or any other nation from encroaching on our rights or liberties'. It raised questions as to whether the State should adopt a policy of:

(*a*) independence in the defence of its territory against any aggressor, or
(*b*) defence as part of the defence scheme of the British empire, or
(*c*) abandoning the defence of the country to British Forces (in which case a special constabulary force would suffice to maintain internal order).

On 14 November of that year the government approved the following policy:

(*a*) the size of the standing army to be retained in normal times should not exceed 10,000 to 12,000 all ranks.

(*b*) The organisation of this force should be such that it would be capable of rapid and efficient expansion in time of need to the maximum strength of the country's manpower. This would necessitate the training of all ranks in duties of a more advanced nature than those normally associated with each rank.

(*c*) The army must be an independent national force capable of assuming responsibility for the defence of the territory of *Saorstát Éireann* against invasion, or internal disruptive agencies, *but it must also be so organised, trained and equipped as to render it capable, should the necessity arise, of full and complete co-ordination with the forces of the British Government in the defence of Saorstát territory whether against actual hostilities or against violation of the neutrality on the part of a common enemy.* (My italics.)

No analysis was made of 'actual hostilities' as against 'violation of neutrality'. An explanatory note stressed that our geographical position would never be used as a base for an offensive against Great Britain. It acknowledged that defence by sea of both Great Britain and Ireland was undertaken by the British navy. Pending a review of the relevant articles of the Treaty providing for this, it was not considered practicable to take any special steps other than to ensure that, if co-operation with the British Forces should become necessary at any time, Irish officers would be capable of commanding mixed forces operating in Irish territory. Staff studies were recommended but ironically, although they had initiated them, these decisions were not formally communicated to the military authorities. They had to wait until the Minister for Defence was introducing the Estimates in the Dáil on 6 May 1926 to find out what the Cabinet's defence policy was. There were obvious flaws in the policy that so emerged.

The idea that we should have a small army in which every man would be trained to NCO standard and every NCO to officer standard was impractical to begin with. Low standards of education, financial constraints and strength restrictions, excessive guard duties and low rates of pay saw to that. The formation of Reserve Forces could no longer be deferred.

On 12 November 1925 the formation of a Special Reserve was proposed, relating army strength to national security. It pointed out that the 25,000 troops required to quickly quell any further rebellion was less than half the number required in the Civil War (1922–3) or a quarter of that employed by the British in the Anglo-Irish War. To successfully resist a foreign aggressor and maintain neutrality at least 100,000 troops would be required. The estimate this time did not cover any serious hostilities on a large scale with north-eastern Ulster. The impracticality of maintaining a standing army of even sufficient strength to deal with internal troubles was acknowledged. A target of 10,000 for the standing army was reaffirmed and reference was made to conscription in Europe and the National Guard militia in the US, as reserve systems which might be considered.

The strength of the army at that point was 17,439 all ranks. The proposition was to put 4,500 Infantry men (privates) on the Special Reserve during 1926–7, and to reduce the standing army to 10,000 the following year by further transfers to the Reserve (Class A). In time further Class A discharges would displace existing Class A to a Class B category, which would be organised into Reserve battalions, under Reserve Officers. The ritual argument about saving well over £300,000 in the first year was put forward. On 18 December 1925 the Minister submitted for approval in the following year's estimates for the establishment under Section 217 of the Act of a Reserve of about 4,500, additional to a standing army of between 10,000 and 12,000 all ranks in normal times.

In a memo to the government dated 18 December 1925 the army restated the mission of dealing with emergencies arising from (*a*) internal disorder (*b*) maintenance of neutrality with or without assistance from a friendly power. It repeated that 25,000 troops (Regular and Reserve) would be required to maintain internal order and that at least 100,000 troops would be required to deter a foreign invader. The Executive Council agreed to these proposals in January 1926, but with the reservation that details as to numbers and cost were to be settled with Finance and insisting on an immediate reduction of the strength of the standing army to 10,000.

A fresh appraisal had to be made of the maintenance of neutrality against an external aggressor. Some understanding with the British in coast defence was essential. Co-operation would be favourably looked at by the Irish when the scheduled review of British rights under Articles 6 and 7 of the Treaty came up the following year. This gesture of co-operation was rebuffed by the British. Although the Chief of Staff (Gen. MacMahon) and a Staff Officer (Capt. Dan Bryan) accompanied members of the government to the Imperial Conference in 1926 to consider mutual coast defence, the British loftily declined to even discuss the matter.

Meanwhile Finance prompted the Minister to state in the Dáil that the ultimate strength of the Reserve would amount to 4,500 men. The Chief of Staff, Peadar McMahon, (on 11 June 1926) angrily refused to accept responsibility for that statement: 'If I, or any responsible military officer advised you that this country could be defended against *anyone* by an Army of 10,000 men plus 4,500 Reservists, we would immediately be deprived of our Commissions. . . . The responsibility for advising you on matters of military policy is mine not the Army Finance Officers.' He related an incident in which the Army Finance Officer had remarked that 'the Minister was nearly walked into it' by incorrect figures on Dominion Armies but that 'luckily we [Finance] advised him not to use them'. The Chief demanded an explanation. The figures given were correct, he said, but apart from that he protested against the system which permitted any civil servant to criticise or veto the professional work of any of his officers. He wanted action which would definitely preclude any such interference in matters of military policy in future.

On a more positive note the Irish public was developing a high regard for the Forces. The army bands had kept up the great start made in winning their hearts. The importance of ceremonial and public relations was realised. As early as 1922 and 1923 the army demonstrated at the grave of Wolfe Tone at Bodenstown. All through the 1920s and early 1930s the *Bóthar Buadha* (Victory) parade was held in Dublin to commemorate Griffith and Collins.[22] In 1927 the army co-operated with the Dublin City Fathers in running a series of pageants, including a Military Tattoo in Ballsbridge, for a Civic Week.[23] In 1926 they impressed the public with their bearing when, proud of their heritage, they turned out to give John Devoy, the old Fenian who had died in America, a great welcome home and a State funeral in Glasnevin.

The famous Army Showjumping Team[24] made its debut in Bray in 1926. It had phenomenal successes all over Europe and America right up to the outbreak of war in 1939, when it was disbanded and the horses sold.

Again in 1926 (September) large-scale manoeuvres involving the Eastern Command and Curragh Camp troops were held. Kilkenny men (B Company 20th Battalion) won a competition for the best trained Infantry company (camping, inspection, drill, guard-marching, tactical operations, range practices and bayonet assault). A sporting boxing tournament between Irish and British army teams was held in Portobello (Cathal Brugha) Barracks. The teams got on very well outside the ring. Boxing continued to flourish, and year after year many national titles were won by the army. There were many successes in the US.

The value of sport to the army in those trying days cannot be overestimated. From its foundation army personnel actively participated in games inside and outside the Forces. It was a unique army in one respect: all ranks were around the same age, and from major-generals down played hurling and football together with their formations. Not until the Emergency did the Army Athletic Association cater for any games except those approved by the Gaelic Athletic Association, though individual officers did play rugby.

Military education was not overlooked. In 1926 a group of officers were sent on a mission to American military institutions (including West Point): Major Gen. Hugo McNeill, Col. M.J. Costello, Col. Joe Dunne, Capt. Paddy Berry, Capt. Seán Collins-Powell, 2nd Lt Charlie Trodden. While in the US Major Gen. McNeill and Col. Costello assumed the ranks of Colonel and Captain respectively, and Capt. Collins-Powell the rank of Lieutenant. The former went to the Command and Staff School in Fort Leavenworth in Kansas, Capt. Dunne, Capt. Berry and Lt Collins-Powell went to the Infantry School in Fort Benning, Georgia. Charlie Trodden went to the Artillery School, Fort Sill, Oklahoma. On their return they set about the slow process of establishing the Military College to replace the Army School of Instruction, now transferred from Kildare to Keane (Pearse) Barracks in the Curragh.

A Cadet Course for Air Corps officers was commenced in the Army School of Instruction in 1926 and subsequently concluded in Baldonnel (Casement) Aerodrome. The first group of Infantry cadets was enrolled in the new Cadet School in 1928. On 2 September 1929 the first class of Regular second lieutenants were commissioned. They made an instant impact on the army.[25]

The Defence Plans Division was set up after the return in 1927 of the military mission to the US. Its ultimate function was the formulation and development of plans covering the organisation, mobilisation, equipment and employment of the Forces to meet possible emergencies and to co-ordinate attendant staff work. The immediate aim was to submit recommendations covering:

(*a*) a suitable doctrine or theory of war on which the defence of the *Saorstát* should be based;
(*b*) suitable tactical doctrines covering the employment of the separate arms and branches of the Service in accordance with the above doctrine of war;
(*c*) any additions or amendments necessary to existing schemes of organisation for the Forces for peace and war required to implement the approved tactical doctrines;
(*d*) tables of equipment and supply for the Forces;
(*e*) general recommendations concerning commands, staff, administration and supply;
(*f*) scheme of military education for the Forces based on the above doctrine of war and tactical doctrines.

One of the most important results to be anticipated from work of the Division was the early establishment of an Irish Military College, forming part of a progressive system of military education for the officers of the Irish army.

The following temporary appointments to the Division were announced:

*Directing Staff*

| | |
|---|---|
| *Director:* | Major Gen. Hugh [*sic*] McNeill, General Staff |
| *Staff Captain:* | Capt. Eamon Rooney, General Staff |
| *Librarian:* | Lt George White, attached General Staff. |

*Section*

| | | |
|---|---|---|
| (1) | *Command*: | Col. Michael J. Costello, General Staff |
| (2) | *Intelligence*: | Comdt D. Bryan, General Staff |
| (3) | *Personnel*: | Capt. Seán O'Sullivan, AG's Branch |
| (4) | *Transport and Supply*: | Capt. Patrick J. Berry, QMG's Branch |
| (5) | *Infantry*: | Major Joseph Dunne, AG's Branch |
| (6) | *Topographical*: | Major Niall MacNiall, General Staff; Capt. Jas. Flynn, Infantry; Capt. Séan Nolan, General Staff; Capt. Thomas Gray, Infantry; Lt Hugh O'Neill. |

*Sub-Sections*

| | | |
|---|---|---|
| (1) | *Artillery*: | 2nd Lt Charles Trodden, Artillery Corps |
| (2) | *Engineers*: | Comdt Peter Slattery |
| (3) | *Signals*: | Comdt J. Smyth, Signal Corps |
| (4) | *Air Corps*: | Capt Gerald J. Carroll, Air Corps |
| (5) | *Ordnance*: | Comdt D. Stapleton, QMG's Branch |
| (6) | *Medical*: | Comdt Charles M. Stuart, Army Medical Service. |

A further fifty -one officers were to hold themselves in readiness (in addition to their other duties) to report for part-time duty to the Director. It included many names which later became well known, such as Major Daniel McKenna, Major John V. Joyce and Major Patrick Mulcahy.[26] On 20 June 1928 the Defence Plans Division submitted a detailed report on

(*a*) preparation for war;
(*b*) a scheme for tactical war organisations;
(*c*) peace establishments embodying a militia system;
(*d*) proposals for the military education of the Defence Forces;
(*e*) summary of proposals and of decisions and directions required.

In July the Minister approved generally of the proposals and agreed that Staff and Service Schools should be set up on the lines of British War Establishments with suitable modifications. War equipment was to be provided for the few permanent units only.

However, no directions were given to put the proposals into effect. No programme was adopted for the provision of equipment or for the provision of necessary trained officers and other ranks.

The strength of the army continued to decrease without reference to its role. The questions posed in 1925 about the probable nature of aggression and the identity of aggressors remained unclarified. The utterances of politicians added further to the 'fudge'.

In 1927 the Minister for External Affairs, Desmond Fitzgerald, declared in the Dáil that it was 'practically inconceivable' that British and Irish soldiers would ever fight each other and must co-operate.[27] He scoffed at the notion of neutrality on the grounds of geographical propinquity, interdependence and mutuality of interests. De Valera on entering the Dáil took an opposite point of view.[28] Strengths continued to decline regardless of policy.

| *Date* | *Officers* | *Other Ranks* | *Total* |
|---|---|---|---|
| 31 March 1923 | 3,600 | 44,576 | 48,176 |
| 31 March 1924 | 1,241 | 15,141 | 16,382 |
| 31 March 1925 | 1,070 | 14,768 | 15,838 |
| 31 March 1926 | 1,053 | 14,469 | 15,522 |
| 31 March 1927 | 911 | 10,661 | 11,572 |

In 1928 the situation got even worse with further draconian demobilisation. Senior officers were offered a voluntary redundancy inducement of a gratuity of two years' pay and allowances; junior officers were offered one year's. Many officers availed of it,[29] and some of them went to America.

A year later senior officers were compulsorily retired on the same conditions. Junior officers were disposed of differently. The 'Hunt Board' of three Colonels, Seamus O'Higgins, Michael Hogan and Joe McLoughlin, was appointed to make recommendations to the Minister on each serving junior officer. As a result about half the junior officers were demobbed with two years' pay. Discipline was enforced to muzzle dissent. In 1928 a new regulation was issued, making it compulsory for officers to wear uniform at all times except when on annual leave. This proved to be very irksome. Passes were hard to come by and there was much evasion while it lasted (about a year).

In 1926 there were twenty-seven battalions. At the end of 1927 there were sixteen; in 1929 there were nine and in 1930 five, with a total strength of 4,706 NCOs and men. The Forces were reaching a low ebb. In the 1930s sport was one of the cheaper means of keeping interest alive. A Sokol PT system from Czechoslovakia was introduced and a Czech training officer was appointed. From his HQ in the Curragh he organised the new system to music throughout the Defence Forces. But on the outbreak of war in 1939 he was recalled to his own country and the army reverted to the old Swedish system. The old post-Civil War establishment apathy to the army had long prevailed, with pernicious consequences.

For self-protection in 1929 a National Defence Association (*Cumann Cosanta Náisiúnta* 1929–30)for officers was formed. It included both serving and Reserve officers. Two of its prominent members, MacEoin and Sweeney, had recently resigned after clashes with the Minister, Desmond Fitzgerald, and the Secretary, Peadar MacMahon. MacEoin's resignation arose from differences over dress, deportment and due deference. Sweeney resigned after a row about the delay in setting up the Military College.

The Association's objects were the cultivation and appreciation of national defence, the development of high standards among officers and the promotion of the welfare of officers and their families. The army journal, *An tÓglach*, was the mouthpiece of the many grievances of officers and of the army in general. Within a year of its foundation the organisation fell foul of the Minister, Desmond Fitzgerald, who had the unenviable task of bringing the victorious Civil War army under political control. Part of the problem lay in the incapacity of more flamboyant senior officers to accept the primacy of politics. Fitzgerald's pedantic manner did not help matters either. *An tÓglach* attacked him. An untimely sexual reference proved to be their undoing, and gave the Minister a pretext to move against them — it stated that restrictions in the marriage establishment were encouraging birth control. That was unmentionable in those days: the Association's days were numbered.

A stormy protest meeting was called. MacEoin challenged Brennan, the Chief of Staff. The exchanges almost came to blows, and nearly every officer present at that turbulent meeting carried a pistol. The outcome was that serving officers were obliged to resign from membership of the Association. The Reserve officers on their own failed to make it a viable undertaking, and the Association was wound up following that stormy rank-pulling (nearly gun-pulling) meeting in McKee Officers Mess on 21 November 1930. It was the worst crisis the army had faced since the mutiny in 1924.

The stability of the State was also beset by menace from the other side. The times were tense. In 1931 armed IRA men chose to hold their Bodenstown commemoration to clash with the army ceremonial. A young second lieutenant was detailed to use his armoured car to ensure the safety of the Minister (Desmond Fitzgerald).

During the parade when it looked as if things might get out of hand he was given the order by an ADC to load his Vickers machine-guns and cover the gates in case shooting started. His Cadet training stood to the young officer, (later Col.) Jim Cogan, and he knew enough about Amritsar (when the British army fired on a large crowd of unarmed civilians) to refrain from loading up. The order was later rescinded.

The election of Fianna Fáil temporarily defused that growing IRA threat, providing a still more crucial test for the integrity of the army with the advent to power in 1932 of its Civil War adversaries, Fianna Fáil, the 'Soldiers of the Republic, Legion of the Rearguard'. Just for a moment the Forces' loyalty to the elected government faltered. To shoot or salute was the stark choice some senior officers saw facing them. They saluted.

Hero of the hour was War of Independence veteran, the Chief of Staff, Major Gen. Michael Brennan, a Clareman. He rejected subversive suggestions from the Chief of Police, Eoin O'Duffy.[30]

The outgoing President, the level-headed W.T. Cosgrave, was aghast when he heard that the army's loyalty had been in doubt. De Valera showed sensitivity, however, and the crisis was quickly over. The axiom that the army was an instrument in the hands of the democratically elected government of the day was finally firmly established. The principle of civilian supremacy, asserted in 1924 with the muffling of the mutiny, was reaffirmed in 1932. It would never again come into question.

At once it was business as usual. The organisation of the Eucharistic Congress in Dublin in 1932 imposed a severe strain on the depleted Defence Forces. Thirty-six officers formed Guards of Honour at Mass in Phoenix Park and at Benediction on O'Connell Bridge. A battalion of infantry administered a camp for foreign visitors in Artane and all available military personnel were on duty on 26 June for crowd control. This was all in addition to heavy guard and security duties. The mounted escort (the colourful Blue Hussars whose passing is regretted to the present day), who first appeared in public at the Congress, had to be drawn in the main from Field Artillery officers, all again in addition to other duties. It was apparent that the permanent Forces were stretched beyond the limit of providing an adequate force to meet an emergency. The long-discussed formation of a proper Reserve could not be deferred for much longer.

From 1926 on there had been various experiments with different classes of Reserves. The Defence Act of 1923 had provided for the Reserve and this provision was given effect in 1927 with the establishment of the A Reserve. Men had been transferred to Reserve units on completion of their army service, and they could be called out in aid of the civil power. In January 1928 the B Reserve was formed. Men were recruited directly into the Reserve after ninety-six days initial training. Between them A and B Reservists manned nine Infantry battalions (6th to 14th) and units of all Corps and Services except Ordnance and Military Police. The positioning of their collar badge numerals distinguished their dress from that of the Regulars. As these Reserves were thought to be inadequate a Volunteer Reserve and an OTC were also established in 1929 (1st City of Dublin Battalion).

It was not required to undergo a period of fulltime initial training, but was permitted to train by weekly parades and weekend camps. It produced many good officers who trained in their spare time and gave good service in the war years (1939–45). In 1931 according to the *Organisation of the Defence Forces (Peace)*, the Reserve had the following components: the Reserve Officers, the A Reserve, the B Reserve, the

Volunteer Reserve and the Officers Training Corps. The Volunteer Reserve then consisted of two units: — the 1st City of Dublin Battalion in Portobello (Cathal Brugha) Barracks and the 1st Cork Field Battery, Collins Barracks, Cork. Both had distinctive collar badges. The Officers Training Corps had a separate organisation.

The formation of an Officers Training Corps (OTC) in 1929 was met with bitter opposition from politicians and from a minority of students. It had units in University College Dublin (established 11 November 1929), Trinity College, Dublin (2 December 1929), University College Cork (2 January 1930), University College Galway (29 January 1930) and the College of Surgeons (9 January 1931). The Dublin OTCs were based in Griffith Barracks and went to Finner Camp — usually around the time of the Scotch Fair (as the annual influx of young, unattached Scots females to the Donegal resorts was called) in mid-July — for their annual training.

When the new government assumed office in 1932 the permanent Force (6,700 all ranks) consisted of five Infantry battalions with elements of the various Corps and Services. The paper strength was as follows:

| | *Officers* | *Other Ranks* | *Total* |
|---|---|---|---|
| Permanent force | 507 | 5,286 | 5,793 |
| A Reserve | 202 | 4,032 | 4,234 |
| B Reserve | – | 3,451 | 3,451 |
| Volunteer Reserve | 23 | 454 | 477 |
| OTC | – | 677 | 677 |
| Total | 732 | 13,900 | 14,632 |

During the year the General Staff reviewed its war plans. In the autumn of 1933 combined exercises were carried out for the first time in six years. Recruiting for the B Reserve was stopped in anticipation of the inauguration of a new Volunteer Force. It was to be organised into three lines to furnish a number of complete units on a territorial and regimental basis. Fourteen to twenty-eight days' initial training was to be supplemented by local drills, weekend and annual camps. Seven days' notice was required to resign. Four Commands were established, within which a number of brigades were to be raised. Military districts, sub-divided into areas, were set up. No cadres were provided. Training and mobilisation duties fell to Depot staffs. Weapons were retained at military posts. Twenty-five Volunteer halls were to be provided (though none materialised before 1938). Recruitment commenced in March 1934.

The initial response to the recruiting drive was good. On 31 March 1935 the overall strength was 11,531, of which 10,000 were First Line. There was a falling-off subsequently in numbers and quality due mainly to deficiencies in training facilities. An exception to this were units like the 11th (Dublin) Infantry Battalion who rivalled the Regulars in professionalism.

In October 1935 when Mussolini invaded Abyssinia (Ethiopia) de Valera's cabinet examined the whole question of the Volunteer Force. The main conclusion reached was a determination not to become the tool of any Great Power (Great Britain was classed as such) and to resist with whatever strength they might possess every attempt to force them into a war against their will. They were going to stay neutral and were prepared to defend their neutrality by force of arms if necessary. Partition clouded a proper estimate of the situation, especially on the consequences of the lack of air and sea power.

The Volunteer Force gave a shot in the arm to *Óglaigh na hÉireann*. A prime recruitment catchment area was reopened. The Volunteers took an oath of allegiance to the State. They were organised into units and controlled by the General Staff under the Minister for Defence. With the rest of the National Forces they were governed by the Defence Forces (Temporary Provisions) Act of 1923.

On 30 July 1934 a new organisation was introduced called the Tactical and Territorial Organisation of the Defence Forces. The Infantry arm was renamed a 'Corps' and organised into ten named regiments as follows:

*Regiment of Rifles*: all Regular, with the five Regular Battalions, 1st to 5th.

*The Regiment of Oriel*: Counties Louth, Meath and Monaghan;

*The Regiment of Leinster*: Counties Kildare, West Wicklow, Wexford and Carlow;
*The Regiment of Dublin*: County and Borough of Dublin and East Wicklow;
*The Regiment of Ormond* (renamed *Ossory* in 1935): Counties Kilkenny, Waterford and Tipperary;
*The Regiment of Thomond*: Counties Limerick and Clare:
*The Regiment of Connaught*: Counties Galway, Mayo and Roscommon;
*The Regiment of Breffni*: Counties Cavan, Longford, Leitrim and Sligo;
*The Regiment of Tírconnail*: County Donegal.
*The Regiment of Uisneach*: Counties Leix, Offaly and Westmeath.

*The Regiment of Pearse* (in effect an OTC) was added on 6 November 1935. The evocative naming of the regiments was an innovation.

A regiment (except Pearse) would have a regular staffed depot, two battalions of A and B Reservists, two battalions of First Line new Volunteer force, two battalions of Second Line, the depot battalion of the regiment being drawn from the Third Line. It was the first scheme to make provision for recruitment into all arms of the service. The Artillery Corps had field batteries numbering from five to twenty-eight, together with light batteries numbering from two to seven. Cavalry was organised into brigades and divisions. To the permanent force of one armoured, one cyclist and one horse squadrons was added four armoured, nineteen cyclist and seven horse squadrons. Grouping was flexible. Training schemes were based on a system of reinforced brigades. The Artillery and Cavalry acquired in time territorial appellations. The outbreak of war prevented the full implementation of this imaginative plan.

In April 1939 new conditions for the Volunteer Force were introduced which laid down age limits of seventeen to thirty years, or seventeen to forty years if candidates had a trade or profession. Ninety days' initial training was required except for those having special qualifications. If a candidate could prove that he could not attend for the ninety days' initial training, local drills, overnight camps and annual training could be substituted. War was threatening. Out of over 7,000 other ranks on the strength on 31 March 1939 only just over 3,000 re-enlisted. They were given new army numbers.

There was also a Second Line (45–55 years) as a back-up. The new condition of service ensured that recruits got the minimum of training necessary to provide a better base for expansion. The Volunteer Reserve and the OTC had been disbanded in 1935. That OTC experiment was a failure. The A Reserve proved to be valuable and reliable; the B Reserve, lacking officers and NCOs, less so.

The new Volunteer project was launched without sufficient preparation. It speaks volumes for the integrity of that Force that it overcame many handicaps and provided backbone for the Forces when the 'Call to Arms' came in 1939 and 1940. On mobilisation they provided a percentage of partially trained officers and NCOs, together with over 6,000 men. Without them, the 1940 expansion would scarcely have been workable.

In the pre-emergency army combat efficiency in the Permanent Force was of necessity low. It was chronically under strength and occupied with guards and duties. In addition it had to supply instructors, cadres and administration for Reserve units. The average yearly strength of the various components of the Defence Forces excluding officers for the period 1930 to 1938 were:

| *Year* | *Regulars* | *A Res* | *B Res* | *Vol. Force* | *Total* |
|---|---|---|---|---|---|
| 1930 | 4,925 | 4,057 | 3,284 | – | 12,266 |
| 1931 | 5,315 | 4,307 | 3,492 | – | 13,114 |
| 1932 | 5,230 | 4,464 | 3,352 | – | 13,046 |
| 1933 | 5,294 | 4,546 | 3,061 | – | 12,901 |
| 1934 | 5,248 | 4,440 | 1,291 | 9,993 | 20,972 |
| 1935 | 5,072 | 4,578 | 1,005 | 11,076 | 21,731 |
| 1936 | 5,188 | 4,544 | 829 | 10,265 | 20,826 |
| 1937 | 5,256 | 4,775 | 593 | 9,631 | 20,255 |
| 1938 | 5,915 | 4,577 | 368 | 9,525 | 20,385 |

That paper strength did not indicate the number of trained men available nor the mobilisation capability of the Reserve.

The organisation providing for the figure of four Reinforced Brigades was largely theoretical. The brigade organisation had been abandoned and the number of Regular battalions reduced to five, distributed over four military districts. The number of districts was reduced to three in 1931. Arms and equipment remained problems for even the most modest organisation.

In 1925 the army had held 42,500 rifles of which 8,000 were serviceable; 797 Lewis light machine-guns; 205 Vickers machine-guns and nine 18-pounder field guns, together with four 4.5" howitzers which were delivered in 1925. No major items of infantry battalion equipment were received in 1928 or 1929. Financial sanction was received on 6 February 1931 to complete the programme for equipping seven battalions and the programme for fourteen (five Regular, seven Reserve and two Volunteer Reserve) was approved in principle. Orders were placed for the purchase of arms, ammunition and equipment accordingly but the purchase of telescopic rifles and range finders was deferred. In 1931 Vickers and other stores were added to the deferred list. At the end of 1932 the stock on hands was as follows: of the 42,500 rifles, 17,600 had been reconditioned; 297 Vickers guns; 797 light machine-guns; 33 telescopic rifles. The Artillery Corps had twenty-five field guns, four howitzers and one half battery of 43" 30 cwt AA guns. There were no anti-tank guns and no mortars other than a few obsolete weapons for which there was no ammunition. There were 29 million rounds of small arms ammunition, 2,500 rounds of artillery ammunition and 43,600 HG grenades. These figures spoke for themselves in terms of relative combat power.

It was originally proposed to complete the partial equipping of another battalion in 1932–33 in addition to the eleven battalions already provided for. In the event no battalion equipment was purchased for that year but three field guns and four 3.7" pack howitzers (previously ordered) were delivered to the Artillery. In 1933–34 Finance suggested that the purchase of the Vickers guns be deferred pending further trials, in spite of the fact that this was the standard British weapon proven in the 1914–18 war! The difficulties of obtaining supplies from the British at short notice were pointed out but Finance persisted in procrastinating.

After the Imperial Conference of 1926 a proposal to maintain liaison with the British principal supply officers committee came to nothing. As a result of the Departmental delays for the second year in succession no battalion equipment was obtained. Sanction was eventually extracted in 1934–35 to purchase fifty Vickers guns and fifty-two range-finders but as the purchases were not completed within the financial year the £5,794 allocated lapsed. They had to be paid for out of the vote appropriate to the year in which they were delivered, thereby reducing the sum available for the purchase of warlike stores in that year by a corresponding amount.

On 18 July 1935 fifty Vickers guns were delivered and by the end of 1937 a further eighty-eight. This practically completed the programme for the partial equipping of the fourteen battalions initially provided for, together with the ten organised Volunteer Force regimental depots in the theoretical four brigades. It was clear that such forces could not be built up effectively without substantial increases in Defence expenditure. The Estimates for 1937–38 showed an increase of £1,029,000 (67 per cent). They were based on the following strengths: Permanent Force 7,300; A Reserve 5,500: B Reserve 750; Volunteer Force First Line 12,000, Second Line 3,000. Considerable expenditure on the Air Corps and anti-aircraft defence was envisaged. Finance demanded an explanation, as a major change of defence policy appeared to be involved. In the end the government decided on 13 January 1937 that normal provisions only were to be made: the increases were abandoned for that year and the army vote and the vote for warlike stores was reduced. The possibility of a supplementary estimate was not ruled out by the Executive Council — some were taking the threat of war seriously.

Financial delays and restrictions persistently hindered the equipping and development of the army. The strength of the already inadequate standing army was required to be kept from 10 to 16 per cent below the Peace Establishment. Promotions of NCOs were restricted. Civil administration exercised an unreasonable control, over and above the necessary normal cut and thrust of such interdepartmental relationships in a democracy. In 1929 Ernest Blythe, presiding over a Council of Defence meeting in his capacity as Acting Minister for Defence, warned that it was essential that the military and civil branches should collaborate but that enquiries, advice or criticism should not involve undue interference by the civil side in the domain of military efficiency. He felt that, the vote having been brought down to a normal figure, the type of penal scrutiny previously practised was no longer necessary. The Department of Defence should be treated as a normal Department, he said, and due weight should be given to the view of the responsible military Chiefs.

The effect of a financial system which resulted in less than 5 per cent of the monies provided for the army over a period of years being available for the purchase of warlike stores ran the risk that all the monies spend on the Forces would be wasted. During 1937 and early 1938 the scheme for four effective Reinforced Brigades (71,655) was costed: £11 million plus an annual expenditure of £2.75 million was required. The exercise became increasingly academic and questionable.

The army, however, could not discharge its duties without reasonable armament and equipment. The following table summarises the financial positions in the years leading up to the outbreak of war:

| *Year* | *Annual Vote* | *Expenditure* | *Savings* | % *Saved* |
|---|---|---|---|---|
| 1924/25 | £3,927,145 | £3,003,164 | £923,981 | 23 |
| 1925/26 | £3,053,117 | £2,804,595 | £248,522 | 8 |
| 1926/27 | £2,483,785 | £2,309,720 | £174,065 | 7 |
| 1927/28 | £2,185,167 | £1,967,935 | £217,232 | 10 |
| 1928/29 | £1,804,433 | £1,760,646 | £ 43,787 | 2 |
| 1929/30 | £1,442,531 | £1,259,501 | £183,030 | 13 |
| 1930/31 | £1,445,032 | £1,173,795 | £271,237 | 19 |
| 1931/32 | £1,442,041 | £1,247,355 | £194,686 | 13 |
| 1932/33 | £1,318,458 | £1,154,416 | £164,042 | 12 |
| 1933/34 | £1,253,334 | £1,160,848 | £ 92,486 | 7 |
| 1934/35 | £1,476,731 | £1,354,886 | £121,845 | 8 |
| 1935/36 | £1,503,368 | £1,339,134 | £164,234 | 11 |
| 1936/37 | £1,529,987 | £1,373,257 | £156,730 | 10 |
| 1937/38 | £1,595,810 | £1,511,501 | £ 84,309 | 5 |
| 1938/39 | £1,995,684 | £1,771,721 | £223,963 | 11 |
| | £28,456,623 | £25,192,474 | £3,264,149 | 11% |

The savings effected on the annual grants voted for the purchase of warlike stores were as follows:

| *Year* | *Annual Grant* | *Sum Expended* | *Saving (Excess)* | *% Saved* |
|---|---|---|---|---|
| 1924/25 | £136,519 | £38,212 | £98,307 | 72 |
| 1925/26 | 49,924 | 194,997 | (145,073) | – |
| 1926/27 | 51,712 | 106,460 | (54,748) | – |
| 1927/28 | 60,716 | 38,154 | 22,562 | 35 |
| 1928/29 | 46,803 | 29,509 | 17,294 | 37 |
| 1929/30 | 72,145 | 35,919 | 36,226 | 50 |
| 1930/31 | 72,962 | 47,015 | 25,947 | 32 |
| 1931/32 | 87,523 | 64,937 | 22,586 | 26 |
| 1932/33 | 51,983 | 32,441 | 19,542 | 38 |
| 1933/34 | 56,672 | 36,583 | 20,089 | 35 |
| 1934/35 | 104,380 | 67,322 | 37,058 | 35 |
| 1935/36 | 71,475 | 64,551 | 6,924 | 10 |
| 1936/37 | 160,683 | 98,259 | 62,424 | 39 |
| 1937/38 | 137,125 | 142,168 | (5,043) | – |
| 1938/39 | 164,807 | 139,667 | 25,140 | 15 |
| | £1,352,429 | £1,136,194 | £189,235(Net) | 14% |

These savings of course represented corresponding deficiencies in purchases. Excluding stores on order, delivery of which was expected by 31 March 1939, the army was deficient £4,723,432 worth of equipment.

It was difficult to formulate policy and build an organisation in such quicksand circumstances. An intelligence submission in February 1936 stated that war was likely to break out in two or three years 'that is, in 1938 or 1939'. It complained about having no military attachés abroad and on receiving no information from the Department of External Affairs who too seemed to adopt a condescending, 'Tim Healy'[31] attitude towards the army.

The problems arising from the adoption of a position of neutrality in the event of a world war had nevertheless to be pursued by the General Staff. They proposed setting up a Council of National Defence to co-ordinate all defence activities and preparations so as to 'make full and proper use of the period of peace still left'. It was not constituted.The interdepartmental supplies committee (appointed in October

1935) examined questions relating to fuel, grain and other foodstuffs but did not deal with warlike stores or explosives. The interdepartmental committee on censorship (set up in 1931 and reconstituted in 1935) was already at work in preparation for the expected war.

By 1936 the General Staff saw clearly the crying need for more energetic action on defence matters, but to get the Department and the government to take notice was a problem. Still confident that any threat to internal security could be disposed of, it concentrated on the intractable problem relating to external aggression. The Chief of Staff (Major Gen. Brennan) submitted to the Minister early in 1936 a memorandum on the military aspects of the 1921 Treaty (Clauses 6 and 7), pointing out that the military implications of these clauses could only be fully appreciated in the light of a general review of the whole strategic and defensive problem of the *Saorstát* (before the new Constitution and the handing back of the Forts). On 19 June of the same year an altered and enlarged memorandum was developed into a military appreciation of the defensive problem and forwarded to the Minister. It indicated that the existing Defence Forces were not capable of defending the country and included two memoranda: one requesting a direction on defence policy submitted by the Defence Council to the Executive Council in 1925; and another entitled *Preparation for War* which was prepared by the Defence Plans Division in 1928.

The following 22 September a hard-hitting memorandum on *Completion of Existing Defence Units* was forwarded. The covering letter stated stiffly that if it was not possible to implement the programme the general organisation of the Volunteer Force should be reduced immediately. That struck a sensitive political chord.

The principal points covered in the memorandum were that:

(*a*) extensive guards and duties had impaired the effectiveness of the Permanent Force (restricted to 5,000) to provide a highly trained cadre for expansion in war;
(*b*) owing to lack of policy or objective the army had neither the organisation nor the material to resist external aggression;

(*c*) the problems of defence involved more than one department and that this required co-ordination;
(*d*) special and early arrangements should be made with the British War Office and other sources if stores were to be delivered in 1937–38;
(*e*) effective defence would require harbour, coast, anti-aircraft and anti-gas defences; field troops; a coast watching service; air and naval services.

A programme was called for which when completed would give four Reinforced Brigades, four Garrison battalions, six Cyclist Regiments. It was made plain that miscellaneous troops, staffs, depots and existing units were deficient in personnel, material and equipment. Many units if mobilised would have practically no armament or equipment. On mobilisation the army could only produce a skeleton of the phantom four brigades and ancillary troops. Only nine of the twenty-four battalions of Artillery required were available. Again it all fell on deaf ears. Normal provision only was made in the estimates for 1937–38 and the proposals were abandoned for that year. The warning that the country had no Coastguard, no Marine Service, a negligible Air Force, no reserves of armament or warlike stores and no assured means of supply in the event of emergency had little effect.

In December 1936, however, the Executive Council assigned responsibility for Air Raid Precautions to Defence. Two military officers were subsequently sent to Britain in that connection. Council made a submission to the government on the subject in June 1937.

On 17 November the Council also approved a concurrent proposal for the motorisation of the army. Trials had been carried out on the feasibility of relying on horse transport in view of an anticipated fuel shortage in war but those trials were unsatisfactory. During the summer of 1937 brigades were concentrated for training on a temporary basis but they were lacking in too much essential equipment for the exercise to be effective.

In August 1937 proposals to amend the Ministries and Secretaries Act[32] to meet defence requirements were postponed on the Minister's instructions pending the enactment of the new Constitution later that year. The following month the Council of Defence directed that Estimates for 1938–39 should be based on existing strengths since no increase had been approved.

However, after further discussions with the General Staff on 25 November 1937 the Minister directed that an estimate be prepared of the strength, nature and cost of the Defence Forces necessary for the maintenance of neutrality on the basis that:

(*a*) no British forces occupy State territory or territorial waters;
(*b*) the border exists, but does not constitute a special problem as regards defence (strategic studies on the problems of border defence in an island context had been done by the army since 1924). The inherent weakness of the 'north east Ulster' situation as regards security was recognised but it was stressed that that did not affect the necessity of taking the best possible steps to secure the defence of the area under the jurisdiction of the Irish government;
(*c*) the question of a special threat to our neutrality from Great Britain did not arise;
(*d*) for the purpose of the estimate it should be assumed that we have to oppose an enemy force of 50,000 supported by naval forces.

Estimates of the strengths required were prepared on 10 December 1937 as follows:

| | | |
|---|---|---|
| 3 divisions (16,000 each) | 48,000 | |
| Corps Troops (Medium Arty, Specialists etc.) | 7,000 | |
| | | 55,000 |
| Local Defence Troops | | 20,000 |
| Fixed Defence Troops | | 20,000 |
| Air Force (12 Squadrons) | | 2,562 |
| Naval Forces | | 3,414 |
| | | 100,976 |

The government's idea was to provide such Defence Forces as would ensure defence against invasion and the prevention of the use of this country as a base against Great Britain. The main thing was to be able to reassure the British that this flank was absolutely secure. After more discussion the scheme was altered up and down and finally steadied at four Reinforced Brigades with an establishment of 71,455. This was submitted to the Minister on 26 January 1938. In effect, it was a reversion to the recurring four-brigade scheme of 1934 on the basis of the maintenance of neutrality and that there be no agreement with the British. The scheme was costed but no further action was taken. Major political developments were afoot.

On 25 April 1938 the Anglo-Irish Agreement provided for the handing over of the Irish Coast Defences and abolished British Treaty rights. This made possible the implementation of a limited neutrality policy for Ireland. The Coast Defences (the Forts) were taken over the following July. The professional bearing of the Irish troops taking over (Artillery and Engineers) made a very favourable impression on all concerned. The following guns were on hand:

| | | | | |
|---|---|---|---|---|
| Cobh | 2 x 9.2"; | 4 x 6"; | 6 x 18-pdr; | 14 x MGs |
| Carlisle | 1 x 9.2"; | 1 x 6" | | |
| Westmoreland | 1 x 9.2 ; | 1 x 6" | | |
| Berehaven | 2 x 6"; | 2 x 4.5"; | 2 x 12-pdrs; | 5 x MGs |
| Lough Swilly (Dunree and Leenane) | 2 x 9.2"; | 2 x 6"; | 4 x 4.45"; | 4 x MGs |

The MGs and 18-pdrs were declined. Military factors predominated the dealings.

In January 1938 the British Chiefs of Staff had been asked to advise on the following questions:[33]

(*a*) For what purpose was it intended to employ the defended ports in Ireland in the event of a major war where their use was needed.

(*b*) If the ports remained in their hands and if on the outbreak of war Ireland were to adopt a hostile attitude would the ports under those conditions be of sufficient importance to them to warrant the additional measures necessary to ensure their security.

(*c*) If the ports had previously been handed over to Ireland and if on the outbreak of war Ireland were to deny them their use, would the importance of the ports be so great as to warrant military operations to regain them.

They acknowledged that it would be most desirable to use Queenstown (Cobh), Lough Swilly, Berehaven and Kingstown (Dún Laoghaire) as bases for both minesweeping and anti-submarine hunting. Berehaven would be vital should Portsmouth prove untenable. The temporary transfer of the Grand Fleet from Scapa Flow to Lock Ewe and Lough Swilly in 1914 showed the desirability of maintaining alternative bases. In preparing their plans for trade protection the Admiralty had always counted upon the use of the ports in Ireland. They had to have control of the ports for two reasons: first, to use them themselves; secondly, to deny them to the enemy. To prevent the ports as they stood being captured by Ireland one Infantry brigade per port plus a division with AA defences for the hinterland would be required. To regain the ports would be a more formidable operation, comparable to the Gallipoli landing, than the reinforcement of existing garrisons; at least three divisions would be required, and it could be an impossible mission.

The case of a war with France (contemplated) was seen by the British Chiefs as quite different from that of a war with Germany. In that case, Ireland's geographical position would make possession of a harbour there as a Main Fleet base of compelling importance. The changing political situation meant that a war with France — or with any European Power for that matter — could be ruled out. Ireland, which had every reason not to forget, did not always appreciate how seriously Britain took the 'business of war' — which they had made their own — when it came to securing the ports. The Chiefs declared that the decision would have to be taken by the Cabinet of the day in the light of existing circumstances.

The use of force was never excluded even if it meant the complete reoccupation of Ireland to prevent its being used as a base for hostile action, either by submarines or aircraft, against Britain or Northern Ireland, or their seaborne trade, or for land operations against Northern Ireland. Nevertheless, the Chiefs continued, to avoid such an intolerable situation they should co-operate with the Irish in every way and be sensitive to de Valera's political problems. When war came and co-operation to the extent anticipated was not forthcoming, that approach was bitterly regretted.

Following the agreement the Irish General Staff reviewed during May 1938 the extent to which the premises set out in the scheme submitted the previous January to the Department now held good. Further proposals were worked out involving the reorganisation of the Volunteer Force and the provision of a garrison battalion for Dublin. During the summer brigades were mobilised, but lack of training personnel and equipment again prevented them from being fully exercised in combined field training as tactical units. The anomalous position of Ireland in the light of the Anglo-Irish Treaty and the international situation had to be worried out and wargamed by the General Staff. 'Certain considerations' had to be weighed up.

In September 1938 GHQ felt compelled to seek an indication of British views on defence, pointing out once more that the actual strength, organisation, armament and equipment of the existing Defence Forces restricted their value to that of an instrument for the preservation of internal order. It was also pointed out that in war arms could only be obtained from Britain or the USA and that the prospect of obtaining arms from the USA against British wishes and in view of the US neutrality law was remote.

The army did not know that Joe Walsh, Secretary of the Department of External Affairs, had insinuated to Eden (British Foreign Secretary) that they were prepared to spend money on the ports in defence of British interests, even if it meant constructing destroyers. A treaty of mutual defence had been mooted which would give the Royal Navy free access in time of war. The vital trade routes were of mutual concern.[34] These would have been vital factors in military estimates. But the Volunteer organisation had been designed to make things too hot for an invader *after* he had landed. It was neither organised nor equipped to *prevent* invasion. Political factors, unionist intransigence, a passionate wish on the part of the people not to be pushed unprepared into the war against its will and recent memories of the Black and Tans' terrorism were factors which clouded clear-cut military estimates. The immovable mission — and the Defence Forces apparently were the only ones to take its implementation seriously — remained the defence of the national territory against invasion or internal disruption agencies. The IRA represented a visible threat to internal security. They could be contained. Defence against external invasion was a different matter. Nothing changed. The nation as a whole had little realisation of the problems arising from the adoption of a neutrality policy. There was a tendency to accept that saying things was the same as doing things. Undefended neutrality would be brushed aside. The country would have to adequately arm itself if a neutrality policy were to have meaning.

In November 1938 the Taoiseach (de Valera), who then happened to be acting as Minister for Defence, called for the War Organisation and plans. From that discussion it became obvious that due to shortage of men and material the four-brigade organisation was unrealistic. A two-brigade revised scheme was finally worked out and costed, providing for a strength of 37,560 all ranks. On 31 December 1938 supplementary proposals were put to provide for air raid precautions, marine equipment, and the erection of factories. A survey of equipment revealed the following deficiencies, even for that attenuated organisation: 294 anti-tank rifles; 3,851 revolvers; 842 bren guns; 17,650 respirators; 32,000,000 rounds of SAA Ball ammunition; 3,020 lbs of explosives; thirty-two 2-pdr anti-tank (there were none in stock; one on order); sixty-four Light Bofors AA guns (none in stock); sixteen Medium AA guns; twelve 4.5" howitzers; sixteen 81 mm mortars; sixty-eight searchlights; sixty-four service aircraft; eleven armoured cars. There were also serious shortages in artillery (Field, AA, Coast) and mortar ammunition.

Finance dismissed the proposals out of hand on 10 January 1939. It assumed that if Britain were at war we should not make any attempt to lend assistance outside our own shores, that we were not liable to attack from any country not at war with Great Britain and that the possibility of any attack from Great Britain might be ignored.[35] Even if such an attack were to be contemplated, it added, the consideration arose as to whether any attempt at formal resistance on our part would not be futile and whether it would not be better for us to make no organised resistance at all in order to avoid unnecessary bloodshed, suffering and economic destruction. It was doubtful, it concluded, if the existence of an army of 37,000 men would really deter Britain from attack if it were imperative for her own military or economic security to deliver it.

What was pertinent in Finance's opinion, however, was a questioning of Britain's agreement to undertake the supply of warlike stores without some guarantee as to Irish intentions. It reckoned that if Britain became powerless, resistance on our part would be futile. With Clausewitzian certitude it pronounced that the possibility of land invasion was remote and that if Ireland were bombarded from the sea or attacked from the air the British would come to its aid. It recommended a return to the drawing board for the military planners and rebuffed them as follows:

> The scheme now submitted does not appear to have been framed on these lines [i.e. a scheme of defence against air attack]. It provides for a miniature army — as armies go — equipped in all its branches. It is a miniature of an army that would be suitable for a country with land frontiers open to attack and invasion. It provides, for example, the increases in medium and light artillery, anti-tank guns and rifles, armoured cars, infantry equipment, engineering equipment and complementary services. A large increase in ammunition and personnel is involved.
>
> Increases in aircraft, anti-aircraft guns, and searchlights are also provided but these are more or less proportionate to the increases in other branches of the army.
>
> No case whatever has been indicated for the necessity to create and maintain these *two* Brigades and it is accordingly suggested that, in the light of above observations, the defence scheme as put forward should undergo a radical review.

Apparently influenced by Douhet's air supremacy heresy[36] of the day Finance nevertheless had a point in countering the provision of a predominantly infantry army. In the US that point would have been thrashed out at War College level, where top soldiers and top civil servants study together.[37] However Finance's conditioned didacticism militated against any exchange of ideas.

This time Defence turned, rebutted the Finance memorandum and proceeded to seek sanction for a War Establishment of 37,500 (all ranks) and expenditure of £5,011,383. Its submission stated, inter alia, the courses of action which had to be addressed:

(*a*) Neutrality, in which we have announced to the world that we have no interest in the war and do not intend to take part in it.

(*b*) Neutrality, with a friendly bias to Britain in which, while not playing an active military part, our economic life is speeded up to give increased supplies to the British of everything we can produce, and in which we allow no activities inimical to their interests to be carried on within our territory.

(*c*) Co-operation with the British to defeat a mutual enemy.

(*d*) Defence against a British attack.

The point made was that if the Dáil decided on complete neutrality or neutrality with a bias to Britain we could find ourselves at war with either Britain's enemies or with the British themselves if either felt we were weak and that they could make use of our territory and resources in their struggle for victory. To be left alone Ireland had to organise in peacetime to resist aggression from any quarter.

There was a swift riposte from Finance. Citing military experience — including analogies with aerial exercises of the Russian and German armies and Franco's ferrying of troops and stores from Morocco — it picked holes in the army's submission. It opined that aeroplane and submarine capacity was incapable of landing large numbers of fully equipped troops in Ireland and that even if they did the existing army should be capable of dealing with them. Ireland should forget about the possibility of an unprovoked attack by Britain. It repeated, however, the point worth debating that undue prominence had been given to the land forces at the expense of air defence. It repeated its suggestion that the scheme for the two Reinforced Brigades (reduced from four) be modified. In spite of that, the government on 30 January 1939 approved the proposed Establishments and sanctioned the defence expenditure. It had already expressed reservations about the erection of munitions factories.

Steps were taken immediately to put the proposed scheme into effect. Officers were dispatched forthwith to Britain to procure supplies, but it was too late. The British had their hands full trying to cope with their own demands. The sending of a senior army officer and a senior civil servant on a similar mission to the US likewise drew a blank.

The question of a munitions factory had been raised as far back as 1926 and 1928. In 1932 the Minister asked for (*a*) a cartridge factory, (*b*) a nitrocellulose plant and (*c*) a nitroglycerine plant. In 1934 the government agreed to the erection of a small arms factory and its operation by the Department of Defence. In 1937 a site was secured in Cullane, Co. Clare, and it was recommended that the project be placed in the hands of Imperial Chemical Industries. That recommendation was held up in Finance, and eventually in February 1939 Defence submitted it directly to the government. Finance then moved, advising that the project was uneconomic and should be abandoned. The government nonetheless adopted the defence recommendations on 14 February 1939, but by that time ICI concluded that it was too late owing to the heavy demands made on them by the British government. ICI indicated that if the project had been decided on six months earlier its completion would not have been affected by the outbreak of war.

Unhelpful also were politicians (with the outstanding exception of de Valera himself). The following selection of quotations provides an insight. 'There is no need for an army in this country' (Deputy Little 1930); 'Any movement designed to organise the young people this country in the use of arms seems to me a great disservice to this country (Deputy Dillon, March 1934); 'Our greatest security lies in having no army at all' (Deputy Anthony, March 1934). The following month he (Deputy Anthony) suggested reducing the army by one half and stated that we would 'still have an army for receiving distinguished visitors with all the necessary paraphernalia and equipped to assist the police in the event of serious civil disturbances'. Dillon added: 'Our country has a population and an area of such a kind as would make it absolutely unthinkable that we could defend this country in arms against invasion by any great power'.

In the debates on the 1936 Estimates he said that any Minister who sought to build an army designed to resist external aggression was an irresponsible fool and that the maintaining of a Volunteer Force was absurd. Deputy Esmonde stated that de Valera's pledge that Ireland would not be used as a base against Britain was worthless as 'the defence forces of this country were quite inadequate and quite incapable. . . .'

In the 1937 Estimates debates Dillon suggested that instead of training a Volunteer force of an infantry and artillery army we should train an 'immense number of pilots capable of operating aircraft to be obtained if the need arose'.

In 1938 Deputy O'Higgins considered that the defence of an island without a navy was a joke and that we should cooperate with Britain. Deputy Dillon said that Britain should pay us to secure her flank so that we could concentrate on aerial arms rather than land forces.

On 8 October 1939, when there was a debate on protection against air attack, Deputy O'Higgins said that 'that army was left without a lead and without a plan because there was no policy'. There was disappointment 'with the scandalous unpreparedness of the army to give either advice or protection to the people of this country'. The Minister for Defence (Frank Aiken) reminded the House that recently a request for £500,000 for the army had been opposed, with the suggestion that the army be abolished.

On 16 February 1939 Deputy O'Sullivan said that in modern war there is no neutrality and that 'the idea of an invasion of this country seems fantastic, absolutely fantastic. . . . If Germans land here, other people will land to wipe them out. . . . The main portion of the defence of the country is not going to be carried on by our military defence forces'.

De Valera had other ideas — the implementation of which demanded absolute dependence on the Defence Forces.

*Ga gascaed ar a ragham indiu,*[38] became very relevant once more.

# 6

## The Emergency
## (1939–45)

On 3 April 1939 Hitler directed his generals to prepare an attack on Poland ('Case White').[1] In the first twenty-four days of the following September the *Wehrmacht* crushed the deficient Polish army. On 3 September Britain and France declared war on Germany. The Dáil introduced emergency legislation. Anticipating an emergency the Volunteer Force had been reorganised the previous spring.

At 11.30 hours on the morning war was declared a British flying boat — a Saro Lerwick I, L 7252 — came down in Dun Laoghaire harbour. No complete explanation for the landing is to hand. Supplies were purchased from Malachy Doyle, a local shop frequented by visiting British crews. It took off at 13.55 hours and headed in a northerly direction. It reappeared in Skerries at 15.40 hours. There is no explanation as to where it was in the intervening period.

At 13.25 hours another RAF seaplane — L 2158, apparently from the same squadron — alighted at Skerries. The crew of four remained aboard while the Squadron Leader, M.C. Collins, came ashore by local boat. The Gardaí facilitated him with a few phone calls but there was no connection with his authorities in Stranraer. Col. P.A. Mulcahy entertained him to lunch in the Officers Mess, Collins Barracks.

Collins stated that he was forced down by stress of weather. He told the Guards that he was unaware that Britain had declared war on Germany and did not know where he was. Gossip in Dun Laoghaire insisted that the exercise was an experiment to ascertain the feasibility of accessing the ports. On instructions from the Department of Defence Squadron Leader Collins was permitted to leave, on the grounds that he was a distressed mariner. L 7252 took L 2158 in tow and both machines left in the direction of Stranraer at about 16.45 hours.

L 7252 was a medium-range smaller version of the Short Sunderland. It had only two engines and was unsuccessful, proving to be unstable both in the air and on the water. It was lost when it ditched in the sea off Pembroke Dock, Wales, on 24 March 1941 while flying with 209 Squadron. This bolsters Collins's weather stress story and casts doubt on Dun Laoghaire's dramatic interpretation of the incident.

On the outbreak of war the 1st and 2nd Reinforced Brigades were organised and mobilised but each was 30 per cent under strength. Five Garrison battalions were mobilised but these were variously between 270 and 590 under strength. None of the War Establishment's eight Rifle battalions had been organised. All units were under strength: many provided for had not been organised. The combat efficiency of the brigades, apart from deficiencies in equipment, was very low.

Strength on mobilisation was 19,136 all ranks: 7,600 Regulars; 4,300 A and B Reservists; 7,236 Volunteers — in all around 50 per cent of the War Establishment. Only four Bofors guns with 2,000 rounds of ammunition, four searchlights and a few other items had been delivered. Orders of £150,000 were outstanding from the British War Office.

Mobilisation overtaxed the understrength overstretched Regular cadre. It comprised five Regular Infantry battalions and representative corps and services units. The 1st Battalion in Galway (*An Chéad Cath*) was Irish-speaking, which gave it a unique élan. The other four battalions — the 2nd and 5th in Dublin, the 3rd (the Bloods)[2] in the Curragh and the 4th in Cork — had their own distinctive *esprit de corps*, and all took great pride in their dress and drills.

Frank Aiken's Volunteers soldiered enthusiastically side by side with Civil War veterans. In the mobilised 10th (*Uisneach*) Infantry Battalion the author and other Volunteers served cheerfully under their platoon commander, Lt ('Score-Card') Larry Clancy, the man alleged to have shot Liam Lynch. That brisk collective training soon received a sharp setback.

On 21 September Finance advised the government to inform Army HQ that the present situation did not constitute a war situation and that, for financial reasons, it was unlikely that they would consider maintaining on a permanent basis more than 18,000 men. 'Emergency Establishments October 1939' were drawn up accordingly.

The country was almost defenceless when the Second World War broke out. The Forces were inadequate and were neither trained nor equipped for war. Defence matters were not taken seriously. The small Permanent Force was constricted by limited Establishments: the purchase of arms and equipment had been restricted to an unviable minimum. Provision for adequate mobilisation stocks of arms and equipment had not been made. The available manpower of the country was not organised for defence.

The 1925 policy for expansion was unrealistic. As we have seen, it laid down that all ranks be trained to take over the duties of the next higher rank, but the low rates of pay militated against that.

Over the years various attempts to secure a general revision of pay rates had met with no success, though the financial position of officers and men was acknowledged to be unsatisfactory. On 2 June 1932 the Chief of Staff pointed out to the Minister that the highest paid Irish officer had a salary equivalence with a British Lieutenant Colonel. Officers got a slight lodging fuel-and-light allowance on 15 November 1930, which was immediately offset by corresponding rent increases and building costs.Enlisted men got nothing. This reflected their position in a society where unemployment was widespread and which saw no occasion to prepare for war.

The Polish lesson was not learned. Some units were demobilised. Exemptions were accelerated. Those not exempted were transferred to make up deficiencies in units retained with the Colours. The army nevertheless pressed for the completion of a War Establishment.

Finance came back with a call for substantial retrenchment and a modification of the War Establishment: it wanted one Reinforced Brigade entirely deleted, combat troops and garrison units reduced and consequential reductions in other branches. The Emergency Establishments of 20,000 were cut back to 15,000. That still did not go far enough for Finance, and in November 1939 it pressed for a reversion to the Peace Establishment. Defence contested this, and on 11 December 1939 the government decided to fix the War Establishment at 29,000 all ranks and to revise the Peace Establishment downward accordingly. The Emergency Establishment was to be based on minimum garrison troops, together with the cadres of two mobile brigades and a number of troops in training. Following a detailed examination (which looked critically at orders for equipment) it was hoped to reduce the Emergency Establishment below 15,530.

The IRA raid on the Magazine Fort in the Phoenix Park in December 1939 did not bring about any change of official attitudes to the army. By 1 January 1940 its strength was 2,600 down on its September mobilisation strength. A further reduction of that strength, 16,500 to 14,454 on 1 April 1940, was effected.

In April 1940 Norway was invaded and a critical phase in the war in Western Europe opened. But exemptions continued until 10 May, when the strength was 13,335. On that day the neutral Netherlands were invaded and the breakthrough at Sedan followed. The Germans reacted angrily when de Valera condemned their invasion of Belgium and Holland. In nine months the German Armed Forces had overrun Poland, Norway and Denmark and defeated the Dutch, Belgians, French and British, forcing the latter into a humiliating withdrawal from Dunkirk (May-June 1940). The English Channel saved Britain — and Ireland — from being overrun. Declarations of neutrality did not save Belgium and Holland.

Reservists of all categories were recalled to the Colours and intensive recruiting started. On 24 May 1940 a Local Security Force was initiated, under the wing of the Garda Síochána. Initially it was armed with shotguns and sporting weapons.

Finance fell silent. On 4 June the government approved a War Establishment of 40,000. A 'Call to Arms' saw political Civil War adversaries, de Valera and Cosgrave, sharing a common platform in College Green on 2 June 1940, appealing to the young men of Ireland to join the army. They did so in droves. Subversives were rejected. Unionist incapacity to make common cause was reckoned with.

On 5 June there was no debate when the Defence Forces (T.P.) No. 2 Bill 1940 was read a second time. Deputy Dillon made amends:

> I feel that we have failed to communicate to the public a true sense of the peril that hangs over this country at the present moment. If we have so failed, that failure is one for which we are all responsible. I want to say deliberately now that I believe this State is in immediate danger of invasion, which, I think, should be resisted by force with all the resources this State can command. I believe that if this country is to be protected from carnage of the most horrible kind we must resist that invasion with all the forces at our disposal.

When a Supplementary Vote came before the Dáil in February 1941 he said:

> I believe it is the essence of financial wisdom to provide whatever money may be necessary, however and wherever we can, to ensure that the defences of this country will be as adequate as we can make them to meet any contingency that may arise. It could be the height of folly to collect money for an invader to collect.

On the other hand he was the odd man out in not supporting the government's policy of neutrality. He favoured crusading for the Allies — something which was not in the national interest and which no other country did voluntarily. America did not enter the war until attacked by the Japanese at Pearl Harbour on 6 December 1941.

On 7 June 1940 the government declared that a state of emergency existed. The Defence Forces Act was amended to authorise the enlistment of personnel for the duration of the Emergency ('Durationists' or 'E-men').

Because of the demands of garrison and protective duties and the problems of training an inrush of recruits and organising new units, only a few columns of little more than company strength could now take the field as mobile units. There were no striking forces capable of offering organised resistance. That did not lead to any spirit of defeatism. On the contrary: memories were still fresh of the successful guerilla campaign against superior British Forces in 1919–21. Some indeed would have been more at home conducting such unconventional war.

But there was a serious shortage of armament, ammunition, and explosives. There were practically no anti-tank weapons. There was a shortage of revolvers and light automatic weapons, and some of the new units raised had to rely on obsolete rifles. Lack of accommodation, deficiencies in bedding and similar difficulties added to the problems presented by the sudden expansions.

In mid-May 1940 the existing Forces were reorganised as follows to prevent subversives collaborating with an enemy:

(*a*) Eleven 'Local Mobile Columns', each of rifle company strength.

(*b*) Three 'Command Reserve Columns', two of battalion strength, one at half battalion strength.

(*c*) One 'General Reserve Column' of one battalion.

That was the height of their capability at that time.

Following the climax in the war situation in May 1940 a decision was taken to increase the effectiveness of War Establishments. Twenty-three thousand were recruited inside four months: the following table reflects the rates of expansion after enlistment for the duration of the Emergency was thrown open on 5 June 1940:

| | *Date* | *Officers* | *NCOs* | *Ptes* | *Cadets* | *Total* |
|---|---|---|---|---|---|---|
| Permanent Service | 1.5.40 | 1,059 | 2,449 | 9,786 | 52 | 13,346 |
| Reserve | do | 197 | 397 | 7,540 | – | 8,134 |
| Total | do | 1,256 | 2,846 | 17,326 | 52 | 21,480 |
| Permanent Service | 31.5.40 | 1,095 | 2,560 | 13,267 | 73 | 16,995 |
| Reserve | do | 165 | 248 | 4,096 | – | 4,509 |
| Total | do | 1,260 | 2,808 | 17,363 | 73 | 21,504 |
| Permanent Service | 30.9.40 | 1,783 | 4,842 | 30,087 | 18 | 36,730 |
| Reserve | do | 49 | 25 | 506 | – | 580 |
| Total | do | 1,832 | 4,867 | 30,593 | 18 | 37,310 |

A difference between the numbers enrolled and those called was explained to some extent by unfavourable Garda reports. Also 2,249 Special Enlistments were effected for one Rifle battalion — the 26th (Old IRA) — and the Engineering units in the Second Line Volunteers. Deficiencies in warlike stores would not stop the War of Independence veterans from fighting for their country.

The Gardaí co-operated wholeheartedly, though they had to be 'disabused' (Gen. Costello's word) of the notion that their cordons could be reinforced by the military. Officering the new army First Line units was met partly through the commissioning of other ranks from the Volunteer Force but initially mainly by the granting of temporary commissions to civilians with previous military experience or with professional or technical qualifications.The Military College ran potential officers' courses. Some Corps, such as the Artillery, produced their own officers.

The two brigades were broken up and a brigade-strength all-arms striking force was provided for each of the four commands. Flexible organisation facilitated concentration. The brigades were subdivided into mobile columns of all arms capable of fighting on their own or co-operating with others as required; they were located at strategic points in each command area. With the exception of the Supply and Transport companies and Engineer units, who were short of drivers and tradesmen respectively, the brigades were fairly well up to strength. Bren gun carriers and armoured cars became available, and the following new units were also formed:

2 Armoured Squadrons
1 Bren Carrier Squadron
2 Cyclist Squadrons

The formation of a brigade in each command area necessitated the raising of thirteen Rifle battalions for garrison duties. Nine of these were to be converted into Infantry battalions to augment the striking forces. Their primary duty was internal security but they had a secondary function as reinforcement for brigade troops.

A scheme for the provision of Second Line units was also evolved. It embraced Rifle battalions, Engineer companies,

Transport companies, Ambulance convoys and Shore companies for the Marine Service. The 26th (Old IRA) Battalion was over strength. Some of its members had taken opposite sides in the Civil War but that was all set aside now. A Construction Corps was also formed for young unemployed unmarried men to undertake certain public works.

Combat training was keyed to producing instant reaction against any aggressor. Whoever made the first move against Ireland became automatically the enemy. Morale and discipline was good. Mobile columns, in co-operation with LSF covering forces, would immediately counter attack Co-operative exercises were practised against assumed enemy landings, including seaplane landings at places like the Shannon Estuary, Lough Ree, Lough Derg etc. Heavy casualties were expected.

St Bricín's and the Curragh Hospitals would be evacuated in the event of air attack. The disposal of Dublin casualties would be effected by means of an ARP scheme to the seven city clearing hospitals. Base hospitals were earmarked in Maynooth and Clongowes Wood College. Auxiliary hospitals were anticipated for Mallow, Ballinasloe and Dublin. Arrangements were made for the recruitment to the Second Line Reserve of twelve surgical teams, Class A and part-time surgical B teams.

The serious problem of providing adequate accommodation for troops, storage and garage facilities was tackled vigorously. Sufficient supplies of bedding and furniture remained scarce, but a big shortage of bed linen was rectified as hitherto withheld financial sanction was finally obtained.

The Forces now enjoyed overwhelming public support. One hundred thousand people turned out during August and September 1940 to see a spectacular Army Show, 'The Roll of the Drum', in the Theatre Royal ('ten soul-stirring scenes'). Gen. Hugo McNeill was its mentor. A clerical correspondent (*Irish Press* 28 August 1940) extolled the army salute: it was a relic of the sign of the Cross, he wrote: the way crusaders used to greet each other as friends. He condemned the fascist salute as a return to imperial Roman practice.

The large influx of recruits and the formation of many new units put a strain on unit administration. Wider powers were given to Command O/Cs and records were decentralised. A special Plans and Operations branch was formed ass part of the General Staff to prepare defensive plans. Dispositions and provision for prompt movement of reinforcements were made accordingly. Air defence and the provision of a Marine Service presented the knottiest problems for the planners. The Air Corps was poorly equipped. Sixteen Service aircraft were available:

| | *Serviceable* | *Unserviceable* |
|---|---|---|
| (*a*) *Fighters* | | |
| Gladiators | 3 | 1 |
| (*b*) *Army Co-operation* | | |
| Lysanders | 5 | 1 |
| (*c*) *Reconnaissance and Bombing* | | |
| Ansons | 6 | 3 |
| Walrus | 2 | 1 |

All these aircraft, except four Ansons at Rineanna, were stationed at Baldonnel. They were all obsolete, though the Gladiator was being used in the East against Italian aircraft and in the British Fleet Air Arm as a converted sea fighter. The remaining aircraft were fitted with armament for their own defence only. There were thirty-two (serviceable and unserviceable) training aircraft:

| | *Serviceable* | *Unserviceable* |
|---|---|---|
| Dragons | 1 | |
| Cadets | 4 | 1 |
| Magisters | 10 | 5 |
| 636 | 1 | 2 |
| 626 | 1 | 2 |
| Hinds | 1 | 5 |

With the exception of three Cadets at Rineanna all of these were also at Baldonnel. Spares were awaited for all the unserviceable machines.

All barracks and posts had perforce to provide their own ground defence against air attack. The small number of AA guns and searchlights remained concentrated for the defence of Dublin. The British Admiralty advised that the supply of Bofors guns ordered would not be delivered. Provision of a Marine Service was equally daunting. Port Control Establishments were set up at Dublin, Cork, Dundalk, Drogheda, Limerick, Waterford, Lough Swilly, Bantry Bay, Rosslare, Fenit, Sligo and Galway. Lough Swilly and Bantry Bay were operated by Military Officers. A Marine Inscription (Second Line Volunteer) was formed consisting of twelve companies of 100 each organised on a district basis to ensure that adequate small craft and personnel were available at all important centres around the coastline. They would assist in blocking channels in the case of invasion. To obstruct navigation channels leading into the Port of Dublin and Dun Laoghaire, vessels and barges would be sunk. Cranes would also be dismantled. This would be done by a special unit of the LDF organised from dock workers and working under the competent Port Authority. The same went for Dundalk, Drogheda and Arklow.

P.V. *Fort Rannoch* was converted to an armed trawler and fitted with a 12-pounder gun. 20 mm Madsen guns were fitted to three motor torpedo boats which were concentrated as a striking force at Haulbowline to attack any invading convoy. A limited number of mines were made in spite of the steel shortage, and arrangements were made to purchase more. The mine-planting vessel *Shark* would mine the entrances to harbours. One battery of 18-pounders was allocated for use against vessels attempting to force an entry into Dublin Harbour. The Coast Watching service functioned satisfactorily.[3] Emergency broadcasting and the destruction of wireless installations (e.g. Malin Head) was provided for.

On 21 September 1940 20,000 rifles were received from the US and a further 10,000 were awaited from the British War Office. There were now sufficient service rifles to meet permanent service requirements and 2,300 more were made available to the LDF. There were enough heavy machine-guns to meet Establishment requirements. The Defence Forces personified the will of the nation to persuade any would-be invader to think again. Down-to-earth work by the dedicated Defence Forces in good days and in bad days rather than political flourishes made that meaningful.

Establishments declined between July and December 1940 as the threat of invasion seemed to recede. Inadequate renumeration and the restricting of enlistment to unmarried men under thirty were factors. The Local Security (Garda) and Defence (Army) Forces provided an alternative outlet for the patriotically motivated. An increase in enlistments in March 1941 was attributable, apart from a renewal of press advertising, to an extension of age limits for single men of up to thirty-five years, and for married men who were qualified motor drivers of up to the age of forty-eight. Once a fortnight the Taoiseach exhorted young men to join up.

The provision of officers to administer and control units continued to present difficulties. Finance refused to agree to the commissioning of a selected number of Regular NCOs. Except for Artillery men, certain Corps and personnel with technical or professional qualifications, all potential officers did a short intensive course in the Military College before being drafted to units as commissioned officers. The number of trained Staff Officers available was limited to Regular Army personnel. Accelerated promotion was essential to meet needs. Equally crucial was the provision of non-commissioned officers, 'the backbone of the army'. Command O/Cs were authorised to promote up to and including the temporary rank of Sergeant. Without this expedient the formation of new units would not have been possible.

By the end of 1940 organisation and training had progressed sufficiently to permit the formation of four additional brigades, three initially, the fourth later. With the exception of anti-tank companies, for which equipment was not available, the original four brigades were practically up to full strength. Divisional staffs were now required for the tactical employment of groups of brigades. GHQ was organised into Forward and Rear Echelons. The organisation now provided for 50,000 men but for the present it was not proposed to exceed the 45,000 in service. Second Line Units, the Marine Service, and the Construction Corps continued to evolve. The former Group A of the Local Security Force became the Local Defence Force under the army. A Garda was appointed Administration Officer for each LDF district which were organised in self-contained unit groups. Emphasis was put on co-ordinated training and combat efficiency. Three battalions in each command were available with supporting artillery, other services and the Local Defence

Forces, to meet coastal or airborne landings. The high standard of training and physical fitness of these battalions greatly enhanced their combat efficiency and the organisation and development of the LDF increased striking power.

In a year combat efficiency had progressed from weak scattered defence by company (and in a few cases battalion) strength columns to defence by formations of all arms, capable of serious fighting, independently or in co-operation. That did not blind a realisation of fire power inferiority. There was still an almost complete absence of the most important weapons, anti-tank, anti-aircraft and automatic. There was a grave deficiency of artillery and mortars and practically no air force. Radio equipment was also seriously deficient. Steps were being taken to reduce the deficiency in transport. All this did not diminish the determination of *Óglaigh na hÉireann* to fight and die rather than surrender. 1916 had taught them how to die to some purpose. Only war itself could have accurately gauged the efficacy of that quality.

Two main plans of defence (involving the Local Defence Force) were prepared: one against a German invasion, one against a British. These were continually modified to meet changing situations. Areas were designated for bridge demolitions and roadblocks. Blockhouses and barriers were erected; open routes agreed. Special provision was made for the defence of aerodromes and harbours. All available anti-aircraft equipment continued to be disposed in the Dublin area. Blackout provisions were made. All this, however, was insufficient for proper air defence. The AA had been a Cinderella among Cinderellas.

In March 1928 four 3" 20-cwt AA guns (two 2-wheeled; two 4-wheeled) were received from England. In October 1929 Lt Maurice McCarthy (later Lt Col.), a founder-member of the Ack-Ack, went to Britain to undergo an Anti-Aircraft Artillery Course. In 1930 an AA Battery cadre was formed, and on 16 September 1931 the 1st AA Battery was established. In September 1938 it was moved from the Curragh (where it had been transferred in 1932) to Dublin to recruit and train a Volunteer Reserve (including officers), which it did very successfully.

In June 1939 four Mark I Bofors (Light AA) were delivered — again from England. They found their way in a cadre capacity to Cork and Limerick. (There were four light batteries but only four guns between them.) Eight searchlights and sound locators were taken over by the anti-aircraft from the Engineers in 1939.

Fourteen gun and searchlight sites were selected in March 1939. Of the eight 3.7" medium guns ordered in 1938 six were delivered in November 1940 (four mobile; two static) but without fire control instruments. The AA Battalion had been formed (from the AA Brigade) in June 1940. The Air Defence of Dublin then consisted of:

(*a*) Air Defence Command;
(*b*) Anti-aircraft Battalion of three Medium and one Light Batteries;
(*c*) Searchlight Battalion (very much under strength);
(*d*) Interceptor or Fighter aircraft from Baldonnel.

Between 31 May and 30 November 1940 guns were allocated to outposts as follows:

*3' 7" Medium*: Clontarf (two static); Ringsend (four mobile);
*3" Medium*: Booterstown (two semi-mobile); Ballyfermot (two mobile);
*40mm AA Bofors*: Baldonnel (two); Hibernian Schools (two) (Collinstown from March 1941);
*Searchlights/Sound Locators*: Howth Summit (one); North Bull (one); South Bull (one); Blackrock Park (one); Sandy-cove (one); Dalkey (one); (two mobile searchlights and sound locator unit units were held in reserve in Ballsbridge);
*12-pounder guns* for ground defence (Battery Commander Capt. R.N. Cooke): Collinstown (one); Hibernian Schools (one) (later Baldonnel); North Bull (one); Sandycove (one);
*6-pounders* (to replace 12-pounders): Hibernian Schools (two).

All these stations were connected by direct telephone line to the Gun Control Room at Air Defence Headquarters,

Eastern Sector in Dublin Castle. The standing orders in force until 1943 were to open fire with all AA guns and machine-guns on all unknown aircraft which were reasonable targets. Fire orders could only be given by the Gun Position Officers (GPOs).

When the Germans reached the French coast (June 1940) the British War Office was begged to complete delivery of the large quantities of equipment ordered, including sixteen 3.7" medium AA guns, sixty LAA Bofors guns, sixty-four searchlights/sound locators and five 12-pounder guns. Churchill was unmoved. On 31 January 1941 he memoed the Dominions Secretary.

> About arms. If we were assured that it was Southern Ireland's intention to enter the war we would, of course, if possible beforehand, share our anti-aircraft weapons with them. . . . Until we are so satisfied we do not wish them to have further arms and certainly would not give them ourselves. . . . Juridically we have never recognised that Southern Ireland is an independent sovereign State and she herself has repudiated Dominion status. Her international status is undefined and anomalous. (*The Second World War,* Vol. III *The Grand Alliance,* London 1950.)

The following November, however, ten 3.7" medium guns (six static, four mobile) and two 40 mm Bofors guns were quietly delivered. The next month a further two 6" guns arrived for the defence of the Shannon Estuary at Tarbert. Ack-Ack initiatives overcame all repository difficulties.

Alerts — sometimes up to three at half-hourly intervals — were a nightly occurrence for AA gun crews. In 1942, probably influenced by the capture of Crete (May 1941) and the surrender of Singapore (February 1942), a redeployment took place to locations in Brackenstown, Brownsbarn, Rineanna and Fort Westmoreland, Spike Island for the defences of airfields and of Cork Harbour. Brackenstown Post took Swords LDF on board and formed close associations with the ground staff in Baldonnel. The LDF at Ringsend and Ballyfermot also integrated well.

The following number of live rounds were fired at intruding aircraft: forty-four 3.7"; forty-four 3"; 217 40 mm and 1,583 .303 (see Epilogue). In 1943 ten of those rounds were fired at a Flying Fortress which flew over Dublin. It landed and after refuelling outside Dublin went on its way again.

Later standing orders were amended. From mid-1943 only a Division or Brigade Commander could authorise the opening of fire against aircraft engaged in bombing or machine-gunning. The last gun position fire control shoot against a German aircraft was on 31 May 1941, the night of the North Strand bombing.

In the spring of 1941 the AA was one of the many units whose training programmes were disrupted by having to assist in the mass slaughter and disposal of beasts affected by a serious outbreak of foot and mouth disease.[4] The disruption did not impair the combat will of this underequipped front-line unit.

Its observational role was supplemented by eighty-nine Coastal Look-Out Posts (LOPs) which were erected on prominent heads around the coast from Inishowen Head in Donegal to Dunany Point in Co. Louth. These did valuable work. Reports on aircraft, shipping and submarines were sent to the local military commander, except in the case of the east coast where messages were sent direct to Air Defence Command in Dublin Castle.

Unscheduled benefits flowed from the introduction of the Coast Watch. In 1940 there had been practically no phones in Leitrim or Mayo. The speedy laying of forty miles of land lines by the Army Signal Corps paved the way for the installation of the first telephone in Belmullet, much to the relief of León Ó Broin, 'Governor' of Connaught. He was one of the Regional Commissioners designated to ensure that the essential functions of government would be carried on in the event of invasion. County commissioners were appointed for the county areas. The military authorities would take over complete control in a number of areas, and the county commissioner would be subject to them. In areas not taken over by the military authorities he would co-operate to the full with them. The importance of unified control and co-ordination at all levels was stressed. Particularism was frowned on.

A more tangible economic bonus was the rubber salvage operation tutored by Comdt Owen Quinn. In 1942 as a result of the war in the Far East and the Allies' stockpiling for the invasion of Europe the supply of rubber was cut off. Rules governing the receivers of wrecks had to be waived, as in the national interest the Coast Watchers kept Dunlops in production with salvaged rubber — 500 tons in one year, almost double the requirements. Once launched the scheme ran itself. The national interest motivated all. The beach-combers got paid, of course, and could also get bicycle tyres and tubes from Dundalk.

The Military had the power. An authorised officer could prohibit, where military requirements demanded, the felling of trees (or even the removal of branches) which were not roadside trees. But it was co-operation that mattered. And in the Mayo telephone installation the co-operation between the Post Office linesmen and the army was most productive. That was the spirit of the times.

Units made do with the weapons they had. Self-reliance was the watchword, 'do it yourself' the motto.

The Great Southern Railway company undertook the manufacture of grenades and an order for 50,000 was placed. A workshop was set up in the Magazine Fort to fill them with explosive. One hundred thousand Molotov Cocktails were issued in barrels to all Commands. Five thousand four hundred anti-tank mines were manufactured by the Corps of Engineers and also issued to Commands. Petrol substitutes were sought. Turf replaced coal. Buildings were renovated. There was, however, a shortage of tentage. Marine vessels were fitted with 12-pounders, Vickers, 20 mm Madsen and Lewis guns. One hundred and six marine mines were manufactured, fifty-two by GSR and fifty-four by Thompson of Carlow. Thirty-seven were filled with high explosive in the Ordnance Corps.

As far back as 1933 Frank Aiken saw no reason why even tanks could not be built at home but Louis Warnant, agent of *Landwerk*, a Swedish firm, was more persuasive. The Department, however, so delayed a second order for a complete squadron of *Landwerk* armoured cars that the German invasion of Denmark prevented delivery. Near panic now set in at this deficiency in armoured cars, with rampageous Germany almost on the doorstep at the French coast.

The inventive Col. J.V. Lawless,[5] having endured many undeserved frustrations, was now grudgingly given his head to design and produce a suitable armoured car. The British at the time had no suitable modern model. GHQ also set up a board of its own to produce one in conjunction with the GSR workers in Inchicore. Lawless approached Thompsons. They were not enthusiastic to begin with. They already had a contract from GHQ for sea mines for harbour defences but the work became so tied up with red tape that there was neither profit nor satisfaction in it.

They were the only ones who held a stock of half-inch steel plate at the time. Lawless eventually persuaded them, and on 10 August 1940 they produced the first vehicle for £200. This compared favourably with the rival GHQ Board's own flawed production costing £600.

Invasion looked imminent and Lawless was instructed to make every effort to acquire plate (then in short supply) to get a full squadron (seventeen) of these new-type cars as soon as possible. Frantic searches were made for steel plate, ranging from inspection of Railway Works at Dublin and Dundalk and the Dublin Dockyard to ship salvage in Donegal by Hammond Lane Foundry. Strangely enough, the Department of Defence refused a request from Industry and Commerce to give Mr Thompson shipping priority for about fifty tons of such plate which he had lying on the quayside in Montreal awaiting cargo space on Irish-bound ships. It took until 1941 to build the full squadron. (Col. Lawless was responsible in 1956 for the re-engining of the *Landwerk* and Leyland armoured cars which gave these cars a new lease of life.[6] He also designed and had built in Cavalry workshops the handy hand-drawn mortar cart).

There was plenty of use for the armoured cars. Churchill was bellicose. Hitler mused that possession of Ireland would help end the war. There was no telling what the IRA would do next. For the Defence Forces the preoccupation was not who the enemy was likely to be but getting combat ready to meet whoever it might be. Buying time to prepare for war was the first essential.

On 3 April 1939 *Abwehr* agent Oscar C. Pfaus sought to establish contact between German Intelligence and the IRA.[7] On 28 March 1940 Ribbentrop appointed his *coup d'état* specialist, Veesenmayer, to foment rebellion in Ireland. In May 1940 a radio link between Germany and the IRA broke down and Nazi agent Dr Herman Goertz was parachuted into Ireland 'to find an Irish quisling'.[8] He had on him a proclamation purporting to suborn the Irish army. By reason of its militant action against England the IRA was regarded as Germany's natural ally.

From 1940 the IRA had been planning something of a major operation on the following lines:

(*a*) a rising on a large scale;
(*b*) extensive gun-running;
(*c*) the support of a foreign power (Germany) including
  (*i*) invasion by parachute;
  (*ii*) landing of troop-carrying aircraft;
  (*iii*) aerial attacks.

To meet this threat in 1940 urgent steps were taken to put designated units on a war footing. Warlike stores costing £1 million were purchased for this specific purpose.

Vessenmayer's idea was to give the Irish a chance to prove themselves and then to give them all they wanted.[9] He could not see why de Valera should not join them in a common front. The initiative, however, had to come from the Irish themselves. The Germans could guide it through men like Sean Russell and Frank Ryan, then living in Germany. Operation Sealion,[10] the German plan to invade England, provided a golden opportunity.

Hitler ordered his preparations to be made for a landing in force in England. His 6th Army prepared for landings in Lyme Bay (southern England), together with simulated landings in Southern Ireland, by five or six divisions from the French Atlantic coast (Operation Green — Landung Irland).[11] Hempel, the German Minister, was to put a flower pot in the window of his legation to signal that Sealion was on its way and that the time for the rising had come. Vessenmayer's man to promote the rising, Sean Russell, died in a German submarine off Galway in August 1940.[12] The

Battle of Britain (September 1940), in which the RAF defeated the *Luftwaffe*, called a halt to Sealion, but did not put a stop to the German threats to Ireland.

Hitler's Chief of Staff was convinced — in spite of activities on eastern border of Germany — that Hitler would invade the British Isles if he could, between 1 July and 12 October 1940. On a separate axis Gen. Student, Commander of the German 11 Airborne Corps, strongly recommended to Hitler a diversionary air attack on Northern Ireland. The author outlined the plan in *An Cosantóir* as follows:[13]

> He {Student] had a force larger than that used for the later invasion of Crete (May 1941) at his disposal: 20,000 paratroops and 12,000 airborne (glider) troops. Using what he called the 'ink and blotting paper' method he would first secure and then expand his base in the triangle between the Northern half of Lough Neagh and the Divis mountains. Strong formations of paratroops were to be dropped at dawn, capturing by sudden attack without prior bombing, the important airfields of Aldergrove, Langford Lodge and Nutts Corner as well as Divis mountains. Simultaneously there would be a drop on Lisburn to destroy aircraft and to cut the railway and road junction in that area. Large numbers of dummies would be dropped in the Mourne and Sperrin mountains. 3" and 4" diameter 'waistcoat pocket' guns with special anti-tank ammunition and a range of up to 7½ miles and new rocket batteries (range 2,200 yards) would increase combat power. From Brittany specially selected aircraft would fly in in daylight to use the captured airfields. If this operation (Viking Raid) failed they would withdraw into Eire and be disarmed there. Hitler counted on Eire's favourable attitude to possible trespass and on her eventual indirect and silent assistance. If a landing had to be made in Eire he had felt that from psychological point of view that the 25th anniversary of the 1916 Rising would be the best time for it. If Eire showed active hostility, so be it. They were ready for any eventuality.

Prior to the war the Department of War Maps and Surveys in Berlin produced detailed military geographical data on Ireland. It was an impressive terrain study marred by silly social comment. Hitler however was making a big mistake in thinking that Eire would stand idly by while the North was being invaded. De Valera — though dubbed 'a Casiabianca of the Protocol' for his condolences on the death of Hitler — did not think twice about dispatching fire brigades from Dublin to help out during the blitz on Belfast (April 1941).

In 1941–42 the international situation remained grave. The spreading of the war to Russia in June 1941 probably lessened the likelihood of an invasion from Germany. But Veesenmayer had not given up hopes of 'fomenting rebellion' and the insertion of agents continued. On the other hand, the entry of America into the war on 6 December 1941 complicated the Irish position *vis-à-vis* the Allies. Also, Japanese involvement curtailed the supply of raw material and further worsened Ireland's precarious supply position. Training, organisation etc. had to be conducted on the basis that the neutrality of the State might be violated at any moment by either belligerent and that the army must be in a constant state of readiness. Fifteen AA men and one Engineer officer killed in a training exercise in the Glen of Imaal on 16 September 1941 reflected the price of attaining such combat readiness.

The strength of the Defence Forces on permanent service on 31 March 1942 (excluding the Construction Corps) was 38,787 all ranks, a decrease of 957 during the year. Recruiting had been poor in spite of the Taoiseach's urgings. The number of officers and men exempted from permanent service or on indefinite leave rose from 857 on 1 April 1941 to 1,733 on 31 March 1942. There were several reasons to explain the low level of recruiting:

(*a*) Low pay: if a soldier married he would have to support his wife on two shillings a day.

(*b*) Exclusion of married men except for certain special services.

(*c*) Plenty of jobs and good money in England.

(*d*) Feeling that danger of invasion had passed. This replaced the patriotic impulse of June 1940.

(*e*) Increase in rural employment due to turf-cutting and tillage.

(*f*) Belief that available arms were insufficient to equip a larger army. The acquisition during 1941–42 of eight 75 mm guns, four Mark II 18-pounders and four Mark I 3.7" AA guns did not alter this impression. It took until March 1942 to decide on the pneumatisation of 3.7" guns.

Wastage during the year amounted to 7,232, including 1,062 deserters (subsequently apprehended) and 368 men discharged for the purpose of being commissioned. There was a weeding-out as follows:

| | |
|---|---|
| Medically unfit | 2,434 |
| Unlikely to become efficient | 117 |
| Services no longer required | 435 |
| | 2,986 |

Older men were placed in administrative posts, leaving the younger men in the field units. The trimmed-down army was far more capable of undertaking prolonged operations than it had been. The Military College was a dynamo of efficiency and stringent standards were set for officers. A small number of Regular NCOs were commissioned as Quartermasters but Finance remained adamant in refusing to sanction the opening up of this desirable source of officer material.

The formation of two divisions and three additional brigades made more apparent the acute shortage of trained staff officers. Field Officers' courses attempted to bridge the gap. Promotion was the spur. The rapid expansion of the army in 1940 and the commissioning of nearly 900 officers left a large number of companies being commanded by 2nd lieutenants and commandants' appointments held by junior officers. This position had greatly impıoved. Much progress was also made in NCO training.

Following the formation of three new brigades it was possible to organise two divisions: the First (Thunderbolt) Division under Major Gen. M.J. Costello in the south and the Second (Spearhead) Division under Major Gen. Hugo McNeill in the north. Divisional staffs concentrated on the training of the divisions as effective Field Forces. The four commands undertook all garrison duties, training of recruits, the organisation of the LDF and the administration of the Construction Corps and the Marine Service. To complete the new brigades and divisions it was necessary to form the following new technical and supply units:

2 Divisional Staffs
3 Brigade Staffs
3 Motor Squadrons, Cavalry Corps
4 Field Companies, Corps of Engineers
4 Field Companies, Signal Corps
3 Field Companies, Supply and Transport Service
1 Field Forces Company, Supply and Transport Service
1 Field Ambulance, Medical Service
4 Field Companies, Military Police Service
4 FA Batteries, Artillery Corps
1 12-Pounder Battery, Artillery Corps
1 Armoured Squadron, Cavalry Corps
6 Cyclist Squadrons, Cavalry Corps
1 Civil Defence Firefighting Company, Corps of Engineers
1 Hospital Company, Medical Service.

Provision was also made for the formation of the Artillery units of an eighth brigade.

Forward and Rear Echelons were firmed-up in all GHQ branches. Provision was made for the appointment of a GOC Field Forces, who would form Field Forces HQ on active service while the Rear Echelon, under the Assistant Chief of Staff, would remain at the Department of Defence. With the exception of certain types of artillery and automatic weapons the seven brigades were practically fully equipped. Organisations were adjusted relative to available equipment. New Second Line units, mainly Hospital companies, Surgical Teams and Ambulance Convoys, were organised. The Marine Service was expanded by the formation of a number of Second Line Shore Companies. LDF battalions, while retaining organisational elasticity, were organised into army-type units coming under Divisional operational control. Five such battalions were organised in Dublin, two in Cork, and one each in Waterford, Limerick and Galway. Anti-aircraft, Field Artillery, Supply and Transport, Engineer, Signal and Medical units were also provided for. In Dublin two Area staffs under Senior Military Officers were set up. The Construction Corps was reorganised into five battalions; two in the Curragh and one in each of the other commands.

Training, however, was adversely affected by the following factors:

(*a*) Rapid expansion in 1940 necessitated posting officers and NCOs with a minimum of training.

(*b*) A proportion of the best officers and NCOs were detached to train the LDF.

(*c*) Cattle burying, turf and timber-cutting and carriage interrupted basic and field training.

(*d*) Continuous running in each Command of Potential Officers' and NCO courses.

(*e*) Conversion of a number of Rifle battalions to Infantry battalions.

(*f*) Formation of two divisions and a new brigade. Recently formed units had to be sub-divided or had to provide cadres at the same time as these units were undergoing field training.

The First Division with headquarters in Cork had three brigades:

1st Brigade: HQ Clonmel: 10th, 13th, and 21st Battalions;
3rd Brigade: HQ Cork: 4th, 19th and 31st Battalions;
7th Brigade: HQ Limerick: 9th, 12th, and 15th Battalions.

The Second Division, whose headquarters were initially in John's Road, Dublin, and then in Maynooth, also had three brigades:

2nd Brigade: HQ Dublin: 2nd, 5th, and 11th Battalions (C Company *Gaelgóirí* of the 11th had provided a large pool of potential officers);
4th Brigade: HQ Mullingar: 6th, 8th, and 20th Battalions;
6th Brigade: HQ Dublin: 7th, 18th and 22nd Battalions (the 22nd subsumed the Regiment of Pearse and also produced many potential officers).

Each brigade had a Field Artillery Regiment, (seven new regiments, including seven anti-tank batteries, were formed); an

Engineer and a Signal Field Company; a Field Ambulance and a Field Company each of Supply and Transport and Military Police; all numbered after their brigade.

In addition there were two independent brigades and three Garrison battalions (14th in Dublin, 17th in Donegal and 24th in the Curragh). The independent brigades were:

5th Brigade: HQ Curragh: 3rd, 16th and 25th Battalions;
8th Brigade: HQ Rineanna: (not fully formed) 1st and 23rd Battalions plus a field artillery battery for operations.

In GHQ a Plans and Operations branch was set up which, with G1 (Training) and G2 (Intelligence), came directly under the Chief of Staff. A Directorate of Cavalry was also set up.

Hard work and attention to detail had raised the fighting efficiency of the Defence Forces to provide a striking force capable of taking the field at any time. De Valera's reassurance to the British that their flank was secure (as well as implying a caution to them) had now more credibility. Defence plans had still to be based on the assumption that the country might be attacked either by the British or by the Germans. In the latter case this would call for a demonstration of a capability to provide a holding and covering force pending the arrival of reinforcements from the North.

The British factor had to be examined at two levels. In January 1938 their Chiefs of Staff recommended waiving,[14] on the grounds that it might politically embarrass de Valera, a complete assurance from Ireland of the availability of the ports and the adequacy of their defences. By the end of 1940 reasoning was less cogent. The British Chiefs of Staff felt that it was imperative to base their naval and air forces in Ireland for two reasons: in defence of their trade and in defence of Irish territory — both vital to their existence.[15] If the Irish, Churchill prodded,[16] withdrew the various cable and watching facilities they had, what would that amount to, observing that they could suspend all connections with England. Although it was not within their province the Chiefs of Staff Committee were of the opinion that the risk of applying economic measures should be accepted. If they were to meet with opposition from Irish elements in driving out the Germans their task would be greatly increased. After capturing the ports it would take about ten divisions to establish a measure of control over the greater part of the country. It was a 'Catch 22' situation for them.

By 8 March 1941 the Committee (Dudley Pound, C.F.A. Portal, R.H. Haining VCIGS) no longer stipulated that they should install defences and provide further forces to protect Irish bases. They reckoned that an invasion of Ireland by the Germans might be attempted by means of an expedition carried in ocean-going vessels, either from French ports or from Norway. Alternatively, the invasion might be attempted as a diversion during an invasion of Britain. If the Germans succeeded in establishing and maintaining themselves in Ireland it would create a mortal threat to both British trade and her west coast ports. The presence there of British naval and air forces would in their opinion be a strong deterrent to an invasion of 'Eire' and, if an invasion were attempted, would make more probable its defeat on arrival. On that reasoning they put forward their requirements as follows:

*Naval*

(*a*) to base light craft in the Shannon and Lough Swilly in order to increase the density of our naval escorts.

(*b*) to base heavy ships in the Shannon to counter any operations against our Atlantic trade by enemy surface forces working from the Biscay ports, and as a deterrent against an invasion of Eire.

(*c*) to install AA and underwater defences and moorings in the Shannon and Lough Swilly.

*Air*

(*a*) to operate reconnaissance and bomber forces from defended bases in Western Eire, where there is much less fog, in order to extend the range of our air reconnaissance and to afford protection to convoys and against invasion.

(*b*) to establish fighters defences for our base in the Shannon, and to base fighters in South-East and Eastern Eire to cover the St George's Channel and the Irish Sea and our own West coast ports, and against the threat of an invasion of Eire.

(*c*) to establish an air defence organisation around the South and East coasts of Eire, in order to enable our fighters to operate with full efficiency.

If the Irish authorities granted these facilities they saw the security of their Atlantic trade as being immensely increased, 'Éire' being reasonably free from invasion and the air defences of their own west ports improved. It might then prove possible to reopen the south-western approaches to ocean trade. The possible effect of US intervention intrigued them, but they kept those cards close to their chest when dealing with de Valera.

In their view the fall of France and the occupation of Norway were incalculable factors rendering null and void the original (1938) appreciation. Those events had given rise to a completely unforeseeable situation. They saw their vital security in home waters as being gravely threatened by their inability to make use of the Irish bases. They would use force if necessary to redress that position. A firm base for their proposition would have been consideration of the indivisible defence of the island against a German invasion. Historic opacity clouded this issue. Also to be reckoned with was a deep-rooted desire in Dublin to spare its defenceless country from the horrors of war. Again, historic attitudes did not help understandings. Then de Valera played his cards.

In '*An Cosantóir*' the author summed up the situation as follows:[17]

> De Valera decided that war was too serious a business to be left in the hands of dilettanti. He delegated total discretion in military matters to Gen. Dan McKenna. McKenna's vocabulary was military. His counterpart in the North at one stage was Gen. Sir Harold E. Franklyn. He had handled the operations around Arras, leading to the evacuation from Dunkirk.
>
> He commanded 8 Corps deployed on the South coast of England to meet the German threat there from July 1940 to May 1941. When the threat of German invasion shifted to Ireland he was appointed GOC Northern Ireland. In 1943 he was appointed Commander-in-Chief Home

Forces. He understood soldiers' language. He and McKenna respected one another as good soldiers.

With the arrival of Cork-born Franklyn in Northern Ireland, hostile snide references to Eire in Orders dealing with the German threat from the South dropped out. Peremptory orders to simply 'Secure Dublin, Baldonnel and Collinstown' gave way to orders demanding mission analysis involving liaison; e.g. to 'Ensure the security of Dublin etc.'

The sortie into Lough Swilly by 61 Division with its sequential skip to Rineanna Aerodrome was put into abeyance. Franklyn's exercises (Exercise 'Bismark') deferred to the Irish susceptibility that they must be seen to take the first 'brunt of attack'. Whether, in a life or death situation, the dogs of war would have dutifully jumped on cue through such face-saving hoops is another matter.

Franklyn's sane soldier approach did not, however, altogether eliminate the Allied threat arising from the German threat. Maffey, the United Kingdom Representative, made mischief out of the presence of Goertz on the loose. Gray, the American Minister, remained a loaded loose cannon at permanent half-cock. The 'Disneyland' *Abwehr* and the IRA played into their hands. The proliferation of competing Nazi organisations created confusion beyond belief. Veesenmayer, the *coup d'état* specialist specially appointed by Ribbentrop to foment rebellion in Ireland, told me some fantastic stories. If only Canaris had not sung every single thing to the British, he ruminated ruefully. Col. Dan Bryan remarked, 'they were going to bring ships where you could not get a row boat'. Veesenmayer's conversations with the Irish Minister in Spain left him believing that 'England's difficulty was Ireland's opportunity'. De Valera's stated policy was to show 'a certain consideration for Britain'. The emphasis — not generally made — was on the 'certain'.

But that 'certain' was not certain enough for the British and the flow of reasoning from their estimates of the situation reinforced their fears.

Northern Ireland expected to be attacked in any of the following ways: by sea and/or air landings without an invasion of Eire; by sea and/or air landings in conjunction with an invasion of Eire (thought to be more probable) or by land from Eire. Any of these operations might be undertaken as a main operation or, more probably, as a diversion in association with an invasion of England. The objectives would probably be the capture of Belfast and Derry and adjacent airfields. It was reckoned that the invading force would embark either at Baltic ports (three divisions), or at Norwegian ports (three divisions), or from French ports south of and including Brest (five divisions). The latter would be the more likely area to be used for the forces to invade Eire. The probability was that part of the force would be sunk or dispersed by naval/air action. Other forms of attack envisaged were employment of one airborne division (8,000 troops) against Eire or Northern Ireland or both which would capture landing places and together with the IRA sabotage and harass: sea plane landings on inland loughs and air bombardment of industrial areas, military HQs or centres of communications. The most likely point for an invasion by sea in Northern Ireland was estimated to be Magilligan beaches.

However, to achieve the greatest measure of surprise and concentration the shortest sea and air routes were likely to be used, while diversions in the Shetlands, Ireland or North of Scotland could not be disregarded. The most favourable area of attack was the area in which fighters and bombers could operate in conjunction and the seaborne expedition could cross under cover of darkness. For this reason the subsidiary or diversionary attack on Ireland would not be of the same intensity as the main attack on England.

Due to the long line of sea communications a direct seaborne attack on Northern Ireland was unlikely. An attack via Eire was obviously the more likely. This contingency gave birth to the controversial 'W' Plan which spawned a sequence of Operation Orders for crossing the border from Northern Ireland into Eire to deal with developments there. They estimated that the Irish army troops were mobile but not numerous enough or sufficiently well equipped to deal unaided with the scale of sea and air landings envisaged: five or more divisions sea-borne, of which at least one was likely to be armoured and one motorised; one airborne division (8,000 men) and some light tanks. Landings were also expected in loughs and in the mouth of the River Shannon.

Initially those Orders took their tone from Churchill's threat to use 'weapons of coercion' to reoccupy the twenty-six counties. He did not agree with the softly-softly approach to Eire and wanted the screws on de Valera tightened steadily. That threat derived directly from the German threat. A dilemma for us was that 'whoever came first is our enemy'. The trouble in December 1940 was that they both nearly came together. The Potential Officers' Course in Kildare at the time (of which I was a member) was literally commissioned in the field, on 19 December 1940. We spent the first night as officers staring into the Curragh sky waiting for German parachutists to arrive.

The Germans were hell-bent on reinforcing their Legation in Dublin. De Valera was equally determined that they wouldn't be allowed to. The rumours were that 'they' got as far as the skies over Rineanna. At the same time our troops on the border had their attentions directed Northwards. The 53 (Welsh) Division in the North was assembled to cross the border on receipt of the codeword 'Hunt' to deal with the German threat in the South.

De Valera had adroitly circumvented Hempel's urgings of Ribbentrop's tempting offer (at Hitler's instigation) of British weapons captured at Dunkirk. Unpredictable hazards remained from unorthodox flirtation with Goertz.

McKenna did things his way. He introduced Franklyn to the Taoiseach. From that day on in the summer of 1941 things changed very considerably. Relationships became more businesslike. Such matters as determining routes for movement and evacuation of refugees from Dublin in the event of heavy hostile bombing were agreed between Irish, Air Raid Precautions (ARP) and British staff officers in Northern Ireland (BTNI). British plans now reflected rather than preempted. Dire shortages of equipment were matters of concern affecting both sides in varying degrees.

In the Irish Army the delivery of twelve more home-produced armoured cars completed the equipping of three Armoured Squadrons.[18] Fixed defences of aerodromes and harbours were strengthened. Twelve extra anti-aircraft guns materialised and mines were got for the harbours. The 6" guns for the defence of Shannon Estuary came by boat. Extensive preparations were made for the blocking of channels and the demolition of docks and port facilities. Blocking off of a large number of areas was provided for.Every detail was prepared in advance and all units and sub-units down to the smallest LDF section knew exactly what to do. The issue of a short simple order by the GOC Field Forces would produce the necessary action. They had come a long way since 1940, let alone 1916. The armament they had was being put to its best use. There was still a deficiency in signal equipment but thirteen Hawker Hectors were received from the British for the Air Corps. Negotiations were opened with the British Air Ministry to purchase three Hurricanes, a Fairey Battle, a Hudson, and a Miles Master which had landed in Ireland and had received a certain amount of damage. Following the report of the Committee of Enquiry into the Air Corps it was decided to radically alter its Establishment. The Reconnaissance and Medium Bomber squadrons were abolished. Two fighter squadrons were provided for: one was actually formed and a cadre was set up for the second. A maintenance unit and a small salvage section were also provided for. A scheme for training sergeant pilots was introduced.

At another level the provision of bands and buglers was attended to. Twenty-five battalions and the Marine Depot at Haulbowline had unit bands. Morale was good, and the rate of desertion which remained high in 1941 decreased in 1942–3. The apathetic civil population, however, was little awake to the besetting danger and was disinclined to share the burden of defence. The paucity of recruiting was a worry. To compensate for that the combat efficiency of the LDF greatly increased, especially in urban areas where collective training was possible.

German aircraft dropped bombs causing casualties and damage to property on Campile, Co. Wexford, (one dead), Borris, Co. Carlow (three dead), the South Circular Road, Dublin (twenty-four injured) and the North Strand, Dublin (twenty dead, 154 injured). Bombs were also dropped in Malin, Co. Donegal. The number of crashes of belligerent aircraft on Irish soil indicated the closeness of the theatre of war. One hundred and sixty-three came down on land; the figure goes up to over 200 if crashes in the adjacent sea are included.[19] Ireland flanked the sea approaches to Great Britain from the south west and the north west. The occupation of the French coast rendered related routes critical.

The Irish government was not insensitive to that situation. While understanding was never more than of eggshell fragility, in March 1941 a verbal agreement between Dublin and the Dominions Office permitted British planes to fly over the neck of territory in the vicinity of Ballyshannon. After Franklyn liaison improved. It did not need any liaison for Dublin to feel spontaneous outrage at the bombing of Belfast.

The German threat induced closer contact. The British prepared information on the German army for the Irish army. Liaison was achieved by use of (*a*) the so-called No. 18 Mission and (*b*) Irish army officers. A named Irish liaison officer was appointed.[20]

Northern Ireland itself was not ready for war.[21] It had hitherto been a training area. Franklyn and McKenna had corresponding difficulties. Apart from understrength units and lack of warlike stores they both had historic sensitive political situations to handle.

McKenna deduced from the blitz that Belfast was as defenceless as Dublin. It underlined their common problems. The skies were the most indivisible area against a common foe. But the everpresent threat of a German landing in Munster had also to be faced up to. What could the Irish army do about that? The British needed to know.

In August 1941 Franklyn toured Ireland as McKenna's guest. In the autumn of 1942 the Blackwater manoeuvres took place.

The 1942 manoeuvres tested the combat efficiency of the army at all levels. The following is a sequence of the principal events:

| | |
|---|---|
| 17 August | Second Division commenced its march from Dublin and the Midlands to the South. |
| September | |
| 1–3 | First exercise: attack on the line of the Blackwater from the northern bank. |
| 6–7 | Second exercise: attack on the line of the Blackwater from the southern bank. |
| 10 | Third exercise; attack on assumed invasion bridgeheads, east and west of Cork Harbour. |
| 13 | Parade of two Divisions, Southern Command troops and Cork City LDF in Cork. |
| 16 | Second Division commenced return march to Dublin. |
| 19–20 | Fourth exercise: Cavalry v. LDF in Co. Wicklow. |
| 26 | Fifth exercise: Attack on Dublin by Second Division. |
| 27 | Parade in Dublin of Second Division, Eastern Command troops and Dublin LDF Units. |

The principal exercise area in the south was the country roughly between Killavullen and Cappoquin, in Co. Waterford. This had been estimated to be a possible German landing place, and the arrival of British reinforcements to help Ireland counter such a landing could be anticipated. Under no circumstances would it be contemplated that the supreme command of the combined military would be placed under a British military general. A naval or air force commander would be marginally less unacceptable but if the boot were on the other foot and Britain were the enemy, a German supreme commander would be unthinkable. The exercises now planned were primarily designed to convince the British of an Irish capability to cover and hold in the event of a German invasion. British observers were present.

The following units took part: the First Division; the Second Division less the 6th Brigade (which was 'minding the house' in Dublin); three Armoured Squadrons; the

Bren Carrier Squadron; eight Cyclist Squadrons; Air Corps Components. For the third exercise in the south troops of the Southern Command and the LDF in Cork City were employed. In the final exercise the 6th Brigade and the LDF participated. One officer and three other ranks were drowned during the Blackwater river crossing. The following points emerged from the exercises:

(*a*) Two complete divisions were for the first time maintained and exercised in the field. They proved to be effective fighting formations marching over long distances with full equipment. All administration was carried out in the field, including provision of full postal services, auxiliary medical facilities and other exercise incidentals. Payment of troops in the field on a large scale for the first time worked satisfactorily.

(*b*) Manoeuvres were carried out in attack and defence.

(*c*) Valuable experience of supply in the field was gained during the concentration marches. This involved the echeloning of supplies and switching to different supply areas to keep pace with the troops. On the whole the advanced supply depots supplied the divisions satisfactorily. However, considerable delays occurred at times in feeding the troops. Due to an insufficiency of motor transport ammunition supply was not practised. The following year's exercise were devoted to this aspect, with the 5th Brigade attacking the 13th and 21st Battalions, two cyclist, two armoured and one motor squadrons.

(*d*) A very high standard of stamina and physical fitness in all ranks, together with a cheerful disregard of prolonged discomfort.

(*e*) Lack of appreciation by the Infantry of Artillery capabilities and limitations, and of the necessity for a co-ordinated fire plan.

(*f*) Necessity to reorganise the Infantry platoon and to provide an Artillery Command organic to the brigade.

(*g*) The necessity for battle drill and battle inoculation. The British provided facilities for this. In the toughest training carried out since its establishment the army proved that it was now an effective and mobile field force, whose further training must be of an advanced and intensely practical nature. A considerable quantity of blank, small-arms and artillery ammunition and pyrotechnics were manufactured for the exercise.

Armament continued to improve. The most important items received during 1942–43 were:

20 4.5" howitzers and trailers
4 3.7" Anti-Aircraft guns
99 Thompson sub-machine guns
6 Anti-Tank guns (2-pounder)
2 40 mm Bofors Anti-Aircraft guns.

Considerable quantities of spare parts for machine guns, light automatics and rifles were also received. The British were not sorry to hand over two 60-pounders which were not fitted with pneumatic tyres. GHQ did not see this as a serious drawback as they had slotted them in a stationery position for coast defence. Irish army gunners, under Capt. Micky Buckley and Battery Sergeant Joe Carroll, fired the museum pieces in the Glen of Imaal.

Still awaited were:

50 3" mortars
2 6" Coast guns
6 4.7" Coast guns
6 60-pounder Field guns
12 6" howitzers.

The provision of officers remained a problem. In view of the poor recruiting figures it was expected that the number of men suitable for training as officers would decrease. The 1942 cadetship examination was confined to persons serving in the Defence Forces at the beginning of that year. Temporary officers were invited to sit for open competitive examination for the Regular Army. If successful, they would be awarded Cadetships. This would require resignation of their temporary commissions.[22] Considerable progress was made in the provision of staff officers but much remained to be done in the training of specialist Intelligence Officers.

Towards the end of 1942, when the results of the autumn exercises were analysed, the following changes in the higher commands were made: O/C Air Corps; Director of Artillery; Director of Signals; Director of LDF; Military Director of Civil Defence; Chiefs of Staff of both Divisions; O/Cs of four brigades; Commandant of the Military College. The new office of Director of Cavalry, Chief Staff Officer Plans and Operations and the vacancy left by the retiring Adjutant General were also filled.

According to the Letter of Instruction No. 30/31/7/42, the object of the exercises had been 'to provide an opportunity for high Commanders to command their troops in the field and to give them practice in co-ordinating the team work of the different components of their commands'. They were also designed to test tactical and technical training, physical fitness and morale and administrative capabilities under severe conditions. The painstaking work of organising, equipping and training over the previous two years had made possible the holding of such exercises. Criticism of defects was merciless: remedial action was swift and unsentimental. There was evidence of good staff work and good leadership but much remained to be done. A high standard obtained throughout the exercises. The following shortcomings, however, were brought to light and heads rolled accordingly.

(*a*) In some instances orders were issued in a haphazard fashion and lacked precision. A reserve company was ordered to cross the Blackwater river but given no mission. Orders were countermanded too frequently.

(*b*) Fieldcraft and reconnaissances were not always carried out with due regard to active service conditions.

(*c*) Control and anti-aircraft discipline during halts was not of a high standard. MT movements, entailing trucking and detrucking, were of an uneven standard.

(*d*) Digging of slit trenches for protection was inadequate.

(*e*) Minor tactics were neglected.

(*f*) Too often co-ordination ceased once an attack was launched. Fire co-ordination fell down.

(*g*) Mortars and anti-tank rifles (often sited conspicuously on roads) were not always employed to the best advantage.

(*h*) There was bunching by some units during river crossings.

(*i*) The need for improvement in Artillery and Infantry co-operation was one of the outstanding lessons.

(*j*) Minefields were not always properly laid. In few cases bridges were not blown. But the Engineers of the Second Division were highly praised for their expert bridge building.

(*k*) The breaking of Cavalry into small groups dispersed it out of brigade control and rendered it ineffective. Cyclist squadrons were not always suitably employed.

(*l*) Intelligence plans were over-elaborate and did not always provide relevant information of the enemy. There were frequent delays in ciphering.

(*m*) Aircraft should have been given specific missions. Aircraft reconnaissance was generally satisfactory though aircraft were not always employed to the best advantage.

The exercises marked the most important milestone in the expansion of the army and the formation of Second Line services and the LDF. Nevertheless by the spring of 1943 combat efficiency was greatly compromised by the fact that all units were greatly under strength. The immediate formation of a Third Division was called for to implement defence plans.

The view then held was that Ireland occupied a position of such strategic importance in regard to Great Britain, to the Continent of Europe and to the Atlantic that an attack on this country by the Axis Powers remained a constant danger. The course taken by the war in Europe only altered matters to the extent that a few days' notice could now be expected. An attack by Great Britain or the US was now considered to be unlikely, but so long as these Powers were unable to overcome the submarine menace to their Atlantic shipping a change might occur at any time.

However, during the period from 1 April 1943 to 31 March 1944 the likelihood of an invasion by either belligerent appeared remote. The Axis was bogged down in Russia (though this did not stop unco-ordinated insertion of compromising agents, presumably still in pursuit of Ribbentrop's instruction to Veesenmayer 'to foment rebellion' and to spy). The Allies at last seemed to have mastered the submarine menace to their Atlantic shipping. Tension was raised nevertheless by the delivery of the 'American Note' to the government — an ultimatum, de Valera called it — demanding the expulsion of the remaining Axis diplomatic staffs. The army hoped that this threat would jerk the public out of its apathy and benefit recruiting. The following table illustrates the decline in strength (all ranks):

| *Date* | *Permanent Service Total* | *Regular Army Component* |
|---|---|---|
| 31.3.43 | 38,394 | 6,644 |
| 31.4.44 | 36,211 | 6,035 |
| 31.3.45 | 32,115 | 5,981 |

The number of officers and men exempted or on indefinite leave increased: recruiting inexorably deteriorated.

Some changes in Establishments were made but no major modification in the general organisation took place in the period, except the implementation of the new platoon organisation. No. 4 Internment Camp staff were established, and a field section added. Garrison Company, Signal Corps and the Detention Barracks Staff, Tintown, Curragh were transferred to No. 1 Garrison Company, Military Police. The Rineanna detachment from the Air Corps Company (Signals), and the Pigeon Service (Signals) were removed from the Establishments. As numbers decreased the focus on individual units sharpened. GHQ inspections were dreaded, as high standards of efficiency were demanded — and achieved.[23]

The Eighth Brigade (though not complete) took shape and assumed responsibility for its mission. The formation of the seven new Artillery regiments was completed (though without further supplies of anti-tank guns being received; these batteries remained as skeleton cadres). The new establishment of the Air Corps became operative. Inter-battalion rifle, light automatic and machine-gun shooting competitions were inaugurated and took on an almost religious significance, such was the pressure. Inter-unit competitions, also, were contested with combat fervour. The result of the supply exercise carried out in the area between Carrick-on-Suir and Dungarvan in 1943 showed up shortcomings, and Corps courses for senior officers were conducted. Battle drill and battle inoculation became routine. More solid soldiering then ever before was carried out.

The School of Cookery established early in 1943 brought about a great improvement in the food, though vegetables were scarce, the butter ration was reduced and supplies of bacon were very limited. Bread baked with a new, more refined flour proved very popular with the troops.

Most of the men had now been serving for four years and the low pay, the discomforts of spartan training, the irksome unavoidable guard duties, cattle burying, turf-cutting, long periods under canvas, public apathy, the feeling that he danger of invasion had passed, all took their toll. Yet the army's loyalty was so dependable and unquestioning that it went unnoticed and was taken for granted by all classes and creeds. The sense of absolute discipline, calm confidence and stoic steadiness shown during the 'American Note' crisis (1944), when the country was rocked with rumours and alarms, was impressive.

Coming up to the invasion of Europe on 5 June 1944 Churchill became more hectoring. He worried that the German 'ambassador' in Dublin 'would send a wireless warning of zero though it was the last he was able to send'.

Irish intelligence exercised stringent surveillance in the Allied interests, but the life or death 'Second Front' hung on threads and no chances could be taken. The slightest risk voided security.

On 32 March 1945 the strength on permanent service was 32,115, a decrease of 4,096 during the intervening year. The Regular Army was down to 5,981. Range practices had to be fitted in with turf-cutting. Uncertainty regarding demobilisation affected training plans. But, subject to the serious drawback that all units were gravely under strength, the army was better trained and more capable of efficient active service than at any time since the beginning of the Emergency. Field Artillery regiments were long enough formed to be able to carry out their technical and tactical training as units or grouped for co-ordinated fire concentrations. In effect a divisional artillery fire power capability was fashioned.

Mines still drifted on the coast and and an intriguing instruction from Major Vivion de Valera, issued on 12 March

1945, stated that they were then to be disposed of in accordance with the procedure in force before the instruction was issued for their salvage.

The war was drawing to a close. It was time to demobilise, look to peacetime, and learning the lessons, to plan for the future defence of the country, against internal subversion and external aggression.

During the Emergency, de Valera had moved ruthlessly against the IRA. Six hundred men were interned in military custody; three were allowed to die on hunger strike and six were executed by firing squad. An indication of the proximity of the external threat was the high number of air crashes. Allied aircraft were repaired and removed, or else purchased by the Department. Allied internees, too, were released in 1943; none of the German internees were released before their time. There were in the region of 270 internees altogether.

Ships were stationed in Irish waters for air-sea rescue. In August 1944 there were 165,000 next-of-kin Irish addresses in the British Forces. There was no obstacle to the free movement of labour to Britain. Food supplies, mainly beef, were fed freely to her. Seven of her oil tankers impounded at the outbreak of war were released.

Communiques concerning submarine sightings were for British consumption. The air corridor over Donegal was a big advantage to the Allies. Crucial weather forecasting was funnelled daily to London. Notwithstanding all this no one doubted Maffey when he said (September 1939) that if the recently vacated Irish ports became vital Britain would seize them. Partition was a factor, but, as de Valera tried to tell Gray in April 1940, it was not a bargaining matter.

The Defence Forces forced them all to count the gains and losses of invasion. The State owes its existence to the Forces. It was a closer run thing than dry recounting can convey. The people will never realise the huge debt they owe to *Óglaigh na hÉireann* in general and to Gen. Dan McKenna in particular. For the Defence Forces it was a time of iron discipline and hard graft soldiering. They had no illusions about their strength, and made the most of what they had. The 1916 *Óglaigh na hÉireann* spirit permeated.

By 15 May 1945 emergency orders were revoked. Military courts, press, postal, telegraph and wireless censorship, registration of foreign residents, and emergency censorship of films were terminated. But the Special Criminal Court which was set up by statute before the Emergency was not affected. Air and Marine Intelligence vacated (with misgivings) Dublin Castle on 21 January 1945, and control establishments were closed down.

Irish neutrality was pragmatic, not doctrinaire. It was a badge of independence, a mark of sovereignty. *Óglaigh na hÉireann* had manned successfully the *bearna baoil* (gap of danger).

# 7

## Post-War Periods
### (1946–69)

The dismantling of the Emergency army gathered its own momentum: finding some suitable Force to replace it turned out it be a more sluggish exercise. The effects of the failure to solve that problem were felt most acutely later on when troops went on active service, first to the Congo in 1960 and later to the border in 1969. 1960 was a turning point, introducing UN peacekeeping service abroad in combat situations; 1969 saw a spillover at home of the troubles in Northern Ireland.

Unfruitful repetitious representations were made year after year to remedy organisational and equipment deficiencies arising from an absence of realistic mission analysis by the civil authorities. Gratuities (Regulars excluded) eased demobilisation. The transition, however, was painful enough for young men who had joined up from school and had got married in a 'Sam Browne'. Exams for the limited entry into the Civil Service cushioned that blow for some. Otherwise rehabilitation was not organised. Recruiting had been stopped on 23 November 1944 for Durationists, Marine Service and Maritime Inscription (Second Line). Infantry battalions were revamped to make do with two rifle companies instead of three: paper Establishments remained unchanged. Seven cyclist squadrons and one armoured car squadron were completely disbanded. The LDF was draining away towards the end of the Emergency. It had reached its peak (106,034) in June 1943. Thereafter it steadily declined, losing more than 80,000 in over two years. This fall was due to the discharge without replacements of non-effective members. A dedicated few kept it going.

The Regular Army was feeling the pinch even more. The perennial paucity of recruits was more critical than ever.

Conscription or some acceptable alternative was mooted. The fact that a small inadequately trained and inadequately equipped army had deterred invasion once did not guarantee a similar immunity in a future, possibly nuclear, war. The Nagasaki and Hiroshima atomic bombs of 1945 had opened a new era.

The United Nations was formed in 1946 — from the victorious Powers initially — to save mankind from totally destroying itself. But the precedents for peacekeeping were not encouraging. The UN superseded the old toothless League of Nations where de Valera in debate had made his presence felt. The result was that if we in Ireland did not provide adequate forces to protect our country, other Powers, for their own security, must do so. The question was how were we to go about it. The pre-Emergency Regular Army with its unattractive conditions of pay and service and crippling guard and garrison duties was not a full role model. In this uncertainty restructuring started off on a wrong foot. The Defence Forces seemed set fair for a becalmed spell in the doldrums.

On 12 February 1945 the government approved an improbable Establishment of 12,500 for the Permanent Force without relating it to any war organisation. A scheme to flesh out even that PDF Establishment misfired. On 25 July provision was made to transfer to the PDF non-regulars on permanent service who had a medical grading of not less than A3 within the age limits of thirty for NCOs and twenty-eight for privates. The following inducements to transfer were offered: (*a*) an extra bounty on top of the gratuity, and deferred pay (*b*) Emergency service to be treated as reckonable service for pension purposes and (*c*) special enlistment leave of four weeks with full pay and allowances, in addition to pre-demobilisation leave of up to three weeks also with full pay and allowances plus free travelling vouchers. The 'E' men were not to be enticed. Apart from anything else, they were disillusioned with the second-class status their rough-cut bulls-wool uniform and poor pay had brought them. This contrasted sharply with the treatment accorded to smartly uniformed free-spending US and British soldiers. At the same time, newspapers disconcertingly reported that eligible recruits were flocking to Belfast at the rate of 350 a month to join the British army.

There was also a disappointing response to efforts to recruit men to the First Line Reserve. Employers were not favourably disposed to granting leave for annual training. There was no national plan.

On 1 November 1945 an Interview Board set about selecting additional officers for the Permanent Force and the First Line Reserve from Volunteer and Emergency officers who were still serving. Three hundred and thirty one officers were kept on in the Permanent Force and 477 on the Reserve. Retentions in the Regular Army in ranks up to Commandant fitted uneasily into a newly enforced seniority system. The influx gave rise to the so-called 'Emergency Hump' which effectively blocked off promotion.

In 1942 Routine Orders invited temporary officers to make a career in the Regular Army. Passing an open competitive examination and successfully completing a course in the Cadet School were prerequisites. At the end of the Emergency, however, that scheme was abruptly set aside and temporary officers who had acquired accelerated promotions in a different league during the Emergency were retained in their ranks without having to revert to Cadet. Rigid insistence on priority for seniority compounded the baffling anomalies thus created. There was no other promotional incentive but a sense of vocation ensured that there was no diminution in dedication or application. That was what being married to the army meant, almost like being in a religious order.

The first stage of demobilisation was fixed to commence on 1 November 1945, the second to follow in January 1946, with the third commencing on 1 September 1946 and concluding on 31 October following, to fit in with the government's intention to revoke the Military Emergency Order with effect from 1 September 1946.

The principal units and formations disbanded were:

2 Division Headquarters Staffs
4 Brigade Headquarters Staffs
4 Infantry Battalions
Anti-Aircraft Battalion, Artillery Corps

2 Supply Companies Supply and Transport Corps
A number of smaller units were also disbanded.

Draft Peace Establishments were then approved. The proportion of senior officers was reduced. It was submitted that the ranks provided for many appointments were too low. There was an acute shortage of senior NCOs.

There were no longer any civilian prisoners or internees in military custody. Military discipline remained steady. Five officers were court-martialled (thirty-six were dealt with summarily) compared with thirteen courts-martial and 101 summary trials in the previous year. Absence without leave was the main other ranks offence. This arose mainly in the Construction Corps and recruits absconding from the Depot in the Curragh:

The following premises were handed back:

| | |
|---|---|
| *Eastern Command* | |
| International Hotel, Bray | 1.4.46 |
| Killarney Wood House | 1.4.46 |
| Ballyfermot | 6.4.46 |
| Santry Court | 20.5.46 |
| St Mobhís Hospital | 31.7.46 |
| *Southern Command* | |
| Rineanna Aerodrome | 10.5.46 |
| *Western Command* | |
| Church Street Hall, Longford | 20.5.46 |
| St Enda's Hospital, Galway | 16.9.46 |

Married quarters were reoccupied. Things were getting back to normal. The exciting times of the Emergency were forgotten and slipping back into the old pre-war rut seemed inevitable.

Disbanding and amalgamation went on over a period of two years (up to 31 March 1947). The face of the Forces changed. Nevertheless during that time they managed to help out, giving assistance with the bad harvest of 1946 and the prolonged freeze-up of 1947.

The Army was still divided into three Commands, Eastern, Southern and Western, plus the Curragh Training Camp.

With the exception of the Curragh Camp, Kildare, Naas Barracks, and the Glen of Imaal, the area administered by the former Curragh Command during the Emergency was now included in the Eastern Command area. Adjustments were made in the boundaries of the Southern and Western Commands (DFR GS4 14/11/46). The Curragh Training Camp had the status of a Command with the primary function of administering, supervising and co-ordinating the principal army training establishments. Training Schools, the Military College, the General Training Depot, Corps and Service Schools (Artillery in Kildare) were centralised there.

The Corps consisted of Air (Baldonnel), Artillery (Kildare), Signal, Army Ordnance, Engineers, Supply and Transport, Medical, Military Police (all Curragh). There were also the Equitation School, (McKee Barracks), the Army School of Music, Portobello (Cathal Brugha) Barracks and the Military Directorate of Civil Defence (GHQ). All Forts, less Westmoreland and Dunree, were evacuated and caretakers appointed. Life was breathed back into '*An Cosantóir*' (the Army Defence Journal, successor to *An tÓglach*, still run by Intelligence Section) after a post-Emergency drop in circulation.

The Air Corps had to deal with the recurring drain of highly skilled technicians to better paid civilian posts. The Naval Service got a new lease of life under its new Director, ex-RN Captain Jerome (1940–56). Personnel were trained in the Marine Depot to take over three new corvettes, and twelve Naval cadets were recruited.

A number of proposals designed to make the Construction Corps more relevant were made. In March 1948, however, it was decided to discontinue it. One Works Company was retained for those who wished to finish their original engagements. Educational training was reintroduced, without, inexplicably, provision for a Directorate. Organisational tables were tidied up. The mortar platoon was incorporated in the Support Company (formerly the Machine Gun Company) of an Infantry battalion; the number of Field Artillery Batteries in the Regiment was reduced from three to two; the Ordnance Research and Production Plant was closed down; a Supply Section with cadre functions was incorporated in Garrison S & T Companies; the Depot, Military Police

Corps was disbanded; the Naval Service was reorganised to provide for a Depot, a nucleus cadre for a flotilla of six motor torpedo boats and complements for six corvettes; the Military College was reorganised into a Command and Staff School, an Infantry School, a Cadet School, a Potential Officers' Wing and a College Administrative Company; the General Training Depot was reorganised into Headquarters, Administrative Section, Recruits Training Section, School of Cookery, School of Physical Culture, 'A' and 'Q' Training Section.

Personnel profiles changed. The reintroduction of age limits, suspended during the Emergency, resulted in the retirement of ninety-seven Regular and fifty Reserve officers.

Four hundred and sixty one temporary officers, fifty-one officers of the General Reserve and 136 Volunteer Force officers were disposed of either by retirement or resignation. Two hundred and forty five old Regular NCOs were found unsuitable for further service and given six months' notice. The strength of the Permanent Force on 31 March 1947 was 8,803 (all ranks), a deficiency of 4,057 from permitted Peace Establishments. The all-ranks strength of the first Line Reserve (which had absorbed Classes A and B and the Volunteer Force) was 5,758, the lowest since 1929. This represented a deficiency of 31,123 all ranks in hypothetical War Establishments, in spite of a pick-up in recruiting following an overdue improvement in conditions of service. Improvements were introduced as regards weekend leave, late passes, civilian attire, reveille and routines, slacks and shoes, duty hours of married personnel, turf-cutting, unnecessary guards and duties, educational and vocational training and a walking out uniform (the 'New Look').

However, a considerable number of short-term and long-term improvements recommended on 14 February 1946 were not implemented, e.g. renovation of barrack rooms, canteens, recreation rooms, provision of married quarters etc. The absence of career planning and limitations on promotion were further handicaps to recruiting. Pay had a long way to go.

On 1 October 1946 army officers after being admittedly underpaid for over twenty years, received an increase in pay backdated to 1 September. In accordance with a submission made on 4 March 1944 — two and a half years earlier —

these increases were designed to bring their pay to the level of other State services, then based on a cost of living figure of 185. A month later the pay of the Civil Service and the Garda Síochána was increased on the basis of a cost of living figure of 270! Thus other State servants, who were already better paid than army officers, were now given a much bigger increase. Officers wondered where they stood or what value was being put on their services to the State.

Demobilisation had denuded the Forces, leaving the country defenceless even though the international situation continued to be tense. In 1947 ideologies divided the world into two hostile camps. All Powers were determined to remain militarily as strong as possible and budgeted for the raising, maintaining and equipping of their fighting forces. Making allowances for developments in atomic and biological warfare, the requirement for up-to-date standardised armament and equipment for the Defence Forces remained urgent. Tactics, techniques and training would have to keep pace. Irish officers on courses abroad gave value for money in this respect. On one course an Irish officer had the distinction of being the only student to achieve the award of 'Distinguished', the highest rating obtainable. The expertise was brought back to professionally restructure the Forces — in thinking, anyway.

The organisation of the Permanent Force and of the *Fórsa Cosanta Áitiúil* had been decided on but higher direction was still awaited on the vitally important question of the First Line Reserve. It was proposed to convert the Maritime Inscription into a First Line Reserve of the Naval Service: organisation and equipment tables for Infantry, Artillery, Engineer and Signal components of the Infantry Division were drawn up. The full scope and span of the Second Line Reserve remained unclarified.

To capitalise on the Emergency experience, *An Fórsa Cosanta Áitiúil* (FCA) replaced the LDF which had been established under the Emergency Powers Order and ceased to exist with effect from 31 March 1946. The FCA was organised into twenty-four territorial areas with ninety-nine battalions and six other formations: an officer of the Permanent Force was in charge in each area. Battalions with geographical labels replaced Groups, e.g. The Collinstown District LDF, which had comprised Swords, Balbriggan and Ashbourne Groups, became the North Co. Dublin Battalion. In Dublin and Cork cities, where the LDF has been organised since 1941, the new FCA retained existing LDF titles, e.g. 41st, 42nd, 43rd, 44th (Dublin) Battalions. Artillery, Cavalry, Engineer, Transport, Signal and Field Ambulance units made the transition to FCA status without change of title. FCA men now had to take an oath and sign on for five years. The officers were commissioned into the Second Line Reserve.

Command was not clear cut by Regular Army standards. The new units were commanded by FCA officers and were grouped into 'areas' as the LDF units had been. The Area Officer was from the PDF but his only command was his cadre, which meant he had no control of cash, transport, rations or clothing. He reported to a Command Staff Officer FCA who was similarly powerless. Training policies and directions were transmitted from him via the Area Officers to the Training Officer. Monitoring and reporting followed this chain of communication. But the FCA unit commanders determined the level of activity and were vested with the powers of Commanding Officer while their troops were up on full-time training. Unlike the Corps units, who worked hand in glove with their parent units and attained high standards, rifle battalions tended to lose contact with the Regulars.

In order to survive, the main concern of each battalion was to maintain an effective strength of 150 in order to qualify for the annual grant-in-aid. The end product was the emergence of independent formations of roughly company strength. They were armed with the Mark 3 Lee Enfield .303 rifle, bayonet, Mills 36 grenade and grenade discharger. Training standards were uneven: PDF battle drills were inapplicable due to a complete absence of automatic weapons. With the relentless run-down of the PDF, however, there was no getting away from the integral importance of the FCA in fashioning credible Defence Forces to meet the needs of the day.

During 1947–48 the international situation saw a worsening of the 'Cold War' between the two main protagonists, America and Russia. Civil war broke out in Greece and only Gen. Clay's leadership and the breathtaking expertise and daring of air crews in the Berlin Airlift of 1948 averted open hostilities. Unrest in Turkey and Czechoslovakia compelled the formation of a military alliance between Great Britain, France, the Netherlands, Belgium and Luxemburg. Geography insisted that this was of direct interest to Ireland. The new alliance could muster twenty-five divisions against the USSR's 200. Russia also had air superiority two to three times greater than the US. The breakdown of time and space had created a global village and iconoclastic isolationism was an ostrich-like luxury no longer realistically on offer to the extent that the island of Ireland could blandly ignore what was happening elsewhere in the world.

GHQ again broached conscription. All the Western European States, with the exception of the defeated countries, had it. The proposal made recalled that on 31 March 1936 the strength of the Defence Forces was: Permanent Force 5,764; 'A' & 'B' Reserves 5,610; making a total of 11,374 all ranks. The supplemental strength of the Volunteer Force at that time was 10,420 all ranks. The difference between the Volunteer Force and the then FCA was that Volunteer Officers had to do at least six months' whole-time training, the NCOs three months', and the bulk of the Volunteers fourteen to twenty-eight days. Even that had not been considered satisfactory, and at the beginning of 1939 the Volunteer Force scheme introduced three months' initial training.

On 7 February 1948 the US Chief of Staff reported that one isolated action might precipitate a conflict and quickly involve nations whose sole desire was for peace. GHQ proposed that our defence policy should be based on the realities of our situation in Western Europe and on an assumption that we would remain neutral in the next war. Our vital strategic position astride the communication and supply routes linking Great Britain and the Western European Powers with the US had to be appreciated. We could be asked to make our ports and airfields available to these Powers and, in the event of our not providing forces to secure them, be requested to permit foreign troops to do so. We would have to co-operate or fight to maintain our neutrality. That took the topic out of the debating society. In spite of an unfriendly regime in Northern Ireland — to which Ireland's being in or out of the Commonwealth made no difference — a measure of co-operation with British and American Forces had been quietly achieved from 1941 onwards. The political will to provide a proper professional Defence Force was essential.

A new government (the First Coalition) came into power in 1948. It would have to either confirm the April 1946 defence policy or formulate a new one. The declaration of a Republic in 1949 made no material difference to that policy.

A defence plan could not be prepared without a knowledge of the organisation, composition and equipment of the Forces to be raised. War Establishments on which Peace Establishments should be based could not be drawn up without this information. On 31 March 1948 the total strength of the Permanent Force was 8,539, representing a deficiency on Peace Establishments of 305 officers, 1,430 NCOs and 2,852 privates. Finance laid down a limitation whereby the number of privates actually in service regulated the number of NCOs permitted. The strength of the First Line Reserve was 5,781. Its expansion was given up, since as no units were organised no establishments were prepared for it.

The position was one of gross unpreparedness. For the first time since 1928 there was no intake of Cadets to the Military College. Eventually in April 1948 twenty-six Cadets were selected, leaving a 74 per cent deficiency for 1947–8. The written examination was discarded in favour of possession of the Leaving Certificate. The quality of candidates presenting themselves was alleged to be not up to pre-Emergency standard. Seventy-six recruits were posted to the 1st Infantry Battalion (Irish-speaking) — an improvement on the miserable immediate post-Emergency responses.

The 1946 Peace Establishment had left the army broadly organised as follows:

*Infantry Corps*: Nine battalions grouped in three brigades of three battalions each (because of low strengths one rifle company in each battalion was not organised).

Generally each combat Corps had a Directorate in Dublin and a Depot and School in the Curragh area (Artillery in Kildare) and in addition:

*Artillery Corps* : three Field Artillery (FA) Regiments, four Fixed Anti-Aircraft Regimental Cadre HQ and Coast Defence Units in each of the Southern and Western Commands.

*Cavalry Corps*: One Armoured and three Motor Squadrons (as it was equipped with obsolete armoured cars it was not organised or trained on a similar basis to British armoured car units).

*Signal Corps*: Three Field Companies, three Garrison Companies and an Air Defence Company (detached to Air Corps).

*Corps of Engineers*: Three Field Companies, four Maintenance Companies, and a Survey Company (detached to Ordnance Survey in the Phoenix Park. See Epilogue).

*Ordnance Corps*: Depot, School Workshops and Stores at Clancy Barracks, Dublin; four Garrison Companies.

*Supply and Transport Corps*: Base workshops in Clancy Barracks, Dublin; three Field Companies and three Garrison Companies.

*Army Medical Corps*: Depot in Curragh; Three Field Ambulance and four Hospital Companies serving Military Hospitals in Dublin (St. Bricíns), Curragh, Cork and Athlone; No 2 Hospital Company (St Bricín's) included a Base Laboratory, Dental Workshops, and Base Depot Medical Stores.

*Military Police Corps*: Three Field Companies; four Garrison Companies and Civil Detention Barrack Staffs; one in the Curragh, the other in Athlone.

*Army School of Music*: Headquarters in Portobello (Cathal Brugha) Barracks where No. 1 Army Band was stationed: No. 2 Army Band in Cork, No. 3 in the Curragh and No. 4 in Athlone. Eight pipe bands were formed.

*Air Corps*: Headquarters, Depot, Schools, Maintenance Unit in Baldonnel with a Fighter Squadron in Gormanstown.

*Naval Service*: Depot in Haulbowline; Corvette Complements (three-ship establishment) and a Motor Torpedo Boat Flotilla; *Sluagh Muiri* (Naval Reserve) four or five Shore Companies.

(The Air Corps and the Naval Service were given the status of separate Commands directly under Army Headquarters.)

*The Army School of Equitation*: McKee Barracks, Dublin.

*Army Nursing Service*: for the first time, on 31 December 1947, age limits became operative.

Because of the shortage of officers and particularly NCOs it was not practicable to organise fully the FCA battalions on an establishment basis. In order to preserve the historical continuity of the 26th Battalion and the 5th Engineer Field Company, eligible members were permitted to continue service in the Second Line of the 26th Battalion LDF: ninety were subsequently appointed to the FCA. Those units stood down in December 1945 and their Colours were handed over for safe keeping to the Army. The Pearse Battalion in Dublin was reorganised with the FCA to cater for the National and Dublin Universities, Royal College of Surgeons and for the senior classes in some Dublin schools and colleges. Demobilisation was wound up: 42,244 gratuity forms had been completed. An impression prevailed of cleaning away dead wood and making a fresh start.

The following naval vessels were sold: *Muirchú*; *Fort Rannoch*; *The Yawl*; *Noray*; three launches, *Faith*, *Shiela* and one belonging to the *Muirchú*; nine ships' lifeboats, and one pulling boat. Four motor torpedo boats were boarded. Horse transport vehicles were retained for barrack duties only. Arcadia Hall, Skerries and Linen Hall were handed back to their owners in November 1945. In 1949 The Hibernian Schools were handed over to the Department of Health for use as a sanatorium.

The army wanted Griffith Barracks back from the Board of Works; the Medical Officer would not recommend the occupation of the huts in Gormanston during the winter months, and the shortage of married quarters for officers, NCOs and men continued to present a serious problem. There was a shortage too of barrack services, particularly in single bedsteads and steel wardrobes. There was also a shortage of forage caps. The disbandment of the youthful Construction Corps in 1948 meant that there was a large quantity of smaller sizes in stock. Finance advised that that someway of enlarging the headgear be found.

But the food got better. Mutton was added to the ration for issue once a week. As against that, soldiers had to go back to turf-cutting. And just as training was progressing the Defence Forces had to provide a passenger-carrying service during a bus strike, as well as giving assistance with the Shannon flooding and aid to the Gardaí.

Civil Defence, whether we stayed neutral or were forced into belligerency, remained a vital element of Irish defence, and a lack of passive measures worried planners. It was unlikely that the air raid shelters, which in the last war were not erected until the most dangerous phase was over, would provide effective protection. By 31 March 1948 nothing much had happened. Units and Establishments were very much under strength despite Gen. McKenna's vigorous protests. Doctrine was still kept up to date by the determined efforts of officers returning from courses abroad.

Gen. McKenna never let up in trenchantly exposing the following problem areas and demanding remedial action: First Line Reserve: re-equipment; technician provision; Second Line Reserve: training, particularly of officers and NCOs; the erection of local halls for the FCA; preparation of War and Peace Establishments; removal of the current obstructive procedure in regard to financial sanction; organisation of effective Civil Defence schemes; and the raising of the pay of all ranks to the level of other State services. His vitriolic presentation did not endear him to departmental mandarins. He retired and was succeeded by Gen. Liam Archer on 1 January 1949. McKenna had served the nation well: his task was a thankless one.

His departure marked the end of an era. His rapport during the Emergency with the British general, Franklyn, was fortunate for both sides. De Valera's delegation of absolute military control to his protegé was inspired. De Valera's detractors, however, would hold that he was just being clever: if anything backfired in liaisons with the British he could always wash his hands of it.

Gen. Liam Archer, the new Chief of Staff, had a different style from McKenna. He knew the Civil Service ropes better, perhaps. He did not, however, varnish the Annual Report (1 April 1948 to 31 March 1949) which showed a wastage of 100 men per month as against a 5.5 intake, but 'for conciseness and clarity' he forebore from making any personal comment.

The drain on the strength of the Permanent Defence Force continued unabatedly. They were one-third under strength. Units could only be partly organised in accordance with the Tables laid down. The First Line Reserve was barely sufficient even to bring units up to Peace Establishment. However, the Military College, Corps Schools, Training Depots and Staffs were maintained as near full strength as possible. For instructional purposes, paper Experimental War Establishments were issued. The College organised and equipped a demonstration battalion accordingly. It was deficient in modern anti-tank guns and projectors, platoon mortars and other equipment. The British and American Military Attachés attended that demonstration which had a knock-on effect in drawing attention to other deficiencies. In Field Artillery 25-pounder gun howitzer stocks amounted to only one-third of the requirements of a normal Infantry Division. In the Air Corps twelve Seafire III single-seater fighter bombers were in service. There were also some of the Anson XIX, Master Mark II, Martinet Target Tower, Magister I, Anson I, and Hurricanes in use as training machines. Propeller-driven aircraft were obsolete and jet-propelled aircraft for both operational and training purposes were required. All that came out of the scrutiny, however, was a proposal to extend the Bay Mechanics Scheme to Signals, Ordnance, Engineers and Supply and Transport Corps.

Only minor adjustments were effected. Establishment for the Legal Section was amended on 3 August 1948 to provide for two commandants as Judge Advocates on the staff of the Deputy Judge Advocate General (see Chapter 4). Provision for the Mounted Escort was discontinued and the Establishment for *An Marc Sluagh* (the Equitation School) was revised (Major Kuleza was appointed Training Officer in January 1949). Gen. McKenna was no longer present as a thorn in the side of the Department so his strictures were not acted upon.

In April 1949 the North Atlantic Treaty, providing for a unified defence plan for the North Atlantic area, was signed by the United Kingdom, France, Belgium and the Netherlands. The existence of Northern Ireland involved the island of Ireland tactically; geography involved it strategically. The policy of the new government remained openly one of neutrality. The new Minister for External Affairs, Sean MacBride, however, seemed to initiate a new departure when he introduced the border as a bargaining factor in negotiations with the Americans on Partition (1949). An advertence to combat power was inescapable in that context.

On 31 March 1950 there were 8,000 all ranks in the PDF and 5,000 in the First Line Reserve. It was obvious that it would fall to the FCA — still a local defence force — to augment the PDF in a call-up situation.

There was still a deficiency in warlike stores: although twelve modern 17-pounder anti-tank guns were received, forty-eight were needed to equip one Division. The United Nations gave its name to participation in the Korean War (1950). The 'Cold War' went on. A foothold in Ireland had obvious advantages to either side. Our preparedness to defend or secure our territory therefore remained of relevance to them. The following year, from 1 April 1950 to 31 March 1951, brought no improvement in our capability to handle a war situation. The flawed 1946 Peace Organisation still obtained. A War Organisation was not yet prepared. Low strengths and lack of resources restricted training. Undeterred the planners forged ahead, giving particular attention to air defence. A coast survey in conjunction with the British was also carried out. As for the Second Line Reserve, the effective strength of the FCA decreased from 25,776 to 21,784 during the year, while the *Sluagh Muiri* increased from thirty-four to 152. There was a shortage of training equipment and ammunition for the obsolete 18-pounder, 4.5" howitzer, 3.7" howitzer and 60-pounder guns was no longer obtainable. 40 mm Bofors anti-aircraft guns and 3.7" heavy AA guns were insufficient for training.

In Coast Defence the five 9.2" guns were in care and maintenance, as were some of the still serviceable 6" guns. The two 4.7" naval guns were obsolete but serviceable. The twenty-one 12-pounders were used only for saluting batteries or training *Sluagh Muiri* in gun drills. The three corvettes were serviceable. Guard duties disrupted Educational Training but in general the Forces kept the best side out.

The Air Corps, for instance, trained direct entrants and apprentices, and the fighter squadron gave demonstrations of air to ground firing. The Artillery did their utmost to give firing demonstrations for the Military College. The Naval Service gave depth charge demonstrations. Engineers demonstrated mine laying, bridge building and demolitions. Cavalry, Supply and Transport, Medicals and Signals left no stone unturned to activate training. It was this drive that kept the deprived Defence Forces going and alive: great credit has to be given for such dedication in unpromising circumstances. There were three Cadet classes in training at one stage with depleted training staffs. The Corps Schools were also active. Three Cadets passed their Army School of Music examinations. (It was becoming increasingly difficult in that sphere to find suitable personnel for pipe bands.)

1951–52 was spent on completion of an Air Defence Plan. Plans for protective forces for airfields were drawn up. The revision of War, Mobilisation, and Peace Organisation was commenced. There was still a deficiency of 5,085 all ranks in the Peace Establishment. It was apparent that there was little prospect of obtaining arms and equipment (including flame throwers) from Great Britain, which was involved in the Korean War. Arms-purchasing missions were then sent to Sweden, France and Belgium. The possibility of getting Artillery equipment from Canada was explored.

In June 1952 a new President, Eamon de Valera, was inaugurated and troops were concentrated in Dublin for ten days for the occasion. The following year saw an overall increase in strength of 2,712. The recruiting campaign had brought in a good type of recruit. Stretched organisations coped to train them. The 10th Field Artillery Battery of the II FA Regiment, for example, had three platoons of recruits in training (Infantry and Artillery) at the one time without any extra staff. This was in addition to its normal battery duties. The success of the recruiting campaign made worse the existing accommodation problems.

Military planning moved forward too. Following the British offer of modern radar equipment within two years, from new production, a review was made of the existing plan for a radar early warning and control and reporting system, taking into account performance of equipment on offer. Availability of equipment determined mobilisation and war organisations. Envisaged was a field force of two divisions; immediate reserves, security troops; aerodrome protective troops. The War Organisation would be a development of the mobilisation organisation differing notably in air defence. Peace Organisations would be revised and related accordingly. Air strip and emergency port surveys were carried out. Members of British Forces attached for Coast Survey returned to Britain in December 1952, but liaison on miscellaneous survey matters was maintained.

Following a government direction in January 1952 time and attention were given to the problem of securing suitable supplies of equipment. Since 1948 the procurement of warlike stores from the British had been most unsatisfactory. A positive British response to representations was now interpreted.

Optimism for progress, however, was tempered in 1953 when the intake of recruits was only 2,463, 50 per cent of the previous year (4,591). Only 40 per cent of those whose term of service expired in 1954 were prepared to extend — a serious wastage. A further recruiting campaign was pessimistically planned.

Plans based on equipment on hand were drafted for the deployment of Air Defence components, comprising one AA Regiment (two HAA Batteries, two LAA Batteries): one Air Corps, one Ground Control Interception (GCI) stations; HQ Air Defence (Dublin); Sector Operation Centre (SOC) (Dublin) and seven Observer Group Centres. They included deployments of AA units in defence of Dublin, Shannon and Collinstown. Due to lack of radar no early warning of the approach of hostile aircraft was possible.

In 1953 Peace, Mobilisation and War Establishments had not yet reached finalisation. The First Line Reserve remained inadequate and there was no change in the Second Line (FCA and *An Sluagh Muiri*) position. In conjunction with the Secretariat work was undertaken on emergency legislation and the compilation of a War Book. The procurement system of 'Forecasting and Indenting' from the British War Office was discontinued for 1954–55. Firm demands would now in theory be accepted, though there was no satisfactory result to ongoing negotiations with the British on the supply of 25-pounder equipment. On the other hand, the British Admiralty dealt very promptly with Naval supply queries and were awaiting word to go ahead with the sale of one minesweeper and two seaward defence boats. They were not prepared to sell modern armoured cars, self-propelled guns or tanks, even though they had sold them to other non-NATO countries such as Sweden and Switzerland. The Cavalry had four obsolete Churchill tanks for which spare parts were not available, two pre-war *Landwerk* out of commission through lack of tracks and seventy-nine obsolete armoured cars of various types, which lacked adequate armoured protection and radio and carried only weapons of small calibre.

The British, for some reason, remained difficult about the supply of guns for Field Artillery, offering eight repairable ones and 35,500 rounds of ammunition, with the uncertainty that they might not have the latest type of fuses. Mobilisation requirements were for two hundred 25-pounder gun-howitzers and 200,000 rounds of ammunition. The army had still (1953) only twenty-four guns and 4,800 rounds of ammunition and no modern mines. An order to the British War Office for 300 shrapnel mines, 200 contact mines and 300 anti-personnel mines had not been met. Of eight obsolescent Seafires only five were now serviceable. Shortly the Squadron would be without operational machines.

In spite of all those difficulties an increased strength of units, supplemented by the First Line Reserve, permitted companies, batteries and cavalry troops to operate independently in the field, thus giving leaders some experience of troop leading and of putting theory into practice.

In 1954 work went on reviewing and redrafting organisations and establishments. The effect of nuclear warfare posed problems. The Americans felt that it was possible to manualise a tactical nuclear doctrine and drill for the battlefield. A state of flux existed in air defence. It was reckoned that about six battalions, separate from the brigade or division organisations, would be required for the protection of vital points and the relief of field units from garrison duties. The possibility of nuclear warfare required that Civil Defence be taken seriously, and protests of neutrality became less relevant in that context.

The IV FA Regiment was converted to a Heavy Mortar Regiment. The British War Office showed more willingness to supply warlike stores. The Infantry School concentrated on a new Staff course, special Reserve Officer courses, and Atomic, Bacteriological, Chemical and Civil Defence courses. The Command and Staff School switched from four-month courses to the controversial long nine-month *selected* Command and Staff courses. Twelve officers qualified in the first Air Staff course at Baldonnel. New classes in French, German, Spanish and Russian commenced in GHQ. In the FCA new Artillery units were formed in the Southern and Western Commands.

On 1 January 1955 the following new members of the Council of Defence assumed office: Major Gen. P. A. Mulcahy, Chief of Staff; Col. J. Hanrahan, Adjutant General; Col. J. Lillis, Quartermaster General. Defence policy was reviewed and the assumption of a period for expansion in an emergency critically examined. On nuclear warfare it was observed that:

(*a*) Nuclear weapons were being integrated in modern armies on the tactical level.

(*b*) Limited warfare on conventional lines could not be ruled out.

(*c*) Increased emphasis was required on the role of the army in support of Civil Defence and internal security.

(*d*) Invasion was more likely to be airborne than seaborne.

(*e*) A need existed to decentralise and disperse field units to reduce transport overheads.

Consequently defence plans were based on the following elements:

(*a*) Limited Air Defence, including Air Defence HQ at which would be co-ordinated HAA, LAA, fighter defences and a control and reporting system.

(*b*) Striking forces to be built up to two divisions after mobilisation.

(*c*) Immediate reserves of two brigades plus one Infantry battalion.

(*d*) Six battalions of security troops to guard vital points.

(*e*) Airfield protection troops: Infantry plus LAA and armoured cars for ground defence of airfield.

(*f*) Port and harbour protection elements.

(*g*) Garrison units, depots, schools etc.

As regards coast defence, while acknowledging the change in character with the introduction of fast surface craft and new techniques in underwater attack, it was reckoned that the retention of at least the 6" equipment was warranted. The three corvettes had been in service for over ten years now without a survey or major refit. The main deficiency in Infantry Corps equipment remained medium-range anti-tank weapons.

In 1956 the outline Scheme of Defence set out in the Memorandum to the Government in 1944 was rigorously fine-combed. As many of the recommendations, such as the creation of a First Line Reserve, had not been implemented the plans envisaged were regarded as faulty. The principal developments during the year affecting those plans were:

(*a*) Establishment of Air Defence HQ staff.

(*b*) Preparation of Revised Observer Corps Plan.

(*c*) Revision of plan for control and restriction of radio transmission during an emergency (Plan Skyline).

(*d*) Approval by the government of the plan for the protection of vital installations and implementation of further steps.

(*e*) Initiation of a study for the employment of the Permanent Force in an immediate emergency.

A revised organisation for the Cavalry Corps was prepared. It was recommended that Naval policy should be concentrated on the seaward defence of our main ports and approaches and that a Seaward Defence School be established. Otherwise reorganisation within existing Establishment strength was proceeded with, and Establishments for other Corps made progress. Stress was laid on the necessity for a high standard in dress, drill and deportment. The importance of night training, weapon training and field craft was emphasised and special attention was directed to specialists, physical training and administration. The Rev. Father Crean was appointed Head Chaplain. (He had landed in Normandy on D-Day and in Arnhem in 1944.) The titles of No. 2, No. 3, and No. 4 Army Bands were changed to The Band of the Southern Command, The Band of the Curragh Training Camp, and the Band of the Western Command respectively. A civilian instructor (Seamus Hayes) was appointed to the Equitation School.

1957–8 saw a recrudescence of IRA activity along the border. Sean Lemass's Fianna Fáil government opened border posts and an internment camp (*An Campa Intheorannach-ta*). On 31 December 1957 120 IRA men were interned in the Curragh. These further security duties on top of existing guard duties and chores put a great strain on the seriously understrength Defence Forces. Reorganisation was imperative and that inevitably involved the FCA, whose officers had greatly benefited from periods of full-time training. In addition, in 1957 the introduction of the Bren light machine-gun and the Gustav sub-machine-gun gave a fillip to the FCA Rifle Battalions. In 1958 the Southern Command reported 'amazingly good results' from the FCA and welcomed 'integration'. The following organisation was proposed:

(*a*) Two brigades in each command comprising the Permanent Force and FCA.

(*b*) Provision by the FCA of units of various arms.

(*c*) Provision of a number of garrison FCA battalions in addition to those included in brigades. Due to the run-down state of the PDF and the First Line Reserve the weapons which could transform the FCA Rifle Battalions and make such a force possible were lying idle.

An 'integrated' force was devised, increasing the number of brigades to six, each brigade containing a mix of PDF and FCA units. A number of battalions were organised whose primary function was the defence of airfields and vital installations. The 20th Battalion in the 2nd Brigade and 21st Battalion in 6th Brigade performed this function. Mobilisation requirements of weapons, equipment and ammunition were based on a force of:

Six Brigade Groups.
Nine Infantry Battalions.
Six Garrison Rifle Battalions.
Other garrison, training and administrative units; miscellaneous air, naval armoured and AA units.

The scheme was implemented with effect from 1 October 1959. Consequences for the FCA Rifle Battalion were:

(*a*) It now became a company of a new Infantry battalion.

(*b*) Medium machine-guns, 81 mm and 60 mm and 84 mm anti-tank were added in line within PDF battalion armament.

(*c*) A PDF Battalion Commander replaced the Area Officer.

(*d*) Former FCA Battalion Commanders (Captains) now became Company Commanders (Commandants) — the same rank as their new PDF Battalion Commander.

(*e*) Curiously, there was no change in Defence Force Regulation R5 — Company Commanders remained responsible for claiming and accounting for the grant-in-aid. A battalion commander had to get the company commander's approval even to use a station waggon. This contrary arrangement apparently arose from a Finance insistence that a condition for the adoption of the 1959 scheme was that it would not involve any extra expenditure.

Another factor was the increasing age of many of the founder members of the Force. Particularism and preoccupation with platoon competitions had made it almost impossible to progress to training at company level. 'Integration' had much to recommend it. The Naval Service also came under review. In addition to its peacetime fishery protection role it now concentrated on the seaward defence of important ports and harbours. A study was made of defence problems arising out of proposals for the reintegration of the national territory in the context of a study of the strategic importance of Ireland during the last two major wars and in the future. Developments in nuclear and other weapons and the reality of the ICBM (Intercontinental Ballistic Missile) were noted. It could not be disinvented.

Still lacking were anti-tank weapons, automatic rifles, artillery and radio equipment, and armoured fighting vehicles.

No progress in the acquisition of radar had been made, but a plan for the Observer Corps was drafted. What was now felt to be the Coast Defence requirement was guns of the mobile twin 6-pounder type to implement the seaward defence of vital harbours and approaches. The Engineer Corps was frustrated by the constant postponements of deliveries of portable power saws, power pumping sets and timber piles. The Engineers had worked miracles (including the building of many churches!) with limited resources over the years.

There were always other levels to Army life. Irish got a new lease of life: courses, including Command and Staff courses, were run through Irish in the Military College. That did not signify that everything else was serene, however. The College complained at the lack of practical experience with troops among incoming student officers. In spite of intense canvassing and pay inducements only seven NCO instructors were found capable of teaching through Irish. Progress was reported in learning French, German and Russian but the declining strengths meant that it was difficult to maintain even the bands. More critically, the organisation for the Infantry Battalion was reckoned to be unsuitable. It should, in line with the 1954 War Organisation, include a Pioneer Assault platoon, a Signal Section and an Anti-tank platoon. A ration change was welcomed as it provided for an evening meal, but cooking equipment and methods of cleaning delph were found wanting.

The Air Corps rejected a thesis that rockets had made it redundant by replacing manual aircraft. These, the Corps maintained, were still the main weapon of strategic air assault. It was a weighty argument to make a point that the armament available suited the aircraft they had. More tellingly, they managed to meet demands from Industry and Commerce to test equipment at Dublin Airport.

1959 GHQ reports (in Irish) to the Minister centred on the integration of the FCA and the building-up of the six-brigade organisation. Peace Establishments (including the revised Tables for the FCA) were promulgated with effect from 1 October 1959, providing a framework for a War Organisation to meet an emergency. Generally speaking, with the exception of a grave shortage of radio equipment, the weapons and equipment for the six-brigade organisation were available. Stocks of ammunition, however, would not allow them to remain in combat for more than a few days.

Civil Defence was receiving renewed attention. British Air Raid Warning Training Schools in London were visited. The strength of the First Line Reserve continued its downward trend. Obsolete air, artillery and cavalry equipment were held on charge. International military developments made no impact on the Departments.

The election of President Kennedy in 1961 marked a change in US military thinking which had global significance. Exclusive reliance on massive retaliation was abandoned in favour of a policy of flexible response which demanded a capability to deal equally with either local emergencies or universal conflict, whether entailing nuclear combat or not.

Khruschev's threat to put Soviet missiles into Cuba highlighted the order of battle and forced consideration in Ireland of the effects of a nuclear exchange. The US nuclear capability was based on six Polaris submarines; 1500 strategic Air Command bombers, fifty-four Atlas and nine Titan ICMBs; sixty Thor and Jupiter IRBMs based in England and Italy and bombers based on aircraft carriers of the 6th and 7th Fleet. Ireland was in the line of fire and astride axes of communication. Fallout made no distinctions or demarcations.

However, domestic problems came first. Ireland was now (1960) sending troops on UN peacekeeping missions (see chapter 8). The IRA intensified its attacks along the border — there were sixty in 1961. They had plenty of weapons: Brens, Stens, Thompsons, rifles, revolvers, explosives. Their active service units were well equipped. The Special Criminal Court had to be reconvened in 1961.

Increased internal security duties were now added to UN and other standard duties. Again, in spite of everything, morale remained high. The Irish soldier has a special talent for dealing with adversity. All he asks are the tools to do the job. Health was good, apart from the dental position which, in line with the rest of the country, was unsatisfactory. Out of an establishment of fifteen dental officers there was a shortage of nine. The Irish Medical Association still advised doctors not to apply for posts in the Defence Forces.

On top of that wide span of duties, Commands, with ever-declining strengths, had to continue organising, training and servicing two brigade groups. In addition, participation in a Civil Defence 'Crash Plan' was required: all on a shoestring.

The Naval Service, for example, was barely stemming the tide and still had no definite policy. They had only one ship in commission, no recruits worth speaking of but were still saddled with a long list of duties. Other Corps and Services were similarly severely strained. The inadequacy and unsuitability of AA equipment in a key area was a grave disability. A positive step, however, was the allocation in 1961 of ten FN rifles to train the 35th Infantry Battalion for the Congo. They were to need them and they put them to good use. 84 mm anti-tank weapons had already been procured for the 34th Battalion.

By 1962 there was no covering up the deficiencies in the 1959 Peace Establishment. Most seriously it failed to provide enough staffs for developing as envisaged the FCA into a combat-worthy organisation. It was practically impossible to get NCOs to fill Congo units, yet Finance continued to impose the percentage limitation. Year after year since October 1959 the army had undertaken three major tasks: 'Integration', the organisation and training of two brigade groups per command; the Congo operation; and a major role in Civil Defence (involving additional training for FCA) without any addition to the Peace Establishment. The Civil Defence 'Crash Plan' clamoured for priority. The steadily declining officer establishment was grossly under strength in junior officers. Once more the army had been given additional onerous tasks but had not been given the means to do them.

The lack of armour and anti-aircraft weapons strictly limited the scope of employment of combat units against a first-class Power but the introduction of the FN rifle and the 84 mm recoilless rifle had greatly increased the combat potential of the Infantry so equipped. A shorter fuse length for grenades was required for the Congo operations.

There was a need for a career training plan for FCA officers and a course training plan for FCA NCOs. The FCA, without being designated as such, were by default performing the role of the First Line Reserve, the bulk of whose officers were too old for combat. A surprise attack could not be opposed initially except with weak and inadequate PDF elements. On the other hand in the Congo the Irish battalions were performing professionally in combat, in their authorised UN role of keeping the peace by enforcement (see Chapter 8).

Military developments at home were not so successful. The combat effectiveness of some units was suspect and the Cuban crisis showed up a lack of weapons and equipment. The capability to engage meaningfully even in a Civil Defence role was questionable. The fifty-year-old Vickers machine-guns needed replacement; Artillery combat and transport vehicles were well obsolete; there were no anti-tank mines, and stocks of ammunition were generally very unsatisfactory. There was a shortage of much needed aircraft, and naval vessels were falling below seagoing standard. The upper age group of the majority of First Line Reserve officers caused increasing concern. Retirement ages (with FCA) were standardised in 1962. There were many complaints too about the supply of uniforms. Rubber-soled boots were being tested to replace the old studded ones and preshrunk socks were tested in the College.

In 1963 things began to look up for the Air Corps with the completion of the first flying course for Aer Lingus pilots and the purchase of helicopters (two Alouette IIIs). A recruiting campaign was very successful and a higher standard of education (to Leaving Certificate standard) was noted among direct entrant technicians. The standard of education among recruits generally continued to increase. This required adaptations to methods of training without diluting the capability to fight as an organised highly disciplined force, the fundamental mission.

In June 1963 President J. F. Kennedy visited Ireland and the army took especial pleasure in honouring him, and taking him to their hearts. He visibly reciprocated. Sadly, before the year was out the Cadets, whom he particularly admired, rendered military honours at his graveside in Arlington following his mindless assassination.

Nearer home, Denmark, Sweden and Norway organised a Scandinavian force of 3,000 men to be placed at UN disposal. This was the first time national forces were earmarked in this way. NATO's nuclear tactical armament had grown rapidly. Almost every Division now had Honest John (tactical nuclear) batteries. The 7th US Army in Germany had 100 Davy Crockett tactical mortars backed by Corps and army missiles and strategic nuclear support. The French were going it alone with their *Force de Frappe.* The outside espionage industry was flourishing and the number of Soviet and Czechoslovakian intelligence agents visiting Ireland showed a marked increase. From the days of Michael Collins intelligence operations in the Irish army had a superb record. Intelligence officers were now posted to each command. IRA infiltration had to be continually guarded against. The main languages favoured by interpreters were Russian, French and German, but Finance refused to sanction payments to more than six officers qualified as French interpreters.

The following casually selected items of what the papers noticed in 1969 gives a random sample of the scope and span of the Defence Forces' activities:

1. Airlift Congo of 38th, 39th Battalions; 2nd and 3rd Armoured Car Squadrons and the 2nd Infantry Group.
2. Departure of Officer Observers to the Middle East.
3. Participation in the RDS Scientific and Technological Exhibition.
4. Coverage by Television Wales of army training including Cadets and track vehicles at CTC.
5. Visit of Premier Adoula and laying of wreath on Congo Plot.
6. Army Mission to Lourdes.
7. The winning of the Aga Khan (showjumping) Trophy.
8. Assistance rendered during the very severe July flooding.
9. Assistance rendered by troops to people in snowbound areas.
10. Funeral of Domhnall O Buachalla.

11. The rescue mission by officers and men in the Glen of Imaal resulting in discovery of dead boy and girl.
12. All-army FCA Shoot.
13. Depot Passing Out Parades.
14. Cadet Commissioning Ceremony.
15. FCA Commissioning Ceremony.
16. Opening of School — Curragh.
17. Public recitals by Bands.
18. Participation in 1913 Commemoration Unveiling Ceremony at the Rotunda and assistance to Telefis Éireann on production of programme on 1913.
19. Cavalry memorial erected at Plunkett Barracks to Congo dead.
20. Helicopter delivery — demonstration to TV and Press at Baldonnel — features in newspapers and on TV.
21. Passing Out Parade of Apprentices — Naas.
22. Air Corps Wings ceremony.
23. Radio Éireann features in *An Ghaeilge* on Cadets and Helicopters.
24. Visit of Mr Andrew Wilson, Military Correspondent from Sunday *Observer.*
25. Operation of passenger service during the bus strike.
26. Features on the Naval Service.
27. Parades, escorts, guards for Ambassadors etc.

When the IRA did not resume combat activities after calling off its border campaign in February 1962 it was possible to concentrate more on UN and routine operations. Individual training in Nuclear Biological and Chemical (NBC) warfare and on Civil Defence (CD) continued as part of normal training in all units.

By 1965 the main planning activities concentrated on:

(*a*) National security legislation.
(*b*) Command structure of the Defence Forces.
(*c*) Siting of National Control and Army HQ.

The ineffectiveness of the 1956 scheme for the protection of vital installations was made known and a new proposal which did not envisage Garda participation was circulated. Communications and telephone requirements from national control/army HQ to lower levels demanded attention. It was a serious weakness that no provision existed for an army HQ Signal Unit or Command Signal Units. The strength of radio and radar mechanics was altogether inadequate (45 per cent of Establishment).

The military involvement with Civil Defence measures persisted. A Board of Officers visited the Total factory in West Germany in March 1966 and made arrangements to purchase Radiac equipment (for delivery in 1977). The raising of special units for overseas service and the disbanding of those returning was now routine. A revision of the 1959 Peace Establishment became more and more urgent. The overall strength of the Permanent Force was 8,249, i.e. 71 per cent of the Peace Establishment. This deficiency created the following difficulties which were repeatedly recited but to no apparent effect:

(*a*) Severe restriction of training and combat effectiveness.
(*b*) Restriction of contribution to UN missions.
(*c*) Limitation on preparation for effective mobilisation — including the training of FCA.

Combat effectiveness was questioned on many levels. Medical opinion was uneasy that the average age of the PDF was higher than desirable. That meant acceptance of a higher sickness rate, especially overseas. (Those medical reports repeatedly remarked that VD was a matter of very minor concern.)

More pertinent queries were directed at Corps roles. The role of Coast Defence was obscure and the question of the provision of Artillery equipment in general remained unclarified. Aircraft numbers also remained unchanged. Chipmunks and Vampires were at the end of their lives but replacements were deleted from the Estimates for economy reasons.

These cuts also affected pay, which remained a vexed question. The Defence Forces were excluded from arbitration. The Chief of Staff recommended to the Minister on 14 January 1966 the establishment of an independent authority of judicial character to adjudicate as required on the remuneration of personnel of the *Forsa Cósanta* (Defence Forces). Nothing resulted from the question of parity of pay between officers of the Forces and the Civil Service. There was a problem of finding an equation for a Lieutenant Colonel who, in addition to being a battalion commander responsible for the lives of 1000 men, was also a barrack O/C answerable for all activities involved in running the equivalent of a small town. An equivalence with an Assistant Principal Officer was patently ludicrous. The matter remained unresolved. It did not make news, as it was to do later. Competing for the headlines then were the continuing escalation of the war in Vietnam; the French defection from NATO; the Rhodesian crisis; changes in British Defence Policy causing ministerial resignations; further Chinese/Russian disagreements; revolt in Nigeria and the overthrow of Nkrumah in Ghana. UN soldier peacekeepers speculated as to where the next trouble spot might be and kept their bags packed.

Unpublicised was the continuing interest by a foreign intelligence service in obtaining Irish passports by illegal means (it took years for the tip of the iceberg to surface). The emergence of ever more splinter groups which tended to act even more irresponsibly than usual increased the difficulties in maintaining surveillance over the IRA. A splinter group blew up Nelson Pillar on 6 March 1966. (The men in the GPO in 1916 had rejected such an idea.) The fiftieth anniversary of the Rising was properly commemorated in military ceremonies by the PDF and the FCA.

The IRA refrained from overt aggressive action against the Forces, which continued to be kept at a dangerously low strength. There was still no move to do anything about replacing the obsolete equipment of the Air, Artillery and Cavalry Corps. With regard to tanks the Comets were of no operational value, the Churchills were not worth maintaining and the *Landwerks* were valueless, except for scrap. The Armoured Car situation was no better. There was no ammunition for the *Landwerks* and Leylands, the Fords were useful only for the initial stages of airport defence and the Panhards without a 90 mm gun were reduced to near impotency. The Beaverettes were not worth their maintenance. None of the Squadron vehicles mounted a gun capable of penetrating 6 mm armour plate. The Cavalry School was understaffed and underestimated.

In the Signal Corps, functioning from a dilapidated Depot, serious maintenance problems remained, although hope had been kindled in 1965 with the sanctioning at long last of technicians' pay for the higher skilled troops. The effort to improve the training of existing grades of technicians was a bright spot. The Apprentice School in Naas — a welcome addition in 1956 to co-ordinate and train apprentices — was functioning satisfactorily. A negative side was the high rate of discharge by purchase of Air Corps apprentices.

1968 saw the Observer Corps on its seventh year without activation. The AA had been firing at ground targets because an air target could not be afforded. In the Naval Service only one 4" quick-firing gun per ship was available to train naval ratings. The Second Line Reserve of that Service was in dire straits without craft or resources. With the resources available *Óglaigh na hÉireann* worked wonders in providing realistic training, and interestingly the Military College spread its wings and trained two classes of Zambian Cadets.

Unit strengths made it difficult to meet ongoing commitments or to make progress on FCA training. A decision was made that as far as possible the general organisation of combat units would be the same for peace and war. Once again the planners found Departmental attitudes to proposals difficult to understand. Submissions were treated with a deafening silence. Planners pleaded for straightforward acceptance or rejection of proposals and, if rejected, for an adequate reason for the rejection. In 1968 a proposal submitted in 1961 was still 'under consideration'. Sectional work practices were incompatible with the general public interest or the fundamental common good.

The claim for parity of pay between officers and civil servants (for want of something better) had been rejected on 7 March 1967. In August 1969 the Defence Forces faced their biggest crisis since the Civil War when the troubles in Northern Ireland boiled over. It was a watershed. The integrity and the security of the State were at issue. It was time for straight talking — and listening. The security of the State depended on the Defence Forces.

# 8

## United Nations
### (from 1960)

*Óglaigh na hÉireann* gives unstinting service to the United Nations in the cause of peace. The 1988 Nobel Peace Prize was awarded to the United Nations Peacekeeping Forces. Unit histories record the actions.

The term 'peacekeeping' as a form of conflict control is not even mentioned, much less described, in the UN Charter.[1] Chapter VI ('peace by persuasion') sets out the means of voluntary settlement of disputes and facesaving. Chapter VII envisages enforcement. Dag Hammarskjold felt that a new chapter of the Charter was needed — to be numbered 'Six and a Half'. Irish initiatives have contributed to this unwritten empirical creation.

'Normal' peacekeeping duties are difficult to define comprehensively. Certain responsibilities sometimes transcended them, giving rise to an accommodating academic vocabulary: 'prophylaxis' for prevention; 'patching-up' for conciliation and 'proselytise' for enforcement.[2]

Ireland became a UN member in 1956 and in 1958 sent volunteer observers[3] on a UN mission to the Middle East (UNOGIL) to investigate a Lebanese complaint about UAR interference and infiltration. The Irish pathfinders were Lt Col. Justin McCarthy, AHQ; Comdt Malachy Higgins, Air Corps and Comdt Gerry Coughlan, Corps of Engineers, Capt. Pat Lavelle, Cavalry Corps and Capt. Rory Henderson, Infantry. The claims concerning infiltration from Syria were not borne out.

Nevertheless the US 6th Fleet landed US marines between Sidon and Beirut causing surprise and alarm to UN HQ. When the US bridgehead expanded world anxiety increased. Eventually a formula was worked out whereby the US would withdraw and be replaced by the UN. Fresh observers arrived for this purpose, bringing the total of Irish observers there to fifty.

The mission was wound down the following December. Capt. Louis Hogan, Capt. Bertie Murphy and Capt. Colm Cox left Operations in Beirut on 16 December 1958. Lt Col. Justin McCarthy and Capt. Pat Jordan were the only Irish UNOGIL observers to transfer to UNTSO (United Nations Truce Supervisory Organisation). In existence since 1948 (the oldest of the UN military organisations) UNTSO is unarmed, made up entirely of officers drawn from seventeen different countries, including the US and the USSR. Its role initially was to supervise the various armistice agreements drawn up between Israel and her Arab neighbours after the first Arab-Israeli war of 1948. Col. McCarthy was appointed to the operational staff of Swedish Chief of Staff, Gen. Van Horn, at Government House, UN Headquarters in Jerusalem, and later, when Van Horn became Force Commander, ONUC (*Organisation des Nations Unies au Congo*), accompanied him to the Congo as his Chief of Operations. His brief but brilliant UN career was tragically cut short in a traffic accident in the Congo shortly afterwards.

During and after the Emergency the Forces had suffered a sort of claustrophobia and were in danger of being treated as nothing more than a glorified gendarmerie. The Congo opened up new horizons and brought a breath of fresh air into role analysis.

In July 1960 the related objectives of ONUC were to help the Congolese government to restore law and order and bring about the speedy withdrawal of Belgian Forces. Irish assistance was requested and, on the recommendation of the Army, granted by the government on the understanding that its role was limited to protecting lives and property and that it had no political part to play. Force was only to be used in self-defence.

Units had to be raised quickly under great pressure: deadlines were met. The honour (and hazards) of pioneering the operation went to Lt Col. Murt Buckley's newly formed 32nd Battalion which was activated on 2 July 1950 (and disbanded on 20 January 1961 on completion of UN service).

Gen. Van Horn revised his original decision to deploy Col. Buckley's battalion in Coquilhatville as the area was low lying, swampy, abounding in hook-worm and mosquitoes. The UN had no stocks of tropical clothing, no mosquito netting. Van Horn changed the battalion's mission to restoring the situation in Kivu province. This was an improvement medically but a disadvantage operationally as greater distances were now involved. East Kivu was over 1,000 miles from Leopoldville. The requirement was for high-powered radio but the UN had no long-range wireless equipment. The only practical means of communication was by air. A good airhead for the battalion was essential. It was planned to fly the Irish battalion direct to not more than three airfields in Kivu province.

All obstacles were overcome. Native armed forces were not disarmed as this would have involved the use of force and loss of confidence. The Belgian settlers were largely unco-operative and often disloyal, though key white workers were encouraged to remain in the area. Not one shot was fired in anger by the 32nd Battalion, though it was a near thing on many occasions, especially with the belligerent Balubakat tribe.

The 32nd Battalion had to learn many things the hard way about kit, conditions, equipment etc. Important lessons were learned about *cafard*, the result of members being removed from the family, and the effects of alcohol on Irish culture and society. Discipline was consistently strict so all problems arising were expeditiously handled. The Congolese population, by Irish standards, was found to be very promiscuous and many were infected with gonorrhea. In all posts facilities for prophylaxis of venereal disease were set up. Chaplaincy was an efficacious antidote in promoting clean living and spiritual welfare. The companies settled in well. The battalion's joint patrols were a major success. The experiences were passed on, but the dangers had to be faced.

The 33rd Battalion under Lt Col. Dick Bunworth, which had followed hot on the heels of the 32nd (August 1960) bore the brunt of the prolonged threats from the unruly Balubakat. It was soon brought face to face with the difference between peacetime soldiering at home and active service with an ambivalent mission in the Congo. Although they carried arms it was dinned into them that they were only to use them in self-defence, that they were in the Congo to help everyone and to harm no one. They paid a high price for trying to keep the peace under such constraints in the hostile environment of Baluba country at Niemba. In carrying out its mission of peace Lt Kevin Gleeson's patrol was ambushed on 11 November 1966 by tribesmen using poisoned arrows. Eight were killed, one died later from wounds, and there were two survivors. Their bravery and self-sacrifice is engraved in blood in proud memory (Appendixes 5 and 6).

The patrol comprised the following:

07500 Lt K. Gleeson
804359 Sgt H. Gaynor
804234 Cpl L. Dougan
809839 Cpl P. Kelly
806115 Trooper A. Browne
808508 Pte T. Fennell
810242 Pte G. Killeen
804536 Pte M. Farrell
802900 Pte M. McGuinn
808214 Pte J. Fitzpatrick
808457 Pte T. Kenny

There were two cars. The party was armed with Bren guns, Gustavs and rifles. Lt Gleeson led in the pick-up truck, Sgt Gaynor driving. They ran into a roadblock of craters and felled trees manned by screaming drugged Balubas. Conscious of his peacekeeping mission Lt Gleeson told the patrol not to fire until he gave the order. He called out the greeting, 'Jambo', and held up his left hand in a peaceful gesture. He got an arrow right through it. Encircled and menaced, the patrol had no option but to open fire.

They were hopelessly outnumbered. Being on a peacekeeping mission they were not deployed for combat. Protecting their comrades' lives was their first concern. Trooper Anthony Browne, the bravest of the brave, was the first Irish soldier to receive the Military Medal for Gallantry. The bodies were brought home and tens of thousands of citizens filed through Baldonnel where they were lying in state. All

Dublin turned out to pay homage at the funeral to Glasnevin on 22 November 1960.

Joseph Fitzpatrick and Thomas Kenny survived, after enduring great hardships. When a patrol under Comdt P. Hogan, the battalion second-in-command, finally came across Kenny, although there were two arrows sticking in him and he was in great pain, he saluted and reported that he was 808457 Pte Kenny, T.

Of five Balubas convicted of the atrocities two were sentenced to three years' penal servitude. The other three got two years. In spite of all this the battalion never wavered in its peacekeeping mission in a savagely violent and strange environment. It gave unswerving service in that role while at the same time remaining an efficient military machine.

In January 1961 Col. Eugene O'Neill's 34th Infantry Battalion took over and got a smoother passage but that, too, took hard work, and luck. Col. H. W. Byrne was now appointed the first Irish Brigade O/C in the Congo. In January 1961 Lt Gen. MacEoin was appointed Force Commander. It fell to Lt Col. John O'Donovan's 1st Infantry Group (May-November 1961), Lt Col. Hugh McNamee's 35th Battalion (June-December 1961) and Lt Col. M. F. Hogan's 36th Battalion to operate under the UN resolution (introduced on 21 February 1961), authorising ONUC to use force as a last resort to prevent civil war in the Congo. The resolution urged that the various Congolese armed units be reorganised and brought under discipline and control, and that Belgian and other foreign military and paramilitary personnel and political advisors not under United Nations Command, as well as mercenaries, be immediately evacuated.

Since mid-March 1961 the mercenary-led gendarmerie had been attacking in order to crush anti-Tshombe forces in Northern Katanga. At the end of April forty-four members of a Ghanaian ONUC detachment were massacred mercilessly by undisciplined and unpredictable armed troops in Port Francqui.

The 1st Infantry Group was formed in response to a UN request to increase the number of Irish troops already in the Congo. This was the first unit of its kind: two Infantry companies commanded by a lieutenant colonel with a very small HQ staff. The organisation had many shortcomings (it was however effectively employed in the early days of the border crisis and later in Cyprus and Sinai) but that did not prevent it performing well under fire in defence of Kamina airbase and pursuing with vigour its mission to maintain peace in the breakaway state of South Kasai. That involved — in addition to the usual protection of refugees and UN workers and maintenance of communication — the prevention of inter-tribal strife between the Kalonji and Kanioka tribes and the maintenance of supply routes between Port Francqui and Elisabethville. There was a strong battalion of Tshombe gendarmerie deployed in Kaminaville.

Shortly after arrival the 1st Infantry Group was involved (with the 35th Battalion) in Operation Rumpunch to detain and repatriate all white mercenaries in Katanga. This involved a strong defence of Katanga airport, which on 14 September was attacked by gendarmes and white mercenaries. The attack was repulsed with losses to the gendarmes of twenty dead and fifty wounded. The 84 mm anti-tank section knocked out the two leading attacking armoured cars. Efforts to penetrate the UN defences, supported by cannon fire and shrapnel bombs from a Fouga jet aircraft, were unsuccessful. Deliberations to send out from Kildare some Bofors AA guns to counter the Fouga were overtaken by events.On 21 September a ceasefire was announced.

During a week of hostilities the UN troops at the disposal of the Base Commander had been increased to include:

| | |
|---|---|
| One Company of Swedish Bn (Ex Elizabethville) | 101 all ranks |
| Two Company of Jat Bn (Indian) (Ex Leopoldville) | 232 all ranks |
| Half-Troop of 2 Recce Regt MSF (Malaya) | 4 all ranks |

Concurrently the 35th Battalion's overall mission was to maintain the UN presence in a secessionist and increasingly hostile Katanga. It was part of a higher formation which directed the battalion's operations more or less closely. It participated actively in Operations Rumpunch, Morthor and Unokat. They cost the battalion a total of three killed and fifteen wounded and were of historic significance. Operation

Morthar was the first occasion in which Irish troops took offensive action against an organised enemy since the formal inception of the army.

In Operation Rumpunch on 28 August 1961 the 35th, after some shooting but incurring no casualties, arrested seventy-three mercenaries and took over the 'New Hospital' and the airport installations. The Katangese gendarmerie and police forces, together with more mercenaries, were running riot in Elizabethville. To restore order and UN control Operation Morthar on 13 September 1961 ordered the 35th Battalion to seize, hold and control the radio station and the railway tunnel, and to be prepared to block them. Friendly forces from the 12th Swedish Battalion, 1st Dogra Battalion and 3/1 Gurkha Battalion supported the Irish Battalion by seizing designated buildings, arresting Katangese Sureté officials and staffs and securing refugee camps. Three Irish armoured cars were placed under command to the Dogra Battalion and two to the Swedish Battalion. The 35th Battalion took all its objectives without trouble but the armoured cars with the Dogra Battalion became involved in heavy street fighting.

A Company of the battalion were not involved in the Elizabethville action, having been allocated an untenable position in remote Jadotville. The company, plus a section of armoured cars, with skilful use of mortars, withstood a siege for four days by an estimated 2,000 gendarmerie, white mercenaries, colonists and a mob.Two attempts were made by the battalion to send a relief force, but coming under heavy fire and air attack they were unable to pass the line of the Lufira river and had to withdraw.

A Company was in an unenviable position. Water had been cut off, reinforcements were not coming and a show of force by UN jets did not materialise. The Irish in good faith entered an agreement to mutually lay down arms in order to save lives as part of its peacekeeping mission. Dishonourably, the Katangese side broke its promises. The outcome was a matter of great chagrin to the company which had shown extraordinary steadiness and coolness under heavy fire. They now displayed the same qualities in frustrating adversity. Meanwhile C Company had come under heavy fire when organising a defensive position around the tunnel. (The unit history gives the heroic details of this and other actions.)

A ceasefire was agreed on 21 September 1961 and prisoners (including the Jadotville company) were released. The Katangese authorities cut off electricity, telephone and water. Fresh supplies had to be flown in. The Katangese eventually denied the UN freedom of movement in Elizabethville. The 35th Battalion HQ was harassed by sniping, mortar and machine-gun fire causing casualties. On 8 December 1961 a composite Irish and Swedish Force (including a platoon of the incoming 36th Battalion) led an attack towards the tunnel. The situation continued to deteriorate.

Operation Unokat on 15–16 December was carried out by two UN brigades. The 36th Battalion (which had just landed) and part of 35th Battalion were in 1st Brigade at the time. The brigade's mission was to attack and capture Camp Massard and block routes Katabia and Don Bosco in order to assist in sealing off Elizabethville city preparatory to the destruction of enemy resistance in the Elizabethville area. One half troop of Indian 120 mm heavy mortar battery was in direct support of the 1st Brigade and was located in the Irish battalion area.

The 36th Battalion had flown to its operational area in the full knowledge of inevitable hostilities. It was the first overseas battalion to have an AA complement and to carry steel helmets. Gendarmerie fired on and damaged landing planes on 7 December 1961. Rotation with the 35th Battalion was carried out under fire. The mission of the 36th Infantry Battalion was to seize and hold the area of the Kasenga to Luxembourg road junction to secure the right flank of the Swedish attack and to be prepared to seize and hold the tunnel (Operation Sarsfield, 16 December 1961). The Irish and Swedish units achieved success in their mission by offensive action, in attack and defence. All companies of the 36th Infantry Battalion had then to organise patrols to control refugees who were looting. The British Chief of Civil Ops, Brian Urquhart, thanked the battalion for a great effort during the days of battle. Killed in action on 16 December 1961 were Lt Patrick A. Riordan, DSM, his radio operator, Pte Andrew Wickham, and Artillery Sgt Patrick Mulcahy, DSM. They showed remarkable bravery under fire and their names are forever proudly enshrined in *Óglaigh na hÉireann's* roll of honour.

The situation remained troublesome in other areas as well. A war party of about two hundred Jeunesse from the refugee camp, armed with bows and arrows, knives and bicycle chains, attacked a camp where they alleged two of their members had been murdered. The break-out was stopped at bayonet point by a platoon of C Company under Capt. Keyes. The gendarmarie started to murder Balubas in the communes. Guerilla warfare was also organised against ONUC among the tribes in Katanga. The battalion reverted to keeping the peace by persuasion, by active patrolling, manning barriers and posts, controlling refugees and escorting workers.

The succeeding 37th Battalion under Lt Col. Don O'Broin, May to November 1962, like the 34th had an easier ride. It did not become involved in any serious outbreak of fighting and its role consisted, in the main, of patrols and security. These exercises, however, could not be taken lightly and were rarely without hazard. Two of the 37th officers, Comdt Jim Crowe and Capt. G.M. (Bertie) Kelly (later Colonels), travelled on from the Congo to West New Guinea (Irian) to join a United Nations Special Force (UNSFI) from August to October 1962 to supervise the ceasefire between the Netherlands and Indonesia under UNTEA (United Nations Temporary Executive Authority).

The 38th Battalion under Lt Col. Paddy Delaney, November 1962 to May 1963, was back in the firing line. On 28 December 1962, after a postponement to allow Mr Tshombe to stop Katangese firing, the Indian Brigade launched an attack. The heavy mortar troop of the 38th Irish Battalion (O/C Capt. — later Col. — T. Boyle, DSM) was under command to the Indian Brigade for this phase. It distinguished itself and was a battle-winning factor in the actions.

On 29 December, the 3rd Ethiopian Brigade captured Simba Hill on the way to Kibushi. The 37th Battalion passed through them and, the way being paved by artillery fire on both sides of the axis of advance from its mortar troop in support, peacefully entered the town. It established excellent relations with the Indian and Ethiopian Brigades, the Belgians outside Elizabethville, the Congolese and the Rhodesian army, with whom contact had to be made.

The 39th Infantry Battalion under Lt Col. Pat Dempsey, April-October 1963, relieved the 38th Battalion and was charged with ensuring the maintenance of law and order in its allotted sector, neutralising quickly and efficiently any attempts to disturb the peace and guaranteeing the freedom of UN troops by patrolling. The numerical disparity with the 38th Battalion precluded the maintenance of all occupied posts. Retrenchment was indicated. However, an order to occupy Dilolo to cut off from Katanga these gendarmerie who had fled to Angola meant that the 39th Battalion, instead of economising in manpower, was to be immediately stretched to breaking point. The order was rescinded on 20 May. While in Dilolo very friendly relations were established with the Portugese army. All ranks projected an excellent public image.

As part of a phase-out schedule for the complete withdrawal of ONUC, the 2nd Infantry Group, under the command of Lt Col. Redmond O'Sullivan, was activated on 28 October 1963 and took up duties in Kolwezi to also ensure, by patrolling, the maintenance of law and order and freedom of movement. As well as the usual run of incidents and tensions they managed to settle a strike at the *Union Minière*—the Irish UN Force was nothing if not versatile! Discipline was very good due, perhaps, to the paternalistic and protective Irish approach towards their men. Other units did not worry whether a man spent the night in his quarters or not so long as he was available for duty when required. A single antisocial act in earlier Irish operations is notable for its rarity: after the December-January fighting following the fall of Kolwezi on 30 December 1962 a soldier was charged with 'demanding the wife of a Congolese'. He was disciplined at once.

The 2nd Infantry Group returned to Ireland on 26 May 1964. On 30 June the United Nations Force in the Congo withdrew according to plan. The military phase of ONUC was completed.

Cyprus was the next area of operations. In spite of complicated constitutional arrangements violent intercommunal strife erupted between the Greek and Turkish communities

The Minister for Defence, Mr Oscar Traynor, with the Army High Command, 1943

The Deputy Garda Commissioner, General W.R.E. Murphy (*seated left*) and the Minister for Justice, Gerald Boland, with the Naas District Command of the LSF during the Emergency

Col. Dan Bryan

The Taoiseach, Mr John A. Costello, accompanied by Major-General Liam Archer, Chief of Staff, inspects a guard of honour of cadets to mark the passing of the Republic of Ireland Act 1949

Sean MacEoin, the legendary 'Blacksmith of Ballinalee' and now Minister for Defence, inspects an FCA guard of honour under the command of Comdt Jim Dukes, April 1951

Preparing to go to the Congo, 1960. The figures in the foreground are (*left to right*) Sgt John Meehan; Sgt P. Lawton; Sgt P. Seymour; Private Dillon; C/QMS Joe O'Donnell and C/Sgt V. Dollard

The funerals of the victims of the Niemba Ambush, 1961

Sgt 'Sixty' Byrne takes out a routine patrol in Cyprus

Irish UN troops guard the Tibnin crossing point in Lebanon

Members of the 25th Irish Infantry group were
amongst the first UNEF troops to
cross the Suez Canal, at 1135 hrs GMT on November 1973

Three corvettes of the naval service

A 'casualty' being brought aboard the L.E. *Eithne* during a simulated air-sea rescue

Prepared for all eventualities

Air Corps helicopters over Baldonnel, 25 September 1987

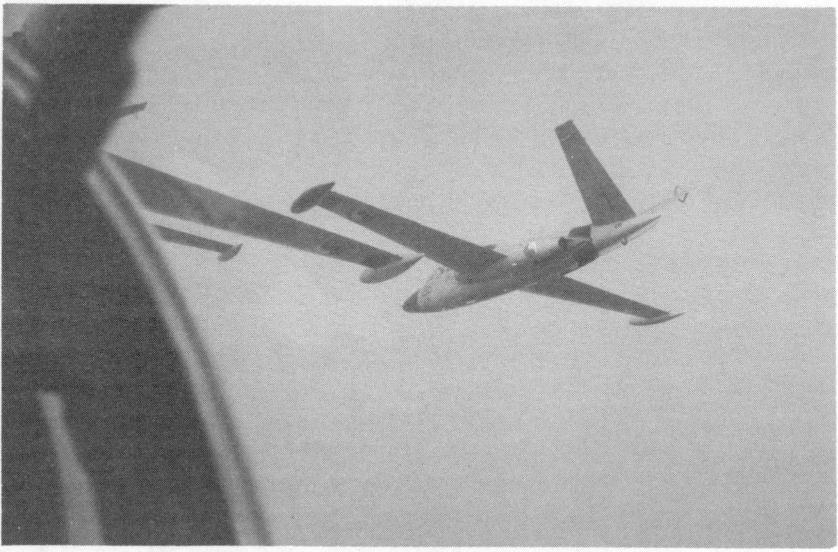

The Air Corps Fouga Magisters over the Shannon area, 23 July 1990

Lieutenant-General William Callaghan

in Cyprus in December 1963. The fighting continued intermittently during 1964, and in an endeavour to restore peace there UNFICYP was then established, with contingents from Austria, Canada, Denmark, Finland, Ireland, Sweden and the United Kingdom. Deployed in sensitive areas, the Force interposed itself between Greek and Turkish military positions or set up adjacent posts to deter recurrence of fighting or, if it did flare up, to quench it by persuasion and negotiations. It required frequent patrolling to remote villages and making the UN presence felt to stop the shooting once it started. *Enosis*, the desire for union with Greece sponsored by Greek leaders, Archbishop Makarios and Gen. Grivas, was a bone of contention.

The mission in effect was to maintain the ceasefire and normal law and order in the best interests of the security and wellbeing of the two communities. In addition, a contribution had to be made to the humanitarian relief programme with the United Nations High Commission for Refugees and World Food Programme and to carry out requested Red Cross/Red Crescent functions.

The 40th Battalion under Lt Col. P.P. Barry, April to October 1964, was the first Irish unit sent to Cyprus to keep the peace between the Moslem Turkish and Orthodox Greek Cypriots. Based in Famagusta it contained the shooting when it broke out, investigated killings and exercised influence by extensive patrolling and sensitive escorting. No means of furthering peacekeeping — including medical cum intercommunal humanitarian work — was neglected. In July the 3rd Infantry Group under Lt Col. T. J. McDonald, July 1964 to January 1965, took over nearby Larnaca district from 1st Battalion Royal Inniskilling Fusiliers in order to maintain peace in that area and to endeavour to restore the situation to normal. The Irish strength in UNFICYP was then the battalion and one group, with Col. J. J. Quinn the Commander of the Irish Contingents and Force Deputy Chief of Staff. He was succeeded by Col. Carl O'Sullivan in November 1964.

The Indian Force Commander (Gen. Thimayya) later decided to rotate the 3rd Infantry Group with 3 Company 28th Swedish Battalion in Paphos district, as the district was considered too large for the Swedes. Shooting was then stopped and conditions were created for ploughing, sowing, harvesting, vaccinations, inoculations and the opening up of mines. Gen. Thimayya wrote at the end of the 3rd Infantry Group's tour a commendation which represented the contributions of each and every Irish unit which served in Cyprus:

> On the occasion of the Group's impending return to Ireland I send warm greetings and grateful thanks to Lt Col. T. J. McDonald and All Ranks 3rd Infantry Group. First in Larnaca, and latterly round Paphos and Polis, you have done a fine job of peacekeeping on behalf of the United Nations. In the process the Group has won golden opinions, not only with UNFICYP itself, but also among all sections of the Cyprus population. Your cheerfulness, friendly approach to others, and resolute performance of any tasks given you combine to make you hard to replace, and we shall miss you greatly. God speed, Good Luck and Thank you.
> *Beannacht Dé libh agus go dteich sibh slán abhaile* (God bless you and a safe return home).

In a subsequent letter the general told Lt Col. P. J. Delaney that *all* the Irish units' devotion to duty would long be remembered by those in UNFICYP who had been lucky enough to serve alongside them. He also paid tribute to the valuable contribution to the work of the Force made by successive Irish officers in the appointments of Assistant Chief of Staff and other key jobs at UNFICYP HQ. On the Irish side (which incidentally had to spend an inordinate amount of time under canvas) there was a keen appreciation of the logistical support provided by British elements.

The 4th Infantry Group under Lt Col. P. D. Hogan, January to July 1965, replaced the 3rd Infantry Group and in April 1965 the 42nd Infantry Battalion under Lt Col. P.J. Delaney took over Morphu District until the following September, when the battalion stood down and was not replaced. Thereafter a succession of Infantry groups rotated every six months, mainly in the Lefka district and then back again to Larnaca until 1973.

The mere presence of the Irish in an area seemed to induce stability. The O/C of the 13th Infantry Group in

Lefka during 1969–70 gave permission to all ranks to bring their wives or girl friends out to Cyprus to visit them; this idea of enlivening the Christmas period was greeted with enthusiasm. Cyprus, however, could never be said to be back to 'normal' but in Irish areas things were as near as could be got to it. That took hard work and manpower.

A major problem therefore, was created for Lt Col. Callaghan's 21st Infantry Group (October 1971 to April 1972) when one of his companies was recalled due to the continuing situation in Northern Ireland. Succeeding groups had to carry on with an attenuated company organisation. Ireland none the less contributed over 9,000 troops to UNFICYP since its inception.

In August 1973 the 25th Infantry Group, similarly organised, took over from a corresponding 24th Infantry Group in Larnaca. For the first time the Infantry Company was drawn exclusively from one battalion, the 12th Infantry Battalion. The mission remained the prevention of a recurrence of fighting, contributing to the maintenance of law and order and a return to normal conditions. The work of UNFICYP over the years was manifest on the surface and there was an appearance of calm and quiet in Cyprus.

At that time (6 October 1973) the outbreak of the Yom Kippur War had shattered the fragile peace between Arab and Jew in the Middle East. In Sinai the Egyptians crossed the Canal and were consolidating their hold over the whole of the East Bank. In the north the Israelis destroyed the Syrian armour and advanced towards Damascus. The UN brought about a ceasefire and on 25 October 1973 decided to send a peacekeeping force (UNEF II) to the Middle East to supervise it. This was on the last complete day of the 24th Infantry Group in Cyprus. The 25th Infantry Group moved in and took over from them.

It had no sooner done that, than it was detailed to be prepared to join the new peacekeeping force in Egypt. The Austrian, Finnish and Swedish Contingent in Cyprus were also involved in the move. UNFICYP responsibilities were handed over to the Force Reserve (16/5 Lancers). The first contingent with Lt Col. Allen O/C the 25th Infantry Group aboard departed Akrotiri RAF base in miserable weather for Cairo on 31 October. Along with the 127 personnel of the Group who departed for service with UNEF II were two Irish MP NCOs of HQ UNFICYP. A rear party of two NCOs — BQMS Tierney and CQMS Darcy — and two privates, Pte Keane and Pte Jordan, were left behind in Cyprus.

Irish capacity for improvisation had to be stretched to the limits to deal with the difficult conditions and lack of facilities they encountered in Cairo. Throughout the night there was sporadic shooting of tracer, flares and automatic fire. Recce (reconnaissance) parties got through Egyptian lines but were prevented by the Israelis from penetrating further into Sinai. Without consultation the harbour party had been moved to Ismailia, complicating arrangements with an incoming Irish augmentation party which came under command O/C the 25th Infantry Group, now numbering 260 all ranks. The Group was ordered to cross the Canal on 9 November — the first UNEF II troops to cross into Israeli-occupied Sinai.

The route led through the heavily fortified positions of the Egyptian 2nd Army on the road to Suez. Death and destruction hung over the battlefield. At this point the Egyptians favoured rigid defensive positions; the Israelis remained relatively mobile. On 11 November the Group commenced reconnaissance patrols in the area. The Israeli Defence Forces did not make their task easy. Irish members of UNTSO were most helpful, particularly Col. Dick Bunworth and his wife, Joan, Capt. Joe Fallon and Capt. Barry Studdert. The wives and families of Irish officers serving in Egypt and Israel rallied in wholehearted support to welcome personnel of the Group on leave from the desert. The Group was blessed in the high quality of its officers, NCOs and men who took this step into an unknown combat situation in their stride.

Hand in hand with the operational task in Sinai went the equally hazardous task of acquiring rations and supplies and of the development of the base camp at Rabah. Activities by Egyptians and Israeli Forces brought positions 501 and 502 under fire several times. At the end of January 1974 a five-stage Disengagement Agreement (Operation Calender) was signed. After that the Irish Battalion controlled the main route between Jerusalem and Cairo and was given the additional tasks of supervising the exchange of prisoners of war, the handing over of bodies and the safe passage of civilians. In March-April they made a new camp, Benburb, in Negela. The Group had performed well in Cyprus, overcome many adversities in Cairo and carried out its mission in Sinai with flair. Its successor, the 26th Infantry Group (commanded by the present Chief of Staff, Gen. Parker) was recalled after six weeks because of the bombings in Dublin. Vacating an important area in Sinai at a crucial time left the UN with a problem. The withdrawal exercise was looked on from afar as a cosmetic charade which ignored serious UN problems on the ground. It left a bad taste.[4] Four years elapsed before Irish troops were to be asked to return to UN duty. Young officers missed this experience. But the withdrawal was not as capricious as some in UN HQ seemed to think. The three car bombs in Dublin and one in Monaghan had killed thirty-two and injured 174.

In retaliation for a PLO commando raid near Tel Aviv on 11 March 1978 which left thirty-seven Israelis dead and seventy-six wounded, the Israeli forces invaded Lebanon on 14–15 March 1978. Following a complaint from the Lebanese government and an American initiative a United Nations Interim Force in Lebanon (UNIFIL) was established to confirm the withdrawal of Israeli Forces, restore international peace and security, assist the return to the government of the Lebanon of its authority in the area and provide humanitarian assistance to the local population. The operation was mounted in an emergency and deployed, without agreement, in haste. Objectives were controversial and ambiguous, terms of reference woolly, and assumptions unrealistic. The precise area of operations was not defined.

The unenviable task of acting as interim Commander of the operation at the outset went to Lt Gen. Emmanuel A. Erskine, a distinguished Ghanaian officer of wide UN experience who was well respected by Irish contingents. He was appointed Force Commander on 12 April 1978 and remained at this post until 14 February 1981 when he was reappointed Chief of Staff UNTSO and succeeded at UNIFIL by Ireland's highly regarded Lt Gen. William Callaghan, who held the post with great distinction until 1986 when he was appointed Chief of Staff of UNTSO.

In order to make UNIFIL operational without delay in 1978 Erskine transferred personnel from the existing contingents: Iranian (UNDOF) and Swedish (UNEF). Later, in response to an appeal by the Secretary General, other countries agreed to provide contingents. In June 1982 Lt Gen. Callaghan commanded the following Force:

*Infantry Battalions*: Fiji (628), France (595), Ghana (557), Ireland (671), Nepal (432), Netherlands (810), Nigeria (696), Norway (660), Senegal (561).
*HQ Camp Command*: Ghana (140), Ireland (51).
*Logistic Units*: France (775), Italy (34), Norway (191), Sweden (144).

Subsequently UNIFIL consisted of a headquarters at Naqoura and six battalions drawn from Fiji, Finland, Ghana, Ireland, Nepal and Norway (total strength 5,126).

To start with UNIFIL did not have a sound political base, a well-defined mandate, clear objectives nor, above all, co-operation of the parties concerned. The intractable Palestinian problem precluded that, and US concern for the Egyptian-Israeli peace treaty (the Camp David Accords) was another impediment.

US support for Israel was strewn with difficulties. Imminent complications internationally were the Iranian Revolution (1979); the seizure of American hostages (1979); and the Russian invasion of Afghanistan (1980). In 1980 also the Iran-Iraq war broke out. The government of Lebanon, even with UNIFIL's assistance, was unable to assert its authority. Israel persistently refused to withdraw to the International Boundary.

There were no clear directions to UNIFIL for handling the proliferating armed elements in the area nor for what to do if the Israelis refused to withdraw. With their egregious allies in South Lebanon — the De Facto Forces (DFF)/ the South Lebanese Army (SLA) — the Israelis repeatedly harassed and obstructed UNIFIL. The Dáil however, while alive to the uncertainties of UNIFIL's role, decided on balance to approve the return of Irish troops to UN duty after four years' rustication.

The Irish Battalion was organised into a Battalion HQ (Tibnin), a HQ Company, three Rifle Companies (A,B,C,) and a Recce (reconnaissance) Company. It occupied an area eleven miles from north to south and eight miles from east to west in the south east of the UNIFIL area of operations, i.e. in the general area Tibnin, At Tiri, Haddathah, Brashit, Haris, As Sultaniyah, Maj Dal-Silm, Quabrikha — an area of approx 140 sq. kms. The terrain is marked by stony hills and deep valleys. The valleys are usually tilled for crops such as tobacco, cereals and some vegetables. The road network is poor. The population, which is almost entirely Moslem, lives in villages, the most prominent of which is Tibnin, where the Irish Battalion had its HQ. The IRISHBATT area is divided into three company areas, A, B, C, with an element in reserve.

IRISHBATT carries out its mission by:

(*a*) Maintaining a village presence.
(*b*) Operating checkpoints.
(*c*) Operating observations posts.
(*d*) Patrolling.
(*e*) Providing humanitarian assistance.
(*f*) Maintaining a curfew.

The main Lebanese factions in the dispute in South Lebanon today with whom UNIFIL comes into contact are:

(*a*) *Amal.* A Shia Moslem organisation which enjoys widespread support in South Lebanon. Its leader is Nabbi Berri, a native of Tibnin who is a minister in the Lebanese government. The organisation is favourably disposed towards UNIFIL. It is opposed to the maintenance by Israel of a security zone in Lebanon and its military wing, acting on its own and in conjunction with others, mounts attacks on the compounds in that area.

(*b*) *Hizbollah.* This is an extreme, Islamic fundamentalist, militant organisation based in the Bekaa Valley. It draws its support from the Shia Moslem population and its funds and inspiration from Iran. It has not had widespread support in

South Lebanon but the ready availability of funds has added to its attractiveness in an area which is economically depressed. It is anti-western in outlook and anti-UNIFIL. The existence of the State of Israel is anathema to it, the Israeli presence in Lebanon abhorrent.

(*c*) *PLO.* The presence of the Palestine Liberation Organisation in Lebanon and its use of that country as a base from which to launch attacks against Israel was the main reason for Israel's two invasions of Lebanon in the past. Prior to 1982 the PLO was a major force in Lebanon, controlling certain key areas, notably Tyre, Sidon and areas of Beirut. In addition to being a thorn in the side of Israel, its activities were resented by a section of the Lebanese population, both Moslem and Christian. This resulted in Israel finding ready allies within Lebanon, when it came to launch its attack against the PLO in 1982. Since that invasion, and the driving out of Lebanon of large numbers of its fighters, the PLO is confined mainly to its camps under the watchful eye of Amal. Consequently PLO members impinge much less on UNIFIL than they did prior to 1982.

(*d*) *SLA.* The South Lebanese Army, more commonly referred to as the DFF (De Facto Forces), is maintained, financed, controlled and trained by Israel. It is the successor to the Christian Militia of Major Haddad who died in 1984. Its initial purpose was to defend the Christian population of South Lebanon from PLO and radical Moslem groups. Israel uses it to maintain a security zone inside Lebanon immediately north of her border as a buffer against would-be attackers. This zone is maintained by manning a number of strong points or compounds on dominating ground, patrolling, and manning checkpoints. The forward positions are heavily armed and equipped, and can call on the physical presence of Israeli personnel and supporting fire from the Israel Defence Forces, including long-range artillery and helicopter gun ships.

From the outset Observer Groups in the UNIFIL area assisted the new force in the performance of its mandate, acting as initial guides, liaison offices, staff officers, advisors and assistants. Apart from a sometimes uneasy relationship between Observer Group Lebanon (OGL) and the new force[5] arising from misconstructions, the role of UNTSO in UNIFIL was positive and generally appreciated. UNTSO's main concerns were the conflict between Israel and Lebanon and Israel and Syria and it works closely with UNIFIL and UNDOF (United Nations Disengagement Observer Force). It still maintains a presence in Egypt and Jordan even though these fronts are now quiet.

The first unit in — always a dangerous operation — was Lt Col. Eric Guerin's 43rd Battalion in May 1979. A recce and planning party from AHQ under Lt Col. Louis Hogan (afterwards Lt General and Chief of Staff) went out to assist with the recce on the ground and with advice on the settling in. It assessed requirements and reported back accordingly. New York advice was that the Irish contingent 'be as self-sufficient as possible in every respect'. Everything from refrigerated road trucks to wall clocks was packed. Never before was a unit so well equipped. In the period 7–19 June 250 truck loads of stores and ammunition were lifted from Tel Aviv airport to Haris. It was all required but, in conventional operations, the Infantry Battalion was organised as a combat unit with limited logistical support capability. It now had the additional problem of handling this vast volume of stores in the forward area and this affected its mobility. But as with all Irish units, problems, no matter how gross, were there to be solved.

The first shots were fired on 23 June 1978 when a patrol of the 43rd Battalion came under machine-gun fire at Rshaf. On 27 June the DFF brought fire to bear on the At Tiri post and the 43rd deployed to defend the village. These DFF attempts to take over this strategic village in the Irish area of operations came to a head in April 1980, in retaliation apparently for Ireland's recognition of the role of the PLO in representing the Palestinian people. Haddad threatened force to drive out the Irish. With the Israelis they did everything in their power to discredit the battalion and have it redeployed — especially after the Nepalese contingent pulled out in late 1980. The Force Commander had good reason for deciding against such redeployment. In April 1980 the

DFF, with the support of the Israeli Defence Forces (IDF), attempted to 'muscle in' on At Tiri[6] by setting up a checkpoint there, and a confrontation involving Erskine's deployment of the Force Mobile Reserve took place. It would have been a serious reverse to have allowed Haddad to control the village and so dominate the Irish area. It would have signalled the end of the mission. On 7 April fire was exchanged and the first Irish fatal casualty — Pte John Griffin — was sustained. Key terrain in the area was Hill 880. The turning point in establishing UNIFIL's credibility in the area was the insistence of the IRISHBATT (46th Battalion) under Col. Jack Kissane, in holding that ground. The defence was a watershed in DFF/UNIFIL relations.

The conclusion of the incident did not, however, end the confrontation. The DFF shelled the Force HQ at Naquora. Irish were wounded and there was widespread destruction of property and equipment. On 18 April Haddad's militias murdered two Irish soldiers, Pte John Barrett and Pte Derek Smallhorne.

There were casualties on both sides but victory went to the Irish, who nonetheless remained conscious that a peace-keeping operation must achieve its objectives without — except as an authorised last resort — recourse to force. The UN Security Council, however, supported the stand taken by adopting Resolution 467 which sanctioned UNIFIL's right to use force in defence of themselves and their positions.

The DFF used small arms, heavy machine-gun, mortar and tank fire indiscriminately against Irish and UNIFIL troops. UNIFIL's fire in response was carefully measured. During this distraction the PLO launched a successful attack and Israel immediately responded by dispatching 250 heavily armed and supported troops into South Lebanon. The Israelis claimed the the PLO had infiltrated through Irish and Nigerian Battalion areas. This was the heart of the matter. The Israelis continued to support the DFF, who continued to try an thwart the UN. The paradox was that there were more advantages than disadvantages for the Israelis in UNIFIL's presence. Israeli actions nonetheless serve to make the full accomplishment of UNIFIL's mission practically impossible. In June 1982 when Israel invaded the Lebanon the UN was left in a rear area. The Israeli withdrawal in 1985 again placed UNIFIL in the front line. Isolated OPs were closed and more secure compounds opened. The ill-fated Multinational Force (MNF) in Beirut collapsed in October 1983 when seventy-eight French soldiers and 241 US Marines were killed by suicide bombing attacks. The Russians, who had been excluded from Middle East diplomacy, now saw to it that UNIFIL did not replace the MNF, though it was requested to do so by the US and French Security Council members.

In Lt Col. Savino's 44th Battalion's time (November 1978 to April 1979) a very tense period of confrontation just stopped short of firing when the Irish first stood their ground. This was the answer to critics who claimed that the Irish 'kid gloves' approach encouraged DFF encroachment. On 9 May 1979 IDF troops of battalion strength supported by tanks crossed the border into the DFF enclave, cleared a minefield in the vicinity of Haule and entered Shaqra village. They were blocked by C Company 44th Infantry Battalion, who were down to fifty strong due to rotation (an overlap weakness later remedied). Negotiations ensued. The IDF wanted to search Shaqra, Brashit and other villages for 'armed elements' (a descriptive term used internationally to described the nineteen Leftist organisations in S. Lebanon) who had attacked the Israeli border area of Ramim during the night 8–9 May 1979. The IRISHBATT refused the IDF this search operation though they did conduct their own search.

The IDF called up reinforcements of twenty armoured personnel carriers. DUTCHBATT armoured elements, followed later by further Dutch, Nigerian, and Senegalese, arrived to support the Irish troops. The IDF backed off. The 44th Battalion had stood up to the aggressors and faced them down. Good discipline and cool heads won through. Its successor, the 45th Battalion, was also subject to shelling and pressure from DFF/SLA. The UN posts in a buffer zone between the UN area and the Israeli border were controlled by the DFF. This made virtual hostages of them and so limited the action which IRISHBATT could take.

On the other side the armed elements were the menace. They indulged in a variety of actions against UNIFIL in spite of political direction. Fijians were killed, Dutch wounded. They were also involved in Kathuska Rocket attacks on Israel, small arms and RPG attacks on the DFF and suicide raids into Israel. In Israeli eyes these were the enemies which the UN should be fighting.

US ambivalence weakened the possibility of UNIFIL accomplishing its mission. A blind eye was turned by them to Israeli support for the DFF with captured 122 mm howitzers, 120mm mortars, 105mm Super Sherman tanks, half tracks, HMGs, MGs, small arms, ammunition, rations and pay. In April 1979 they raked the IRISHBATT area with artillery fire (181 shells) while the Irish were responsible for the safety of the Lebanese troops coming under operational control. The shelling did not stop the Lebanese army being deployed as planned. Haddad's 'Independent Lebanon' ploy was foiled when the 44th Battalion opposed him at Brashit by deploying all its armoured vehicles and heavy mortars. The 44th Battalion had faced a very difficult and dangerous situation and, considering the amount of shelling, HMG fire and small arms fire directed at that battalion, the lack of casualties is amazing. The same could be said of every battalion that has served with UNIFIL.[7]

Lt Col. Peter Feeley recalled writing letters home to the sound of gunfire assuring the folks at home that everything was quiet out there. Coming up to Christmas 1989 the constant 'plastering' of A Company positions in the Lebanon did not make the headlines. Being under fire was routine now. The following serious incidents which occurred during 1989 index that situation:

(*a*) 24 February: Pte McNeela killed in Haddathah by DFF gunfire.

(*b*) 21 March: Cpl Heneghan, Pte Armstrong and Pte Walsh killed by landmine explosion near Brashit.

(*c*) 17 May: A billet in Camp Shamrock containing ten soldiers was hit by a tank round fired by the DFF. Two soldiers were injured.

(*d*) 21 December: Direct hit by tank round on UN position at Quabrikha.

In the UNIFIL area there is a high incidence of War Debris/EOD (bomb disposal) activity in every tour: air-dropped unexploded cluster grenades, shells of various calibres, land mines and hand grenades. The most bizarre EOD call (to the 44th Battalion) concerned a coffin (occupied). Bomb disposal officers joke about another hazard: the fondness of scorpions for nestling up to unexploded bombs. Improvised explosive devices (IEDs), e.g. roadside bombs, are a particular menace. Tragically, Lt Kevin Murphy (son of Major Gen. Kevin Murphy, the retired Adjutant General) was murdered by one of these devices. Proper armament and equipment give no protection against murder.

The UNIFIL Irish contingent is supported by fourteen Panhard M3 armoured personnel carriers (APCs) and four Panhard H-90 armoured cars which mount the heaviest armament of any UNIFIL contingent.[8] A Force Mobile Reserve[9] (FMR) was set up in January 1987 to which the Irish contribute a personnel element: one lieutenant colonel (O/C); one captain (Troop Commander) and around twenty other ranks (with RSM, BQMS). This broadens vehicle experience (e.g. with the Finnish-developed Sisu APCs). This reserve unit is ready to move at a moment's notice to any threatened UN position. In addition to the Sisu were three Panhard AML 90 'Lynx' vehicles. The FMR embodies mobility and fire power — some of the many faces of UNIFIL. It is a strong, Irish-led, multinational 'fire brigade' for self-defence with enough fire power to be taken notice of. In addition the Irish also provide a component of UNIFIL HQ. The security of their own HQ in Tibnin — Camp Shamrock — is also a source of concern, as are position 6-28A and the new De Facto Forces Compound near Tallusah.

The Irish Panhard APCs have done their bit for UNIFIL. They are now been replaced by Sisu armoured personnel carriers (recalling the 'might-have-beens' for an Irish defence industry). The Steyr rifle has also been introduced to the battalion.

Ireland has been a contributor to UNIFIL since its inception and has already contributed in excess of 16,000 all ranks.

Irish officers under Lt Col. T. Ryan also supervised a ceasefire between India and Pakistan on the India-West Pakistan border from September 1965 to March 1966 (UNIPOM: United Nations India-Pakistan Observer Mission). A number of Irish observers from UNTSO were also deployed to that mission for a short period. UNIPOM terminated in 1960 when both parties fulfilled the Security Council's resolution by withdrawing. UNMOGIP (United Nations Military Observer Group in India and Pakistan) strength was reduced to forty-five drawn from the some ten contributing countries.

Ireland was not initially one of the countries contributing to UNMOGIP. Although it was established in 1949, the Irish did not participate until Brig. Gen. James Parker (present Chief of Staff) was appointed Chief Military Observer in 1987. It had its origin in the conflict between India and Pakistan over the status of the state of Kashmir. In 1989 it consisted of thirty-nine observers, stationed along the ceasefire line, who reported to the Secretary General on observance of the ceasefire, and investigated complaints by the parties. The current Chief Observer of UNMOGIP is Brig. Gen. Enright.

In addition, at UN request, an Irish inspection team visited the Iran/Iraq war in 1984.

There was a time when Irish troops might have envied Imperial soldiers their chances of foreign travel; not any more. Empires have withered away leaving in their wake a growing peacekeeping requirement. The 'world's policeman' has a new role, Chapter Six and a Half (a mixture of persuasion and force) and has new meanings. The Irish are acceptable everywhere because of their adaptability to all sorts of operations.

Prior to 1988 a United Nations Peace Mission had been classified as either a Peace Mission or an Observer Mission. With the signing of the Geneva Accords in April of that year a new concept was born, that of a Good Offices Mission.

The United Nations Good Offices Mission in Afghanistan and Pakistan (UNGOMAP) was established to cater for the new idea. The Accords, which were the result of several years of intense diplomatic activity by Diego Cordovez of Ecuador, who was acting as representative of the Secretary General of the United Nations, were signed by Afghanistan and Pakistan, High Contracting Parties, and by the USSR and the US, the guarantors. The Accords included four instruments which provided for:

(*a*) A bilateral agreement between Afghanistan and Pakistan on non-interference and non-intervention in each other's internal affairs.

(*b*) A bilateral agreement between Afghanistan and Pakistan on the voluntary return of refugees to Afghanistan.

(*c*) A declaration of international guarantees signed by the USSR and the US.

(*d*) A declaration on inter-relationships to deal with the withdrawal of foreign (Soviet) troops from Afghanistan and to set out a time-frame for its implementation.

Major Gen. Rauli Helminen of Finland took over as the Deputy Representative of the Secretary General in the Mission area.

One Irish officer, Lt Col. Patsy McHale, was seconded from UNTSO and arrived in Islamabad (Pakistan) in April 1988. Four more were sent direct from Ireland (Comdts H. Quirke, J. Quilty, J. Martin and M. Verling). All five arrived in the Mission area on 2 May; two were deployed to Islamabad in Pakistan and three to Kabul in Afghanistan. The Irish officers based in Kabul were involved in the monitoring of the withdrawal of the Soviet troops from Afghanistan which was completed on 15 February 1989. The officers on the Pakistan side were involved in the investigation of complaints of interference and intervention in each other's internal affairs by both High Contracting Parties. They were also to confirm the voluntary return of refugees from Pakistan to Afghanistan.

Evocative of other Irishmen in different uniforms in Kipling's time, the Irish officers in this mission in the line of duty had to journey up the Khyber Pass and to the foothills of Hindu Kush.

Later that year in a relatively adjacent part of the field the ceasefire between Iran and Iraq became effective on 20 August 1988, and the United Nations Iran/Iraq Military Observer Group (UNIIMOG) was established by Resolution 619 of the Security Council. The observer group of 350 military officers includes fifteen Irish officers. In addition to the officer observers an Irish Military Police unit of thirty-eight all ranks is serving with UNIIMOG. It is deployed in Iran and Iraq with its HQ in Baghdad. The mission of UNIIMOG is as follows:

(*a*) To establish agreed ceasefire lines.
(*b*) To monitor the ceasefire.
(*c*) To investigate violations of the ceasefire.
(*d*) To prevent changes in the status quo.
(*e*) To supervise the withdrawal of all forces to internationally recognised borders.
(*f*) To reduce tension and build confidence between Iran and Iraq.

Operations by the observers are carried out by conducting mobile patrols, maintaining liaison with both sides and investigating violations of the ceasefire. Brig. Gen. James Kelly was Assistant Chief Military Observer, Iran Operations, for the first year of operation of UNIIMOG.

The next year saw a return of *Óglaigh na hÉireann* to Africa when the United Nations Transition Assistance Group (UNTAG) in Namibia was established by UN Security Council Resolution 435 on 1 April 1989. It consisted of three battalions drawn from Malaysia, Kenya and Finland, 300 military observers and 1,700 logistic support troops. There were also 500 civilian police drawn from various countries including fifty from Ireland. The mission of UNTAG was to assist the Special Representative of the Secretary General of the United Nations in the fulfilment of his mandate. This involved the monitoring of the South West African Peoples Organisation (SWAPO), the South African Military and Police Forces (including the dismantling of those Forces to agreed levels) and the supervision of elections in November 1989. Concurrent with the carrying out of its mission, the withdrawal of Cuban Forces from Angola was supervised by the United Nations Assistance Verification Mission. Two of the twenty Irish officers serving with UNTAG were located in Angola. The other eighteen were located in the southern part of Namibia in Keetmanshoop and Luderitz. The Irish observer involvement terminated in March 1990.

Towards the end of 1989 another continent, Central America, was opened up as a new area of operations for the Irish. There is no need to stress the sensitivities involved. The United Nations Observer Group in Central America (ONUCA) was established by Security Council Resolution 644 of 7 November 1989. Its purpose was on-site verification of the security undertakings in the Guatemala Agreement of 7 August 1987. The countries involved are Costa Rica, El Salvador, Guatemala, Honduras and Nicaragua. These countries have undertaken to cease aid to irregular forces and insurrectionist movements operating in the region and the non-use of the territory of one State for attacking others. The headquarters of the Group was located at Tegucigalpa in Honduras with an HQ and liaison office in each of the capitals of the five countries. Patrols and surveillance were operated from thirty-three verification sites along the border in the area, using helicopters, patrol vessels and vehicles. The deployment of 260 military observers took place in three phases. Two colonels, two lieutenant colonels and two commandants went out at the beginning of December 1989. They were followed at the end of February by two more lieutenant colonels and three commandants. A lieutenant colonel and seven commandants went out at the end of January to be followed by two more lieutenant colonels and three commandants at the beginning of March 1990. It was anticipated that the mission would last for one year. A further phase involving thirteen Irish observers was planned. The senior appointments held are Chief Operations Officer in HQ ONUCA and Chief Observer Group Costa Rica.

All these missions have a limited mandate which must be renewed in the Security Council each time it falls due, or let lapse. UNTSO, on the other hand, has an open-ended mandate and is used by the Secretary General to plan and start up all or almost all new missions. Consequently Irish officers have been involved in the initial stages of all the following missions:

(*a*) ONUC
(*b*) UNFICYP
(*c*) UNEF II
(*d*) UNDOF
(*e*) UNIFIL
(*f*) UNIPOM

(*g*) UNGOMAP (*i*) UNTAG
(*h*) UNIIMOG (*j*) ONUCA

In addition since 1976 an Irish officer has been deputy to the Military Advisor to the Secretary General at UN HQ in New York.

It is a matter of intense pride to the Defence Forces that three of its officers, graduates of the Military College's Cadet School, have held the highest command in UN military operations.[10] Lt Gen. Sean MacEoin, DSM was Force Commander ONUC 1961–2 with 20,000 multinational UN troops under his command. U Thant, the UN Secretary General, stated that it was under him that law and order was restored, tribal strife kept in check and the people in the cities and the interior succoured. He also stated that Lt Gen. MacEoin had welded the UN Force into an efficient one which acted with great discipline and restraint in trying conditions, including that most difficult of all operations, peace by enforcement, such as Operations Morthar, Rumpunch and Unokat. In recognition of his service in the Congo he was awarded the Distinguished Service Medal (First Class). The University of Dublin(Trinity College) awarded him an honorary degree of LL.D in July 1968.

Major Gen. James J. Quinn, DSM was appointed Force Commander in Cyprus, a post he held from December 1976 until February 1981. In recognition of his service in Cyprus he was awarded the Distinguished Service Medal (First Class). He had also given distinguished service as Deputy Chief of Staff in the Congo under Gen. MacEoin in 1961–2.

Force Commander in the war-wracked Lebanon for the longest period was Lt Gen. W. Callaghan. He commanded the sorely tried United Nations Interim Force in Lebanon (UNIFIL) from February 1981 to May 1986. His legendary performance in that protracted and taxing task has been internationally acclaimed. He was awarded the Distinguished Service Medal (First Class) in 1984, and in March 1986 he received an Honorary Doctorate of Law (LL.D. *Honoris Causa*) from the National University of Ireland. He was also awarded the *Légion d'Honneur* (France) and the Lebanese authorities conferred on him the National Cedar Decoration of Commander's Rank.

Tribute must also be paid to the magnificent performance abroad of the NCOs and men. The way they handled themselves and situations abroad is a matter for deep national pride. Every soldier abroad is conscious of being an ambassador of his country.

Service with the UN has resulted in the award of six Military Medals for Gallantry, seven Distinguished Service Medals (First Class), thirty-nine Second Class and thirty-four Third Class. Nearly every Chief of Staff since the regularisation of *Óglaigh na Éireann* has seen active service, either in the War of Independence or with the UN.

The involvement which began in a small way in 1958 in acceding to a UN request to send officer observers to Lebanon has grown consistently in response to demand. Ireland has been involved in peacekeeping with troops in the Congo, Cyprus, Sinai and Lebanon and observers in the Middle East, West New Guinea (West Iran), Pakistan, Iran/Iraq, Afghanistan, Namibia and Central America. To date over 30,000 men for peacekeeping have been supplied. Rotating commitments (as on 31 December 1989) are as follows:

| | *Offrs* | *NCOs* | *Ptes* | *Total* |
|---|---|---|---|---|
| (*a*) United Nations Truce Supervision Organisation (UNTSO) | 22 | – | – | 22 |
| (*b*) United Nations Force in Cyprus (UNFICYP) | 2 | 6 | – | 8 |
| (*c*) United Nations Military Observer Group in India & Pakistan (UNMOGIP) | 1 | – | – | 1 |
| (*d*) UN HQ (NY) (UNNY) | 1 | – | – | 1 |
| (*e*) United Nations Interim Force in Lebanon (UNIFIL) | | | | |
| 66 Infantry Battalion | 53 | 215 | 390 | 658 |
| 21 Irish Component | 5 | 35 | 14 | 54 |
| Force HQ Staff | 13 | – | – | 13 |
| Force Mobile Reserve | 2 | 12 | 3 | 17 |
| Force MP Company | 2 | 10 | – | 12 |
| (Total - UNIFIL) | (75) | (272) | (407) | (754) |

| | | | | |
|---|---|---|---|---|
| (*f*) United Nations Good Offices Mission Afghanistan/Pakistan (UNGOMAP) | 5 | – | – | 5 |
| (*g*) United Nations Iran/Iraq Military Observer Group (UNIIMOG) | 18 | 25 | – | 43 |
| (*h*) United Nations Transition Group in Namibia (UNTAG) | 20 | – | – | 20 |
| (*i*) United Nations Observer Group in Central America (ONUCA) | 18 | – | – | 18 |
| Grand Total | 162 | 303 | 407 | 872 |

Continued participation in United Nations service reflects credit on the nation as a whole and is of particular benefit to the Forces. It provides operational experience and leadership challenges not otherwise available. It reinforces training and develops and practises skills. Working as part of an International Force or Observer Group also gives an opportunity to weigh up Irish strengths and weaknesses *vis à vis* other nationalities. UN peacekeeping is the next century's best hope of averting major devastating conflict. The Irish government's decision to participate in UN peacekeeping was momentous and farsighted, especially now that neutrality seems destined to achieve a new significance.

Overseas service has attractions for the troops: a good record is essential for a soldier to be selected for such service and this provides incentives for consistent good performance and improving standards. When they do go abroad they get the added satisfaction of finding out that nobody does it better. All ranks and the country benefit.

# 9

## Aid and Assistance
(from 1969)

In 1969 the outbreak of violence in Northern Ireland overshadowed normal work to a very great extent. It constituted a greater menace to the State than the IRA eruption in the 1950s which had necessitated the reintroduction of internment. New Establishments had to be prepared, new units deployed, vital installations protected. There was inevitably less emphasis on long-term planning. The day-to-day requirements took precedence.

Initially, UN operations in Cyprus and the Middle East were maintained. A three-phase mobilisation scheme was planned. Planning studies and liaison with Civil Defence continued. Something had to be done about the inadequate stocks of all types of ammunition and explosives. The chronic low-strength problem came to a head in August 1969 when it became necessary to call up the First Line Reserve.

To further frustrate matters infantry battalion organisations were constantly changing, causing confusion in staff Tables and in accounting for weapons and equipment. Command staffs had to contend with peace, mobilisation, UN Infantry group and home-based Infantry group organisations, most of which were dissimilar. It felt that the basic organisation for an Infantry battalion should be established in such a way that it could be readily adjusted by adding or subtracting companies, platoons or sections. This would facilitate the tailoring of border units to specific missions. Headquarters, Headquarter Company and the Infantry Company HQ should be common to all organisations. If these had to be altered because of the introduction of new weapons and techniques the changes should be common to all organisations.

Another defect in military preparedness was the scarcity of young officers and NCOs. The average age of officers was forty-two and of the NCOs forty and a half.

Internal security situations were not new. They were always there but times were changing and a new look was needed at keeping the peace — either by persuasion or by force. Aid to the civil power began at home — it was not enough to be performing brilliantly abroad.

To meet the immediate threat at home in August 1969 the 14th, 15th and 16th Infantry Groups were quickly formed and quietly deployed in Dundalk, Castleblaney, Cootehill and Cavan. The requirements to provide personnel for these new groups at instant notice, as well as for UN Cyprus contingents and many other activities, in addition to maintaining the training and administration commitments of permanent and FCA units, placed a severe strain on resources. Marshal Foch listed public opinion as a principle of war. It was a resource that now had to be cultivated. Consequently, while for security reasons the Infantry groups deployed silently, more publicity was given to the establishment of refugee camps and field hospitals. The Defence Forces found themselves involved in a newly expanding role, of providing, in changing times, a new dimension of traditional aid to the civil power — a complex operation.

The primary responsibility for the maintenance of law and order rests with the civil power, the Garda Síochána. Provision also exists in law for the Defence Forces to aid the civil power if needs be. Since 1969 subversive threats to the very institutions of the State have proclaimed this need. The IRA have carried out raids for weapons and military equipment, large-scale robberies on banks and cash in transit, kidnappings of prominent businessmen, riots and fomentations of public disorder and the illegal importation of arms and equipment. These threats imposed an intolerable burden on the civil power, and in response to that threat the government authorised the calling out of the Permanent Defence Forces when it became clear that the Gardaí, organised and equipped as they are, could not act as sufficient deterrent to armed elements within the State. Previously, in the 1940s and 1950s, internment in the Curragh was invoked to contain such a threat.

In 1973 the 27th Infantry Battalion was activated and given operational responsibility for the area of the border stretching from Dundalk to Cavan — a major task for one unit. In 1976 a further unit, the 29th Infantry Battalion, was activated to share responsibility for a portion of that large stretch. It took over posts in Cavan and Cootehill and the new barracks in Monaghan. It quickly became closely knit into the local community while still maintaining its essential role of border security. The 28th Battalion, from Finner Camps and Rockhill House, looked after the left flank to Donegal: Manorhamilton, Lifford, Malin Head.

The original 27th, 28th and 29th Battalions had Civil War origins: the 27th under Comdt James Hancock in the Kerry Command with headquarters in Tralee; the 28th under Comdt Tim O'Donnell in the Limerick Command with headquarters in Gort; the 29th under Comdt Michael Stephenson, later Comdt Luke Hegarty, in the Curragh Command with headquarters in the Curragh. These units were disbanded in the 1924 demobilisation when the army was reduced from fifty-five Infantry battalions to twenty-seven. No one took their activation as an omen but if the authority of the State — including the sole right to declare war — continued to be usurped the outcome could be ominous indeed, if democratic rule were to be upheld in the teeth of threats and intimidation masquerading as patriotism.

Prior to 1969 there were no permanent military posts located north of a line from Gormanstown to Mullingar and Galway. Now, the three newly activated Infantry battalions (27th, 28th, 29th) and a Cavalry Squadron have been established and ten permanent military posts developed in the border area. The Minister for the Defence told the Dáil (quoted in the *Irish Independent*, 11 July 1985) of the scale of activity up to 1984 '. . . 12,000 military parties were supplied to the border area for operational duties; about 13,500 checkpoints were set up and 16,500 patrols sent out into the road network along the border area'. O/C 27th Battalion (Lt Col. Hogan) codified operational procedures which were widely adopted.

In carrying out these duties it is painful for members of *Óglaigh na hEireann* to see the once honourable name of the

IRA — integral to its traditions — so sullied and traduced. Gardaí and a member of the PDF have been murdered by the subversives. No one has yet been brought to book for the murder of the married soldier and the young trainee policemen during the Don Tidey rescue operation in 1983.

It is obvious that in dealing with an enemy of this ruthless lawlessness and fundamentalist fanaticism members of *Óglaigh na hÉireann* must be properly armed and equipped. Consideration of the scope and span of the aid to the civil power will reinforce this requirement.

These tasks range from the provision of permanent guards on all military posts and certain vital installations (prisons; explosives factory; Central Banking facility; Government Buildings) to supplying armed parties and escorts for cash, explosives and prisoner movements within the State. In addition there are requirements to provide for specialist tasks, such as bomb disposal, search teams, presence at blasting and air and naval support to the Gardaí.

Air Corps co-operation with the army prior to 1969 was nominal. To the best of its ability it used helicopters supplemented by Dove aircraft. But its equipment generally was obsolete: Chipmunks (17 years old); Provosts (16 years); Vampires (14 years); Dove 176 (17 years); Dove 194 (17 years). To meet the subversion threat to the State and to retain a limited conventional capability all equipment had to be modernised.

The Air Corps is now equipped with the following type of aircraft and navigates with sophisticated avionics by day and by night.

(*a*) British Aerospace Hawker Siddley 125 for ministerial air transport service.

(*b*) Aerospatiale Gazelle helicopters for pilot training and VIP transportation.

(*c*) Beech King Air for fishery protection duties, VIP transportation, air ambulance and search and rescue.

(*d*) Cessna FR 172 for army co-operation.

(*e*) Marchetti SF 260 WE for flying instruction and photographic reconnaissance.

(*f*) SA 365 Dauphin helicopter for search and rescue and fishery protection duties.

(*g*) CM 17 Fouga for advanced pilot training.
(*h*) Aerospatiale Alouette III helicopter for army co-operation and air ambulance.

The Navy, taking gun-running attempts into account in addition to other aspects, has also an important part to play in internal security. With the extension of the exclusive fishery limit to twelve miles and the assumption of responsibility in 1977 for a 200-mile exclusive economic zone the Naval Services' role has been enlarged. In order to preserve a conventional naval role and meet the increased demands of fishery protection the Naval Service has the following vessels:

(*a*) *LE Eithne* helicopter patrol vessel, armed with a Bofors 57 mm automatic gun.
(*b*) *LE Aoife* offshore patrol vessel.
(*c*) *LE Aisling* offshore patrol vessel.
(*d*) *LE Deirdre* offshore patrol vessel.
(*e*) *LE Emer* offshore patrol vessel.
(*f*) *LE Orla* coastal patrol vessel.
(*g*) *LE Ciara* coastal patrol vessel.

(*LE Orla* and *LE Ciara* are ex-RN vessels. All others are built in Cork.) The offshore patrol vessels are armed with Bofors 40 mm and 20 mm guns and the coastal patrol vessels are armed with 76 mm Oto-Melara automatic guns.

The results of the Dublin Institute for Advanced Studies/Hamburg University Rapids I and II experiments indicate that Irish continental shelf mineral rights are more extensive than originally thought. That is going to require further policing and patrolling by the air and naval services. In addition the fleet manages to do two resupply runs a year to the Irish troops in Lebanon.

Up to the current internal security emergency the Cavalry Corps in particular had been badly hit. The Tank Squadron was seen as an expensive joke: if tanks were obtained free of charge they could not be maintained, let alone used. There was no equipment, not even a suitable Establishment for the Armoured Squadron. The Motor Squadron had been equipped apparently on the assumption that the enemy would have no armour and that Irish soldiers would be bullet proof. There was no other explanation for a concept which backed up 7.62 mm gunned armoured cars by troops in soft-skinned vehicles. There have now been improvements arising out of internal security demands. In the field of armoured vehicles the Defence Forces have purchased both Panhard and Timoney APCs, Panhard AML 60s and AML 90s and the Scorpion Combat Reconnaissance Tracked Vehicle. (In UNIFIL the Panhard is to be replaced by the Sisu — see Chapter 8.)

The bomb disposal men of the Ordnance Corps (no women here yet) are of course on active service every day of their lives. Considerable expertise has been developed in both techniques and equipment in Explosive Ordnance Disposal and in Specialist Search Team activities, which are in use both in the Lebanon, on the Dublin–Belfast railway line and more extensively as required. The robot is an Irish Ordnance Corps invention and many countries are purchasing it. The task of bomb disposal is, to date, in the exclusive control of the Defence Forces Explosive Ordnance Team (EOD). Otherwise the Gardaí do the direct interfacing with the people. The policy, except during a brief period in 1976 when the defence provisions of the Emergency Powers Act were enacted, is that the Defence Forces keep a low profile. It was never envisaged that armed soldiers, with a statutory policeman in attendance, would come to searching ladies' handbags in the street. The quick-change role of the soldier trained for conventional warfare is a demanding one. What, indeed, is conventional? Unconventional war may become the norm for the rest of the century and beyond, whether or not its legality is to be established. It may take an all-out application of chapter VII of the UN Charter ('Peace by Enforcement') to contain local conflicts or spill-overs. Resurgent nationalism and fundamentalism are forces to be reckoned with. Security in its wider sense remains a prime preoccupation. The threat to the security of the State was so serious that endemic resistance to providing money to re-equip the Defence Forces was reduced. These are some of the infantry and support weapons included among the purchases made as part of a re-equipment programme:

(*a*) Steyr 5.66 Aug Al which replaces both the FN rifle and the Gustaf SMG.
(*b*) .5 inch Browning heavy machine-gun.
(*c*) Long-barrel 81 mm mortar.
(*d*) 105 mm light field gun.
(*e*) Milan anti-armour missile system.
(*f*) RBS 70 air defence missile system.

In this context may be mentioned the Army Ranger Wing established in 1980 (*Sciathán Fhiannóglaigh an Airm*), in the news in 1990 for succouring civilians stricken by the flooding in Portlaoise. The term '*Fiannóglach*' links the traditions of '*Na Fianna*' (see note 1 Chapter 1) with *Óglaigh na hÉireann.* They specialise in small-unit tactics and long-range patrolling. High standards are exacted in physical endurance, marksmanship and individual military skills. In aiding the civil power they specialise in VIP security, search operations, aircraft hijacking and hostage situations. Flexibility is their main characteristic. The range of incidents which arise in aiding the civil power is wide: attacks on Garda stations; rioting; raiding; burnings; bombings; prisoners escaping; kidnapping; assassination; shootings of police; smuggling of arms by sea. There are also security requirements for visits such as those of the British Prime Minister and the Pope.

There is still a lack of appreciation from predictable sources of the effort involved. The day in, day out border operations have to go on. The border is not a natural delineated physical feature which would yield to normal terrain analysis, though of course local commanders have to analyse the terrain factor in their sectors. It is 448 kilometres long, with 291 crossings, some which are cratered and blocked. It is a political contrivance which bisects property and people but that consideration is irrelevant to the troops on the ground who have a military mission to accomplish. It is manned by *Óglaigh na hÉireann* as follows:

*E Command* = 6 Military Posts
(1) 27th Inf. Bn: Dundalk, Castleblaney, Gormanston.
(2) 29th Inf. Bn: Cootehill, Monaghan, Cavan.
(3) Helicopter: Monaghan.
(4) Fixed wing aircraft: Gormanston.

(5) Bomb Disposal Team: Dundalk.
(6) Specialist Search Team(s): Dundalk/Cootehill.

*W Command* = 4 Military Posts
(1) 4th Cav. Sqn: Longford, Ballyconnell.
(2) 28th Inf. Bn. Finner, Lifford, Rockhill.
(3) Helicopter: Finner.
(4) Bomb Disposal Team: Finner.
(5) Specialist Search Team: Finner.

The legal position regulating that deployment is:

(*a*) Military operate in aid to the civil power (Garda Síochána)
(*b*) Military provide armed protection for Garda Síochána.
(*c*) Military have *no* special statutory powers currently in force to stop civilian vehicles, to detain civilians or to search houses.

The following are the main tasks arising:

(*a*) Mobile patrolling.
(*b*) Road checkpoints/Permanent checkpoints.
(*c*) Searches of unoccupied houses.
(*d*) Searches of areas such as woods.
(*e*) Specialist search.
(*f*) Bomb disposal (EOD).
(*g*) Escorts.
(*h*) Sealing of small sector of border for limited period.
(*j*) Vital installation protection.
(*k*) Extraditions/support operations.

With regard to the use of force the military are governed by Common Law and Statue Law.

In general:

(*a*) North-South security contact is maintained by the RUC and the Garda Síochána. This was enhanced by the Anglo-Irish Agreement of 1985.
(*b*) Military parties are on twenty-four hours' immediate standby in each military post.
(*c*) Procedures operate under the Anglo-Irish Agreement.

The following statistics for 1988 gives some idea of the legwork involved:

*Type of duty* (1988)

| | |
|---|---|
| 1. Military parties supplied for border operations (from half section (5) to company size (120) for periods of from a number of hours to one week) | 21,788 |
| (*a*) Patrols | 11,788 |
| (*b*) Snap checkpoints | 9,725 |
| (*c*) Searches | 275 |
| 2. Permanent border checkpoints | 5 |
| 3. Cash in transit | 1,997 |
| 4. Explosives escorts | 499 |
| 5. Prisoner escorts | 135 |
| 6. Guards on explosives factory and mines | 365 |
| 7. Military presence at blasting | 545 |
| 8. Prison guards | 732 |
| 9. Guard on government buildings | 365 |
| 10. Guards on Sandyford (British Ambassador's residence) | 365 |
| 11. Guards on docks, ships, courts (including Special Criminal Court) | 106 |
| 12. EOD | 165 |
| (*a*) On the border | 19 |
| (*b*) Non-border | 146 |

In addition to the heavy workload imposed by aid to the civil power the Defence Forces have also provided assistance to the civil authorities in times of natural disasters and major emergencies.The Defence Forces have also been called on by the civil authorities to maintain essential services to the community during periods of industrial action.

The following are samples of disasters/emergencies: Whiddy Oil Tanker (January 1979); Snow Hazard (January 1982); CIE Train Accident Kildare (August 1983); Air India Disaster (June 1985); Hurricane Charlie (August 1986); Salvage of *Yarrawonga* (June 1989). In the snow-in 115 military and 156 air missions were carried out covering food and fuel deliveries; air ambulance; hospital supplies; food drops; road and pavement cleaning, etc. For Hurricane Charlie, catering facilities were provided for flood victims in the Ballsbridge area and engineering support at Templeogue, Bray and Avoca. *LE Eithne* and Air Corps personnel were involved in the salvage of the *Yarrawonga.*

The Defence Forces are only called in in the public interest as a last resort. Members have, however, been called on to man sewage pumping stations, mend burst water mains, operate fire fighting services, provide essential courier services, collect refuse, distribute emergency petrol and oil supplies, run an emergency bus service for disadvantaged citizens, secure prisons, help with emergency ambulance cases and clean up to prevent hazards to the public health. Demands made to maintain essential services to the community during periods of industrial action are always irksome, distasteful and often outside the scope of normal capabilities. Properly authorised maintenance of essential services to the community is, however, paramount and *Óglaigh na hÉireann* does its duty as and when properly ordered to do so. The Defence Forces are truly the people's army, and all these tasks give them a chance to show it. Such chores, ill-fitting as they are, like the others such as police support and UN commitments, give the Forces an acceptable visible public image and attract for them resources that might not otherwise be allocated.

The disadvantage, however, is that all these activities tend to deflect the Forces from its primary role of defence. The *gendarme* side of internal security is perhaps more proper to the Gardaí. UN involvement demands deployment in some cases in a manner never intended. On the other hand, overseas service offers a training medium for professional skills without which the Defence Forces would be bereft. Internal security, in the final analysis, has the added dimension of fashioning a facility to expand in response to a significant realignment in the Northern Ireland political military balance.

There is no need for any of these issues to cloud or delay the overdue reform in the Defence Forces to enable it to fulfil its primary role of defence. Representative bodies can have no impact on operational matters; discipline, organisation and operations are specifically outside their scope. Good order and military discipline remain paramount and preparation for war the *raison d'être* of *Óglaigh na hÉireann.*

# Epilogue

The essence of *Óglaigh na hÉireann* is an *esprit de corps* which, as Clausewitz said, 'is the cement which binds together all qualities which taken together give an army military value'. It is the spirit which interlaces the soul of the Forces with the ethos of the people. A mere recitation of happenings will neither capture nor convey this spirit.

Ordnance Survey maps are fundamental tools of military science. Integral to their production is the Survey Company of the Corps of Engineers. The present (1990) Assistant Director is Comdt M.C. Walsh (traditionally the Commissioner of Valuation is Director). The military association goes back to the origins of mapping in the last century. On 10 July 1791 the Ordnance Survey of the British Isles was established and in 1824 the Ordnance Survey, with Col. Colby as its Director, came to Ireland and is in the Phoenix Park (Dublin) ever since.

Its first task was to carry out for taxation purposes an unprecedented six inches to one mile survey (with field boundaries included in the 1830s). In 1842 the survey of all thirty-two counties was completed. In 1887 a resurvey of Ireland at 1:2500 scale was commenced and completed in 1914. A new six-inch series was derived from the larger survey. The indispensable half-inch series was also completed in 1918. In 1922, indicative of what the new State was up against from all sides, less than two hundred staff remained on to maintain an archive of over 25,000 maps. In time, with the efficient use of technology the new management maximised the value of that invaluable archive created over the years.

The Construction Corps also tends to be forgotten. It was founded in 1940 as a non-combatant section of the Defence Forces. It was a social experiment clumsily handled and hardly thought through. Initially elderly Reserve officers from rural backgrounds officered deprived city youngsters who were posted to isolated areas like Nad bog in Connemara. This was remedied in time, though barrack commanders continued to regard the youngsters as ready-made fatigue parties. In spite of obstacles the Construction Corps had many achievements to its credit. It felled trees and cleared scrub in Virginia, Co. Cavan, built roads in north Wicklow, worked on an Irish Tourist Board Scheme in Tramore, planted trees in the Curragh, built roads to the mines in Arigna and runways in Baldonnel which involved rerouting rivulets. They suffered from unrealistic expectations and fears. Some, with European examples in mind, saw in the experiment a social cure-all; others were reminded of the Hitler Youth. Dressing the youths in soldiers' uniforms may not have been the best idea.

The famous Army Jumping Team is, happily, recording its own history (see *Cosantóir*, March 1990). In other parts of the field, the 1956 founding of the Army Apprentice School saw Lt Gen. Dan McKenna's 1947 idea being productively born. Female personnel of all ranks have served in UNIFIL. A more than passing salute must be given to Irish Shipping which braved submarines and mines for the country during the war.

It was not always appreciated in the war years that the Anti-Aircraft Battalion was a front-line unit. Clontarf, Ringsend, Ballyfermot, Booterstown, Sandycove, Dalkey and North Bull all opened fire on unauthorised aircraft which had to take avoiding action (see pp. 191–2). Any current defence plan must still heavily rely on air defence. The Ack-Ack is also producing its own honourable history to coincide with the sixtieth anniversary of its founding on 16 September 1931.

Any defence plan must also rely on well-trained Reservists and so reap from the investment in education. The differences in definition between First and Second Line Reserve no longer apply. Age and neglect over the years has withered the First Line Reserve down to less than 800. There was no annual training in 1988 or 1989, therefore even this figure is not verifiable. The all-purpose Second Line Reserve (FCA/SM) is restricted to 15,000 since 1983. The State has a maximum of 15,800 Reserve contracts. A comparison between some European States illustrates how out of line is our ratio of Regular and Reserve troops.

| *Country* | *% GDP* | *Regular Forces* | *Reserve Forces* |
|---|---|---|---|
| Portugal | 3.2 | 66,500 | 190,000 |
| Turkey | 4.8 | 645,400 | 951,000 |
| Sweden | 2.7 | 67,000 | 709,000 |
| Switzerland | 1.8 | 20,000 | 625,000 |
| Austria | 1.2 | 54,700 | 186,000 |
| Finland | 1.4 | 34,400 | 700,000 |
| Ireland | 1.4 | 13,600 (1986) | 15,800 (1986) |

(Source: *Military Balance*)

The LDF and their successors, the FCA, have served the Nation well. In the 1969 internal security crisis and subsequently the FCA has played an important, positive and patriotic role. Since integration in 1959 they benefited greatly from close association with Regular units who had clear operational responsibilities with armament to match. In spite of difficulties and occasional failures the integration scheme proved, overall, to be successful. Security demands on brigade staffs and other factors have, however, directed a temporary reversion to command guidance. Since 1983 63,000 man-pay-days had been allowed annually. Six thousand FCA out of the allowed 15,000 strength are thereby denied both gratuity and attendance at annual camp. This affects the integrity of the FCA. Officer and NCO training, weapon instruction and other specialist training have suffered. This of course affects the Force's capability to participate effectively in putative paper national defence plans.

In a national defence plan, for defence purposes the State would be divided into key zones and security zones, geared to meet a two-division plus enemy attack capability. The Reserve units would provide the static defence in key areas and have a high air defence capability. In security areas an emphasis would be on combat, engineer, assault, pioneer capabilities in the Austrian/Swiss style. There would be no time (nor air cover) for the obsolete Second World War 'mobilisation' procedures. The defence of the State depends upon trained troops who are instantly available.

The Reserve Force needs to be revitalised into a mainly single-category adjunct that is viable, instantly available and contractually enforceable. In the absence of Continental-type conscription the Territorial Army in Britain offers a model which has the added advantage of developing relevant workforce and management skills. Trade unions recognise the value of this start-up training. The gains to the State from such would be enormous and constitute, in the absence of possible defence industries, an economic investment. It would make manifest, internally as well as externally, that Ireland takes seriously its international standing as a sovereign independent nation. It would provide a patriotic outlet antidotal to subversive organisations and a civic counterweight to apathy and cynicism. Integration is a two-way traffic and it would help to affirm the status of the military profession by integrating more closely the Permanent Defence Force with the society it serves. As things stand the reality is that even the most modest of emergency/contingency planning, which must totally depend on an available capable Reserve, could not be implemented.

Nowadays of course, no project can be contemplated which does not take the economic realities of the country into account viz., uncertain economic future, the extraordinary external debt and the necessary constraints on public spending. The old time 'mobilisation' concept, dependent on crude stockpiling and duplicated infrastructures, falls at the first cost-effective fence. The following comparison does not reveal the full story. On the one hand most of the Irish defence budget is heavily involved in the internal security and law and order needs of the State, wherein the Defence Forces perform military police roles, some of which may, perhaps, be more proper to the Garda Síochána. On the other hand, there is no added value to the economy from defence industries (opportunities for an ammunition factory and armoured personnel carrier production were not capitalised). There is also an inherent imbalance. Eighty-two per cent of the 1982 budget was allotted to pay and allowances, yet that clearly was not enough. This left 18 per cent for capital investment, the greater part of which was absorbed by day-to-day logistic support and building maintenance, leaving a tiny fraction for defence hardware and transport.

The logical conclusion is that the maintenance of a credible defence system in Ireland with the monies available must rely on a well-educated territorial Reserve, run by professional cadres with appropriate pay, conditions and prospects.

*Relative Defence Expenditure 1987*

| *European Neutrals* | *US $ GDP 1987* | *Defence* | % |
|---|---|---|---|
| Ireland | 28.11 bn | 434.52 m | 1.49 |
| Switzerland | 171.00 bn | 4.43 bn | 1.8 |
| Austria | 117.65 bn | 1.449 bn | 1.2 |
| Finland | 86.96 bn | 1.29 bn | 1.48 |
| Sweden | 159.00 bn | 4.43 bn | 2.7 |
| *European NATO States* | | | |
| United Kingdom | 606.69bn | 31.92 bn | 5.2 |
| France | 877.05 | 29.58 bn | 3.37 |

(Source *Military Balance* 1989)

Unlike its old battle-scarred neighbours in Britain and Europe, the new Irish State has little direct experience in 'the business of war'. There is a belief in funding circles that war could never happen in Ireland and that even if it did someone else would take care of it.

Irish politicians of all hues show little aptitude to debate seriously current defence issues, let alone the future evolution of defence policy. The annual debates on defence estimates incline towards the trivial, the superficial and the parochial.The Cuban crisis of 1962 was an exception.

The most comprehensive parliamentary debate was in 1981 (*Parliamentary Debates* Vol. 327 No. 8 1431–1490). The primary role of the Defence Forces was defined as defence of the State against external aggression. The army, whatever its size or potential, was seen as an outward and practical manifestation of the nation's sovereignty and of its determination to maintain and protect that sovereignty in the context of the political intention to remain militarily neutral. The 1945 world order scenario no longer suffices and fresh responses are now required.

The decline in global hegemony of the US and the USSR however has not resulted in a dawn of sweetness and light among the released nations. Old ethnic hatreds surface, suppurate and destabilise. Unbridled nationalism (soccer hooliganism may be a manifestation) which contributed to so many wars in the past seems set fair to continue to do so in the future. The uncoupling of the Warsaw Pact and the consequential decoupling of NATO paradoxically increased those dangers. The reunification of Germany is pivotal in such situations. The Western European Union (France, Benelux, West Germany, Italy and the UK) is stirring itself. The institutions of the EC are struggling to find a unified coherence within the Helsinki process and the collapse of the Warsaw Pact. An analysis of the courses of action open to Israel in 1974 may not lead to the ruling out with absolute certitude the possibility of a limited nuclear war. Anything could happen in the Middle East. Oil accentuates the global village cliché. Radioactivity knows no frontiers. Current eruptions and erosions could force new military responsibilities on Ireland. A clinical estimate is imperative

A positive response can be made to Gen. Mulcahy's 1923 postulation about what the country wants an army for and what the army can do for the country. The Cause lies within the Oath:

> I, do solemnly swear (or declare) that I will be faithful to Ireland and loyal to the Constitution and that while I am a member of the Defence Forces I will obey all lawful orders issued to me by my superior officers and that while I am a member of the Permanent Defence Force I will not join or be a member of or subscribe to any political organisation or society or any secret society whatsoever and that, if I become a member of the Reserve Defence Force, I will not, while I am a member of the Reserve Defence Force, join or be a member of or subscribe to any secret society whatsoever.

The State's legitimacy and right to existence is constantly challenged by illegitimate revolutionary organisations. Its destruction is their declared aim, though it suits those organisations not to publicise the fact until they judge the time to-be ripe.

The Northern Ireland question remains an unresolved issue which retains the potential for Civil War on the island. *Óglaigh na hÉireann* acts as a deterrent. One futile bitter Civil War has been one too many. The primary role of the Defence Forces, however, remains the defence of the State against *external* aggression. The problem of who that aggressor might be has to be examined in the context of the political decision to remain militarily neutral and to uphold the United Nations Charter. Neutrality obliges Ireland to deny, *by force of arms if necessary*, the use of national territory to *all* belligerents. There is no guarantee of immunity in merely righteously protesting our neutrality. Irish ports and airports are spans in the 'Atlantic Bridge' between Europe and the US, rendering them key terrain. The development of Anglo-Irish relations has virtually eliminated the possibility of one party using military force against the other.

The EC is not an immediate factor in the urgent requirement to formulate a coherent Irish defence policy for the twenty-first century, even though economic, political and military realities become inseparable, and the distinct terms 'security' and 'defence' are misused interchangeably in the European complex of which we are part.

The disintegration of the Warsaw Pact has stranded NATO and changed the geopolitical landscape. The cold war is over. Phony idealogical walls have crumbled but out of the dust endemic nationalistic barriers have arisen. Eastern European countries may seek sanctuary in full EC membership. Irish neutrality could be a lubricant here. Russia has acceded to East Germany being a member of a NATO whose mission is now in the melting pot. Ireland's special family relationship with the US could bridge gaps. Russian and American soldiers may soon keep the United Nations peace side by side in Cambodia or in the Middle East: *Óglaigh na hÉireann* is a sought-after catalyst in such contexts. West Germany was the mainstay of the EC, a United Germany will be a pillar of the UN.

In the vacuum now existing the European Community must look to its own security. Ireland as a fully committed member State could not remain indifferent to a Community security problem which impinged on Irish interests. She would have to consider participation in that unique type of arrangement in which catering for neutrality would be a factor.

*Óglaigh na hÉireann* has a proven and proud record of keeping the United Nations peace both by persuasion and by force. The pace of events has pushed the Community beyond the limitations of considering only the economic and political aspects of security. Ireland's participation in a common security concept could involve a new EC security role for the Defence Forces. Russian tanks driving for the Channel ports is no longer the main fear for Europe. The unexpected and an overspill from local conflicts is. It is becoming increasingly impossible to reconcile existing State frontiers with demanding and explosive nationalism. Ireland, paradoxically, has a major peacekeeping role to play, within a United Nations framework, in containing confrontations arising from raging nationalism and fundamentalism. It is a pre-1914 situation, except for the blessings of the United Nations and the European Community. Ireland, fortunately for all concerned, is an active member of both communities and has a faithful, tried and trusted instrument of policy in *Óglaigh na hÉireann*.

*Rapproachment* between the two former 'Cold War' adversaries — USSR and the US — indicates the emergence of a new partnership of nations with hopes of a new global order enabling the UN (with Ireland) to enforce the rule of law world wide. There have been chilling military lessons to be drawn from the Chernobyl nuclear disaster. The danger of nuclear war may not come from the Super Powers but from a reckless subversive maverick (or a desperate suicidal state) which has managed to lay hands on a nuclear capability. The world has become a very small place: there are no remote areas any more. Of the different kinds of neutrality armed neutrality is the most credible option.

With regard to the part of the Defence Forces' mission requiring defence of the State against internal subversion, it has to be said that any condoning of concealing caches of smuggled arms poses a serious threat to the Primacy of Politics, the Authority of democratically elected governments and the Sovereignty of the State. *Sinne Fianna Faíl* (opening words of the Irish national anthem, 'soldiers are we').

# Appendix 1

## Members of the General Staff and General Officers Commanding

### COMMANDERS IN CHIEF

| NAME | RANK | DATE |
|---|---|---|
| P.H Pearse | Gen | June 1922–Aug 1922 |
| Michael Collins | Gen | Nov 1913–May 1916 |
| Richard Mulcahy[1] | Gen | Aug 1922–Aug 1923 |

### CHIEFS OF STAFF

| NAME | RANK | DATES |
|---|---|---|
| Eoin O'Duffy[2] | Gen | Feb 1922–July 1922 |
| Richard Mulcahy | Gen | July 1922–Aug 1922 |
| Sean MacMahon[3] | Gen | Aug 1922–Mar 1924 |
| Peadar MacMahon[4] | Lt Gen | Mar 1924–Mar 1927 |
| Daniel Hogan | Lt Gen | Mar 1927–Feb 1929 |
| Sean McKeon | Lt Gen | Feb 1929–June 1929 |
| Joseph Sweeney | Maj Gen | June 1929–Oct 1931 |
| Michael Brennan[5] | Maj Gen | Oct 1931–Jan 1940 |
| Daniel McKenna | Lt Gen | Jan 1940–Jan 1949 |
| W.A. Archer | Maj Gen | Jan 1949–Jan 1952 |
| W.A. Egan | Maj Gen | Jan 1952–Dec 1954 |
| P.A. Mulcahy | Maj Gen | Jan 1955–Dec 1959 |
| John McKeown | Maj Gen | Jan 1960–Dec 1960 |
| S. Collins-Powell | Maj Gen | Jan 1961–Mar 1962 |
| John McKeown | Lt Gen | Apr 1962–Mar 1971 |
| P.J. Delaney | Maj Gen | Apr 1971–July 1971 |
| T.L. O'Carroll | Maj Gen | July 1971–July 1976 |
| Carl O'Sullivan | Maj Gen | July 1976–Aug 1978 |
| | Lt Gen | Aug 1978–June 1981 |
| Louis Hogan | Lt Gen | June 1981–Apr 1984 |
| Gerald O'Sullivan | Lt Gen | Apr 1984–Feb 1986 |
| Tadhg O'Neill | Lt Gen | Feb 1986–Oct 1989 |
| Jim Parker | Lt Gen | Oct 1989– |

1. Gen Mulcahy was also Minister for Defence from January 1922 to March 1924.
2. Gen O'Duffy was also appointed "Inspector General and General Officer Commanding Forces" in March 1924 as a consequence of the Army Mutiny. While he held the appointments officially until February 1925, he did not act in either from November 1924.
3. Maj Gen J. Sweeney was acting Chief of Staff for seven days in March 1924 following Gen MacMahon's departure.
4. Lt Gen MacMahon later became Secretary of the Department of Defence.
5. Maj Gen Brennan was also appointed "Inspector General" from 1928 to 1931.

## ADJUTANTS-GENERAL

| NAME | RANK | DATES |
|---|---|---|
| Gearóid O'Sullivan | Lt Gen | Feb 1922–Mar 1924 |
| *Hugo McNeill | Col(A/Maj Gen) | Mar 1924–June 1924 |
| Hugo McNeill | Maj Gen | June 1924–Oct 1925 |
| Michael Brennan | Maj Gen | Oct 1925–Oct 1928 |
| Joseph Sweeney | Maj Gen | Oct 1928–Feb 1929 |
| Seamus O'Higgins | Col | Feb 1929–Feb 1932 |
| Liam O'hAodha | Col | Feb 1932–Dec 1942 |
| James Flynn | Col | Jan 1943–Jan 1949 |
| James McGoran | Col | Jan 1949–Jan 1952 |
| James Flynn | Col | Jan 1952–Dec 1954 |
| James Hanrahan | Col | Jan 1955–Apr 1957 |
| Patrick Hally | Col | Apr 1957–Apr 1962 |
| Seán Collins-Powell | Maj Gen | Apr 1962–Jan 1969 |
| J.P. Emphy | Col | Jan 1969–Apr 1972 |
| H.W. Byrne | Col | Apr 1972–Sept 1975 |
| Carl O'Sullivan | Col | Sept 1975–July 1976 |
| P.J. Dempsey | Col | July 1976–Apr 1978 |
| P.J. Carroll | Maj Gen | Apr 1978–Mar 1980 |
| William Callaghan | Maj Gen | Mar 1980–Feb 1981 |
| W.E. Prendergast | Maj Gen | Feb 1981–Jul 1984 |
| B. Cassidy | Maj Gen | Jul 1984–Apr 1987 |
| C.J. McGuinn | Maj Gen | May 1987–Mar 1989 |
| J. Parker | Maj Gen | Mar 1989–Oct 1989 |
| F. Murphy | Maj Gen | Oct 1989–June 1990 |
| J.N. Bergin | Maj Gen | June 1990– |

## QUARTERMASTERS-GENERAL

| NAME | RANK | DATES |
|---|---|---|
| Sean MacMahon | Lt Gen | Feb 1922–Aug 1922 |
| * Seán Quinn | Col | Aug 1922–Jan 1923 |

| | | |
|---|---|---|
| Séan O'Muirtuile | Lt Gen | Jan 1923–Mar 1924 |
| Felix Cronin | Col | Mar 1924–June 1924 |
| Felix Cronin | Maj Gen | June 1924–Mar 1927 |
| Seán McKeon | Maj Gen | Mar 1927–Feb 1929 |
| Joseph Sweeney | Maj Gen | Feb 1929–June 1929 |
| E.V. O'Carroll | Col | June 1929–June 1932 |
| J.J. O'Connell | Col | June 1932–June 1935 |
| E.V. O'Carroll | Col | June 1935–Oct 1940 |
| Liam Egan | Col | Oct 1940–Oct 1949 |
| Patrick Mulcahy | Col | Oct 1949–Oct 1952 |
| Felix Devlin | Col | Oct 1952–Dec 1954 |
| James Lillis | Col | Jan 1955–Apr 1958 |
| Liam Egan | Maj Gen | Apr 1958–Dec 1959 |
| Séan Collins-Powell | Col | Dec 1959–Dec 1960 |
| J. McPeake | Col | Jan 1961–Sept 1962 |
| P. Curran | Col | Sept 1962–Feb 1968 |
| W. Donagh | Col | Feb 1968–Mar 1971 |
| C. O'Sullivan | Col | Mar 1971–Sept 1975 |
| W. Mullins | Col | Sept 1975–July 1978 |
| M.J. Murphy | Col | July 1978–Aug 1978 |
| M.J. Murphy | Maj Gen | Aug 1978–Dec 1980 |
| Louis Hogan | Maj Gen | Dec 1980–June 1981 |
| J.F. Gallagher | Maj Gen | June 1981–Apr 1984 |
| D. Byrne | Maj Gen | Apr 1984–Dec 1985 |
| J.J. Barry | Maj Gen | Dec 1985–Feb 1987 |
| V.F. Savino | Maj Gen | Feb 1987–July 1989 |
| F. Murphy | Maj Gen | July 1989–Oct 1989 |
| F O'Connell | Maj Gen | Oct 1989– |

* denotes acting appointment

**ASSISTANT CHIEFS OF STAFF**

| NAME | RANK | DATES |
|---|---|---|
| H. McNeill | Maj Gen | Oct 1925–Oct 1927 |
| F. Cronin | Maj Gen | Mar 1927–May 1928 |
| F. Bennett | Col | Nov 1931–June 1932 |
| H. McNeill | Maj Gen | July 1932–May 1937 |
| M.J. Costello | Col | May 1937–Nov 1939 |
| H. McNeill | Maj Gen | Aug 1940–June 1941 |
| L. Archer | Col | June 1941–Jan 1949 |
| J. Flynn | Col | Jan 1949–Jan 1952 |
| W. Egan | Col | Jan 1952–Jan 1952 |
| J. Lillis | Col | Feb 1952–Jan 1955 |
| J. Flynn | Col | Jan 1955–Sept 1961 |
| R. Callanan | Col | Sept 1961–July 1962 |

| | | |
|---|---|---|
| J.P. Emphy | Col | Aug 1962–Jan 1969 |
| H.W. Byrne | Col | Jan 1969–Apr 1972 |
| C. Shortall | Col | Apr 1972–Sept 1975 |
| P. Dempsey | Col | Sept 1975–July 1976 |
| J. Quinn | Col | July 1976–Dec 1976 |
| R. Bunworth | Col | Dec 1976–Mar 1978 |
| R. O'Sullivan | Col | Mar 1978–Feb 1979 |
| R. O'Sullivan | Brig Gen | Feb 1979–June 1979 |
| W. Callaghan | Brig Gen | June 1979–Mar 1980 |
| W. Prendergast | Brig Gen | Mar 1980–Feb 1981 |
| V. Crawford | Brig Gen | Feb 1981–Apr 1982 |
| S. Casey | Brig Gen | Apr 1982–Nov 1983 |
| D. Byrne | Brig Gen | Nov 1983–Apr 1984 |
| J.J. Barry | Brig Gen | Apr 1984–Dec 1985 |
| F.K. Murphy | Brig Gen | Dec 1985–Feb 1986 |
| L.S. Moloney (NS) | Comdre | Feb 1986–Dec 1988 |
| S. Murphy | Brig Gen | Mar 1989– |

**GENERAL OFFICERS COMMANDING EASTERN COMMAND**

| NAME | RANK | DATES |
|---|---|---|
| D. Hogan | Maj Gen | 1922 |
| D. J. Reynolds | Col | 1927 |
| J.H. McGuinness[1] | Col | 1927 |
| L. Hayes | Col | 1928 |
| M. Hogan | Col | 1929 |
| S. O'Higgins | Col | 1932 |
| T. McGrath | Maj | 1932 |
| F. Bennett | Col | 1933 |
| S. McGoran | Col | 1935 |
| L. Hoolan | Col | 1940 |
| H. McNeill | Maj Gen | 1946 |
| W. Egan | Col | 1951 |
| S. McGoran | Col | 1952 |
| P.A. Mulcahy | Col | 1953 |
| L. Egan | Maj Gen | 1955 |
| R.J. Callanan | Col | 1958 |
| J.P. McNally | Col | 1961 |
| P.J. Hally | Col | 1963 |
| J.H. Byrne | Col | 1970 |
| J.J. Quinn | Col | 1972 |
| J.J. Beary | Brig Gen | 1976 |
| M.J. O'Brien | Brig Gen | 1979 |
| P.J. Daly | Brig Gen | 1980 |

| | | |
|---|---|---|
| G. O'Sullivan | Brig Gen | 1981 |
| V. F. Savino | Brig Gen | 1984 |
| P.F. Monahan | Brig Gen | 1987 |

1. E Comd was divided into Dublin Districts North & South in June 1927. No overall OC was appointed.

## GENERAL OFFICERS COMMANDING SOUTHERN COMMAND

| NAME | RANK | DATES |
|---|---|---|
| E. Dalton | Maj Gen | Aug 1922 |
| D.J. Reynolds | Maj Gen | Jan 1923 |
| M. Brennan | Maj Gen | Feb 1924 |
| S. McMahon | Lt Gen | Oct 1925 |
| L. Hayes | Col | Jan 1927 |
| F. Brennan | Col | Nov 1928 |
| J.J. McCabe | Col | July 1933 |
| J. McLaughlin | Col | Oct 1938 |
| J. Hanrahan | Col | Apr 1939 |
| M.J. Costello | Col | Nov 1939 |
| J. Hanrahan | Col | May 1941 |
| S. McGoran | Col | July 1946 |
| J. Hanrahan | Col | Jan 1949 |
| S. Collins-Powell | Col | Jan 1955 |
| P. Curran | Col | Dec 1959 |
| W. Donagh | Col | Sept 1962 |
| C. O'Sullivan | Col | Feb 1968 |
| W. Rea | Col | Mar 1971 |
| T. McDonald | Col | June 1973 |
| R. Bunworth | Col | Sept 1975 |
| P.P. Barry | Col | Dec 1976 |
| W. O'Carroll | Brig Gen | Apr 1978 |
| K. Nunan | Brig Gen | Oct 1979 |
| J.F. Gallagher | Brig Gen | June 1980 |
| B. Cassidy | Brig Gen | Nov 1983 |
| T.J. Waters | Brig Gen | July 1984 |
| D. Byrne | Brig Gen | June 1981 |
| F.N. O'Connell | Brig Gen | Aug 1986 |
| J. Kissane | Brig Gen | Oct 1989 |

## GENERAL OFFICERS COMMANDING WESTERN COMMAND

| NAME | RANK | DATES |
|---|---|---|
| Seán McKeon | Lt Gen | 1922 |
| Joseph Sweeney | Maj Gen | Feb 1925 |

| | | |
|---|---|---|
| Administered by | | |
| OC, Curragh Command | | 1927 |
| Liam Hoolan | Col | Oct 1934 |
| Charles McAllister (Acting) | Maj | Mar 1939 |
| Sean McCabe | Col | Aug 1939 |
| Joseph Sweeney | Maj Gen | Dec 1939 |
| Felix McCorley | Col | Dec 1940 |
| James Hanrahan | Col | Nov 1946 |
| Patrick A. Mulcahy | Col | Jan 1949 |
| Liam Egan | Col | Oct 1949 |
| Seán Collins-Powell | Col | Oct 1951 |
| Thomas D. Fox | Col | Jan 1955 |
| Austin X. Lawlor | Col | Oct 1958 |
| J.P. Emphy | Col | Mar 1961 |
| H.W. Byrne | Col | Sept 1962 |
| C.E. Shortall | Col | Jan 1969 |
| M.J. Buckley | Col | Apr 1972 |
| M.J. Murphy | Col | Sept 1975 |
| J.M. Stewart | Brig Gen | July 1978 |
| L. Hogan | Brig Gen | Mar 1980 |
| V. Crawford | Brig Gen | Dec 1980 |
| T.J. Hartigan | Brig Gen | Feb 1981 |
| T. O'Neill | Brig Gen | Feb 1984 |
| F.K. Murphy | Brig Gen | Feb 1986 |
| P.M. Dixon | Brig Gen | Aug 1989 |

## GENERAL OFFICERS COMMANDING CURRAGH CAMP AND CURRAGH COMMAND

| NAME | RANK | DATES |
|---|---|---|
| J.J. O'Connell | Lt Gen | May 1922 |
| P. McMahon | Lt Gen | July 1922 |
| J.A. Sweeney | Maj Gen | Mar 1924 |
| S. McKeon | Maj Gen | Feb 1925 |
| J.A. Sweeney | Maj Gen | June 1927 |
| H.H. McNeill | Maj Gen | Oct 1928 |
| J. McLoughlin | Col | Sept 1930 |
| J.A. Sweeney | Maj Gen | Oct 1931 |
| J. O'Higgins | Col | Jan 1940 |
| T.J. McNally | Col | Aug 1940 |
| S. Collins-Powell | Col | Nov 1944 |
| J. Lillis | Col | Oct 1951 |
| A.T. Lawlor | Col | Feb 1952 |
| P. Curran | Col | Jan 1959 |

| | | |
|---|---|---|
| W. Donagh | Col | Dec 1959 |
| J. Cogan | Col | Sept 1962 |
| J.J. Quinn | Col | Feb 1968 |
| T. McDonald | Col | July 1972 |
| C.J. Burke | Col | July 1973 |
| P.J. Dempsey | Col | July 1974 |
| P.D. Hogan | Brig Gen | Sept 1975 |
| D. Hurley | Brig Gen | June 1979 |
| K. Nunan | Brig Gen | June 1980 |
| S.F. Casey | Brig Gen | June 1981 |
| T. McDunphy | Brig Gen | Apr 1982 |
| J.B. Egan | Brig Gen | July 1983 |
| C.J. McGuinn | Brig Gen | Nov 1984 |
| P.A. Maguire | Brig Gen | June 1987 |
| P. Grennan | Brig Gen | Aug 1988 |
| K. Duffy | Brig Gen | July 1990 |

**GENERAL OFFICERS COMMANDING THE AIR CORPS**

| NAME | RANK | DATES |
|---|---|---|
| W.J. McSweeney | Maj Gen | 1922 |
| T. Moloney | Maj | 1924 (Killed in air crash) |
| C. Russell | Col | 1924 |
| J. Fitzmaurice | Maj | 1927 |
| T. McLaughlin | Col | 1929 |
| T. Liston | Maj | 1930 |
| P.A. Mulcahy | Maj | 1935 |
| W. Delamere | Col | 1943 |
| P. Quinn | Col | 1946 |
| W. Keane | Col | 1960 |
| K. Curran | Col | 1966 |
| P. Swan | Col | 1969 |
| J. O'Connor | Col (Later Brig Gen) | 1974 |
| W. Glenn | Brig Gen | 1980 |
| J. Connolly | Brig Gen | 1983 |
| B. L. McMahon | Brig Gen | 1984 |
| P. Cranfield | Brig Gen | 1989 |

(Before the appointment of Major Moloney, Baldonnel was commanded for short periods by Comdt Daly, Col P. O'Connell (1 week) and Col Gilheaney (5–6 weeks).)

**FLAG OFFICER COMMANDING THE NAVAL SERVICE**

| NAME | RANK | DATES |
|---|---|---|
| J.O'Higgins | Col | Sept 1939 |
| A. Lawlor | Col | Jan 1940 |

| | | |
|---|---|---|
| S. O'Muiris | Commander | May 1941 |
| H.S. Jerome | Capt (NS) | Dec 1946 |
| T. McKenna | Capt (NS) | Dec 1956 |
| P. Kavanagh | Capt (NS) | June 1973 |
| P. Kavanagh | Commodore | Nov 1979 |
| L.S. Moloney | Comdre | Sept 1980 |
| W.J. Brett | Comdre | Feb 1986 |
| J. Deasy | Comdre | Jan 1990 |

**COMMANDANT OF THE MILITARY COLLEGE**

| NAME | RANK | DATES |
|---|---|---|
| P.A. Maguire | Col | July 1984 |
| P.A. Maguire | Brig Gen | Jan 1986 |
| W. McNicholas | Brig Gen | June 1987 |
| A. Brophy | Brig Gen | May 1989 |
| M. Downing | Brig Gen | June 1990 |

(*Note*: The appointment, Commandant Military College, was upgraded to the rank of Brig Gen in January 1986.)
*Source*: The Irish Defence Forces Handbook

**PREVIOUS COLLEGE COMMANDANTS**

| NAME | RANK | DATES |
|---|---|---|
| H. McNeill | Maj Gen | 1930–32 |
| M. Costello | Col | 1932–37 |
| H. McNeill | Maj Gen | 1937–39 |
| L. Egan | Col | 1939–40 |
| S. Collins-Powell | Col | 1940–42 |
| T. P. Gallaghar | Col | 1943–45 |
| C. J. O'Donoghue | Col | 1945–50 |
| J. Lillis | Col | 1950–51 |
| T. Ó hUigín | Col | 1951–52 |
| D. Bryan | Col | 1952–55 |
| T. Feely | Col | 1955–57 |
| S. Mac Eoin | Col | 1957–59 |
| S. Emfi | Col | 1960–61 |
| H. O'Broin | Col | 1961–62 |
| C. Ó Suilleabháin | Col | 1962–68 |
| T. L. Ó Cearbhaill | Col | 1968–71 |
| F. E. Mac an Leagha | Col | 1971–75 |
| P. T. P. Quinlan | Col | 1975–76 |
| W. O'Carroll | Col | 1976–78 |
| T. J. Ryan | Col | 1978–80 |
| E. Condon | Col | 1980–80 |

| | | |
|---|---|---|
| D. Byrne | Col | 1980–81 |
| H. Crowley | Col | 1981–82 |
| D. Ó Riain | Col | 1982–83 |
| C. Cox | Col | 1983–83 |
| T. Waters | Col | 1983–84 |

# Appendix 2

## From General Routine Orders No. 14, 18 January 1923

**Section 49.—Commands: Re-organisation of.**
The existing Commands will cease to operate on and after the 20th instant. On and after that date the Army will be divided into the following Commands:

(1) The *DONEGAL COMMAND* which includes:—

The Six-County Area Border from Lough Foyle to Swanlinbar. The road from Swanlinbar to the County Leitrim border south of Gorloch. Along the County Leitrim border to Dowra. From Dowra to Loch Allen, and along the North and West coast of Loch Allen to the County Leitrim border at Aghamore. Along this border to a point where it joins the Sligo border at Altagowlan. The direct road from this point across the mountains to Riverstown, thence the road to Drumfin, Knockaltideen, on to Owenmore River. By the river to the road north of Templehouse Lake and on to Killaran. The road across the Ox mountains by Ladies Brae to Doonflin Lower and thence the road to Easky *via* Dromore. All the roads above mentioned defining the boundary to be included in this Command.

(2) The *CLAREMORRIS COMMAND* which is bounded:—

The Donegal Command boundary line from Easky to the point north of Templehouse Lake, by the lake and along the Owenmore river to Gloonashin. The road to Duninadden and along this road to the County Mayo border. The line of the County border to Gloonfed thence the road to Dunmore and on to Newtownbellew. The road by Lismoyle, Glentane, across M.G.W. Railway line and Woodlawn Station and on to Kilreakle *via* New Inn, thence on to the Dunkellin River and to Dunbulcaun Bay. The roads mentioned above, on the boundary, to be included in the Command Area.

(3) The *ATHLONE COMMAND* bounded:—

From the point north of Templehouse Lake along the Donegal Command boundary line to the point on the Co. Leitrim border south of Gorloch. Along the Leitrim border to Newtowngore. Along the road to Carrigallen *via* Duganny, thence the road to Arva, Granard, Rathowen, Ballynacargy. Along the Royal Canal to the point where it meets the M.G.W. Railway and straight across to Lough Ennel at Ladestown House. Along the Western shore of Lough Ennel and along the road to Tyrrells Pass. The road from Tyrrells Pass to Philipstown and on to Cloneygowan, thence the road to Stradbally *via* Killeen, Carryhinch House, Huntingdom, Ballybrittan, Rossmore cross roads and the Buttock cross roads. From Stradbally to Swan *via* Tinahoe. The road to Ballinakill, Spink, and on to Rathdowney. From Rathdowney to Errill, Lisduff Station, Boggaun, Ballycahill to Killen, Goldings Cross, Gortalough, Garrangreen Lower, Currabaha Cross across to Moonsha Glen. The road across Knockacraheen Hill to a point where the road crosses Nenagh River near Ballycronode House. From this point along the road to Toomevara, Gloughjordon *via* Modreen, thence the main road to Portumna, Killimor *via* Gortymaddon, Mullagh, to Kilreakle. From Kilreakle the Claremorris Com-mand boundary to Templehouse Lake. All roads and places men-tioned above to be in the Command.

(4) The *DUBLIN COMMAND* bounded as follows:—

The Six-County boundary from Carlingford Lough to Swan-linbar. The road from Swanlinbar to the County Leitrim border south of Gorloch, thence the Athlone Command boundary line to Swanlinbar. The road from Swan *via* Gurteen to Leighlin Bridge and on to Newtownbarry *via* Fennagh, Myshall. From Newtownbarry to Clohalan, Ferns and the straight road to Ford, and then on to the coast. The roads and places mentioned on the Southern Boundary line from Swan to Ford to be included in the Command.

Refer to Curragh Boundary which is not included in the Dublin Command.

(5) The *WATERFORD COMMAND* includes:—

The river Blackwater from Youghal to Lismore. From Lismore the road across the mountains to Ballyporeen. From Ballyporeen a straight line to be drawn to Knockacolla north-west of Cahir. From this point along the river to Golden and on to the Multeen river to where it joins the road at Hollyford. From this point the road by Milestone, Inch, Curreeny Cross and on the Dolla. The road from Dolla to the Athlone Command boundary line at the point where it crosses the Nenagh river. From this point the Athlone Command boundary line to Swan and from Swan the Dublin Command boundary line to the coast at Ford. All places and roads mentioned from Ballyporeen to Dolla to be included in the Command.

(6) The *LIMERICK COMMAND* bounded:—

The Claremorris Command boundary line from Dunbulcaun Bay to Kilreakle. The Athlone Command boundary line from Kilreakle to the point where it crosses the Nenagh river. The Waterford Command boundary line from this point to Ballyporeen. The road from Ballyporeen to Doneraile *via* Mitchelstown and Kildorerry. From Doneraile to Ballyclough and on to Kanturk and Newmarket, thence the road to Kingwilliamstown *via* Clamper Cross. From Kingwilliamstown the County Cork boundary to a point where it joins the Glydagh river. Along the Glydagh river to the river Feale, and along the Feale to Abbeyfeale. From Abbeyfeale the road to Listowel, and along the light railway to Ballybunion. The road from Ballyporeen to Doneraile and Mitchelstown, Kildorerry and Doneraile, Abbeyfeale and Listowel and Ballybunion, and the light railway to be included in the Command.

(7) The *KERRY COMMAND* bounded:—

From Ballybunion along the Limerick Command boundary to Kingwilliamstown. From Kingwilliamstown the County Cork boundary to Ardgroun Harbour.

(8) The *CORK COMMAND* included:—

From Ardgroun harbour along the Cork Command boundary to Kingwilliamstown. The Limerick Command boundary from Kingwilliamstown to Ballyporeen. The Waterford Command boundary from Ballyporeen to Youghal. Kingwilliamstown, Newmarket and Kanturk and the roads between these places to be included in the Command. Also the road from Kanturk to Doneraile. The road from Ballyporeen to Lismore and Youghal to be included in the Cork Command. Rathmore on the Cork border will also be included.

(9) The *CURRAGH COMMAND* which includes:—

The road Kildare to Milltown and on to Newbridge and the canal from Newbridge to Kilcullen and the road from Kilcullen to Kildare. All these roads are included in this Command.

# Appendix 3

## From General Routine Orders, No. 16, 24 January 1923

**Section 61.—Reorganisation.**

The new Battalion in course of formation will be numbered as follows, and described as Infantry Battalions by numbers, for example . . . the 21st Infantry Battalion.

| Battalion being formed in | With H.Q. at | To be known as |
|---|---|---|
| *Dublin Command* | Keogh Barracks | 1st and 55th Infantry Battalions. |
| | Portobello Barracks | 8th and 56th Infantry Battalions. |
| | Collins Barracks | 13th and 57th Infantry Battalions. |
| | Mountjoy Gaol | 16th Infantry Battalion. |
| | Tallaght | 24th Infantry Battalion. |
| | Gormanstown | 37th Infantry Battalion. |
| | Dundalk | 49th and 58th Infantry Battalions. |
| | Clones | 21st Infantry Battalion. |
| | Cavan | 53rd Infantry Battalion. |
| | Mullingar | 45th Infantry Battalion. |
| | Naas | 33rd Infantry Battalion. |
| | Navan | 48th Infantry Battalion. |
| | Carlow | 20th Infantry Battalion. |
| | Gorey | 50th Infantry Battalion. |
| *Athlone Command.* | Athlone | 5th Infantry Battalion. |
| | Longford | 23rd Infantry Battalion. |
| | Boyle | 22nd Infantry Battalion. |
| | Maryboro | 51st Infantry Battalion. |
| | Roscrea | 2nd Infantry Battalion. |
| *Donegal Command.* | Drumboe | 3rd Infantry Battalion. |
| | Donegal | 46th Infantry Battalion. |
| | Sligo | 35th Infantry Battalion. |

| Battalions being formed in | With H.Q. at | To be known as |
|---|---|---|
| *Claremorris Command.* | Claremorris | 52nd Infantry Battalion. |
| | Ballina | 26th Infantry Battalion. |
| | Galway | 4th Infantry Battalion. |
| | Westport | 44th Infantry Battalion. |
| | Tuam | 34th Infantry Battalion. |
| *Limerick Command.* | Limerick City | 7th Infantry Battalion. |
| | Nenagh | 11th Infantry Battalion. |
| | Gort | 28th Infantry Battalion. |
| | Ennis | 12th Infantry Battalion. |
| | Tipperary | 18th Infantry Battalion. |
| | Newcastle | 31st Infantry Battalion. |
| | Charleville | 39th Infantry Battalion. |
| *Kerry Command.* | Tralee | 27th Infantry Battalion. |
| | Castleisland | 19th Infantry Battalion. |
| | Kenmare | 17th Infantry Battalion. |
| | Killarney | 6th Infantry Battalion. |
| | Cahirciveen | 9th Infantry Battalion. |
| *Waterford Command.* | Waterford | 14th Infantry Battalion. |
| | Kilkenny | 47th Infantry Battalion. |
| | Clonmel | 25th Infantry Battalion. |
| | Templemore | 36th Infantry Battalion. |
| | Wexford | 41st Infantry Battalion. |
| *Cork Command.* | Cork City | 10th Infantry Battalion. |
| | Bandon | 15th Infantry Battalion. |
| | Bantry | 30th Infantry Battalion. |
| | Macroom | 32nd Infantry Battalion. |
| | Kanturk | 38th Infantry Battalion. |
| | Fermoy | 40th Infantry Battalion. |
| | Youghal | 42nd Infantry Battalion. |
| *Curragh Command.* | Curragh— | |
| | 3 Garrison Battalions | 29th, 43rd and 54th. |
| | 7 Reserve Battalions | 59th to 65th. |

# Appendix 4

## INTELLIGENCE REPORT ON 2ND NORTHERN DIVISION AS IT STOOD IN 1922

The majority of the northern units joined the regular army: only a very few took the other side during the civil war. When heavy demobilisation sparked off the 1924 Mutiny their retention was resented by the mutineers. The commander-in-chief, Dick Mulcahy, called for comprehensive reports on the build-up to that situation. Major Dan McKenna ('Q' Branch, GHQ, formerly of 2nd Northern Division) supplied the following report, probably through the Director of Intelligence.

SUBJECT—POSITION OF 2ND NORTHERN DIVISION IN 1922
(1) As directed in your communication of the 5th ultimo, I submit hereunder a report on the position of the 2nd Northern Division in 1922. As the Military situation in the North at this time was based on a political objective, it is necessary for me to explain the position from both sides, so that you may clearly understand how matters stood.
(2) After the Treaty was signed, the late General Collins who was then Chairman of the Provisional Government, and the mouthpiece of the new order of things, impressed strongly on the Nationalists of the Six Counties that, although the Treaty might have an outward expression of Partition, the Government had plans whereby they would make it impossible, and that Partition would never be recognised even though it might mean the smashing of the Treaty.
(3) About the beginning of February, 1922, the late General Collins advised the Northern Bishops to induce all Catholic Teachers to ignore the Northern Educational Authorities, and that he would pay them full salary whether dismissed or not. He advised all Councils and Boards with a working Nationalist majority to ignore the authority of the Northern Local Government Board.
(4) In the same month, General O'Duffy with the authority of the late General Collins and General Mulcahy, started operations against the "Specials" and British Military in the Six Counties, which resulted

in shooting a number of "Northern" Government Officials and Police; capturing a few Barracks, and destroying several thousand of pounds worth of "Northern" Government property. These activities had their results. Special murder gangs were organised in Belfast and let loose on the Catholic population of the Six Counties, with the result that several families were completely wiped out, whilst others, who were a little more fortunate, succeeded in obtaining refuge in the Free State.

(5) In May, 1922, General O'Duffy gave an undertaking to the Officer Commanding, 2nd Northern Division, that he would provide him with barracks in the Free State for the purpose of training some hundreds of men, with the intention of an invasion of the Six Counties in the late Summer. He also gave an undertaking that he would supply the men in training with food, clothing and all the necessary equipment of a fighting force. At this time, the "Northern" Government assisted by the British, conducted a general round up of all suspected men. Six hundred were interned, and it is generally surmised that fifty thousand left the Area.

(6) About the month of July, it appeared that the Free State Government had their hands full in the South and they deemed it advisable to cancel activities in the North. A Conference was called of Northern Officers, which assembled at Portobello Barracks on the 2nd August, 1922. The following G.H.Q. Staff were present: Commander-in-Chief (Late General Collins), presiding, also present, Chief of Staff, Adjutant-General and Director of Organisation. The following decisions were arrived at:

1. That all I.R.A. Operations in the Six Counties would cease forthwith.
2. That men who were unable to remain in the Six Counties would be handed over a Barrack at the Curragh Camp, where they would be trained under their own officers to such tactics as would be applicable to the nature of fighting in the Six Counties.
3. That these men would not be asked to take any part in the activities outside the Six Counties.
4. That N.V.R. Forms would be presented for the purpose of receiving an allowance for the men.
5. That the organisation in the Six Counties would remain unchanged and be carried on in the same way as it was in Ireland previous to 1918.

(7) I annex hereto for your information, copy of a communication to the Officer Commanding, 2nd Northern Division, received from General Mulcahy, dated 17th August, 1922. The Officers and men

were transferred to the Curragh a few days later, and it then became evident that the objective was to absorb all the Units in the National Army and sever connection with the Organisation in the Six Counties.

From this time on, a good many of the Officers and quite a number of the men resented what they termed "this sale" and at once showed antagonism to the Government. The Division, therefore, became badly split. The Officers in sympathy with the Government advised the men to join the Army, and left each officer free to choose for himself. A number of the officers and men joined the Army, and the remainder were disbanded on the 31st March, 1923.

(8) The Divisional Staff were as follows: Divisional Officer Commanding — THOMAS MORRIS. As this officer was a pretty prominent figure about G.H.Q. for some time, you are, I presume, in possession of all particulars regarding him. Deputy Divisional O/C — DANIEL McKENNA. Divisional Adjutant — FRANK STRONG. This Officer did not join the Army. Divisional Intelligence Officer — JAMES MALLON. This officer joined the Army in March, 1923. I might mention that I was responsible for his not joining sooner. He was left with the Division until it was disbanded for the purpose of advising the men and keeping them out of the Irregular ranks. Divisional Engineer — THOMAS KELLY. This Officer joined the Army in the Autumn of 1922. He resigned in the Autumn of 1923, and joined the Garda Siothchana. Divisional Director of Training — EDWARD CONWAY. This Officer did not join the Army.

(9) Prior to the 2nd August, 1922, the Divisional Staff performed the same duties as in Pre-Truce days. After the 2nd August, 1922, the Divisional O.C., Adjutant and Quartermaster had their Headquarters in Donegal and endeavoured to keep in touch with the Division from there. The Deputy Divisional O.C. was put in charge of the men at the Curragh.

The Divisional Intelligence Officer spent most of his time in the Division until October when he reported to the Curragh and remained there until he joined the Army. The Divisional Engineer came to the Curragh with the Unit and remained until he joined the Army. The Divisional Director of Training reported to the Curragh with the Unit and remained until it was disbanded.

(10) Divisional Officers who did not join the Army were paid on a flat rate of £5.0.0. per week until 31st March, 1923. Divisional Officers who joined the Army were also paid on a flat rate of £5.0.0. until they were gazetted.

(11) I might add that the general impression of our supporters in the North was, and is, that the Treaty created a serious and thorny

position for the Six Counties at first, but the misleading and uncalled for tactics of those in authority in the first year were responsible for the wholesale evacuation of the Nationalists, which resulted in another plantation in the Summer and Autumn of 1922. In addition, it resulted in the disfranchisement of Catholic areas for local Government purposes, and the wiping out of those having Nationalists ideas.

(12) I am well aware of the fact that a great deal of the information given above was not asked for in your communication, but I am of opinion that it may be useful to you, hence it is submitted.

---

(Copy of Communication referred to in Paragraph (7))

*OGLAIGH NA h-EIREANN*

Oifig: Chief of General Staff
Bearraic Phortobello,
Baile Atha Cliath.
17th August, 1922.

To:
Commadt-General
2nd Northern Division.

A Chara,

(1) You will make arrangements for the transfer immediately to the command of Comdt. Sweeney, the Posts that you now hold in his area.

(2) You will report at once the number of your men that are in those Posts, and arrangements will be made to have them brought forthwith to the Curragh.

(3) Comdt. Sweeney has instructions to receive and store for you whatever arms and munitions belonging to your area which are now in these Posts. He will make arrangements to release them as required.

Beir Beannacht,

(signed) *RICHARD MULCAHY*, General
Chief of General Staff.

# Appendix 5

## UN Casualties

### CONGO—ONUC

| Rank/Name | O/Seas Unit | Home Unit | Cause of Death |
| --- | --- | --- | --- |
| Coy Sgt F. Grant BSD | 33 Inf Bn | 12 Inf Bn | Died after operation 3/10/60 |
| Col J. McCarthy BSD | HQ ONUC | HQ 4 Bde | Traffic Accident 27/10/60 |
| Lt K. M. Gleeson | 33 Inf Bn | 2 Fd Engr Coy | Niemba Ambush 8/11/60 |
| Sgt H. Gaynor | 33 Inf Bn | 2 Mot Sqn | Niemba Ambush 8/11/60 |
| Cpl P. Kelly | 33 Inf Bn | 5 Inf Bn | Niemba Ambush 8/11/60 |
| Cpl L. Dougan | 33 Inf Bn | 5 Inf Bn | Niemba Ambush 8/11/60 |
| Pte M. Farrell | 33 Inf Bn | 2 Hosp Coy | Niemba Ambush 8/11/60 |
| Tpr T. Fennell | 33 Inf Bn | 2 Mot Sqn | Niemba Ambush 8/11/60 |
| Tpr A. Browne BMC | 33 Inf Bn | 2 Mot Sqn | Niemba Ambush 8/11/60 |
| Pte M. McGuinn | 33 Inf Bn | 2 Fd Engr Coy | Niemba Ambush 8/11/60 |
| Pte G. Killeen | 33 Inf Bn | CTD(E) | Niemba Ambush 8/11/60 |
| Pte P. Davis | 33 Inf Bn | 2 Fd Engr Coy | Accidental shooting 10/11/60 |
| Cpl L. Kelly | 33 Inf Bn | 3 Inf Bn | Accidental shooting 24/12/60 |
| Cpl L. Kelly | HQ ONUC | Dep MPC | Traffic Accident 30/8/61 |
| Tpr E. Gaffney | 35 Inf Bn | 1 Armd C Sqn | Killed in action 13/9/61 |

| Rank/Name | O/Seas Unit | Home Unit | Cause of Death |
|---|---|---|---|
| Tpr P. Mullins | 35 Inf Bn | 1 Mot Sqn | Killed in action 15/9/61 |
| Cpl M. Nolan | 35 Inf Bn | 1 Tk Sqn | Killed in action 15/9/61 |
| Cpl M. Fallon | 36 Inf Bn | 5 Inf Bn | Killed in action 8/12/61 |
| Sgt P. Mulcahy BSD | 36 Inf Bn | 6 Fd Arty Regt | Killed in action 16/12/61 |
| Pte A. Wickham | 36 Inf Bn | 2 Inf Bn | Killed in action 16/12/61 |
| Lt P.A. Riordan BSD | 36 Inf Bn | 5 Inf Bn | Killed in action 16/12/61 |
| Cpl J. Geoghegan | 36 Inf Bn | 15 Inf Bn | Accidental shooting 28/12/61 |
| Cpl J. Power | 36 Inf Bn | CTD (E) | Natural Causes 7/3/62 |
| Capt R. L. McCann | HQ ONUC | CTD (W) | Traffic accident 9/5/62 |
| Cpl J. McGrath | 38 Inf Bn | 4 Hosp Coy | Traffic accident 21/3/63 |
| Comdt T. M. McMahon | HQ ONUC | HQ W Comd | Natural Causes 28/9/63 |

**CYPRUS—UNFICYP**

| Rank/Name | O/Seas Unit | Home Unit | Cause of Death |
|---|---|---|---|
| Cpl W. Hetherington | 4 Inf Gp | CTD (E) | Traffic accident 19/7/65 |
| Coy Sgt W. MacAuley | 41 Inf Bn | Dep MPC | Natural Causes 22/2/65 |
| Sgt J. Hamill | 4 Inf Gp | Dep Cav | Traffic accident 7/4/65 |
| Coy Sgt J. Ryan | 6 Inf Gp | 5 Inf Bn | Died 4/10/66 in St Bricins subsequent to repatriation 1/7/66 |
| Capt C. McNamara | 9 Inf Gp | 2 Grn S&T Coy | Natural Causes 16/1/68 |
| Cpl J. Fagan | 10 Inf Gp | 2 Mot Sqn | Traffic accident 10/6/68 |
| Lt R. B. Byrne | 11 Inf Gp | 4 Inf Bn | Natural Causes 28/10/68 |
| Tpr M. Kennedy | 12 Inf Gp | 1 Armd C Sqn | Drowned 1/7/69 |
| Pte B. Cummins | 20 Inf Gp | 2 Inf Bn | Natural Causes 11/6/71 |

**LEBANON—UNIFIL**

| Rank/Name | O/Seas Unit | Home Unit | Cause of Death |
|---|---|---|---|
| Pte G. Moon | 43 Inf Bn | 4 Inf Bn | Traffic accident 25/8/78 |
| Cpl T. Reynolds | 44 Inf Bn | 2 Grn S&T Coy | Traffic accident 24/12/78 |
| Pte P. Grogan | HQ UNIFIL | 28 Inf Bn | Drowned 10/7/79 |
| Pte S. Griffin | 46 Inf Bn | 1 Fd Engr Coy | Killed in action 16/4/80 |
| Pte T. Barrett | 46 Inf Bn | 4 Inf Bn | Killed in action 18/4/80 |
| Pte D. Smallhorne | 46 Inf Bn | 5 Inf Bn | Killed in action 18/4/80 |
| Sgt E. Yates | 47 Inf Bn | 2 Mot Sqn | Traffic accident 31/5/80 |
| Cpl V. Duffy | 47 Inf Bn | 6 Fd Sig Coy | Traffic accident 18/10/80 |
| Pte J. Marshall | 48 Inf Bn | 6 Fd S&T Coy | Natural Causes 17/12/80 |
| Coy Sgt J. Martin | HQ UNIFIL | 4 Grn MP Coy | Natural Causes 10/2/81 |
| Pte H. Doherty | 49 Inf Bn | 28 Inf Bn | Killed in action 27/4/81 |
| Pte K. Joyce | 48 Inf Bn | 1 Inf Bn | Missing 27/4/81 |
| Pte N. Byrne | 49 Inf Bn | 6 Inf Bn | Traffic accident 22/6/81 |
| Pte G. Hodges | 50 Inf Bn | CTD (S) | Died in Dublin Hospital after fire UNIFIL 20/3/82 |
| Cpl G. Morrow | 52 Inf Bn | 2 Inf Bn | Killed in action 27/10/82 |
| Pte G. Burke | 51 Inf Bn | 5 Inf Bn | Killed in action 27/10/82 |
| Pte T. Murphy | 52 Inf Bn | 2 Inf Bn | Killed in action 27/10/82 |
| Cpl G. Murray | 55 Inf Bn | 2 Grn MP Coy | Accidental shooting 9/10/84 |
| Tpr P. Fogarty | 59 Inf Bn | 1 Tk Sqn | Traffic accident 20/7/86 |
| Lt F. A. Murphy | 59 Inf Bn | AAS | Killed in action 21/8/86 |
| Pte W. O'Brien | 60 Inf Bn | 6 Inf Bn | Killed in action 6/12/86 |

| | | | |
|---|---|---|---|
| Cpl D. McLoughlin | 60 Inf Bn | 28 Inf Bn | Killed in action 10/1/87 |
| RSM J. Fitzgerald | HQ UNIFIL | 1 Fd Arty Regt | Shooting accident 24/2/87 |
| Cpl G. Bolger | 61 Inf Bn | 12 Inf Bn | Natural Causes 29/8/87 |

**MIDDLE EAST—UN TRUCE SUPERVISION ORGANISATION (UNTSO)**

| Rank/Name | O/Seas Unit | Home Unit | Cause of Death |
|---|---|---|---|
| Comdt T. P. Wickham | Observer | Mil Col | Shot in Syria 7/6/67 |
| Comdt M. Nestor | Observer | HQ C Comd | Landmine explosion Beirut 25/9/82 |
| Gnr P. Cullen | 62 Inf Bn | 2 Fd Arty Regt | Accident 17/3/88 |
| Pte P. Wright | 63 Inf Bn | 27 Inf Bn | Accidental shooting 21/8/88 |
| Pte M. McNeela | 64 Inf Bn | 27 Inf Bn | Killed in action 24/2/89 |
| Cpl F. Heneghan | 64 Inf Bn | 1 Inf Bn | Killed in action 21/3/89 |
| Pte M. Armstrong | 64 Inf Bn | 28 Inf Bn | Killed in action 21/3/89 |
| Pte T. Walsh | 64 Inf Bn | 28 Inf Bn | Killed in action 21/3/89 |
| Sgt C. Forrester | 65 Inf Bn | 2 Fd Arty Regt | Natural causes 21/5/89 |
| Comdt M. O'Hanlon | 66 Inf Bn | HQ C Comd | Accidental shooting 28/11/89 |

*Source*: The Irish Defence Forces Handbook

# Appendix 6

## Nominal Roll of Recipients of An Bonn Míleata Calmachta (The Military Medal for Gallantry) and of An Bonn Seirbhise Dearscna (The Distinguished Service Medal)

The Military Medal for Gallantry is the highest military honour in the State. The medal may be awarded in recognition of the performance of any act of exceptional bravery or gallantry(other than one performed on War Service) arising out of, or associated with Military Service and involving risk to life or limb. There are three classes: with honour, with distinction and with merit which equate with the three classes prior to 13 December 1984, 1st class, 2nd class and 3rd respectively.

To date only seven awards of the medal have been made, six 2nd class awards and one 3rd class award.

**BMC (MMG) RECIPIENTS**

| **Rank Name** | **Class** | **Date of Incident** | **Location** |
|---|---|---|---|
| Tpr Browne, Anthony | 2nd Class | 08.11.60 | Niemba Ambush, Republic of the Congo. |
| Capt Ainsworth, Adrian | " | 07.04.80 | At Tiri, South Lebanon. |
| Lt Bracken, Anthony | " | 08.04.80 | At Tiri, South Lebanon. |
| Cpl Jones, Michael | " | 08.04.80 | At Tiri, South Lebanon |
| Pte Daly, Michael John | " | 07.04.80 | At Tiri, South Lebanon. |
| Comdt Lynch, Michael | " | 25.09.82 | Beirut, Lebanon. |
| Pte Metcalfe, Thomas | 3rd Class | 25.07.81 | Portlaoise Prison Co. Laois. |

The Distinguished Service Medal may be awarded in recognition of individual or associated acts of bravery, courage, leadership, resource or devotion to duty (other than any such acts of duty performed on War Service) arising out of, or associated with, service in the Defence Forces and not meriting the Award of An Bonn Míleata Calmachta. The medal may be awarded in the following classes; with Honour, with Distinction and with Merit. These classes equate with 1st Class, 2nd Class and 3rd Class respectively as in the case with the Military Medal for Gallantry in awards made prior to 13 December 1984.

**BSD (DSM) RECIPIENTS**

| **Rank Name** | **Class** | **Date** | **Location/ Incident** |
|---|---|---|---|
| Lt Gen McKeown, John | 1st Class | Jan 61 – Mar 62 | FC ONUC. |
| Comdt Nunan, Kevin | 1st Class | – | Mulangwoshi River. |
| Capt Magennis, Arthur J. | " | Sep 61 | Elizabethville. |
| Cpl Connolly, Charles | " | Dec 61 | Elizabethville. |
| Comdt O'Shea, Patrick | " | Aug 77 | Muckish Mountain. |
| Sgt Byrne, William | " | Aug 77 | Muckish Mountain. |
| Armn Sherry, Owen | " | Aug 77 | Muckish Mountain. |
| Cpl Doohan, James | " | Apr 79 | Naquora. |
| Lt Gen O'Sullivan, Carl | " | – | Chief of Staff. |
| Maj Gen Quinn, James J. | " | Dec 76 – Feb 81 | FC UNFICYP. |
| Lt Gen Hogan, Louis | " | – | Chief of Staff. |
| Lt Gen Callaghan, William | " | – | FC UNIFIL. |
| Pte Connolly, Anthony R. | 2nd Class | Sep 60 | Manono. |
| Cpl O'Sullivan, Michael | " | Sep 61 | Kilubi. |
| Cpl Kavanagh, John | " | Sep 61 | Lufira Bridge. |
| Cpl Gregan, Patrick J. | " | Dec 61 | The Congo. |
| Cpl Francis, Gerald | " | Dec 61 | The Congo. |
| Cpl Allen, William | " | Dec 62 | Katanga. |
| Sgt Shaughnessy, George | " | Sep 61 | Elizabethville. |
| Sgt Rowland, Michael | " | Sep 61 | Elizabethville. |
| Sgt Quirke, John | " | Dec 62 – Jan 63 | Katanga. |
| Sgt Johnston, Alfred | " | Sep 60 | Kisenyi Post, Goma. |
| CQMS Cotter, James | " | Mar 63 | The Congo. |
| Coy Sgt McLoughlin, William | " | 1961 | The Congo. |
| Coy Sgt Hegarty, Walter T. | " | 1960–1961 | The Congo. |

2nd Class

| | | | |
|---|---|---|---|
| Coy Sgt Carroll, Daniel | " | – | The Congo. |
| SM Norris, Patrick | " | Dec 61 | Elizabethville. |
| Lt Riordan, Patrick A | " | Dec 61 | The Congo. |
| Lt Murphy, Anthony T. S. | " | Sep 61 | Kamina Base. |
| Lt Feely, Peter J. | " | – | Elizabethville. |
| Capt Quinlan, Thomas | " | Sep – Dec 61 | Katanga. |
| Capt Purfield, Michael | " | Sep 61 | The Congo. |
| Capt Norton, John J. | " | Dec 61 | Elizabethville. |
| Capt McCorley, Rodger E. | " | Sep 61 | Elizabethville. |
| Capt Lavery, James K. | " | Dec 62 | Kipushi. |
| Capt Boyle, Thomas | " | Dec 62 – Jan 63 | Katanga. |
| Comdt Flynn, James | " | Oct 61 | The Congo. |
| Comdt Fitzpatrick, Joseph M. | " | Dec 61 | Elizabethville. |
| A/Comdt Browne, Columba B. | " | – | Matadi. |
| Lt Col Hogan, Michael F. | " | – | The Congo. |
| Lt Col Barry, Patrick P. | " | Sep 60 | Manono. |
| Col McCarthy, Justin J. | " | Aug – Oct 60 | The Congo. |
| Comdt McMahon, Brian L. | " | Mar 70 | Glendalough. |
| Sgt Dunne, Thomas | " | Mar 70 | Glendalough. |
| Cpl Brady, Michael J. | " | Mar 70 | Glendalough. |
| Sgt Murray, Richard | " | Mar 77 | Glendalough. |
| Comdt O'Shea, Patrick | " | Mar 77 | Glendalough. |
| Capt Loughnane, Donal | " | Aug 77 | Muckish Mountain. |
| Armn Byrne, David | " | May 77 | Glendalough. |
| Comdt Flynn, James J. | " | Jul/Aug 74 | UNFICYP. |
| Capt Croke, Thomas | " | Aug 72 | Powerscourt. |
| Cpl Kelly, Terence | " | Aug 72 | Powerscourt. |
| Cpl Ring, John | " | Aug 72 | Powerscourt. |
| Lt Col O'Sullivan, Gerald | " | Aug 74 – Jul 76 | UNFICYP. |
| Comdt Fallon, Joseph A.C. | " | Apr 73 – Dec 75 | UNTSO and UNEF. |
| Sgt Lordon, Maurice | " | Apr 79 | Naquora |
| Pte Dillon, Michael | " | Apr 79 | Brachit. |
| Pte Douglas, Colin | " | Apr 79 | Naquora. |
| Pte Burke, Michael | " | Apr 79 | Brachit. |
| Sgt Power, John | " | Apr 80 | OP RAS. |
| PO McIntyre, Michael | " | Nov 81 | LE Aisling. |
| Pte Doyle, Edward | " | Dec 81 | Brachit. |
| Lt Cdr Robinson, James A. | with distinction | Jun 85 | Air India Disaster. |
| PO Mahon, Muiris S. | " | Jun 85 | Air India Disaster. |

| | | | |
|---|---|---|---|
| LS McGrath, John M. | " | Jun 85 | Air India Disaster. |
| AB Brown, Terence J. | " | Jun 85 | Air India Disaster. |
| Pte Wall, Patrick | 3rd Class | 1961 | The Congo. |
| Pte Murray, John | " | – | The Congo. |
| Pte Murray, James | " | Dec 61 | The Congo. |
| Pte Madigan, Peter | " | – | The Congo. |
| A/Cpl Doyle, Aiden T. | " | 1961 | The Congo. |
| Cpl Keenan, John | " | – | The Congo. |
| Pte Doolan, Christopher | " | Sep 61 | The Congo. |
| Pte Clarke, John | " | Dec 61 – May 62 | The Congo. |
| Cpl Woodcock, Anthony | " | Dec 61 – May 62 | The Congo. |
| Cpl O'Neill, Francis | " | – | The Congo. |
| Cpl Nolan, Edward | " | – | Port of Matadi. |
| Cpl Kealy, John J. | " | – | The Congo. |
| Cpl Feery, James W. | " | Dec 61 | The Congo. |
| Cpl Fallon, James | " | – | The Congo. |
| Sgt Whelan, William | " | – | Port of Matadi. |
| Sgt Ryan, John | " | — | The Congo. |
| Sgt O'Sullivan, William J. | " | – | The Congo. |
| Sgt O'Reilly, John J. | " | Oct – Dec 60 | The Congo. |
| Sgt Maguire, Thomas | " | – | The Congo. |
| Sgt McCormack, Patrick J. | " | Oct 60 | Kabalo. |
| Sgt McCaffrey, James | " | – | The Congo. |
| Sgt Mulcahy, Patrick | " | Dec 61 | The Congo. |
| Sgt Mannix, Daniel | " | – | The Congo. |
| Sgt Hayes, Patrick | " | – | The Congo. |
| Sgt Hartley, William | " | – | The Congo. |
| Sgt Daly, John | " | – | Port of Matadi. |
| Sgt Connolly, Richard | " | – | The Congo. |
| Sgt Cashman, Joseph P. | " | – | The Congo. |
| Sgt Ahern, Daniel | " | Nov 63 | Kolwezi. |
| Coy Sgt Walsh, Christopher | " | — | The Congo. |
| Coy Sgt Grant, Felix | " | 1960 | The Congo. |
| Armn O'Sullivan, Richard | " | Aug 77 | Muckish Mountain. |
| Chaplain Dunne, Edward | " | Apr 79 | Naquora. |
| Sgt Smith, Michael | " | Sep 79 | South Lebanon. |
| Cpl Mullins, Noel | " | Oct 78 | South Lebanon. |
| CPO Tumulty, Patrick | " | Nov 81 | L. E. Aisling. |

*Source*: The Irish Defence Forces Handbook

# Notes

Chapter 1 (pp. 1–29)

1. Lit.: 'Soldiers of Ireland'.
2. Lit.: 'Association of Women'.
3. F.X. Martin ed., *The Irish Volunteers 1913–1915* (Dublin 1963) p.111. (Emphasis added.)
4. Ibid., pp. 188–9.
5. Military Archives, A/0122 Group V Item IV (1916 Royal Commission of Inquiry). See also Kevin Nowlan ed., *The Making of 1916* (Dublin 1969) p.130 and *Old Diplomacy: Reminiscences of Lord Hardinge of Panhurst* (London 1947).
6. Indicative of the balance of power in Europe at the time, the Pope sang a *Te Deum* Mass in thanksgiving for King William's victory.
7. F.X. Martin, op. cit., pp.170–83. Essential reading.
8. G.A. Hayes McCoy, *A History of Irish Flags*, pp. 194 et seq.
9. *An tÓglach*, 10/3/23 p. 9.
10. Military Archives, A/0102(III).
11. Nora Connolly O'Brien, *The General Plan of Campaign 1916*; Military Archives, A/0102(II).
12. Ibid., A/0102(I).
13. *An tÓglach*, 16/1/26 p.4.
14. His interest in military theory impressed Connolly. In fact, however, his plan for a national uprising was unrealistic — childish according to F.X. Martin in *Clogher Record 1986* pp. 184–5. For Connolly's impatience to get on with the Rising see 'Irishmen in Scotland 1916', *An tÓglach*, 17/3/62.
15. G.A. Hayes McCoy, 'A Military History of the 1916 Rising' in Nowlan, op. cit., pp. 257 and 309 (n. 29). The Fenians who raided Canada in 1866 used the initials IRA.
16. The tricolour was hoisted by West Cork man, Gearoid O'Sullivan, first Adjutant General of *Óglaigh na hÉireann* who served until his resignation after the mutiny in 1924. He was later a deputy in Dáil Éireann for Carlow and Wicklow.
17. For greater detail see 'A Military History of the 1916 Rising', op. cit.; P.J. Hally, 'The Easter Rising in Dublin: The Military Aspects', part I *The Irish Sword* vol. 7, no. 29; Part II ibid., vol. 8, no. 30; Eoghan O'Neill, 'The Battle of Dublin 1916', *An Cosantóir*, May 1986. Military Archives and PRO records also refer.

18. 'The Dark of the Dawn', *An tÓglach*, 16/1/26, pp. 3–6; 'The Defence of the GPO' from the narratives of M.J. Staines and M.W. O'Reilly, *An tÓglach*, 23/1/26, pp. 3–6; Eamon Lynch, 'James Connolly', ibid., vol. I, no. 5. p. 5; 'Irishmen in Scotland', ibid., vol. I, no. 4, p.4.
19. W.J. Brennan-Whitmore, 'Easter Week, 1916, The Occupation of the North Earl Street area', *An tÓglach*, 30/1/26, pp. 3-6; 'The Defence of the North Earl Street area', ibid., 6/12/26, pp.3-6.
20. Charles Saurin, 'Hotel Metropole Garrison', *An tÓglach*, 13/3/26, pp. 3–4; ibid., 20/3/26, pp. 3–6.
21. L. Turner, 'The Defence of Messrs Hopkins and Hopkins, O'Connell St, Dublin in Easter Week 1916', *An tÓglach*, 5/6/26, pp. 3-6.
22. L. Turner, 'The Kimmage Garrison in 1916', *An tÓglach*, 1/5/26, pp. 3–5; Ernie Nunan, 'The Kimmage Garrison; 1916', ibid., vol. 2, no. 12, p. 9.
23. J.J. Reynolds, 'Four Courts and North King St area in 1916', *An tÓglach*, 15/5/26, pp. 3–6; 22/5/26, pp. 3–4; 29/5/26, pp. 3–4; 12/6/26, p. 6; Summer 1971, p. 19.
24. Thomas Young, 'Fighting in South Dublin; with the Garrison in Marrowbone Lane during Easter Week 1916', *An tÓglach*, 6/3/26.
25. G.A. Lyons, 'Occupation of the Ringsend Area in 1916', *An tÓglach*; 10/4/26, pp. 3-11; 17/4/26, pp. 3–8; 24/4/26, pp. 3–4.
26. *An tÓglach*, 10/4/26, p. 6; Earl of Longford & T.P. O'Neill, *Eamon de Valera* (London 1970) p. 38; Margaret Ward, *Unmanageable Revolutionaries* (Brandon Press 1983) pp.110–11.
27. *An tÓglach*, 10/4/26, pp. 10–12; John McCann, 'The Defence of Clanwilliam House, 1916'; *The Kerryman*, 11/3/39.
28. J.V. Joyce, 'Easter Week 1916; the Defence of the South Dublin Union', *An tÓglach*, 12/6/26, pp. 3–5; ibid., 17/3/62, p. 3; President Sean T. O Ceallaigh unveiled a memorial to the deceased members of the 4th Battalion Dublin Brigade at Harolds Cross, Dublin, in September 1954. The six companies of the battalion (seven with the formation of the G Company in 1920) all had honourable records in the 1920/21 period.
29. 'The Fight at Ashbourne' from the narrative of Capt. Joseph Lawless, *An tÓglach*, 31/7/26, pp. 3–5; ibid., Easter 1961, p. 8. The 5th Battalion singularly accomplished its mission. It was composed mostly of North County Dublin (Fingal) men. After being rearrested, Ashe died on 25 September 1917 from forcible feeding unskilfully performed. His funeral was a great national occasion. Michael Collins delivered the graveside oration. In many eyes Ashe redeemed Kerry, which had allowed Casement under only a small escort to be moved to London.

Austin Stack had been unfairly blamed by some for this lack of support. See Richard Mulcahy, 'The Work of Thomas Ashe', *An tÓglach*, vol. I, no. 6.
30. P. Colgan, 'The Maynooth Volunteers in 1916', *An tÓglach*, 8/5/26, pp. 3–5; 22/5/26, p. 5.
31. M. Reynolds, 'Cumann na mBan in the GPO', *An tÓglach*, 27/3/26, pp. 3–5; Nora O'Daly, 'The Women of Easter Week', *An tÓglach*, 3/11/26, pp. 3–6.
32. 'A Military History of the 1916 Rising', op. cit., pp. 261 et seq.
33. The Volunteers, the Irish Citizen Army and the Ancient Order of Hibernians.
34. J.J. Burke, 'The Citizen Army in 1916', *An tÓglach*, 20/2/26, pp. 3–4.
35. See note 14.
36. Anon., 'Easter Week 1916, Dublin Castle from the Inside: The narrative of one who was there', *An tÓglach*, 13/2/26, pp. 3–6.
37. See F.X. Martin, article in *Clogher Record 1986*, no. 3, pp. 206–11.
38. Charles Steinmayer, 'Evacuation of the GPO 1916', *An tÓglach*, 27/2/26, pp. 3–5.
39. 'A Military History of the 1916 Rising', op. cit., pp. 298–304; see also Florence O'Donoghue, 'Plans for the 1916 Rising', *University Review*, vol. III, no. 1; Denis Crowley, 'An Embryonic Army on Parade', *An Cosantóir*, Nov. 1989, p. 13.
40. The executions went on daily for over a week and halted only when the matter was raised in the House of Commons by John Dillon. There was one execution in Cork in 1916. A family named Kent of Fermoy defended their home against an RIC raid but were eventually overpowered. One of the three brothers was tried by court-martial and executed. See also León Ó Broin, *W.E. Wylie and the Irish Revolution 1916–1921* (Dublin 1989), pp. 31 ff.
41. Willie Redmond represented East Clare. After he was killed in action de Valera succeeded him (10/8/1917). (De Valera's opponent was Paddy Lynch K.C. who later became Attorney General.) In 1917 Sinn Féin won by-elections in Roscommon (Count Plunkett) and Longford (Leo McGuinn). After de Valera's success it won Waterford (Dr White) and Armagh (P. MacCartan). John Redmond, who died in March 1918, was succeeded by his son, also a captain in the British Army. He was elected with a substantial majority over his Sinn Féin opponent, White.
42. W.B. Yeats, 'Easter 1916', *Selected Poetry* ed. A. Norman Jeffares (London 1917) p. 93 — written 25/9/1916.
43. *Irish Press*, 13/12/89, pp. 4–5.
44. Military Archives, A/0122.
45. Ibid., A/0122 II.

Chapter 2 (pp. 30–68)

1. J.C. Beckett, *The Making of Modern Ireland 1603–1923* (London 1988), p.441: 'Ireland was quickly passing under the most dangerous of all tyrannies — the tyranny of the dead.'
2. 'Largely' but not 'totally' as the contemporary press testified. See also Earnan de Blaghd, 'Ireland in 1915, National Spirit at its lowest Scale', *An tÓglach*, vol. I, no. 5, pp. 4–8; ibid., no. 6, pp. 3, 10.
3. Earl of Longford & T.P. O'Neill, *Eamon de Valera* (London 1970), p. 56.
4. The Irish Republican Brotherhood was founded in 1858. Its members were known as Fenians and the Fenian Brotherhood was the official name of the corresponding organisation in the USA. Separating Ireland from England was the aim of both. No means by which this could be accomplished were excluded. Founder members of both organisations were: John O'Mahony, James Stephens, Michael Doheny, Thomas C. Luby, Diarmuid O'Donovan Rossa, John O'Leary, Edward Duffy, Charles Kickham and John Devoy. Sam Maguire (d. 1927), the Ulster Protestant who presented the All-Ireland football cup, was also a member.
5. In April 1919 de Valera took over from Brugha who had been elected temporary President the previous January. Cabinet Ministers included Cathal Brugha (Defence), Michael Collins (Finance), Count Plunkett (Foreign Affairs), W.T. Cosgrave (Local Government), Countess Markieviecz (Labour). When de Valera went to America in June 1919 Griffith took over the Presidency and held it until his arrest on 26/11/1920. Collins then became acting President until de Valera's return in December 1920. Griffith reassured the Dáil that de Valera's absence could not be construed as a retreat from the front line.
6. Oscar Traynor, 'The Defence Brigade', *An tÓglach*, vol. I, no. 6, p. 5, Christmas 1962. Charles Dalton, *With the Dublin Brigade*, (London 1929) pp. 34–35; 'A Tribute to Oscar Traynor', *An tÓglach*, Summer 1964.
7. De Valera was later to proclaim that the Volunteers were a 'national army of defence', not 'a praetorian guard'. See Robert Kee, *The Green Flag* (London 1972), vol. III, p. 137; *An tÓglach*, vol. I, no. 5, p. 7; Dan Breen, *My Fight for Irish Freedom* (Dublin 1924); Desmond Ryan, '*Sean Treacy and the Third Tipperary Brigade*' (Dublin).
8. These executions went on up to the truce (11/7/1921); no belligerent status had been accorded to *Óglaigh na hÉireann*.
9. Confidential source.
10. 'Tomás Mac Curtain', *An tÓglach*, vol. I, no. 8, Winter 1963.

11. Michael Quirke, 'The Battle of Kilmallock', *An tÓglach*, 18/12/26, pp. 16–18.
12. 'Traolach Mac Suibhne', *An tÓglach*, vol. I, no. 8, Winter 1963, pp. 1, 3.
13. Rapparees were armed bands made up mainly of ex-soldiers from the Jacobite armies grouped to protect Roman Catholics against the emergence of a rapacious Protestant ascendancy under William and Mary.
14. He had previously been arrested in May 1918 during the East Cavan by-election and imprisoned with de Valera in England. De Valera escaped from Lincoln Jail (3/2/1919). See Longford & O'Neill, op. cit., chapter 7, p. 77.
15. *An tÓglach*, 16/12/26, p. 8.
16. Longford & O'Neill, op. cit., p. 123. Lt Gen. 'Mickey Joe' Costello in the course of an interview said that if they had listened to de Valera they would have been wiped out in a week. What he wanted was another spectacular 'like a Battle of Clontarf' (1014). When de Valera came back from America at Christmas 1920 he disagreed with the form the campaign had taken, particularly with street ambushes and flying column activities. He wanted major battles with up to 500 Volunteers taking part. This was swiftly rejected by Collins and Mulcahy and the guerilla war went on. See also interview with Lt Gen. Sean Clancy. For the Custom House burning see *An tÓglach*, vol. 1, no. 5 (Custom House) Memorial November 1962.
17. Tom Barry, *Guerilla Days in Ireland* (Cork 1948) p. 20–27. Training was hard, and discipline of necessity harsh.
18. Ibid., p. 208 et seq. Barry was a master of tactics.
19. Arms and grenades were also manufactured locally on a small scale.
20. On another level Montgomery criticised the sub-standard contemporary British military educational system. See Montgomery, *Memoirs* (London), chapter 3 and 4, pp. 34–58.
21. Confidential source.
22. Ernie O'Malley, *On Another Man's Wound* (Dublin 1979). O'Malley was a brilliant organiser and daredevil leader whose deeds of valour subsequently won for him the appointment of O/C Second Southern Division.
23. See T.P. Kilfeather, *The Connaught Rangers* (Tralee 1969) and Sam Pollock, *Meeting for the Cause* (London 1969). Later, after a long struggle, the survivors were awarded trifling pensions based, believe it or not, on the length of their service in the British Army.

24. Beckett, op. cit., p. 455.
25. The evening papers of 8 July 1921 contained an extract setting forth the terms from a special edition of the *Irish Bulletin* — an underground daily news sheet which circulated internationally countering the British version of the war. Published by the Minister for Propaganda of the First Dáil, Desmond Fitzgerald, and edited by Kathleen Napoli McKenna (d. 1988).

Chapter 3 (p. 69–113)

1. Tom Barry, *Guerilla Days in Ireland* (Cork 1948) p. 162.
2. *Hearst Newspapers* 6/2/22. De Valera's fancies for large-scale actions involving 500 men and for attacks on Beggars Bush, Headquarters of the Auxiliaries were regarded risibly. See also Earl of Longford & T.P. O'Neill, *Eamon de Valera* (London 1970) p. 121. Barry, op. cit., p. 193.
3. *Irish Defence Forces Handbook* 1968, p. 2.
4. Calton Younger, *Ireland's Civil War* (London 1968) p. 226.
5. Charles Townshend, *The British Campaign in Ireland* (OUP 1975) pp. 19, 195-8; Longford & O'Neill, op. cit., pp. 121, 131.
6. Ibid. Liaison H.Q. was established in the Gresham Hotel.
7. Younger, op. cit., p. 256–60; Cabinet conclusions 23/22 (5/4/22) and 24/22 (1) (10/4/22).
8. Michael Brennan, *The War in Clare* (Dublin 1980) p. 105. Brennan sent two officers, Michael Hogan (later GOC Claremorris Command) and Ned Lynch, to London in 1921 to purchase arms with £1000 received from Cathal Brugha for that purpose. They raided Chelsea and Windsor Barracks, were arrested, sentenced to long terms of imprisonment but released within a year. Collins was in London at the time trying to negotiate the Treaty. He was kept in the dark by Brugha about the compromising undertaking. The incident added to the ill-feeling between the two of them. Collins referred to him irreverently as 'Charlie' (the English version of his name). See also Uinsionn MacEoin, *Survivors* (Dublin 1987) pp. 139–40.
9. S.P. Irwin, 'The Birth of an Army', *Irish Times* 3/1/66. Lt Col. Sean Clancy felt these hours were somewhat exaggerated, but Tom Barry's men trained intensively from 8 a.m. to 6 p.m., followed by lectures in the evenings.
10. Townshend, op. cit., p. 199 (G.O. C.–in–C WSR 1 Oct. 1921 CP 3377. CAB 24127).
11. 400,000 Irishmen fought 'for the freedom of small nations' in the Great War. 50,000 were killed in action unsung.
12. Correspondence and interviews with Lt Gen. Sean Collins-Powell and Lt Col. Sean Clancy.

13. J.C. Beckett, *The Making of Modern Ireland 1603-1923* (London 1988) p. 452. The Northern State was already functioning as such under the pre-treaty Government of Ireland Act (1920). The Treaty signatories believed Lloyd George's blandishments.
14. Longford & O'Neill, op. cit., p. 138.
15. Ibid., pp. 146, 157.
16. Ibid., p. 144.
17. Ibid., pp. 148–9; Griffith was not committed to republicanism. However, he hated all Englishmen, particularly Childers, who was also intensely disliked by Lloyd George for his disloyalty to Britain. Both Barton and Childers had British Army service.
18. Ibid. When prior to the Truce, de Valera suggested that Collins should go to America, he retorted, 'The long "hure" won't get rid of me as easily as that'. On the other hand, around the same time when Tom Barry was called to GHQ and was introduced to President de Valera by Collins he found that the two men chatted amiably. He (Barry) found Brugha taciturn and the tension between him and Collins palpable. De Valera posed Barry the all-important question, 'How long can the Cork Flying Columns keep the field against the British'. De Valera said that Collin's suspicions of a plot against him were quite unjustified.
19. Ibid., p. 150.
20. Beckett, op. cit., p. 452; communications of the time were unsophisticated. De Valera's support was expected. Opposition from Brugha and Stack was anticipated. Collins felt that as the enemy was now fully familiar with the names of the leaders, neither the army nor the people could stand another dose of Lloyd George's 'terrible war'. The 'trucileers' allegedly felt otherwise.
21. Ibid., p. 454. The Battle of the Boyne (1690) was a skirmish in the prevailing continental power struggle, between Dutch and English royal rivals. Few battles in history have paid such disproportionate dividends and caused so much lasting misery to the losers.
22. Ibid., p. 455. See also Margaret Ward, *The Unmanageable Revolutionaries* (Brandon 1983) pp. 173–7; includes P.O. O'Hegarty's 'Furies' reference.
23. Longford & O'Neill, op. cit., p. 116.
24. Townshend, op. cit., p. 17.
25. Longford & O'Neill, op. cit., p. 182.
26. Younger, op. cit., p. 221.
27. Longford & O'Neill, op. cit., p. 171.
28. Ibid., p. 182.
29. FOR: Richard Mulcahy, Chief of Staff; Eoin O'Duffy, Deputy Chief of Staff; 'Ginger' O'Connell, Assistant Chief of Staff;

Gearóid O'Sullivan, Adjutant General; Sean McMahon, Quartermaster General; Emmett Dalton, Director of Training; Diarmuid O'Hegarty, Director of Organisation; Piaras Beaslaí, Director of Publicity; Michael Collins, Director of Intelligence.

AGAINST: Liam Mellowes, Director of Purchases; Rory O'Connor, Director of Engineering; Sean Russell, Director of Munitions; Seamus Donovan, Director of Chemicals. Younger, op. cit., p. 252. (An excellent painting by Leo Whelan of the General Staff of the IRA now hangs in the Officers Mess, McKee Barracks.)

30. E. Neeson, *The Civil War in Ireland* (Dublin 1981) p. 51.
31. Younger, op. cit., p. 244.
32. *Irish Defence Forces Handbook*, op. cit., p. 2.
33. See Ronan Fanning, 'The Impact of Independence' in *Bicentenary Essays Bank of Ireland (1783–1983)* (Dublin 1983) p. 83–6.
34. I*rish Defence Forces Handbook*, op. cit., p. 2 gives 4,000 as the figure. Capt. Martin Bell's recall of 12,000 seems nearer the mark.
35. Younger, op. cit., p. 232.
36. Interview with Comdt Vinny Byrne (July 1989) in company of Capt. Martin Bell.
37. Letter from Lt Col. Sean Clancy.
38. *An tÓglach*, 7/4/23 p. 16–17; *Irish Defence Forces Handbook*, op. cit., p. 6.
39. *Irish Defence Forces Handbook*, op. cit., p. 2.
40. Neeson, op. cit., 52; Younger, op. cit., p. 232; M. Tierney & M. MacCurtain, *The Birth of Modern Ireland*, p. 158. Neeson differs on the date and credits the 3rd Tipperary Brigade under Denis Lacy rather than Ernie O'Malley with the raid. The haul was 300 rifles; 20,000 rounds of ammunition, two armoured cars, two armoured Lancias; ten ordinary Lancia cars and Crossley tenders; two other cars; seven machine guns and hundreds of boxes of grenades. O'Malley makes no mention of the raid in his book *On Another Man's Wound*. In Tipperary 33 rifles and two machine guns and ammunition were captured.
41. Neeson, op. cit., p. 56–60. Captured: 1,500 rifles; 55 Lewis guns; 6 Maxim guns; three Vickers guns; 500,000 rounds of ·303 ammunition; 1000 revolvers; 1000 ·455 automatic pistols with ammunition, 3000 hand grenades and a quantity of rifle grenade throwers.
42. Longford & O'Neill, op. cit., p. 185.
43. Ibid., p. 187.
44. Ibid.
45. Interview with Major Gen. James Lillis, March 1988. Pretruce, Lillis had been a prisoner of the British in Rath Camp. He devised an ingenious method of an envelope within an envelope

to smuggle out information. He typified the brains and talent that made up the early *Óglaigh na hÉireann.*

46. Seán McBride subsequently defected to the Irregulars and continued in active opposition to successive governments until 1937 when the new constitution allowed his conscience to conform.
47. Dorman Smith (later Major Gen. Dorman O'Gowan whose attitudes to subversives later became eccentric and questionable) was sacked with Auchinleck by Churchill prior to the Battle of Alamein (1942). He was determined to 'get even' with Churchill and did secure a retraction from him. See Lavinia Greacen, *Chink* (London 1990).
48. Letter (2/10/87) from Col. James Flynn: Adjutant General 1943–5; 1946–8; 1952–4; Assistant Chief of Staff 1949–51; 1955–61.
49. Kevin O'Higgins entered the army when the war began and held senior rank at Army HQ.
50. Lt Col. W.P.G. Donnelly who served in WWI, the War of Independence and the Civil War. A founder member of the Artillery Corps.
51. Chief of Staff 1931–40.
52. Interview with Captain Martin Bell (7/1/88). Martin opined that in a way these few shots could be called opening rounds of the Civil War. See also Dan Breen, *My Fight for Irish Freedom* (Dublin 1924).
53. Interview with Major Gen J. Lillis (March 88).
54. Longford & O'Neill, op. cit., p. 188.
55. Kevin O'Higgins, 'Civil War and the Events which led to it' (memo from Lt Col. Seán Clancy, retired).
56. Interview with Capt. Martin Bell. He was part of the escort which brought a load of these rifles from Beggars Bush to the Four Courts.
57. See Fanning, op. cit., p. 69.
58. Younger, op. cit., p. 291.
59. 'Sir Henry Wilson was an ardent upholder of the Ulster Unionists and he was consulted by the Six County Government in connection with the situation there — Sir James Craig announced that the post had only been accepted by Sir Henry on condition that he got an absolutely free hand and all his requirements for the protection of the Six Counties Government. He has bitterly attacked Lloyd George for what he saw as a sell-out.' *Irish Independent* 23/6/22. His assassination is ascribed to Collins who regarded him as the evil genius behind the programmes. Dunne and Sullivan were hanged in London.
60. P.J. McCarthy, 'The RAF and Ireland 1922–26' *Irish Sword*, vol. XVII, no. 68, p. 183–5. Around the time of Wilson's assassina-

tion it was rumoured that Brugha and a party had been detailed to travel to London to assassinate the entire British cabinet. Events overtook this.

61. The Four Courts caucus had also been making demands on Dublin firms for money under the pretext of a Belfast boycott which had no authorised existence but which they felt, not without justification, Collins condoned. The leader of the raiding party, Leo Henderson, was captured. (He was later o/c 26th Battalion during the Emergency with Frank Thornton from the Free State side as his adjutant.)
62. *Irish Independent*, 22/6/22. Both the MacEoin and Cooney families were well-known in Co. Longford. MacEoin commanded the Midland Division. He was captured by the British, tried by court-martial in the City Hall Dublin, sentenced to be hanged but released after truce because he was a Dáil deputy.
63. Mrs Mc Grath had pleaded in vain for Gen. MacEoin at his court-martial.
64. The majority were not against the Treaty. Out of 620, 283 votes, anti-treaty candidates won 133,864, pro-treaty panel candidates 239,193, non panel 247,276. Out of 128 seats the anti-treaty group got 35. See Michael Hopkinson, *Green Against Green* (Dublin 1989), chapter 14; MacCurtain, *The Birth of Modern Ireland*, op. cit., p. 160.
65. Longford & O'Neill, op. cit., chapter 16.
66. Younger, op. cit., p. 257.
67. Ibid., p. 285.
68. Neeson, op. cit., p. 71.
69. J.P. Duggan, 'Artillery in the Civil War', *An Cosantóir*, Nov. 1988. Comdt Johnny Doyle who fired the 18-pdr on the Four Courts claimed as a result to have been the first Artillery Officer in the Irish army.
70. Churchill quipped 'Better a State without archives than archives without a State'. Younger, op. cit., p. 324.
71. Letter from Lt Col. Sean Clancy. Later sold to him by the State. Re-sold 1988.
72. As recalled in part by Cahir Davitt. Capt. Martin Bell recalls that the term 'District' was in use for a long while. Commands were not formally established until February 1923; brigades later. It seems to have been, understandably, *ad hoc* up to that. 'South-Western' had been a designated district — Ennis. 'Division' from the old IRA organisation was also in common usage.
73. Military Archives. Comdt Young's list.
74. Neeson, op. cit., p. 90; quotation from Thomas Davis's *Fontenoy 1745* (London 1914) pp. 328–31.

75. Peter Verney, *Anzio 1944: An Unexpected Fury* (London 1978). 'I had hoped that we were hurling a wild cat on to the shore but all we got was a stranded whale [Churchill].' Maj. Gen. W.R.E. Murphy was born in Bannow, Co. Wexford, and educated at Queens and UCD. He joined the British Army in 1914. Before retiring from that service, in 1919, he had reached the rank of Acting Brigadier-General, commanding the 91st Brigade. With service in Italy, he won the DSO, Military Cross and Bar, 1914 Star, Service Medal and Victory Medal. Italy awarded him a Silver Medal for Valour, and a Croce di Guerra. He was mentioned four times in despatches. He joined the National Army in 1922, and became Commandant General, GOC Kerry Command. On 3 May 1923, he resigned from the army to join the Garda Síochána. He died in 1975.
76. Flood's brother, Frank, had been hanged by the British in Mountjoy Gaol in March 1921; another brother, Harold, was a Company Commander (B Company) of the 10th Uisneach Battalion during the Emergency (1939–45). Later Tom became a Christian Brother. He took over Collins Barracks from the British in 1922. Another brother, Alfie, became Deputy Commissioner of the Garda. The eldest brother, Sean, was in Perth Gaol, having been 2 i/c to Eoin Duffy in Fifth Northern Division. Their sister Treasa was equally intrepid. A remarkable, patriotic family.
77. Orderly officers in McKee Barracks Dublin, where Paul was a finicky Camp Commandant, smiled when they heard this story. Major Gen. P. Mulcahy alleged that Lt Col. Paul never forgave the Artillery Corps for that incident.
78. Other appointments: Fionan Lynch, deputy O/C South West; Comdt Gen. Kevin O'Higgins, assistant A.G., Comdt Gen. Joseph McGrath, Director of Intelligence, Major Gen. Diarmuid O hEigeartaigh (Governor of Mountjoy) General Staff Officer, Comdt Gen.
79. Neeson, op. cit., chapter 22.
80. The following barracks were burned: Victoria (Collins) Cork; New (Sarsfield) Limerick; Clonmel; Tipperary; Fermoy; Buttevant; Tralee; Renmore (Mellowes) Galway; Castlebar. The Dublin Brigade saved the Dublin Barracks and MacEoin's Midland Division saved Athlone and other midland and western installations. The Curragh, Mullingar, Naas, Kilkenny and Wexford were also saved.
81. The Westport landings consisted of a composite force commanded by Mayoman, Gen. Joe Ring. He had given distinguished service against the British in West Mayo and a few weeks later

was killed in action in the Ox Mountains by Michael Kilroy's republicans. When the ship bearing the Government forces was sighted in Clew Bay Kilroy dispatched a man on a bicycle (there was no telephone system in Mayo) to Castlebar (10 miles away) with instructions to burn the Gaol and the Military Barracks at once and retreat toward Newport. This was done, but an attempt to burn the Post Office was foiled by the intervention of a local priest. No opposition was encountered by the troops but in a follow up operation westwards from Castlebar heavy fighting took place around Newport and Westport.

82. The Dublin Guards landed at Fenit after a rough sea journey. The tide was misjudged and the landing delayed. Some waded ashore. Many were wounded, eight were killed. The bodies were brought back to Dublin; ill-feeling was aroused. Breaches of discipline occurred on both sides. This was more serious in the pro-treaty side, as they purported to be the Regular Army.

83. Hogan's party consisted of Clare and Galway men. Hogan was sent by Brennan at Brugha's instigation to London to purchase arms during the truce. He was later GOC Claremorris Command. Retired 1940 to become manager of Dublin Airport. See *An tÓglach* 28/7/23, p. 2 and chapter 5.

84. He was appointed Major General, GOC Kerry Command on 2 January 1923. It was a meteoric rise without adequate preparation from Captain the previous Spring. Its rapidity may have shot him through his ceiling. On the ground he was a fearless fighter and proved it in 1916 and in the War of Independence. He commanded the ASU and took part in all dangerous operations including Bloody Sunday. He rejoined the Army during the 'Emergency', but was only given the rank of Captain in the Construction Corps. He had left the Army in 1924. His General's rank was recognised when he was given a military funeral in the early 1950s.

85. Neeson, op. cit., p. 156–62; Younger, op. cit., chapter 20. There are many theories as to the identity of the assassin. J. Anthony Gaughan holds that an ex-British Army marksman fighting for the anti-treaty side did it. One of his bullets which ricochetted upwards from the road near where Collins lay in a prone position hit the Commander-in-Chief in the back of the head, fatally wounding him. The theory leaves fixed opinions unmoved and ballistic experts unconvinced. It is argued that firing a rifle in a ditch was no place for a Commander-in-Chief. (For a comparison see Montgomery's *Memoirs* (London) chapter 4 on Lord Gort's command of the BEF.) But this was an ambush: and he felt safe enough in his own Co. Cork. See also Capt. Feehan,

*The Shooting of Michael Collins,* RTE's evocative, interesting documentary, and Meda Ryan, *The Day Michael Collins was shot* (1989).

86. Neeson, op. cit., p. 162; Barry, op. cit., p. 183.
87. Paddy O'Keeffe (afterwards Gen. Sec. GAA) was then O/C Barracks. He had unsuccessfully queried the order to burn the barracks, reasoning that if they won they would need it and if they lost, why destroy the people's property. Though Cork city and county were in anti-treaty hands a number of old Volunteer officers came forward and served on in the Defence Forces for many years afterwards.
88. Hopkinson, *Green Against Green,* pp. 161–2.
89. Harold O'Sullivan's lecture on 'The Civil War in North Louth 1922–3', Military History Society of Ireland, Field Day Visit to Dundalk 27 August 1989.
90. Younger, op. cit., pp. 494, 503.
91. Neeson, op. cit, p. 184; Army Archives HQ 2nd Southern command 12/10/22.
92. Beckett, op. cit., p. 459.
93. Childers, son of Professor Robert Childers of London, was educated at Hailesbury and Trinity College, Cambridge. Served as a trooper in the Boer War in 1900 — on leave from his position as Clerk in the British House of Commons (which he held until 1910). A relative of Huge C.K. Childers, Chancellor of the Exchequer in Gladstone's Ministry from 1882 to 1885; a convert to Home Rule even before Gladstone himself; responsible for the financial clauses of the first Home Rule Bill; the author of a book dealing with the financial aspect of an Irish settlement. From 1910 to 1914 Childers was active politically and published *The Framework of Home Rule.* As expert yachtsman, in 1903 had also published a best-selling novel, *The Riddle of the Sands,* based on his experience sailing amongst the islands and sandbanks off Germany's Baltic coast. With his yacht, *Asgard* took part in the famous Howth gun-running episode when he brought 900 rifles and 29,000 rounds of ammunition from the Continent and landed them in Howth for the Irish Volunteers in July 1914. Served with distinction in the 1914–18 war; rose to Major, won DSO with RAF. On the Secretariat of the Irish Convention of 1917–18. Thought the best solution of the Irish question was on the lines of Dominion Home Rule. On demobilisation from Air Force returned to Ireland; became converted to the Republican ideal. Elected to Dáil Éireann for Wicklow in May, 1921. Spoke ably against the Treaty in the Dáil debates. See also Longford & O'Neill, op. cit., p. 200.

94. It was a ·32 Spanish Automatic No. 10169 and remained in the possession of Judge Cahir Davitt for many years until on 4 November 1939 he returned it to the Childers family.
95. P.S. O Hegarty, *The Victory of Sinn Fein* (Dublin 1924); *Irish Independent*, 15/3/23; *Freeman's Journal*, 16/3/23. Derrig was later a Fianna Fáil Minister of Education.
96. Neeson, op. cit., p. 191.
97. Seán Mc Garry T.D. was an old IRB man who had fought in the 1916 Rising.
98. Deasy was sentenced to death by court-martial in Clonmel in April 1923. At his own request he saw Dick Mulcahy and signed an appeal to his comrades. (He became a lifelong friend of Mulcahy.) He served over a year in Mountjoy jail and on release was again court-martialed. Manhandled by Irregulars. Sentenced to death. Again reprieved. On outbreak of war in 1939 rejoined army. Rose to rank of Commandant.
99. *An tÓglach*, 24/3/23, p. 3–9.
100. John Canon Pigott (d. 23/8/89) was among the first three priests to answer Collins's call for chaplains. He received Collins's body after the *Béal na Bláth* ambush. He gave the last sacraments to Dick Barrett, Rory O'Connor, Joe McKelvey and Liam Mellowes. Breandan O Cathaoir, ed., 'Canon Pigott', in the *Bray Historical Record*, no. 4, 1990
101. *An tÓglach*, 24/3/23, p. 2 'Is fearr súil sa chluaid ná dhá shúile sa doras' ('The insurmountable authority of the proverb will have to cover my approach', MacNeill explained).
102. *An tÓglach*, 11/8/23, pp. 4–6: Ibid., 1/9/23, pp. 3–4.
103. Ibid., 1/9/23, pp. 12–13.
104. Ibid., 5/5/23, p. 13.
105. Ibid., 11/8/23, pp. 7–8.
106. Ibid., 3/11/23, pp. 9–10.
107. Ibid., 7/4/23, p. 3.
108. Ibid., 2/4/23, p. 3.
109. Ibid., 5/5/23, p. 3.
110. Ibid., p. 22.
111. Ibid., 6/10/23, pp. 1, 3–6, 8; *The Call to Arms* (Dublin 1945), p. 128.
112. *An tÓglach*, 24/2/23, p. 5; W.P. Delamere,'The Air Corps' in *The Call to Arms*, op. cit., p. 103.
113. Richard Cooke, 'The Artillery Corps', in *The Call to Arms*, op. cit., pp. 193–204; J.P. Duggan, 'The Artillery Corps', *An Cosantóir*, February 1947, p. 22. Data collected by the late Capt. Frank Whitty, who made a great contribution to the pursuit of excellence in the Corps. See also *An tÓglach*, 16/6/23, pp. 8–9.

114. Liam McNamee, 'The Cavalry Corps', *An Cosantóir*, January 1976.
115. *An tÓglach*, 19/5/23; T.J. McKenny, 'The Army Medical Service'; in *Call to Arms*, op. cit., p. 51; 'The Army Nursing Service', ibid., p. 155. Mark Cooney, 'The Army Medical Corps', *An Cosantóir*, October 1967, pp. 529–35; Comdt Brigid Lyons-Thornton (ret'd), 'Women and the Army', *An Cosantóir*, November 1973, pp. 364-5; Col. J. Laffan MD (ret'd), 'Lt Brigid Lyons-Thornton: Our first female Lt', *An Cosantóir*, October 1987.
116. *An tÓglach*, 10/3/23, p. 11–14; R.H. Greene, 'The Signal Corps', p. 63.
117. F.J. Henry, 'The Military Police Service' in *Call to Arms*, op. cit., p. 151; *Defence Forces Handbook*, op. cit., p. 43–4.
118. C. Sauerzweig, 'Army School of Music', in *Call to Arms*, op. cit.
119. See note 109 and 110.
120. *An tÓglach*, 19/5/23, p. 18.
121. Liam Egan, 'Q', *Call to Arms*, op. cit., p. 89.
122. *An tÓglach*, 30/6/23, (Transport), pp. 7–9; ibid., 14/7/23 (Supplies), pp. 5–7.
123. *An tÓglach*, 20/10/23 and 3/11/23; J. T. Murphy, 'Supply and Transport', op. cit., p. 73.
124. T. McGrath, 'The Army Ordnance Corps', *Call to Arms*, op. cit., p. 113; *An tÓglach*, 2/6/23 pp. 5–7.
125. *An tÓglach*, 6/10/23.
126. Neeson, op. cit., pp. 198–9. See chapter 6.
127. *An tÓglach*, 16/6/23, pp. 3–6.
128. Longford & O'Neill, op. cit., p. 223.
129. Neeson, p. 202, note 7.
130. Surprised by Lt Frank Curran's section (the bank gave him a gold watch for his bravery).
131. Longford & O'Neill, op. cit., p. 220, makes it 82. The usual figure quoted is 77. The bodies of all the executed prisoners were handed over to their relatives some time during 1924.

Chapter 4. (pp. 114–137)

1. Earl of Longford & T.P. O'Neill, *Eamon de Valera* (London 1970) pp. 203-4, and chapters 14-17.
2. J.C. Beckett, *The Making of Modern Ireland 1603-1923* (London 1988) p. 459.
3. Longford & O'Neill, op. cit. pp. 200-201; Finance, Austin Stack; Home Affairs, P.J. Ruttledge; Local Government, Seán T. O'Kelly; Economic Affairs, Robert Barton; Defence, Liam Mellowes (then in Mountjoy Jail).
4. Longford & O'Neill, op. cit., p. 204.

5. Michael Hopkinson (Dublin 1989), *Green Against Green*, pp. 91-2. After the mutiny the force was disbanded; reconstructed 18/8/22. When the British evacuated the Depot in the Phoenix Park the Gardaí moved in. O'Duffy replaced Staines but returned for a short period to Army in March 1924 when a mutiny occurred there. Sacked in 1933, he became leader of the Blueshirts — an Irish-style quasi-fascist organisation. He had a good military record in the War of Independence but his political wisdom was later found wanting.
6. Davitt was called to the Bar aged 21 in January 1916. In August 1920 Austin Stack made him a Circuit Court Judge in the Dáil courts. In August 1922 Eamonn Duggan referred him to Hugh Kennedy (Law Advisor to Provisional Government) who offered him the post of Judge Advocate General. After much soul-searching he accepted. He did not identify with the fighting men.
7. Davitt had known O'Higgins slightly as a student in UCD. From 1914-17 O'Higgins had been a solicitor's apprentice, but political involvements disrupted his studies.
8. Davitt's own personal recall. Eamonn de Barra who took the anti-treaty side maintained that Collins was drinking heavily at the time. Davitt never mentioned any such problem.
9. Theodore Cunningham Kingsmill Moore was elected to the Senate for the Dublin University constituency. He subsequently became a High Court, and ultimately a Supreme Court, Judge. In the *Handbook of the Irish Rebellion* published by the *Irish Times* (May 1916) his name appears as one of those who assembled in the College to defend it against the Insurgents. He was called to the Bar in 1918 which suggests that he could not have been very long in the R.A.F.
10. Paddy McGilligan subsequently became Minister for Industry and Commerce and as such was responsible for the Shannon Scheme and the E.S.B. He became a Minister in 1926, later Minister for External Affairs, Finance, and was also Attorney-General.
11. Had been a solicitor's clerk; brother of John Carrig, solicitor in Ballina firm, Bourke, Carrig and Loftus.
12. Second son of Professor Robert Donovan, leader writer of the *Freeman's Journal* and Professor of English Literature UCD. Later became Assistant Secretary of the ESB.
13. O'Connell School's man. Joined British Army as a private, served as a commissioned officer throughout most of war (Royal Dublin Fusiliers). Studied for Bar on demobilisation. Became Attorney General in 1950 and Judge of the High Court in 1951. His brother became Head Chaplain in the Army.

14. In 1923 became Private Secretary to Kevin O'Higgins (Justice). He spent a period — unhappily — with Charles Bewley in the (First) Irish Legation in Rome.
15. The first court-martial was of an ex-British Army NCO, Sergeant Major Dixon. He did not think much of an order which had been given by his commanding officer, Captain Caprani, during operations in Co. Cork. He advised his men not to obey it and was charged with mutiny and insubordination. He had to come to Dublin for trial. Road and rail communications were non-existent. He was sent by sea with the other accused, unescorted. He marched them from the Quays to Portobello (Cathal Brugha) Barracks and reported himself and his accused men to the orderly officer. He was not so much concerned with his own predicament as with the general style of conducting the court-martial, making unfavourable comparisons with ones he had experienced in the British army.
16. Allegedly became a Customs Officer when Fianna Fáil came to power in 1932. The same name crops up intriguingly in Hempel's telegrams, J.P. Duggan, N*eutral Ireland and the Third Reich* (Lilliput Press 1989).
17. Charles Wyse Power, subsequently a Circuit Judge for the Western Circuit. Henry Conner became a District Justice in Co. Cork. Trant McCarthy, another Dublin Fusilier, was the most famous criminal solicitor of his day. Hearne went to Dept of External Affairs in 1929. (He had been assistant parliamentary draughtsman from 1923 to 1929.) In the 1930s he did a lot of League of Nations work, attending international conferences etc. He was Irish Ambassador to Washington from 1950 until his retirement in 1960. He died in 1968.
18. Letter, 20/10/87. Capt. Cooke S.C. served in the Artillery Corps during the emergency period. He had been in the OTC (Officers Training Corps). A highly efficient gunner, he retains a great affection for what he used to refer to in the war years as 'The National Army' (Interview, 31/12/89).
19. Letter, 2/10/87. Col. Flynn was a brillant unassuming officer.
20. Power took a transfer to Donegal to replace McMenamin, who left to become State Solicitor for the county.
21. His salary was fixed at £1,200 p.a. Colonel Hodnett's was increased to £900 p.a. at this point.
22. Davitt remained adamant that the reprisal executions of O'Connor, Mellowes, McKelvey and Barrett were fully justified as he held that the Four Courts Executive were responsible for starting the Civil War. He pointed out that no members of the Dáil were shot afterwards. Ernie O'Malley, he felt, should not have 'got away with it'. Comdt O'Connor AMS ordained otherwise.

23. Transferred from Kerry, he became Command Legal Officer in the Curragh when it became a separate Command in the Spring of 1923. Later brought by Davitt to GHQ to work on the new Defence Forces Act.
24. Dorothy MacArdle, *The Irish Republic* (Dublin 1951) p. 858.
25. Collins was impatient with abstractions: 'What we fought for at any particular time was the greatest measure of freedom available at that time.' See Hopkinson, op. cit., pp 36–9; Beckett, op. cit., 453; Longford & O'Neill, op. cit., chapters 13 and 14.
26. *Irish Defence Forces Handbook*, p. 5; Maryann Valiulis, *Almost a Rebellion*, (Cork 1988); review by Comdt Peter Young, *An Cosantóir* 1986, pp. 18-19.
27. Interview with Capt. Martin Bell.
28. Dáil Report 19/3/24, p. 2229.
29. *The Irish News and Belfast Newsletter* 10/3/24 PRO Prem 1/43.
30. Ibid.
31. PRO Prem 1/43.
32. It is difficult to separate the facts from the myths in the mutiny. Col. Dan Bryan (Director of Intelligence) used to recall would-be mutineers muttering into their pints of 'coops de tat'. Other stories are that the Old IRA did not approve of the execution of old comrades by the other side. A Dundalk man is alleged to have been told by Dick Mulcahy, when he interceded for his captured brother's life, that he need have no worries; that it was the 'new crowd' they were after. The 'new crowd' had apparently been less than prominent in the pre-truce fighting. MacNeill's brother had been shot by Comdt Charlie McGoohan's Regulars in Sligo and this apparently made MacNeill acceptable to the mutineers: 'the only man in the army who could hope to get into that room and come out alive'. Bryan MacNeill was very highly regarded by the Dublin Brigade IRA. O'Higgins's foiling of the raid is seen as proof of his cleverness.
33. According to Cahir Davitt. See also Valiulis, op. cit.
34. Resentment at what had been hitherto seen as the hijacking of the title 'IRA' seemed to have abated after the 'Old IRA' irregularities embarrassed. During the Civil War Free State soldiers had written 'Official IRA' on the sides of their armoured cars.

Chapter 5 (pp. 138–177)

1. F.X. Martin, *The Irish Volunteers* (Dublin 1963) p.vii.
2. *An tÓglach*, 24/2/23, p.9.
3. Ibid., 24/2/23, p.11.
4. Ibid., 10/6/22. This issue (vol. iv, no 3) refers to demobbed British Army Officers being threatened, 'in every case the ukase

has been issued by individuals who do *not* belong to the Regular troops of the IRA'.

5. Ibid., 10/3/23, p. 15.
6. Ibid., 24/3/23, p. 23-4. Thanks to Professor Brian Ó Cuív (Dias) for record of remuneration paid to Ó Suilleabháin for teaching Irish classes in 20 Kildare St (1913-16).
7. Ibid., 7/4/23, p. 2; See also Udo E. Troster, 'Anfgabe P — a Plan for Gun Running', (1914) *An Cosantóir,* October 1989, p. 33-37.
8. *An tÓglach* 21/4/23, p.2.
9. Ibid., 5/5/23, p.2.
10. Ibid., 19/5/23, p.2.
11. Ibid., 2/6/23, p.2.
12. Ibid., 16/6/23, p.2.
13. Ibid., 30/6/23, p.2.
14. Ibid., 14/7/23, p.2.
15. Ibid., 28/7/23, p.2.
16. Ibid., 11/8/23, p.2.
17. Ibid., 1/9/23, p.2.
18. Ibid., (5/5/23), p.22.
19. Ibid., 17/11/23, p. 14; Ibid., 1/12/23 p. 18 (General Staff Organisation Memo No. 9). *Irish Defence Journal,* pp. 607. 'Fitz Brassy' learned his English from brother officers with amusing effect: 'Good morning Mr Mulcahy isn't it a "hure" of a day'.
20. *An tÓglach,* 19/5/23, p. 18.
21. Ibid., p. 19-20.
22. Later an annual Easter parade was enjoyed by younger generations. It was suspended because of Border duties.
23. Tattoos were subsequently held in 1935 and 1945: the 1945 one was an end-of-the-Emergency spectacular.
24. Original team — Captains Jed O'Dwyer i/c, Dan Corry and Cyril Harty — won worldwide fame.
25. Two went on to achieve high rank: Gen. Pat Hally, a School of Artillery Larkhill and Camberley graduate, to become Adjutant General; and Gen. Pat Curran, a Fort Leavenworth graduate, to become Quartermaster General.
26. D. McKenna, Chief of Staff 1940-49; J. Joyce, President Military Courts; Military History Bureau; P.A. Mulcahy, first Director of Artillery, Air Corps, Artillery again and Chief of Staff (1955-60).
27. Dáil Debate on Defence Forces (Temporary Provisions) Bill 1927 (3/2/27).
28. Patrick Keatinge, *A Place among the Nations* (Dublin 1978) p. 86; Dáil Debates 21: 14 56 (16/11/27).
29. Including Comdt Seán Haughey, father of Charles J. Haughey T.D.

30. O'Duffy was sacked in 1933. See chapter 4, note 5.
31. Healy was regarded as a snob who looked down on the senior officers fighting in the Civil War. He was the first Governor General of the Irish Free State. See chapters 3 and 4.
32. Minister and Secretaries Act 1924: An Act for constituting and defining the Ministers and Department of State.
33. PRO CAB 53 35 X/K5593. Report of Chief's of Staffs' Subcommittee on Defended Ports in Ireland.
34. Robert Fisk, *In Time of War* (London 1983) p. 25; Earl of Longford & T.P. O'Neill, *Eamon de Valera* (London 1970) p. 303-4; PRO CAB 26/263 (4.3.36; May '36).
35. Military Archives File no 3/157. Memo on Defence Estimates attached to personal letter of 16/1/39 (for MF to MD).
36. *The Douhet Theory and its application to the Present War, German Air Historical Branch Study NN.* 1944; Ronald Wheatley, *Operation Sea Lion* (London 1958) pp. 58, 132.
37. There is no war college in the Military College (the British had an Imperial Staff College equivalent). The Military College Senior Officers' course, which purports to be proportionately in lieu of a war college course, does not normally cater for top civil servants.
38. The Cadet School (Military College) motto. The question put by hero Cuchulainn to his opponent Ferdia each morning during their protracted duel in the Red Branch Knights Saga (1st Century BC) 'What feat of arms will we perform today' became a burning question.

Chapter 6 (pp. 178–217)

1. Matthew Cooper, *The German Army 1933-1945* (London 1978) pp. 169-76.
2. Noel Conway, *The Bloods* (Dublin 1972).
3. Comdt Owen Quinn is the expert on the Coast Watching Service. He has gone through all its log books and is compiling a dossier for Army Archives. See his articles in *An Cosantóir*: 'A Coast Watcher Remembers (1940-45)', April 1983; 'Coast Watch', January 1988. There were 18 Coast Watching districts each commanded by a District Officer (2nd Lt). There were 3 to 8 posts in each district (a total of 80), each manned by a corporal and seven men. Total strength was 666.
4. There were a number of solicitors among the rank and file of the AA at the time (1941). The author, then a Lieutenant in the 11th Field Artillery Battery (Cyril Mattimoe's two-in-a-row shield-winning 'Greyhounds') was in charge of a party from McKee Barracks digging a mass grave at Dunboyne. He was charged with kicking an AA soldier, having indicated with his foot that

all digging implements had to be disinfected before leaving the field. The Command O/C (freedom fighter Col. Liam Hoolan) dismissed the case. Col. Hoolan said 'I often feel like giving these fellows a kick in the arse myself, but it's better to charge them'.

5. A member of the family with a fine combat record in 1916 (Ashbourne). Author's Brigade Commander (4th) in late 1940s.
6. Denis McCarthy & A.J. English, *Armoured Fighting Vehicles of the Army*. This is essential reading and is a fine example of the most meticulous research. See also series of articles in the following issues of *An Cosantóir*: Sept. 74; Aug. 75; Dec. 75; May 76; Feb. 77; Sept. 77; Aug. 78; Feb. 80; May 81; July 81; Nov. 81; Jan. 82; May 82; March 83; Apr. 84; Oct. 84; Jan. 85; Nov. 85 (Military Archives).
7. Enno Stephan, *Spies in Ireland* (London 1963). This seminal original work, without which much would never have been uncovered, has not got the credit it deserves. See also Carolle Carter, *The Shamrock and the Swastika* (Pacific Books, Calif. 1977) and J.P. Duggan, *Neutral Ireland and the Third Reich* (Dublin 1989).
8. *Daily Express* (24/5/47) reporting Geortz's suicide by taking poison.
9. J.P. Duggan, *Herr Hempel at the German Legation in Dublin 1937-1945*, TCD thesis 1979, appendix XXIV.
10. Ronald Wheatley, *Operation Sealion* (London 1958).
11. Duggan, TCD thesis, op. cit., appendix XI.
12. Duggan, *Neutral Ireland and the Third Reich*', op. cit., p. 293
13. J.P. Duggan, 'The German threat — Myth or Reality', *An Cosantóir*, Sept. 1989; *Neutral Ireland and the Third Reich*, op. cit., p. 139; Robert Fisk, *In Time of War* (London 1983),pp. 137, 337-8, 157, 434-6, 482; *Irish Independent* 25/26/4/49, two articles by General Student: 'A German Airborne Attack in the North' and 'Airfields around Belfast as Paratroop Objectives'.
14. PRO CAB 53 X/15 5593; Duggan, TCD thesis, op. cit.; appendix V.
15. *Base Facilities in Eire. Note by the Chiefs of Staff* 6 November 1940 and 6 December 1940. PRO Prem 3 127/3A 153655.
16. Prem 3/126 3A 153655 (3/12/40).
17. Duggan, 'The German threat — Myth or Reality' op. cit.; see also TCD thesis, op. cit., appendix XXIV.
18. See note 6.
19. Another example of valuable meticulous research into crashes is to be found in the meritorious work of A.P. Kearns (Dublin) and John Quinn (Belfast) (Military Archives).
20. PRO WO 166/272 153887 (30/5/41 and 24/11/81).
21. PRO WO 166–1172 – 1 XC 153764 June 1940.

22. This later gave rise to a number of anomalies, when temporary officers were retained in attained their accelerated ranks (it had been easier to get promoted as a temporary officer) without having to go back to Cadet School. Author reverted to Cadet from temporary First Lieutenant in 1942 and re-emerged as a regular Second Lieutenant in 1944. After the West Point manner — with a few homegrown refinements — it was impressed on a Cadet that he was the lowest form of life. Having been an officer it was hard to take. Seniority then religiously froze promotional prospects — anomalies and all. See chapter 7.
23. Training Diaries, not always related to reality, were occasionally passports to fame. Junior Officers had nightmares about soldiers' socks. A well-known dug-in GHQ Inspection Officer (temporary) used the aim corrector back to front. It was mostly sweat and blood and swift punishment — a reign of terror, some would have said. It didn't stop jokes; it is a pity that they were not recorded, as some of them were very good.

Chapter 8 (pp. 249–278)

1. *The Blue Helmets* (NY 1985) foreword by Javier Pérez de Cuellar, UN Secretary General.
2. R.E. Asgood and R.W. Tucker, *Force, Order and Justice* (John Hopkins Press); J.P. Duggan, 'The Management of Force', *An Cosantóir*, Sept. – Dec. 1971.
3. P. Lavelle, 'UNOGIL Silver Jubilee 1958-83'; *An Cosantóir*, June 1983; C. Cox, 'Lebanon Diary 1958', ibid.
4. E. D. Doyle, 'The beginning of UNIFIL', *An Cosantóir*, October 1988; Ray Murphy, 'Establishing UNIFIL', ibid., April 1987.
5. E.A. Erskine, *Mission with UNIFIL* (London 1989). See also G.J. McMahon, 'A Book Review', *An Cosantóir*, December 1989.
6. Ray Murphy, 'Background to the 1980 Battle at Tiri — a personal assessment', *An Cosantóir*, October 1988.
7. D. Bracken, 'Lebanon Ten years and Twenty-One Peace keeping Battalions Later', ibid.
8. D.J. McCarthy. 'Armoured Vehicles of the Force Mobile Reserve UNIFIL', ibid.
9. T. O'Donnell, 'The Force Mobile Reserve — A Tp Comd's View', ibid.
10. *The Irish Defence Forces Handbook*, 1988 pp. 62-3.

# Sources

Interviews; *An tÓglach* (with particular reference to 1926 issues for first-hand accounts of 1916 Rising); *The Irish Sword,* Confidential documents were sources for earlier part of book, Richard Mulcahy, J.J. 'Ginger' O'Connell, Michael Collins, and James J. O'Donovan papers are in University College Dublin Archives and National Library of Ireland. The bulk of primary source documentation came from Military Archives. Cataloguing and computerisation of those collections is in progress. German material is in the Imperial War Museum and of course in the Bonn, Koblenz and Freiburg Archives. 'Emergency' material as broadly indicated hereunder from 'the other side of the hill' is accessible in PRO Kew.

PRO:
(*a*) *General*

| | | |
|---|---|---|
| Prem 1; | Prem 3; | CAB 53 |
| WO 166: | 1172 – 87 | (1939 – 41) |
| (BTNI) | 6842 – 9 | (Jan. – Dec. 42) |
| | 14402 – 7 | (Jan. – Dec. 44) |
| | 16665 – 73 | (Jan. – Dec. 45) |
| | 655 – 6 | (53 Div) |
| | 744 – 6 | (61 Div) |
| | 204 – 7 | (3 Corps) |
| | 271 – 3 | (VI Corps BNTI Order of Battle) |
| | 6681 – 90 | (BNTI) |
| Imperial War Museum | MI 14/402 | |

(*b*) *Selected items*
Prem 1/43: Mutiny in State Army. Protests from Lord Londonderry to Mr Henderson (1924).

| | |
|---|---|
| CAB 53 35<br>12 January 1938 | Defended Ports in Ireland<br>(Previous paper No COs 652) (waiving insistence on formal undertaking to secure a satisfactory agreement). |

| | |
|---|---|
| Prem 3 127/1 (1940) | Neutrality. |
| Prem 3 127/3A (1940-42) | Necessity for Base Facilities in Eire — vital, German U Boats in West Coast ports. Churchill's consideration of military reaction. Measures to secure the use of Irish Ports. Projected operational sectors and stations in Ireland. Alternative naval bases (to Foyle and Swilly) in Bantry Bay. |
| Prem 3 127/2 (1941) | British and U.S. planes allowed to fly to and from Donegal Bay in vicinity of Lough Erne. Necessity for Base Facilities in Eire: 'We need to base naval and air forces in Eire for two reasons: In defence of our trade and in defence of Eire territory, both vital to our existence.' Effect of U.S. Intervention (8/3/41) — only substantial change from 1940 appreciation. |
| No 166/1172/1 (1939-40) | Defence of Vulnerable Points in NI (Sept. 1939). Role of troops in NI: primary, war against Germany; secondary, internal security. Map showing dispositions 53 (Welsh Div). NI Defence Schemes: ('under no circumstances will any movement of troops be made through the territory of Eire'). Fall of France (June 1940). BTNI formed from 6 Corps with HQ in Lisburn: exercising general control wef 12/7/40 incl. mov. of 53 Div across border (Codeword 'CROMWELL'). War Diary 1 Intelligence Summary June/July 1940. |
| No 160/1172/2 (1941) | Invasion by land from Eire — air raids in Belfast — striking force to cross border (Codeword 'HUNT') NI Defence Scheme — 'W' plan (in author's possession) War Diary. Concentration of 3 Corps and command of 61 Div and 231 AC Sqn Codewords. |
| WO 166/1173 | Organisation — Lord Gort's visit — Belfast Bombing — War Diary. |

| | |
|---|---|
| WO 166/1174 (1939) | War Organisation and Equipment. |
| WO 166/1175 (1939-40) | Troop Movements. |
| WO 166/1183 (1941) | New organisation: Northern area: HQ Ballymena. Southern area: HQ Armagh. 61 Div. Location Statement. 'An enemy attack on N. Ireland alone is unlikely, more probable is a simultaneous attack on Éire and N. Ireland'. |
| WO 166/1184 (1941) | 'Molotoff' [*sic*] cocktails — War Diary HQ. NI District Armagh. Southern area. |
| WO 166/204 (1941) | 3 Corps: Operation Instructions No. 17 and 18. 'W' Plan for moving South: '3 Corps will ensure the security of DUBLIN and the aerodromes at COLLINSTOWN 01644 and BALDONNEL 00329 with the utmost speed and thereafter will be prepared to destroy any enemy forces in Eire!' Liaison Officers (18 Mission; see WO 178 2) assumed that initial invasion would take place on south and west coasts: RABBITS: two hours' notice. Border closed on codeword 'ASHTRAY' — HUNT cross border. By end of 1941, Green Plan superseded 'W' Plan. Assembly for Ops 20 21 replaced Instr. No. 18, 'Please burn forthwith the copies of 3 Corps operation Instruction No. 18 held by you and render destruction certificates to this HQ'. Someone, it seems, omitted to carry out that order. Special idea — British 'On 22 June (1941) Comd. 53 Div was sent for to GHQ at Athy . . .' Routes, 3 Corps Order of Battle, 'Div's despatch LOs to meet EIRE LOs as laid down in 3 Corps letter S403500 dated 1 Jul. '41. |
| WO 166/207 (1941) | Assembly for 'W' Plan (Special Adm Instruction). Every effort to obtain closest co-operation with Gardai. '3 Corps will cross the border' (HUNT). On securing DUBLIN 3 Corps responsible for traffic control west |

| | | |
|---|---|---|
| | | and south of line COLLON — CLONTARF. 3 Corps Medical Exercise SERPENT (28–30 Jul 41; 'Every second vehicle will carry the Eire flag and the Union Jack!' 'Rd DUBLIN — MULLINGAR will be kept clear of refugees and non-residential civilian traffic'. Locations of Adm Units of 3C Tps and Div Sup Units in concentration area. |
| WO 166/271 (1940) | | The Defence of Northern Ireland — Plan X 61 Div (less Lough Swilly Striking Force). 'Invasion from Eire'. Order of Battle. |
| No 166/272 (1941) | | 'W Plan' (26/4/41). 'W' Plan superseded by Green Plan. (16/12/41) 3 Corps *ensures* security of Dublin, Collinstown and Baldonnel. 61 Div (less two Bde Gps) secures area of Mullingar. Improved liaison between British and Irish armies. '*The operation planned with a view to securing LOUGH SWILLY for use as a fleet anchorage is held in abeyance.* Should it be necessary, after the commencement of operations in Ireland to deny this anchorage to the enemy, troops for this purpose will be found from BTNI' (Franklyn) 'Ensure Security' (involving mission analysis) replaces peremptory 'Secure' in previous operations orders. 'HUNT': Liaison achieved by use of<br>(a) No. 18 mission }<br>(b) Eire Liaison officers } 153887<br>Ex 'BISMARCK'. (Gen. Franklyn's Command Post and Terrain exercise):- |
| 1 Jul 41 | Dawn | Attack on England. |
| 2 Jul | 0500 hrs | Landing WATERFORD. Bombs CORK. |
| | 0600 hrs | Landing CORK. Bombs DUBLIN and LIMERICK. |
| | 0800 hrs | BALDONNEL, COLLINSTOWN captured. |
| | 0900 hrs | Landing LIMERICK–GALWAY–WESTPORT. |
| | 2000 " | Landing CORK–GALWAY–WESTPORT–LIMERICK. |
| | 2205 " | Fighting in LARNE. |

| | | |
|---|---|---|
| | 2245 " | Air-raid DUBLIN. |
| | 2250 " | IRA attack SHANES BELVOIR. |
| | 2330 " | Air raid BELFAST. |
| 3 Jul | 0230 " | Air raid BELFAST ends. |
| | 0800 hrs | LIMAVADY bombed. |
| | 0845 " | Parachute attack LIMAVADY. |
| | 0915 " | DERRY bombed [Not Londonderry! This is Franklyn!] |
| | 0945 " | Air-raid DERRY clear. |
| | 1000 " | Parachute attacks ALDERGROVE. |
| | 1005 " | MAGILLIGAN bombed. |
| | 1040 " | First landings MAGILLIGAN. |
| | 1040 " | SOS from EIRE: |

'On 4 July at 13.20 hrs the bridge and the main streets Athlone were heavily contaminated with liquid mustard. At 13.45 hrs the enemy was driven back across GRAND CANAL at ROBERTSTOWN. 500 prisoners taken. Heavy fighting between NAAS and KILCULLEN.'

Ex 'Mercury' (6 Nov. 41): Campaign on Eastern Front stalemated. Germany invades Ireland to further attack England. Small bodies of Eire troops holding out near KILKENNY, NEW ROSS, LIMERICK. No. 3 Corps at KELLS.

| | |
|---|---|
| WO 166/655 (1939/40) | Border area activity. 'Every indication of something in nature of a civil war in the near future in Ireland'. 53 Div. (less one Inf Bde) prepared to march into Southern Ireland in the event of a German invasion. Feeling in Dundalk that British invasion more likely than a German one. |
| WO 166/656 (1941) | 'Whole of Ireland is open to invasion at any time' 53 Div. Op. Instr. No. 1 (6/5/41): 53 Div. will secure DUBLIN and the aerodrome at COLLINSTOWN and BALDONNEL, preparatory to occupying Br. heads or the R. LIFFEY to the SW and getting in touch with 5 Div. Routes etc. etc. |
| WO 166/744 (1939-41) | 3 Corps, 61 Div. Lough Swilly operations and operational role in Eire. To secure Lough Swilly north of incl INCH ISLAND for use as an anchorage for the Royal Navy. Use of gas by Germany expected. 328 Inf Bde. Donegal |

| | |
|---|---|
| | Bay/Lough Swilly Ops: to move SOUTH to join 3 Corps. Gen. H.E. Franklyn, July 1941: co-operation replacing coercion. Landing grounds exist at Curragh, Phoenix Park, Oranmore and Fermoy. Numerous loughs in West where seaplanes could land. |
| WO 166/746 (Dec 1940) | Op. Instr. 1 is concerned with operations in the Lough Swilly area. Op. Instr. 2 ('W' Plan) deals with a possible advance Southwards into Eire. [This was at the height of Churchillian 'weapons of coercion' hectoring.] 'Closest contact will be maintained with all Eire forces, *including LSF if friendly.* |
| WO 178/2 (1941/2) | Mission No 18 (Liaison) Dublin Evacuation Plan. Visit to BTNI: 'W' Plan. Ex BISMARCK: (see No 166/272) Visit/Tour of Lt Gen. Franklyn as Gen. McKenna's guest (July 1941). First consignment of equipment handed over (18/12/41) (second in January). 20 Jan 1942 U.S. troops landed in N.I. Coast Defence reconnaissance (Gens McKenna and Franklyn. |
| Imperial War Museum MI 14/402. | Operation 'Green' German plans for invasion of Ireland. (For Operation Order see J.P. Duggan, *Herr Hempel at the German Legation in Dublin* TCD thesis, 1979, appendix XI, op. cit.) |

# Bibliography


Barry, Tom, *Guerilla Days in Ireland*, Cork 1948.

Béaslaí, Piaris, *Michael Collins and the Making of a New Ireland*, vols 1 and 2, Dublin 1930.

Beckett, J.C., *The Making of Modern Ireland*, London 1988.

Bell, J. Bowyer, *The Secret Army*, London 1970.

Breen, Dan, *My Fight for Irish Freedom*, Anvil 1978.

Brennan, M., *The War in Clare 1911 – 1921*, Dublin 1980.

Bowman, John, *De Valera and the Ulster Question*, Oxford 1983.

Buckland, Patrick, *Irish Unionism 1: The Anglo-Irish and the New Ireland 1885–1927. Irish Unionism 2: Ulster Unionism and the Origins of Northern Ireland 1866–1922*, Dublin 1973.

Carroll, J. T. *Ireland in the War Years 1939–45*, Newton Abbot 1975.

Carter, C.J., *The Shamrock and the Swastika: German Espionage in Ireland in World War II*, Palo Alto California 1977.

Carty, James, *Ireland: from the Great Famine to the Treaty of 1921*, Dublin 1968.

Clarke, D. *Seven Assignments*, London 1948.

Conway, Noel, *The Bloods*, Dublin 1972.

Coogan, Tim Pat, *The IRA*, London 1970.

Cooper, Martin, *The German Army 1933–45*, London 1978.

Cunningham, Hugh, *The Volunteer Force*, London 1975.

Deasy, Liam, *Towards Ireland Free: The Reality of the Anglo-Irish War 1920–21 in West Cork. Reflections, Corrections and Comments*, Anvil 1974.

Duggan, J.P., *Neutral Ireland and the Third Reich*, Dublin 1989 (with particular reference to Sources p. 271). *Herr Hempel at the German Legation in Dublin 1937–45*, TCD thesis, 1979.

Erskine, Emmanuel, *Mission with Unifil — An African Soldier's Reflections*, London 1989.

Fisk, Robert, *In Time of War*, London 1983.

Forde, Frank, *The Long Watch*, Dublin 1981. *Maritime Arklow*, Dublin 1988.

Franklyn, H.E., *The Story of One Green Howard in the Dunkirk Campaign*, Yorkshire 1966.

Gwynn, Denis, *The History of Partition (1912–1925)*, Dublin 1956.

Gwynne, Stephen, *John Redmond's Last Years*, London 1919.

Hayes-McCoy, G.A., 'A Military History of the 1916 Rising' in Nowlan, Kevin, *The Making of 1916*, Dublin 1969.
Hogan, J.J., *Badges: Medals: Insignia*, Dublin 1987.
Hopkinson, Michael, *Green Against Green*, Dublin 1989.
Keatinge, Patrick, *A Place among the Nations: Issues of Irish Foreign Policy*, Dublin 1978.
Kee, Robert, *The Green Flag*, vols I and II, London 1987.
Kilfeather, T.P., *The Connaught Rangers*, Tralee 1969.
Lee, J., *The Modernisation of Irish Society*, Dublin 1975.
Liddell-Hart, B.H., *History of the Second World War*, London 1976.
Longford, Earl of & O'Neill, T.P., *Eamon de Valera*, London 1979.
MacArdle, Dorothy, *The Irish Republic*, Dublin 1951.
McCaughran, Tom, *The Placenames of Niemba*, Dublin 1966.
MacCurtain, Margaret, *A History of Ireland*, Dublin 1969.
MacEoin, Uinsionn (ed.), *Survivors*, Dublin 1987.
Maher, Jim, *The Flying Column West Kilkenny 1916–21*, Dublin 1988.
Martin, F.X., *The Irish Volunteers 1913–1915*, Dublin 1963.
Morrison, George, *The Irish Civil War — an illustrated History*, Dublin 1981.
Neeson, E., *The Civil War in Ireland*, Dublin 1981.
Nowlan, Kevin, *The Making of 1916. Studies in the History of the Rising*, Dublin 1969.
Nowlan K, & William, T.D., *Ireland in the War Years and After*, Dublin 1969.
Ó Broin, León, *Protestant Nationalists in Revolutionary Ireland: The Stopford Connection*, Dublin 1985.
Ó Broin, León, *W.E. Wylie and the Irish Revolution 1916–1921*, Dublin 1989.
O'Malley, Ernie, *On Another Man's Wound*, London 1961. *The Singing Flame*, London 1978.
Packenham, F., *Peace by Ordeal*, London 1962.
Pollock, Sam, *Mutiny for the Cause*: the story of the revolt of Ireland's 'Devils Own' in British India, London 1969.
Smith, Raymond, *Under the Blue Flag*, London 1980.
Stephans, Enno, *Spies in Ireland*, London 1963.
Taylor, Rex, *Michael Collins*, London 1961.
Tierney, M., *Eoin Mac Neill, Scholar and Man of Action*, Oxford 1980.
Townshend, Charles, *The British Campaign in Ireland 1919–21*, London 1973.
Urquart, Brian, *A Life in Peace and War*, N.Y. 1987.
Valiulis, Maryann, *Almost a Rebellion: the Irish Army mutiny of 1926*, Cork 1988.
Verrier, Anthony, *International Peacekeeping*, London 1988.

West, Nigel, *M15 British Security Operations 1909–45*, London 1981.
Wheatley, Ronald, *Operation Sealion*, London 1958.
William, T.D. (ed.), *The Irish Struggle 1916–20*, London 1966.
Younger, Calton, *Ireland's Civil War*, London 1968.

## Selected Miscellaneous (Pamplets/Periodicals etc.)

*The Last Post*, National Graves Association, 1976.
*The Blue Helmets*, A review of United Nations Peace-keeping, N.Y. 1985.
*Basic Facts about the United Nations*, N.Y. 1970.
*Easter Fires*, Waterford 1943.
Martin, F.X., *The Scholar Revolutionary: Eoin MacNeill 1967–1945 and the making of the new Ireland. Easter 1916: An inside report on Ulster.*
Hally, P.J., 'The Easter 1916 Rising in Dublin, The Military Aspects': Part I *The Irish Sword*, vol 7, no 29; Part II *The Irish Sword*, vol 8, no. 30.
O'Neill, Eoghan, 'The Battle of Dublin 1916', *An Cosantóir*, May 1966.
Student, Kurt, 'A German Airborne Attack on the North' *Irish Independent*, 25.4.47. 'Airfields around Belfast as Paratroop Objectives', ibid., 26.4.47.
*An tÓglach* (particular reference to 1926 editions for 1916 material).
*An Cosantóir* (particular reference to April 1987 and October 1988 for UNIFIL material and in general for the various excellent unit and corps histories).
*The Irish Defence Forces: A Handbook*, 1985 (N.B.).
Permanent Missions to the United Nations No. 245, N.Y. 1979.

# Index

E



F

M